Other Books and Series by Jeff Bowen

Applications for Enrollment of Choctaw Newborn Act of 1905 Volumes I thru XX

Choctaw By Blood Enrollment Cards 1898-1914 Volumes I thru XVIII

I0223050

Visit our website at **www.nativestudy.com** to learn more about these
and other books and series by Jeff Bowen

CHOCTAW BY BLOOD ENROLLMENT CARDS

1898-1914

VOLUME XIX

TRANSCRIBED BY

JEFF BOWEN

NATIVE STUDY
Gallipolis, Ohio
USA

Native Study LLC
Gallipolis, OH
www.nativestudy.com

Library of Congress Control Number: 2020911767

ISBN: 978-1-64968-115-7

Made in the United States of America.

This series is dedicated to
Mike Marchi,
who keeps my spirits up.

CREEK CENSUS.

SECOND NOTICE.

Members of the Dawes Commission will be present at the following times and places for the purpose of enrolling Creek citizens, as required by Act of Congress of June 10, 1896:

At Muskogee, Nov. 8 to 30, 1897, inclusive.
At Wagoner, Nov. 8 to 13, " inclusive.
At Eufaula, Nov. 8 to 13, " inclusive.
At Sapulpa, Nov. 15 to 20, " inclusive.
At Wetumpka, Nov. 15 to 20, " inclusive.
At Okmulgee, Nov. 22 to 30, " inclusive.

All persons who have not heretofore enrolled before the Dawes Commission should appear and enroll. Parents and guardians can enroll their families and wards.

TAMS BIXBY,
FRANK C. ARMSTRONG,
A. S. McKENNON,
THOS. B. NEEDLES,
                                    Commissioners.

The above illustration is similar in nature to what was found throughout Indian Territory for different tribes as far as postings on bulletin boards, public centers, or wherever they could be read so people would be notified of where and when they needed to be for enrollment with the Dawes Commission.

This is a picture of the Dawes Commission at Camp Jones in Stonewall, Indian Territory on September 8, 1898.

The images below are of two of the original cards given on the microfilm. The cards given in this book have been formatted to fit on one page and still give all the information found on the original cards.

Introduction

This series of Choctaw Enrollment Cards for the Five Civilized Tribes 1898-1914 has been transcribed from National Archive Film M-1186 Rolls 39-46.

The series contains more than 6100 Choctaw enrollment cards. All of the cards list age, sex and degree of blood, the parties' Dawes Roll Numbers, and date of enrollment by the Secretary of Interior for each person. The contents also give the enrollee's parents' names as well as miscellaneous notes pertaining to the enrollee's circumstances, when needed. Most entries indicate whether or not a spouse is an Intermarried White, with the initials I.W.

Enrollment wasn't as simple a process as most would think just by going through these pages. The relationships between the Five Tribes and the Dawes Commission were weak at best. There were political battles going on between the tribes and the U.S. Government as it was, but the struggles didn't stop there. Each tribe had its own political factions pulling it from every direction. On top of everything else, people from every corner of the United States were trying to figure how to get in on the spoils (Money and Land Allotment) by means of political favor. Kent Carter, author of *The Dawes Commission*, describes the continuous effort required to enroll the different tribes and the pressure the Commission incurred from people all over the country who tried to insinuate themselves into the equation:

"In May 1896 the Dawes Commission Returned To Indian Territory for its third visit, establishing its headquarters at Vinita in the Cherokee Nation. It now had to process applications for citizenship in addition to negotiating allotment agreements; these circumstances make the narrative of events more confusing because the commission attempted the two tasks concurrently. The commissioners resumed making their usual speeches to tribal officials and public gatherings to promote negotiations, but now they inevitably had to respond to questions about how the application process for citizenship would work. They also began receiving letters from people all over the United States asking how they could 'get on the rolls' so they could 'get Indian land'."[1]

For the actual process of Choctaw enrollment, "A commission was appointed in each county of the Choctaw Nation under an act of September 18 to make separate rolls of citizens by blood, by intermarriage, and freedmen; it was to deliver them to recently elected Chief Green McCurtain by October 20, but he rejected them even before they were completed because of charges that people were being left off for political reasons. On October 30, the National Council authorized establishment of a five-member

---

[1] *The Dawes Commission* by Kent Carter, page 15, para. 1

commission to revise the rolls within ten days and then directed McCurtain to turn them over to the Dawes Commission on November 11, 1896. The Choctaws hired the law firm of Stuart, Gordon, and Hailey, of South McAlester to represent the tribe at all proceedings held by the Dawes Commission,"[2] another indication that throughout the Commission's efforts there was always controversy between the tribes and the negotiators.

When completed, this multi-volume series will contain thousands of names, all of them accounted for in the indexes carefully prepared by the author. Hopefully this work will help many researchers find their ancestors and satisfy the questions that so many have had about their Native American heritage.

Jeff Bowen
Gallipolis, Ohio
NativeStudy.com

---

[2] *The Dawes Commission* by Kent Carter, page 16, para. 5

Choctaw By Blood Enrollment Cards 1898-1914

RESIDENCE: Choctaw Nation 3ᵈ Dist ~~COUNTY~~.
POST OFFICE: Stringtown, Ind. Ter

Choctaw Nation

Choctaw Roll
(Not Including Freedmen)

CARD No.
FIELD No. **5401**

Dawes' Roll No.	NAME	Relationship to Person First Named	AGE	SEX	BLOOD	TRIBAL ENROLLMENT		
						Year	County	No.
13688	₁ Bond, Mary	First Named	49	F	1/2	1896	Jacks Fork	1873
13689	₂ " Cornelius	Son	19	M	1/4			1874
13690	₃ " Eliza	Dau	14	F	1/4			1875
13691	₄ " Sallie Ann	"	11	"	1/4			1876
13692	₅ " Emeline	"	8	"	1/4			1877
13693	₆ " Esther	"	5	"	1/4			1878
	7							
	8							
	9							
	10							
	11							
	12							
	13							
	14							
	15							
	16							
	17							

ENROLLMENT
OF NOS. 1-2-3-4-5-6 HEREON
APPROVED BY THE SECRETARY
OF INTERIOR Mar. 19, 1903

TRIBAL ENROLLMENT OF PARENTS

	Name of Father	Year	County	Name of Mother	Year	
1	Alexander Billie	Dead	Choctaw Roll	Ah-Saweaha Billie	Dead	Chick
2	Jesse Bond		Jacks Fork Co ~~Choctaw Roll~~	No.1		
3	" "		" "	No.1		
4	" "		" "	No.1		
5	" "		" "	No.1		
6	" "		" "	No.1		
7						
8	All on Choctaw Census Record No.2 Page 76					
9	No1 Wife of No1 on Choctaw Roll Card #1900					
10	No4 on '96 Roll as "Sally Ann Bond" ~~Nos 1 to 6 inclusive originally enrolled on Chick Card~~					
11	~~#648. Transferred to this card Oct. 16, 1902.~~					
12						
13						
14						
15					~~Date of Application for Enrollment.~~	
16						
17					Sept. 26"/98	

Choctaw By Blood Enrollment Cards 1898-1914

RESIDENCE: Choctaw Nation COUNTY. **Choctaw Nation** Choctaw Roll CARD NO.
POST OFFICE: South Canadian Ind Ter. *(Not Including Freedmen)* FIELD NO. **5402**

Dawes' Roll No.	NAME	Relationship to Person First Named	AGE	SEX	BLOOD	TRIBAL ENROLLMENT Year	TRIBAL ENROLLMENT County	TRIBAL ENROLLMENT No.
13694	1 Cheadle, Lucy B		28	F	1/4	1896	Tobucksy	2364
13695	2 " Jas. Pushmataha	Son	7	M	1/8	"	"	2365
13696	3 " Mary Almeda	Dau	5	F	1/8	"	"	2366
13697	4 " Martin Douglas	Son	3	M	1/8	"	"	2367
13698	5 " George Rector	"	2mo	"	1/8			
13699	6 " Kiska Harkins	"	8mo	"	1/8			
	7							
	8							
	9							
	10							
	11	ENROLLMENT OF NOS. 1-2-3-4-5-6 HEREON						
	12	APPROVED BY THE SECRETARY						
	13	OF INTERIOR MAR 19						
	14							
	15							
	16							
	17							

TRIBAL ENROLLMENT OF PARENTS

	Name of Father	Year	County	Name of Mother	Year	County
1	George Harkins	Dead	Choctaw Roll	Mary Harkins	1897	Tishomingo
2	Elias R. Cheadle		" "	No.1		
3	" " "		" "	No.1		
4	" " "		" "	No.1		
5	" " "		" "	No.1		
6	" " "		" "	No.1		
7						
8	No1 Also on Choctaw Census Record #2, Page 96: Wife of Elias R. Cheadle on Choctaw Card #4679					
9	" 2 " " " " " " " " as "James P Cheadle" On '96 Roll "James P Cheadle"					
10	" 3 " " " " " " " " "Almeda " " " "Almeda M " "
	" 4 " " " " " " " " "Martin D " " " "Martin D. " "
11	" 5 Affidavit of Physician to be supplied; Received Oct 11" 1898					
12	" 6 Born Dec 18" 1901: Enrolled Sept 6" 1902					
13	Nos. 1 to 6 inclusive originally enrolled on Chick card #772. Transferred to this card Oct 11, 1902.					
14						
15						Date of Application for Enrollment.
16						
17						Sept. 29"1898

2

Choctaw By Blood Enrollment Cards 1898-1914

RESIDENCE: Choctaw Nation 3ʳᵈ Dist ~~COUNTY.~~
POST OFFICE:

Choctaw Nation

Choctaw Roll *(Not Including Freedmen)*

CARD NO.
FIELD NO. **5403**

Dawes' Roll No.	NAME	Relationship to Person First Named	AGE	SEX	BLOOD	TRIBAL ENROLLMENT		
						Year	County	No.
13700	₁ Harkins, Annie		28	F	1/4	1896	Blue	5920
13701	₂ " Willis	Son	5	M	1/8	"	"	5921
13702	₃ " Clara	Dau	3	F	1/8	"	"	5922
13703	₄ " Lillie	"	1 1/2	"	1/8			
13704	₅ " Lee	Son	10mo	M	1/8			
13705	₆ ~~DIED PRIOR TO SEPTEMBER 25, 1902~~ Grover	"	~~11da~~	"	~~1/8~~			
	7							
	8							
	9							
	10							
	11	ENROLLMENT						
	12	OF NOS. 1-2-3-4-5-6 HEREON APPROVED BY THE SECRETARY OF INTERIOR MAR 19 1903						
	13							
	14							
	15							
	16							
	17							

TRIBAL ENROLLMENT OF PARENTS

Name of Father	Year	County	Name of Mother	Year	County
₁ Henry James		Atoka Co Choctaw Roll	Lorenna James	Dead	Chick residing in ~~Choctaw N. 3ʳᵈ Dist~~
₂ William Harkins		Blue Co Choctaw Roll	No.1		
₃ " "		" "	No.1		
₄ " "		" "	No.1		
₅ " "		" "	No.1		
₆ " "		" "	No.1		
7					
₈ No1 on Choctaw Census Record No2, Blue County Page 250 Husband William M Harkins					
₉ " 2 " " "					Choctaw Card 4442
10 " 3 " " "					
" 5 Enrolled Decʳ 13" 1899					
11 " 6 Born June 13" 1902: Enroll... 4" 1902					
12 Nos 1 to 6 inc... ginally enrolled on Chick. card No. 774. Transferred					
13 to this ca... 17, 1902.					
No4 Proof of birt... and filed Oct. 31, 1902.					
14 No 6 died Aug 3, 1902. Enrollmen... d by Department July 8, 1904					
15					Date of Application for Enrollment.
16					
17 Ardmore I.T.					Sept. 29" 1898

3

Choctaw By Blood Enrollment Cards 1898-1914

RESIDENCE: Choctaw Nation ~~COUNTY~~.   **Choctaw Nation**   Choctaw Roll   CARD No.
POST OFFICE: South Canadian Ind Ter   *(Not Including Freedmen)*   FIELD No. **5404**

Dawes' Roll No.	NAME	Relationship to Person First Named	AGE	SEX	BLOOD	TRIBAL ENROLLMENT Year	TRIBAL ENROLLMENT County	TRIBAL ENROLLMENT No.
IW 1044	1 Morgan, Robert A		30	M	I.W.			
13706	2 " Alice	Wife	30	F	1/4	1896	Tobucksy	7863
13707	3 " Helen Lee	Dau	2mo	F	1/8			
13708	4 " William Allen	Son	1mo	M	1/8			
	5							
	6							
	7							
	8							
	9							
	10							
	11							
	12							
	13							
	14							
	15							
	16							
	17							

ENROLLMENT
OF NOS. 1 HEREON
APPROVED BY THE SECRETARY
OF INTERIOR Oct 21 1904

ENROLLMENT
OF NOS. 2-3-4- HEREON
APPROVED BY THE SECRETARY
OF INTERIOR Mar 19 1903

TRIBAL ENROLLMENT OF PARENTS

	Name of Father	Year	County	Name of Mother	Year	County
1	Wm Morgan		non-citizen	Louisa Morgan		non-citizen
2	Allen G. Lee (I.W.)		Choctaw Roll	Lucy Lee		Choctaw Roll
3	No.1			No.2		
4	No.1			No.2		
5						
6	No.2 on '96 Roll as Alice F. Lee					
7	" " on Choctaw Census Record Page 331, No.2					
8	" 3 Enrolled Nov. 3ʳᵈ 1899					
9	" 4 Enrolled Sept 21ˢᵗ 1901					
10	Nos 1.2.3 and 4 originally enrolled on Chick. Card #807 and					
11	transferred to this card Oct. 17, 1902.					
12	For children of Nos 1 and 2 see NB (Mar 3, 1905) #391					
13						
14						
15						
16					Date of Application for Enrollment.	#1 & 2
17	P.O. [Illegible] I.T. 1/18/03					Sept. 29,1898

4

Choctaw By Blood Enrollment Cards 1898-1914

RESIDENCE: Choctaw Nation 1st ~~County~~ Dist.
POST OFFICE: Sans Bois, Ind Ter

Choctaw Nation

Choctaw Roll
(Not Including Freedmen)

CARD No.
FIELD No. **5405**

Dawes' Roll No.	NAME	Relationship to Person	AGE	SEX	BLOOD	TRIBAL ENROLLMENT		
						Year	County	No.
13709	1 Scott, George W	First Named	26	M	1/8	1896	Sans Bois	11095
	2							
	3							
	4							
	5							
	6							
	7							
	8							
	9							
	10							
	11							
	12							
	13							
	14							
	15							
	16							
	17							

ENROLLMENT OF NOS. 1 HEREON APPROVED BY THE SECRETARY OF INTERIOR Mar. 19, 1903

TRIBAL ENROLLMENT OF PARENTS

	Name of Father	Year	County	Name of Mother	Year	County
1	G.W. Scott	Dead	Non-citizen	Eliza Scott	Dead	Chickasaw Roll
2						
3						
4						
5	No1 on '96 Roll as Geo. W. Scott					
6	No1 on Choctaw Census Record No.2 Page 417					
7	" Wife and children of, on Choctaw Card #2837					
	No1 originally enrolled on Chickasaw Card No. 679					
8	transferred to this card Oct. 17, 1902					
9						
10						
11						
12						
13						
14						
15						
16				Date of Application for Enrollment.	Sept. 27-1898	
17						

5

Choctaw By Blood Enrollment Cards 1898-1914

RESIDENCE: Choctaw Nation ~~COUNTY~~ ▮▮▮ **Nation**
POST OFFICE: Waupaunuka Ind Ter

Choctaw Roll CARD NO.
(Not Including Freedmen) FIELD NO. **5406**

Dawes' Roll No.	NAME	Relationship to Person First Named	AGE	SEX	BLOOD	TRIBAL ENROLLMENT Year	County	No.
13710	₁ Billis, Louvina	First Named	42	F	Full	1896	Atoka	1820
13711	₂ Page, Lewis	Son	15	M	"	"	"	1821
13712	₃ " Benton	StepSon	10	"	1/2	"	"	1822
13713	₄ " Alice	" Dau	8	F	1/2	"	"	1823
13714	₅ Dick, Thomas	Son	11	M	1/2	"	"	3597
	₆							
	₇							
	₈ No1 is wife of Jackson Billis Choctaw Card #316							
	₉ No2 On 96 Roll #10548 as Lewis Peach							
	₁₀ No4 on '96 Roll #10549 as Ada Peach							
	₁₁ No5 Son of Martin Dick Choctaw Card #4315							
	₁₂							
	₁₃							
	₁₄ ENROLLMENT OF NOS 1-2-3-4-5 HEREON							
	₁₅ APPROVED BY THE SECRETARY OF INTERIOR							
	₁₆							
	₁₇							

TRIBAL ENROLLMENT OF PARENTS

	Name of Father	Year	County	Name of Mother	Year	County
₁	Pe-lish-tubby	Dead	Chickasaw Roll	Sha-to-ho-ye	Dead	Chickasaw Roll
₂	Wall Page	"	" "	No.1		
₃	Jackson Billis		Atoka Co Choctaw Roll	Nancy Billis		Chick residing in Choctaw N. 3ʳᵈ Dist
₄	" "		" "	" "		" " "
₅	Martin Dick		" "	No.1		
₆						
₇	No1 On 96 Roll as Lorina Billis: On Choctaw Census Record #2 Page 74 as "Lorina					
₈	"2 " " " " " Willis "	" "	" " " " " " " " " Willis			
₉	"3 " " " " " Benton "	" "				
	"4 " " " " " Alice "	" "	" " " " " " " " "			
₁₀	"5 " " " " " "Thomas Dicks" "	" "	" " " " " " " 149			
₁₁						
₁₂	Nos 1 to 5 inclusive originally enrolled on Chick. card #819 and					
₁₃	transferred to this card Oct. 17, 1902.					
₁₄						
₁₅						
₁₆						
₁₇				Date of Application for Enrollment.	Sept. 29,1898	

Choctaw By Blood Enrollment Cards 1898-1914

RESIDENCE: Choctaw Nation   ~~COUNTY.~~   **Choctaw Nation**   **Choctaw Roll** *(Not Including Freedmen)*   ~~407~~

POST OFFICE: Waupaunuka Ind Ter

Dawes' Roll No.	NAME	Relationship to Person First Named	AGE	SEX	BLOOD	TRIBAL ENROLLMENT		
						Year	County	No.
13715	1 Dick, Elizabeth	First Named	55	F	1/2	1896	Atoka	3615
	2							
	3							
	4							
	5							
	6							
	7							
	8							
	9							
	10							
	11							
	12							
	13							
	14							
	15							
	16							
	17							

ENROLLMENT OF NOS. 1 HEREON APPROVED BY THE SECRETARY OF INTERIOR MAR 19 1903

TRIBAL ENROLLMENT OF PARENTS

	Name of Father	Year	County	Name of Mother	Year	County
1	Thomas Homer	Dead	Choctaw Roll	Melvina Goforth	Dead	Chickasaw Roll
2						
3						
4						
5						
6	No1 On 96 Roll as Lizzie Dick					
7	Also on Choctaw Census Record #2 Page 149					
8	No.1 originally enrolled on Chickasaw card #825. Transferred to this card October 17, 1902.					
9						
10						
11						
12						
13						
14						
15					Date of Application for Enrollment:	
16						
17					Sept. 29"1898	

Choctaw By Blood Enrollment Cards 1898-1914

Choctaw Nation

Choctaw Roll
(Not Including Freedmen)

CARD No.
FIELD No. 5408

Dawes' Roll No.	NAME	Relationship to Person First Named	AGE	SEX	BLOOD	TRIBAL ENROLLMENT		
						Year	County	No.
13716	1 Harkins, Sophia	First Named	30	F	1/4	1896	Blue	5892
	2							
	3							
	4							
	5							
	6							
	7							
	8							
	9							
	10							
	11							
	12							
	13							
	14							
	15							
	16							
	17							

ENROLLMENT OF NOS. 1 HEREON APPROVED BY THE SECRETARY OF INTERIOR MAR 19 1903

TRIBAL ENROLLMENT OF PARENTS

Name of Father	Year	County	Name of Mother	Year	County
1 Namus McCurtain	Dead	Choctaw Roll	Elizabeth Dick	1897	Chick residing in Choctaw N 3ʳᵈ Dis
2					
3					
4					
5					
6 No 1 On Choctaw Census Record No 2 Page 250					
7					
8 No.1 originally enrolled on Chickasaw Card No 826. Transferred to this card October 17, 1902.					
9					
10					
11					
12					
13					
14					
15					
16				Date of Application for En	
17				Sept.	

8

Choctaw By Blood Enrollment Cards 1898-1914

RESIDENCE: Pontotoc		COUNTY. Choctaw Nation				Choctaw Roll (Not Including Freedmen)		CARD NO.
POST OFFICE: Wiley Ind. Ter								FIELD NO. 5409

Dawes' Roll No.	NAME	Relationship to Person First Named	AGE	SEX	BLOOD	TRIBAL ENROLLMENT		
						Year	County	No.
DEAD.	1 Cealey, Cephus	First Named	23	M	Full	1896	Blue	2876
	2							
	3							
	4							
	5 No. 1 HEREON DISMISSED UNDER ORDER OF THE COMMISSION TO THE FIVE CIVILIZED TRIBES OF MARCH 31, 1905.							
	7							
	8							
	9							
	10							
	11							
	12							
	13							
	14							
	15							
	16							
	17							

CANCELLED

Applicant died prior to ratification of Choctaw-Chickasaw agreement Sept. 25, 1902.

TRIBAL ENROLLMENT OF PARENTS

	Name of Father	Year	County	Name of Mother	Year	County
1	Sampson Cealey	Dead	Chickasaw Roll	Serena Cealey	Dead	Chickasaw Roll
2						
3						
4						
5						
6	No1 On Choctaw Census Record No.2 Page 117					
7	" Husband of Susan Cealey Choctaw Roll Card 318					
8						
9	No.1 originally enrolled on Chickasaw card No. 840. Transferred to this card Oct. 17, 1902.					
10						
11	No.1 died in 1900, proof of death filed Nov. 26, 1902.					
12						
13						
14						
15						
16				Date of Application for Enrollment.		Sept. 29" 1898
17						

Choctaw By Blood Enrollment Cards 1898-1914

RESIDENCE: Choctaw Nation 3rd Dist ~~COUNTY~~.
POST OFFICE: Stringtown Ind. Ter.

Choctaw Nation

Choctaw Roll (Not Including Freedmen)

CARD NO.
FIELD NO. **5410**

Dawes' Roll No.	NAME	Relationship to Person First Named	AGE	SEX	BLOOD	TRIBAL ENROLLMENT Year	TRIBAL ENROLLMENT County	TRIBAL ENROLLMENT No.
13717	1 Watson, Edna	Named	16	F	1/2	1896	Jacks Fork	14086
13718	2 " Jonas J.	Son	3mo	M	1/4			
	3							
	4							
	5							
	6							
	7							
	8							
	9							
	10							
	11							
	12							
	13							
	14							
	15							
	16							
	17							

ENROLLMENT OF NOS. 1-2- HEREON APPROVED BY THE SECRETARY OF INTERIOR MAR 9 1903

TRIBAL ENROLLMENT OF PARENTS

Name of Father	Year	County	Name of Mother	Year	County
1 Jesse Bond		Jacks Fork Co Choctaw Roll	Mary Bond	1897	Chick residing in ~~Choctaw N. 3rd Dist~~
2 Julius Watson		" "	No.1		
3					
4					
5					
6 No1 on Choctaw Census Record No.2 Page 487					
7 " wife of Julius J Watson Choctaw roll card #1895;					
8 Nos 1 and 2 originally enrolled on Chickasaw Card #1045. Transferred to this card Oct. 17, 1902					
9 For child of No1 see NB (Mar 3 '05) #414					
10					
11					
12					
13					
14					
15					~~Date of Application for Enrollment.~~
16					
17					Oct. 10"1898

Choctaw By Blood Enrollment Cards 1898-1914

						TRIBAL ENROLLMENT		
es' No.	NAME	Relationship to Person First Named	AGE	SEX	BLOOD	Year	County	No.
19	1 Bond, Calvin	First Named	21	M	1/2	1896	Jacks Fork	1881
	2							
	3							
	4							
	5							
	6							
	7							
	8							
	9							
	10							
	11							
	12							
	13							
	14							
	15							
	16							
	17							

RESIDENCE: Choctaw Nation **COUNTY.**
P.O. OFFICE: Stringtown Ind. Ter
Choctaw Nation
Choctaw Roll (Not Including Freedmen)
CARD NO.
FIELD NO. 5411

ENROLLMENT
OF NOS. 1 HEREON
APPROVED BY THE SECRETARY
OF INTERIOR MAR 19 1903

TRIBAL ENROLLMENT OF PARENTS

	Name of Father	Year	County	Name of Mother	Year	County
1	Jesse Bond		Jacks Fork Co Choctaw Roll	Mary Bond	1897	Chick residing in Choctaw N. 3rd Dist
2						
3						
4						
5						
6	No1 On 96 Roll as "Campbell Bond"					
7	" On Choctaw Census Record #2, Page 76					
8	" Husband of Sallie Bond Choctaw Card #3993					
9	No.2 originally enrolled on Chick Card No. 1047. Transferred to this card Oct. 17, 1902.					
10						
11	Calvin Bond is now the husband of Mary Hays on Choc. Card #4023.					
12						
13						
14						
15					Date of Application for Enrollment.	
16						
17					Oct. 10"1898	

11

Choctaw By Blood Enrollment Cards 1898-1914

RESIDENCE: Choctaw Nation COUNTY. **Choctaw Nation**
POST OFFICE: Stringtown Ind. Ter

CARD NO.
FIELD NO. **5412**

Dawes' Roll No.	NAME	Relationship to Person First Named	AGE	SEX	BLOOD	TRIBAL ENROLLMENT		
						Year	County	No.
13720	1 Noah, Annie	First Named	27	F	Full	1896	Jacks Fork	9860
13721	2 " Rindie	Dau	10	"	1/2	"	" "	9863
13722	3 " Robert	Son	5	M	1/2	"	" "	9864
13723	4 " Reuben	"	3	"	1/2	"	" "	9865
	5							
	6							
	7							
	8							
	9							
	10							
	11	ENROLLMENT OF NOS. 1-2-3-4 HEREON APPROVED BY THE SECRETARY OF INTERIOR MAR 19 1903						
	12							
	13							
	14							
	15							
	16							
	17							

ENROLLMENT OF PARENTS

	Name of Father	Year	County	Name of Mother	Year	County
1	Hus-cha	Dead	Chickasaw Roll	Te-ho-ya	Dead	Chickasaw Roll
2	David Noah		Jacks Fork Choctaw Roll	No.1		
3	" "		" "	No.1		
4	" "		" "	No.1		
5						
6	All on Choctaw Census Record No2 Page 384					
7	No.2 On '96 Roll and on Choctaw Census Record as "Ranty Noah"					
8	Nos. 1,2,3 and 4 originally enrolled on Chickasaw Card #1058. Transferred to this card Oct. 17, 1902					
9						
10						
11						
12						
13						
14						
15					Date of Application for Enrollment.	
16						
17	P.O. Stratford Okla 11/2/10				Oct. 10"1898	

12

Choctaw By Blood Enrollment Cards 1898-1914

RESIDENCE:	Choctaw Nation
POST OFFICE:	Caddo Ind Ter

COUNTY. **Choctaw Nation**   Roll (including Freedmen)

CARD NO.

FIELD NO. **5413**

Dawes' Roll No.	NAME Blue	Relationship to Person First Named	AGE	SEX	BLOOD	TRIBAL ENROLLMENT		
						Year	County	No.
13724	1 Turnbull, George W		37	M	1/2	1896	Blue	12418
13725	2 " Jesse James	Son	4mo	"	1/4			
I.W. 1432	3 " Ettie	Wife	21	F	I.W.			
	4							
	5							
	6							
	7							
	8							
	9							
	10							
	11							
	12							
	13							
	14							
	15							
	16							
	17							

ENROLLMENT
OF NOS. 3 HEREON
APPROVED BY THE SECRETARY
OF INTERIOR JUN 12 1905

ENROLLMENT
OF NOS. 1-2- HEREON
APPROVED BY THE SECRETARY
OF INTERIOR MAR 19 1903

TRIBAL ENROLLMENT OF PARENTS

	Name	Year	County	Name of Mother	Year	County
1	Leroy T	Dead	Choctaw Roll	Mary J Turnbull	1897	Tishomingo
2				Ettie Turnbull		Non-citizen
3	Bates		Non citizen	Rosie York	" "	" "
4						

5 No 1 Also on Choctaw Census Record #2, Page 449
6   " Father of Emma Turnbull, Choctaw Card #353
7   " Husband of Ettie Turnbull, noncitizen. Evidence of marriage filed March 25" 1901
8 No 2 Enrolled March 25, 1901
9 For child of No 1 see NB (Apr 26-06) Card #859
  Nos 1 and 2 originally enrolled on Chick Card #1072. Transferred
10   to this card Oct. 17, 1902.
11 No. 3 placed on this card Dec 19, 1904, under an order of the Commission
12   of that date, issued in accordance with the instructions of the Secretary
13   of the Interior of Dec. 8th, 1904. (I.T.D. 11870-1904). Construing the affidavit
  of Ettie Turnbull of March 15, 1901 to the birth of Jesse James Turnbull
14   an application for her enrollment as an intermarried Choctaw.

15 PO address
16   Emet Ind Ter
17   12/17/04

DATE OF APPLICATION
FOR ENROLLMENT.
Oct. 10" 1899

13

Choctaw By Blood Enrollment Cards 1898-1914

POST OFFICE: Tuskahoma, Ind. Ter   (Not Including Freedmen) FIELD NO. 5414

Dawes' Roll No.	NAME	Relationship to Person First Named	AGE	SEX	BLOOD	TRIBAL ENROLLMENT Year	County	No.
13726	1 Impson, Louisa	Named	58	F	Full	1896	Jacks Fork	6340
13727	2 Anderson, Tandy	Son	23	M	1/2	"	" "	461
13728	3 Anderson, Ida	Dau	17	F	Full	"	" "	6341
13729	4 Anderson, Clarence J	Gr Son	2mo	M	1/2			
	5							
	6							
	7							
	8							
	9							
	10							
	11							
	12							
	13							
	14							
	15							
	16							
	17							

ENROLLMENT OF NOS. 1-2-3-4- HEREON APPROVED BY THE SECRETARY OF INTERIOR MAR 19 1903

TRIBAL ENROLLMENT OF PARENTS

	Name of Father	Year	County	Name of Mother	Year	County
1	Hotubby Moore	Dead	Chickasaw Roll	Hettie Anderson	Dead	Chickasaw Roll
2	Allington Anderson	"	Choctaw Roll	No.1		
3	Sydney Burris	1897	Chick residing in Choctaw N. 3rd Dist	No.1		
4	Jackman Anderson	1896	Choctaw Roll	No.3		
5						
6						

7 No1 Also on Choctaw Census Record #2, Page 268

8 " 2 " " " " " " " 19 Husband of, Lyles Hotubbee on Choctaw

" 3 " " " " " " " 268 Card #1993 Sept 12

9 " 3 Now the wife of Jackman Anderson on Choctaw Card #1883. Evidence of marriage

10 requested May 13th 1902. Received and filed June 9" 1902

11 " 4 Born March 8" 1902, enrolled May 13" 1902

12

13 Nos 1 to 4 inclusive originally enrolled on Chickasaw Card #1082 and

14 transferred to this card Oct. 17, 1902.

15 For child of No2 see NB (Mar 3 '05) #416

16 Date of Application for Enrollment. For Nos 1 to 4

17 Oct. 10"1898

14

Choctaw By Blood Enrollment Cards 1898-1914

Dawes' Roll No.	NAME	Relationship to Person First Named	AGE	SEX	BLOOD	TRIBAL ENROLLMENT		
						Year	County	No.
DEAD	1 Anderson, Nicholas		30	M	1/2	1896	Jacks Fork	463
13730	2 Clay, Louisa	niece	16	F	3/4	"	" "	6342
	3							

No. 1 HEREON DISMISSED UNDER ORDER OF THE COMMISSION TO THE FIVE CIVILIZED TRIBES OF MARCH 31, 1905.

ENROLLMENT
OF NOS. 1 HEREON
APPROVED BY THE SECRETARY
OF INTERIOR MAR 19 1903

TRIBAL ENROLLMENT OF PARENTS

	Name of Father	Year	County	Name of Mother	Year	County
1	Allington Anderson	Dead	Choctaw Roll	Louisa Impson	1897	Chick residing in Choctaw N. 3rd Dist
2	Gooden "	"	Chick residing in Choctaw N. 3rd Dist	Nancy Anderson	Dead	" " " "
3						
4						

5 No1 On 96 Roll as "Nicholas E Anderson" Also on Choctaw Census Record No2 Page 19

6 Husband of Amanda Anderson, Choctaw Roll, Card #357

No2 on 96 Roll as "Louisa Impson" Also on Choctaw Census Record No2 Page 268

8 Nos 1 and 2 originally enrolled on Chick. Card No. 1083. Transferred to this card Oct. 17, 1902.

9 No.1 died in 1899; proof of death filed Dec. 6, 1902.

10 No2 now wife of Andrew Clay on Choctaw card #1875; evidence of

11 marriage filed Dec. 26, 1902.

12	
13	
14	
15	
16	
17	[Illegible] IT 4/16/05

Date of Application for Enrollment.   Oct. 10"1898

Choctaw By Blood Enrollment Cards 1898-1914

RESIDENCE: Choctaw Nation 3ᵈ Dist COUNTY.
POST OFFICE: Doer IT 11/1/104[sic]

Choctaw Nation

Choctaw Roll ████ No.
(Not Including Freedmen) No. **5416**

Dawes' Roll No.	NAME	Relationship to Person First Named	AGE	SEX	BLOOD	TRIBAL ENROLLMENT Year	County	No.
13731	1 Thompson, William C	Named	23	M	1/4	1896	Kiamitia	12361
13732	2 " Ella	Sis	19	F	1/4	"	"	12362
13733	3 " Lewis	Bro	16	M	1/4	"	"	12363
13734	4 " Burney	"	14	"	1/4	"	"	12364
	5							
	6							
	7							
	8							
	9							
	10							
	11							
	12							
	13							
	14							
	15							
	16							
	17							

ENROLLMENT
OF NOS. **1-2-3-4** HEREON
APPROVED BY THE SECRETARY
OF INTERIOR **MAR** 19 1903

TRIBAL ENROLLMENT OF PARENTS

	Name of Father	Year	County	Name of Mother	Year	County
1	Robert Thompson		Kiamitia Co Choctaw Roll	Siney Thompson	1897	Chick residing in Choctaw N. 3ᵈ Dist
2	" "		" "	" "	"	" " " "
3	" "		" "	" "	"	" " " "
4	" "		" "	" "	"	" " " "
5						
6	All on Choctaw Census Record No2, Page 448, Kiamitia Co					
7	No4 On '96 Roll as "Burnie Thompson"					
8	No1 " " " " "W" C. " "					
9	Nos 1,2,3 and 4 originally enrolled on Chick. Card #1084 and					
10	transferred to this card Oct. 17, 1902.					
11						
12						
13						
14	P.O.					
15	Marlow, Okla 1/1/11					
16						
17					Date of Application for Enrollment.	Oct. 10"1898

16

Choctaw By Blood Enrollment Cards 1898-1914

RESIDENCE:			ctaw Nation				Choctaw Roll	CARD NO.	
POST OFFICE							(Not Including Freedmen)	FIELD NO. **5417**	

Dawes' Roll No.	NAME	Relationship to Person First Named	AGE	SEX	BLOOD	TRIBAL ENROLLMENT		
						Year	County	No.
13785	1 Anderson, Zadick		20	M	1/2	1896	Jacks Fork	532
	2							
	3							
	4							
	5							
	6							
	7							
	8							
	9							
	10							
	11	ENROLLMENT						
	12	OF NOS. 1 HEREON APPROVED BY THE SECRETARY						
	13	OF INTERIOR MAR 19 1903						
	14							
	15							
	16							
	17							

TRIBAL ENROLLMENT OF PARENTS

	Name of Father	Year	County	Name of Mother	Year	County
1	Solomon Anderson	Dead	Chickasaw Roll	Lucy Anderson	Dead	Chickasaw Roll
2						
3						
4						
5						
6	No1 On 96 Roll as "Verdick Anderson"					
7	" On Choctaw Census Record No2 Page 22 as "Verdick Anderson"					
8	No. 1 originally enrolled on Chick. Card #1085. Transferred					
9	to this card Oct. 17, 1902.					
10						
11						
12						
13						
14						
15					Date of Application for Enrollment.	
16						
17					Oct. 10"1898	

Choctaw By Blood Enrollment Cards 1898-1914

RESIDENCE: Choctaw Nation 3ᵈ Dist COUNTY.
POST OFFICE: Durant, Ind. Ter.

Choctaw Nation

Choctaw Roll
(Not Including Freedmen)

CARD NO.
FIELD NO. **5418**

Dawes' Roll No.	NAME	Relationship to Person First Named	AGE	SEX	BLOOD	TRIBAL ENROLLMENT		
						Year	County	No.
13736	1 Thompson, Leo Edward	First Named	2	M	1/4	1896	Blue	12410
	2							
	3							
	4							
	5							
	6							
	7							
	8							
	9							
	10							
	11	ENROLLMENT						
	12	OF NOS. 1 HEREON APPROVED BY THE SECRETARY						
	13	OF INTERIOR MAR 19 1903						
	14							
	15							
	16							
	17							

TRIBAL ENROLLMENT OF PARENTS

	Name of Father	Year	County	Name of Mother	Year	County
1	Greenwood Thompson		Blue Co Choctaw Roll	Thompson, Minnie	1897	Chick residing in Choctaw N. 3ʳᵈ Dist
2						
3						
4						
5						
6	No1 Also on Choctaw Census Record No.2 Page 449 as "Leo Ed. Thompson"					
7	" On 96 Roll as Lee Ed Thompson					
8	No.1 originally enrolled on Chick. Card No 1091; Transferred to this card Oct. 17, 1902.					
9						
10						
11						
12						
13						
14						
15						
16					Date of Application for Enrollment,	
17						Oct. 10"1898

18

Choctaw By Blood Enrollment Cards 1898-1914

RESIDENCE: Choctaw Nation 1st Dist COUNTY. **Choctaw Nation**   Choctaw Roll   CARD NO.
POST OFFICE: Ward, Ind. Ter   *(Not Including Freedmen)*   FIELD NO. **5419**

Dawes' Roll No.	NAME	Relationship to Person First Named	AGE	SEX	BLOOD	TRIBAL ENROLLMENT Year	County	No.
13737	1 Burgevin, Josephine	First Named	22	F	1/4	1896	Sans Bois	4649
DEAD.	2 " Basil Duke	Son	7mo	M	1/8			
13738	3 " Agnes Elberta	Dau	2mo	F	1/8			
13739	4 " Herbert Spencer	Son	1mo	M	1/8			
	5							
	6							
	7							
	8							
	9							
	10							
	11							
	13							
	14							
	15							
	16							
	17							

ENROLLMENT OF NOS. 1-3-4- HEREON APPROVED BY THE SECRETARY OF INTERIOR MAR 19 1903

No. 2 HEREON DISMISSED UNDER ORDER OF THE COMMISSION TO THE FIVE CIVILIZED TRIBES OF MARCH 31, 1905.

TRIBAL ENROLLMENT OF PARENTS

	Name of Father	Year	County	Name of Mother	Year	County
1	William Goforth	Dead	Non-citizen	Jensie Goforth	Dead	Chickasaw Roll
2	Francis E Burgevin	" "	No1			
3	" " "	" "	No1			
4	" " "	" "	No1			
5						
6	No1 On '96 Roll as "Josephine B. Goforth"					
7	" On Choctaw Census Record #2, Page 197 as Josephine Goforth					
8	"2 Enrolled June 16' 1899					
9	"3 Enrolled May 24' 1900					
	"4 Enrolled Aug. 13' 1901					
10	Nos. 1,2,3 and 4 originally enrolled on Chick. Card #1093 and transferred to this card Oct. 17, 1902.					
11	No2 Died Nov. 23, 1899, proof of death filed Oct. 29, 1902.					
12	For child of No 1 see NB (Mar 3'05) #404					
13						
14						
15					DATE OF APPLICATION FOR ENROLLMENT.	#1
16						Oct. 10"1898
17						

Choctaw By Blood Enrollment Cards 1898-1914

RESIDENCE: Choctaw Nation 3ᵈ Dist COUNTY.
POST OFFICE: Coalgate, Ind. Ter

Choctaw Nation

Choctaw Ro███
(Not Including Free███

CARD NO.
FIELD NO. **5420**

Dawes' Roll No.	NAME	Relationship to Person First Named	AGE	SEX	BLOOD	TRIBAL ENROLLMENT		
						Year	County	No.
13740	1 Thompson, Cyrus R	First Named	29	M	1/4	1896	Atoka	12448
ᴵᵂ606	2 " Clemmie	Wife	27	F	I.W.	"	"	15110
13741	3 " Valley	Dau	8	"	1/8	"	"	12451
13742	4 " Preemon C	Son	6	M	1/8	"	"	12449
13743	5 " Cyrus Waverly	"	4	"	1/8	"	"	12450
13744	6 " James H	"	1 1/2	"	1/8			
13745	7 " Joseph B	"	8mo	"	1/8			
13746	8 " Robert H	"	3mo	"	1/8			
	9							

10 Marriage Certificate filed in office of Dawes Commission
11 Nos 2,3,4 & 5 admitted by Dawes Commission
12 Choctaw Case #75 and No Appeal taken
13 Nos 1 to 8 inclusive originally enrolled on
14 Chickasaw Card #1101. Transferred to this card
15 October 17, 1902.
16 For child of Nos 1&2 see NB (Mar 3'05) #3
17

ENROLLMENT
OF NOS. 1-3-4-5-6-7-8 HEREON
APPROVED BY THE SECRETARY
OF INTERIOR MAR 19 1903

ENROLLMENT
OF NOS. 2 HEREON
APPROVED BY THE SECRETARY
OF INTERIOR FEB -8 1904

TRIBAL ENROLLMENT OF PARENTS

Name of Father	Year	County	Name of Mother	Year	County
1 Robert Thompson		Gaines Co Choctaw Roll	Siney Thompson	1897	Chick residing in Choctaw N. 3ʳᵈ Dist
2 James Gammons	Dead	Non-citizen	Martha Gammons		Non-Citizen
3	No.1		No.2		
4	No.1		No.2		
5	No.1		No.2		
6	No.1		No.2		
7	No.1		No.2		
8	No.1		No.2		Thompson"

9 No1 On 96 Roll as "Cyrus W Thompson On Choctaw Census Record #2 Page 450 as "Cyrus W
10 " 2 " " " " " "Clamey " " " " Intermarried Roll Page 107
11 " 3 " " " " " "Valley " " " " Census Record #2, Page 450
  " 4 " " " " " "Preman C " " " " " " " "
12 " 5 " " " " " "Cyrus W " " " " " " " " as "Cyrus W
13 Thompson" Admitted by Dawes Com as "Waverly"
14 " 6 Affidavit of Attending Physician to be supplied; Received Oct 21" 98
  " 7 Enrolled Aug 10" 1899
15 " 8 Enrolled May 21" 1901
16 #1 to 6 inc
17 4/21/02 PO Atoka IT

Date of Application for Enrollment
Oct. 11" 1898

20

Choctaw By Blood Enrollment Cards 1898-1914

RESIDENCE:	Tishomingo	COUNTY.	Choctaw N...		Roll (Not Including Freedmen)	CARD NO.		
POST OFFICE:	Emet, Ind. Ter.					FIELD NO. **5421**		

Dawes' Roll No.	NAME	Relationship to Person First Named	AGE	SEX	BLOOD	TRIBAL ENROLLMENT		
						Year	County	No.
1747	1 McKinney, Clara Louisa	First Named	11	F	1/4	1896	Chickasaw Dist	9428
1748	2 " Ben A	Bro	9	M	1/4	"	"	9529
1749	3 " Mattie	Sis	7	F	1/4	"	"	9530
	4							
	5							
	6							
	7							
	8							
	9							
	10							
	11	ENROLLMENT						
	12	OF NOS. 1-2-3- HEREON APPROVED BY THE SECRETARY						
	13	OF INTERIOR MAR 19 1903						
	14							
	15							
	16							
	17							

TRIBAL ENROLLMENT OF PARENTS

	Name of Father	Year	County	Name of Mother	Year	County
1	Ben F. McKinney	1897	Pickens Co Of 79	Maggie McKinney	Dead	Chick. Roll
2	" " "			" "	"	" " "
3	" " "			" "	"	" " "
4						
5						
6						
7	No1 On '96 Roll as "Louisa McKinney"					
8						
9	Nos 1,2 and 3 originally on Chickasaw Card No 1104. Transferred to this card Oct. 17, 1902.					
10						
11						
12						
13						
14						
15						
16				Date of Application for Enrollment.	Oct. 11" 98	
17						

Choctaw By Blood Enrollment Cards 1898-1914

Choctaw Nation

Choctaw (Not Including)

Dawes' Roll No.	NAME	Relationship to Person First Named	AGE	SEX	BLOOD	TRIBAL ENROLLMENT		
						Year	County	No.
13750	1 McGee, Ellis	First Named	48	M	1/2	1896	Jacks Fork	8887
13751	2 " Sol	Son	14	"	3/4	"	" "	8888
13752	3 " Esau	"	11	"	3/4	"	" "	8889
13753	4 " Isom	"	9	"	3/4	"	" "	8890
13754	5 " Mary	Dau	7	F	3/4	"	" "	8891
	6							
	7							
	8							
	9							
	10							
	11	ENROLLMENT						
	12	OF NOS. 1-2-3-4-5- HEREON APPROVED BY THE SECRETARY						
	13	OF INTERIOR MAR 19 1903						
	14							
	15							
	16							
	17							

TRIBAL ENROLLMENT OF PARENTS

	Name of Father	Year	County	Name of Mother	Year	County
1	Isaac McGee	Dead	Chickasaw Roll	Angeline McGee	Dead	Chickasaw Roll
2	No.1			Susan McGee		Chick residing in Choctaw N. 3rd Dist
3	No.1			" "		" " " "
4	No.1			" "		" " " "
5	No.1			" "		" " " "
6						
7	No.1 On 96 Roll as "Ellis Magie" Also on Choctaw Census Record #2 Page 358 as "Ellis Magie"					
8	" 2 " " " " " "Sol " " " " " " " " " " "					
9	" 3 " " " " "Ason " " " " " " " " " "Ason Magie"					
	" 4 " " " " "Ison " " " " " " " " " "					
10	" 5 " " " " "Mary M " " " " " " " " "					
11	Nos 1 to 5 inclusive originally enrolled on Chick. Card #1127 and transferred to this card October 17, 1902.					
12						
13						
14						
15					Date of Application for Enrollment.	
16						
17					Oct. 11" 1898	

Choctaw By Blood Enrollment Cards 1898-1914

hoctaw Nation ~~COUNTY~~,
Featherston, Ind Ter — **Choctaw Nation** (Not Including Freedmen) FIELD NO. **5423**

NAME	Relationship to Person First Named	AGE	SEX	BLOOD	TRIBAL ENROLLMENT		
					Year	County	No.
13755 rhey, Allen	First Named	25	M	1/2	1896	Sans Bois	2101
6							
7							
8							
9							
10							
11							
12							
13							
14							
15							
16							
17							

ENROLLMENT
OF NOS. 1 HEREON
APPROVED BY THE SECRETARY
OF INTERIOR MAR 19 1903

TRIBAL ENROLLMENT OF PARENTS

	Name of Father	Year	County	Name of Mother	Year	County
1	Wallace Carney		Sans Bois Co Choctaw Roll	Susie Carney	Dead	Chickasaw Roll
2						
3						
4						
5						
6						
7	No1 Husband of Susan Carney, Choctaw Roll card #365					
8	" On Choctaw Census Record, Sans Bois Co, Page 85[?]					
9	No.1 originally enrolled on Chick. Card on Chick. card #1153. Transferred					
10	to this card Oct. 18, 1902					
11	For child of No.1 see NB (March 3, 1905) #1102					
12	" " " " " " (April 26, 1906) #429					
13						
14						
15					Date of Application	
16					for Enrollment.	
17					Oct. 11" 1898	

Choctaw By Blood Enrollment Cards 1898-1914

Choctaw Nation   ~~(Not Including Freedmen)~~ Roll   CARD NO.   FIELD NO. **5424**

Dawes' Roll No.		NAME	Relationship to Person First Named	AGE	SEX	BLOOD	TRIBAL ENROLLMENT Year	County	No.
13756	1	Perry, Coleman		41	M	3/4	1896	Sans Bois	10064
~~DEAD~~	2	" Hattie	Wife	30	F	1/2	"	" "	~~10065~~
~~DEAD~~	3	" Isaac	Son	7	M	5/8	"	" "	~~10067~~
13757	4	" Jefferson	"	5	"	5/8	"	" "	10068
13758	5	" Becky	Dau	6mo	F	5/8			
	6								
	7								
	8	No. 2 and 3 HEREON DISMISSED UNDER ORDER OF THE COMMISSION TO THE FIVE							
	9	CIVILIZED TRIBES OF MARCH 31, 1905.							
	10								
	11	ENROLLMENT							
	12	OF NOS. 1-4-5 HEREON APPROVED BY THE SECRETARY							
	13	OF INTERIOR MAR 19 1903							
	14								
	15	No. 2 and 3 HEREON DISMISSED UNDER							
	16	ORDER OF THE COMMISSION TO THE FIVE CIVILIZED TRIBES OF MARCH 31, 1905.							
	17								

PARENTS

	Name of Father	Year		Name of Mother	Year	County
1	Jackson Perry	Dead	Chickasaw Roll	Salina Perry	Dead	Chickasaw Roll
2	~~Wallace Carney~~		Sans Bois Co Choctaw Roll	~~Susie Carney~~	"	" " "
3	No.1			No.2		
4	No.1			No.2		
5	No.1			No.2		
6						
7	No 1,2,3 & 4 on Choctaw Census Record No.2 Page 390					
8	No 5 Enrolled Aug 1st 1899					
9	~~Nos. 1 to 5 inclusive originally enrolled on Chickasaw Card #1144 and~~					
10	~~transferred to this card Oct 18, 1902.~~					
11						
12	~~No 2 Died Feb 10, 1900, proof of death filed Nov. 13, 1902~~ ~~No 3 Died March 20, 1900 proof of death filed Nov. 13, 1902~~					
13						
14						
15					#1 to 4	
16					Date of Application for Enrollment.	
17					Oct. 11" 1898	

Choctaw By Blood Enrollment Cards 1898-1914

RESIDENCE: Choctaw Nation COUNTY. **Choctaw Nation** Choctaw Roll CARD No.
POST OFFICE: Featherston, Ind. Ter (Not Including Freedmen) FIELD No. **5425**

Dawes' Roll No.	NAME	Relationship to Person First Named	AGE	SEX	BLOOD	TRIBAL ENROLLMENT		
							County	No.
	ore, Austin		30	M	Full			21
2								
3								
4								
5								
6								
7								
8								
9								
10								
11								
12								
13								
14								
15								
16								
17								

ENROLLMENT
OF NOS. 1 HEREON
APPROVED BY THE SECRETARY
OF INTERIOR MAR 19 1903

TRIBAL ENROLLMENT OF PARENTS

	Name of Father	Year	County	Name of Mother	Year	County
1	No-ub-by	Dead	Chickasaw Roll	Emeline	Dead	Chickasaw Roll
2						
3						
4						
5						
6	No1 On w Census Record No.2 Page 345					
7	" Hu f Lily Moore, Choctaw Roll Card #367					
8	No.1 ori nrolled on Chickasaw Card No. 1145. Transferred to th ard Oct. 18, 1902					
9						
10						
11						
12						
13						
14						
15						
16					Date of Application for Enrollment.	Oct. 11" 1898
17						

25

Choctaw By Blood Enrollment Cards 1898-1914

RESIDENCE: Choctaw Nation ~~COUNTY.~~ **Choctaw Nation**   Choctaw Roll   CARD NO.
POST OFFICE: Springtown Ind Ter   *(Not Including Freedmen)*   FIELD NO. **5426**

Dawes' Roll No.	NAME	Relationship to Person First Named	AGE	SEX	BLOOD	TRIBAL ENROLLMENT Year	County	No.
13760	₁ Whistler, Dora	First Named	18	F	3/4	1896	Jacks Fork	3052
13761	₂ Calvin, Ella M	Dau	1 1/2	"	3/8			
13762	₃ Carnes, Melvin C	Son	3mo	M	7/8			
13763	₄ Whistler, Mamie	Dau	17mo	F	7/8			
	₅							
	₆							
	₇							
	₈							
	₉							
	₁₀							
	₁₁	ENROLLMENT						
	₁₂	OF NOS. 1-2-3-4 HEREON APPROVED BY THE SECRETARY						
	₁₃	OF INTERIOR Mar. 19 1903						
	₁₄							
	₁₅							
	₁₆							
	₁₇							

TRIBAL ENROLLMENT OF PARENTS

	Name of Father	Year	County	Name of Mother	Year	County
₁	Wᵐ B Anderson	1897	Chick residing in ~~Choctaw N. 3ʳᵈ Dist~~	Lizzie Anderson	Dead	Chick residing in ~~Choctaw N. 3ʳᵈ Dist~~
₂	Morris Calvin	Dead	Choctaw Roll	No.1		
₃	Ellis H Carnes	1897	" "	No.1		
₄	Robinson Whistler	1896	Jacks Fork	No.1		
₅						

₆ No1 on '96 Roll as "Dora Calvin" also on Choctaw Census Record #2 Page 24 as Dora Calvin
₇ " Wife of Ellis Harris Carnes, Choctaw Roll, Card #368
~~No3 Enrolled May 16th 1899~~
₈ For child of No.2 see NB. (Apr 26, 1906) Card No. 16
₉ Nos 1,2 and 3 originally enrolled on Chick. Card #1147 and
₁₀ transferred to this card October 18, 1902.
~~For child of No1 see NB (March 3, 19050 Card No. 1109~~
₁₁ ~~No.1 is now wife of Whistler Robinson, Choctaw Card 4578 Nov. 8, 1902~~
₁₂ No4 Born June 13, 1901 Enrolled Nov. 8, 1902
₁₃ Evidence of marriage between No1 and R.J. Whistler received
~~and filed Nov. 15, 1902.~~

						#1 & 2
₁₆						Date of Application for Enrollment.
₁₇	P.O. Connersville 2/20/06					Oct. 11ᵗʰ 1898

26

Choctaw By Blood Enrollment Cards 1898-1914

RESIDENCE: Choctaw Nation ~~COUNTY.~~
POST OFFICE: Scipio, Ind. Ter.

Choctaw Nation

Choctaw Roll *(Not Including Freedmen)*

CARD NO.
FIELD NO. **5427**

Dawes' Roll No.	NAME	Relationship to Person First Named	AGE	SEX	BLOOD	TRIBAL ENROLLMENT		
						Year	County	No.
13764	1 Anderson, Rhodes	Named	24	F	1/2	1896	Tobucksy	109
13765	2 " Dora	Dau	7	"	1/4	"	"	110
	3							
	4							
	5							
	6							
	7							
	8							
	9							
	10							
	11	ENROLLMENT						
	12	OF NOS. 1-2- HEREON APPROVED BY THE SECRETARY						
	13	OF INTERIOR Mar. 9, 1903						
	14							
	15							
	16							
	17							

TRIBAL ENROLLMENT OF PARENTS

	Name of Father	Year	County	Name of Mother	Year	County
1	Thomas Folsom	dead	Choctaw Roll	Jennie Folsom	Dead	Chick residing in Choctaw N. 1st Dist
2	Andie Anderson		Tobucksy Co Choctaw Roll	No.1		
3						
4						
5						
6	No.1 on Choctaw Census Record #2, Page 5; Wife of Andie Anderson Choctaw Roll Card 370					
7	No.2 " " " " " " "					
8	~~Nos. 1 and 2 originally enrolled on Chick. Card No. 1156. Transferred~~					
9	~~to this card Oct. 18, 1902~~					
10						
11	For child of No.1 see NB (Apr 26. 1906) Card No. 240					
12						
13						
14						
15					Date of Application for Enrollment.	
16						
17					Oct. 12"	

Choctaw By Blood Enrollment Cards 1898-1914

RESIDENCE: Choctaw Nation ~~COUNTY~~.
POST OFFICE: McAlester, Ind. Ter.

Choctaw Nation
(Not Including Freedmen)

Choctaw Roll

CARD No.
FIELD No. **5428**

Dawes' Roll No.	NAME	Relationship to Person First Named	AGE	SEX	BLOOD	TRIBAL ENROLLMENT Year	County	No.
13766	1 Ott, Katsie ~~DIED PRIOR TO SEPTEMBER 25, 1902~~	First Named	38	F	Full	1896	Tobucksy	9922
13767	2 " Joe	Son	6	M	1/2	"	"	9924
13768	3 " Simeon	"	5	"	1/2	"	"	9925
13769	4 " Sallie	Dau	1	F	1/2	"	"	
13770	5 " Sam	St. Son	15	M	1/2	1896	Tobucksy	9923
13771	6 Eddy, Ida O	Dau	12	F	1/2	"	"	3702
13772	7 " Elsie O	"	9	"	1/2	"	"	3701
	8							
	9							
	10							
	11							
	12							
	13							
	14							
	15							
	16							
	17							

ENROLLMENT
OF NOS. 1-2-3-4-5-6-7 HEREON
APPROVED BY THE SECRETARY
OF INTERIOR Mar 19 1903

TRIBAL ENROLLMENT OF PARENTS

	Name of Father	Year	County	Name of Mother	Year	County
1	~~Johnson Perry~~	Dead	Chickasaw Roll	~~Lizzie Perry~~	Dead	~~Pontotoc~~
2	Willie Ott		Tobucksy Co Choctaw Roll	No.1		
3	" "		" "	No.1		
4	" "		" "	No.1		
5	" "		" "	Liza Ott	Dead	~~Chick residing in Choctaw N. 1st Dist~~
6	Sam Eddy	Dead	~~Chick residing in Choctaw N. 1st Dist~~	No.1		
7	" "	"	" " " "	No.1		
8	No1 Wife of Willie Ott Choctaw Roll Card #371					
9	Nos 1,2,3 & 5 on Choctaw Census Record No2 Page 386					
10	Nos 6 & 7 " " " " " " 154					
11	No7 On ,96 Roll as "Elsie Eddy"					
12	Nos 1 to 7 inclusive originally enrolled on Chick. Card #1157. Transferred to this card Oct. 18, 1902.					
13	No.1 died before Sept. 25, 1902. Enrollment cancelled by Department May 2, 1906.					
14	For child of No5 see NB (Apr 26-06) Card #423.					
15						
16					Date of Application for Enrollment.	
17	No.5 Celestine I.T.				Oct. 12th 1898	

28

Choctaw By Blood Enrollment Cards 1898-1914

RESIDENCE: Choctaw Nation ~~COUNTY.~~
POST OFFICE: Durant Ind. Ter.

Choctaw Nation

Choctaw Roll (Not Including Freedmen)

CARD No. FIELD No. **5429**

Dawes' Roll No.	NAME	Relationship to Person First Named	AGE	SEX	BLOOD	TRIBAL ENROLLMENT		
						Year	County	No.
IW 1045	1 Spears, David Freeman	First Named	46	M	I.W.	1896	Blue	15060
DEAD	2 " Caroline	Wife	48	F	3/8	"	"	11584
13773	3 " Julia Ann	Dau	6	"	3/16	"	"	11585
13774	4 Thompson, Dora Ellen	Step Dau	11	"	3/16	"	"	12402
	5							
	6 No1 Admitted by Dawes Comm Case 805 No Appeal							
	7 Marriage License & Certificate on file							
	8							
	9							
	10							
	11 ENROLLMENT							
	12 OF NOS. 3-4- HEREON APPROVED BY THE SECRETARY							
	13 OF INTERIOR MAR 19 1903							
	14 NO. 2 HEREON DISMISSED UNDER ORDER OF THE COMMISSION TO THE FIVE CIVILIZED TRIBES OF MARCH 31, 1905.			ENROLLMENT OF NOS. 1 HEREON APPROVED BY THE SECRETARY OF INTERIOR OCT 21 1904				
	17							

TRIBAL ENROLLMENT OF PARENTS

Name of Father	Year	County	Name of Mother	Year	County
1 Clayborn Spears	Dead	Non-Citizen	Ann Spears	Dead	Non-citizen
2 Sam Colbert	"	Chickasaw Roll	Lousanna Colbert	"	Chickasaw Roll
3 No.1			No.2		
4 Henry Thompson	Dead	Non-citizen	No.2		
5					
6					
7 No1 On '96 Roll as "B F Spears" On Choctaw Intermarried Roll Page 101					
8 " 2 " " Census Record " 429					
9 " 3 On 96 Roll as "Julia A Spears" " " " " " 429					
10 " 4 " " " " "Dora Thompson" " " " " " " 449					
11					
12 Nos 1 to 4 inclusive originally enrolled on Chick. Card #1162 and transferred to this card Oct. 18, 1902.					
13 No2 died April 25, 1899, proof of death filed Dec. 19, 1902.					
14					
15					
16			Date of Application for Enrollment.	Oct. 12" 1898	
17					

Choctaw By Blood Enrollment Cards 1898-1914

Choctaw Nation

Choctaw Roll (Not Including Freedmen)   CARD NO. ▮▮▮▮

Dawes' Roll No.	NAME	Relationship to Person First Named	AGE	SEX	BLOOD	TRIBAL ENROLLMENT		
						Year	County	No.
13775	1 Folsom, Levina C	Named	52	F	3/4	1896	Blue	4357
13776	2 " Lewis L	Son	28	M	7/8	"	"	4358
13777	3 " Robert E	"	21	"	7/8	"	"	4360
13778	4 " Nannie A	Dau	14	F	7/8	"	"	4361
13779	5 " Maud H	"	11	"	7/8	"	"	4362
13780	6 " Ava V	"	6	"	7/8	"	"	4363
13781	7 " Roy E	Gr. Son	3mo	M	7/16			
	8 No1 Her Husband and father of children on this Card							
	9 as Alfred Wright Folsom on Choctaw Card #374							
	10 No3 Husband of Laura Folsom non-citz; Evidence of							
	11 marriage filed April 25" 1902 7-5908							
	12							
	13 Nos 1 to 7 inclusive originally enrolled on							
	14 Chickasaw Card No. 1168. Transferred to this							
	15 card October 18, 1902.							
	16							
	17							

Left margin: ENROLLMENT OF NOS. 1-2-3-4-5-6-7 HEREON APPROVED BY THE SECRETARY OF INTERIOR MAR 19 1903

TRIBAL ENROLLMENT OF PARENTS

	Name of Father	Year	County	Name of Mother	Year	County
1	Robert Colbert	Dead	Chickasaw Roll	Mah-lo-ta-ka	Dead	Chickasaw Roll
2	Alfred W. Folsom		Blue Co Choctaw Roll	No.1		
3	" " "		" "	No.1		
4	" " "		" "	No.1		
5	" " "		" "	No.1		
6	" " "		" "	No.1		
7	No.3			Laura Folsom		Non-citizen
8						
9	No1 On 96 Roll as "Piney C. Folsom" On Choctaw Census Record No.2 Page 186 as "Piney C. Folsom"					
10	" 2 " " " "Lewis L " " " " " " " " " " " "					
11	" 3 " " " "Robt. L " " " " " " " " " " 187					
12	" 4 " " " " " " " " " " "					
13	" 5 On 96 Roll as "Maud A Folsom" " " " " " " " " " as "Maud A Folsom"					
14	" 6 " " " "Ava N. " " " " " " " " " " " "Ava N. " "					
15	" 7 Born Jan 29" 1902; Enrolled April 25" 1902					
16	No3 is now the husband of Harriet Risener					
	on Choctaw card #3681: 12/22/02					
16					Date of Application for Enrollment.	
17	No4 P.O. Academy IT 10/23/05				Oct. 12" 1898	

Choctaw By Blood Enrollment Cards 1898-1914

RESIDENCE: Choctaw Nation   ~~COUNTY.~~   **Choctaw Nation**   **Choctaw Roll** (Not Including Freedmen)   CARD N
POST OFFICE: Nelson, Ind. Ter.   FIELD N

Dawes' Roll No.	NAME	Relationship to Person First Named	AGE	SEX	BLOOD	TRIBAL ENROLLMENT		
						Year	County	No.
IW607	1 Woods, Robert A	First Named	36	M	I.W.	1896	Kiamitia	15184
13782	2 " Mary A	Wife	26	F	1/4	"	"	13770
13783	3 " Lillie May	Dau	6	"	1/8	"	"	13771
13784	4 " Arthur	Son	2	M	1/8			
13785	5 " Ida Belle	Dau	4mo	F	1/8			
	6							
	7							
	8							
	9							
	10							
	11							
	12							
	13							
	14							
	15							
	16							
	17							

ENROLLMENT
OF NOS. 1 HEREON
APPROVED BY THE SECRETARY
OF INTERIOR FEB -8 1904

ENROLLMENT
OF NOS. 2-3-4-5 HEREON
APPROVED BY THE SECRETARY
OF INTERIOR MAR 19 1903

TRIBAL ENROLLMENT OF PARENTS

Name of Father	Year	County	Name of Mother	Year	County
1 Robert A Woods	Dead	Non-citizen	Elizabeth Woods	Dead	Non-Citizen
2 Robert Thompson		Gaines Co ~~Choctaw Roll~~	Siney Thompson	1897	Chick residing in Choctaw N. 1st Dist
3 No.1			No.2		
4 No.1			No.2		
5 No.1			No.2		
6					
7 No1		On Choctaw Intermarried Roll Page 116			
8 " 2		" " Census Record " 482			
9 " 3 On '96 Roll as "Lila M Woods" " " " " " " 482 as "Lila M Woods"					
" 4 Affidavit of attending Physician to be supplied. Received Nov 2nd 1898					
10 " 5 Enrolled May 12" 1899					
11 Nos. 1 to 5 inclusive originally enrolled on Chickasaw Card No. 1167 and transferred to this card Oct. 18, 1902.					
12					
13					
14					
15					
16					#1 to 4
17				Date of Application for Enrollment.	Oct. 12" 1898

Choctaw By Blood Enrollment Cards 1898-1914

RESIDENCE: Choctaw Nation ~~COUNTY~~.
POST OFFICE: Nelson, Ind. Ter.

Choctaw Nation

Choctaw Roll
(Not Including Freedmen)

CARD NO.
FIELD NO. 5432

Dawes' Roll No.	NAME	Relationship to Person First Named	AGE	SEX	BLOOD	TRIBAL ENROLLMENT		
						Year	County	No.
13786	1 Pierce, Ed	First Named	28	M	1/4	1896	Kiamitia	10440
13787	2 " Belle	Wife	28	F	1/4	"	"	10441
13788	3 " Hattie	Dau	6	"	1/4	"	"	10442
13789	4 " Alice	"	5	"	1/4	"	"	10443
13790	5 " Siney	"	2	"	1/4			
13791	6 " Susan J	Mother	55	"	1/2	1896	Kiamitia	10444
13792	7 " Robert L	Bro	23	M	1/4	"	"	10445
13793	8 " Henry C	Son	5mo	"	1/4	ENROLLMENT OF NOS. 10 HEREON APPROVED BY THE SECRETARY OF INTERIOR MAY 21 1904		
13794	9 " Ella May	Dau	3mo	F	1/4			
IW850	10 " Maudie May	Wife of Nº7	22	F	I.W.			
	11 ENROLLMENT OF NOS. 12345678&9 HEREON APPROVED BY THE SECRETARY OF INTERIOR MAR 19 1903							
	14 Nos 1 to 9 inclusive originally enrolled on Chick. Card No 1168.							
	15 Transferred to this card Oct. 18, 1902.							
	16 For child of Nos 7&10 see NB (Ap 26-06) Card #408							
	" " " " 1&2 " " (Mar3-05) " #278							
	17 " " " " 7&10 " " " " " #1386							

TRIBAL ENROLLMENT OF PARENTS

Name of Father	Year	County	Name of Mother	Year	County
1 Robert Pierce	Dead	Non-Citizen	No.6	1897	Chick residing in Choctaw N, 3rd Dist
2 Robert Thompson		Gaines Co ~~Choctaw Roll~~	Siney Thompson	1897	" " 1st "
3	No.1		No.2		
4	No.1		No.2		
5	No.1		No.2		
6 Wm Stewart	Dead	Chickasaw Roll	Matilda Stewart	Dead	Chickasaw Roll
7 Robert Pierce	Dead	Non-Citizen	No.6		
8	No.1		No.2		
9	No.1		No.2		
10 D W Wood		non citizen	Julia Wood		noncitizen
11 Nos 1,2,3,4,6,&7 on Choctaw Census Record No2, Page 400					
12 No5 Affidavit of attending Physician to be supplied. Received Nov 7" 1898					
13 " 7 Husband of Maudie May Pierce on Chickasaw Card #D.369 Sept 22nd 1902					
" Now at San Antonio, Texas, Member 4th Texas Volunteers; On 96 Roll as "Robt L Pierce"					
14 " 8 Enrolled May 17" 1899					
15 " 9 Born May 23rd 1902: Enrolled Sept 4" 1902				#1 to 7 inc	
16 No10 transferred from Chickasaw card D369 April 13, 1904			Date of Application for Enrollment.		
17 See decision of March 15, 1904			Oct. 12" 1898		

Choctaw By Blood Enrollment Cards 1898-1914

Choctaw Nation

Choctaw Roll
(Not Including Freedmen)

CARD NO.
FIELD NO. **5433**

Dawes' Roll No.	NAME	Relationship to Person First Named	AGE	SEX	BLOOD	TRIBAL ENROLLMENT		
						Year	County	No.
13795	1 Wesley, Elias		24	M	1/2	1896	Tobucksy	13000
	2							
	3							
	4							
	5							
	6							
	7							
	8							
	9	ENROLLMENT						
	10	OF NOS. 1 HEREON APPROVED BY THE SECRETARY						
	11	OF INTERIOR mar 19 1903						
	12							
	13							
	14							
	15							
	16							
	17							

TRIBAL ENROLLMENT OF PARENTS

	Name of Father	Year	County	Name of Mother	Year	County
1	Te-i-nin-tub-by	Dead	Choctaw Roll	Icy Wade	1897	Chick residing in Choctaw N. 1st Dist
2						
3						
4						
5			No1 On Choctaw Census Record No.2, Tobucksy Co, Page 463			
6			" Husband of Siley Wesley Choctaw Roll Card #377			
7			No.1 originally enrolled on Chickasaw Card No. 1169. Transferred			
8			to this card Oct. 18, 1902.			
9			For child of No1 see NB (Mar 3, 1905) #1387			
10						
11						
12						
13						
14						
15						Date of Application for Enrollment.
16						
17						Oct. 12"1898

Choctaw By Blood Enrollment Cards 1898-1914

Dawes' Roll No.	NAME	Relationship to Person First Named	AGE	SEX	BLOOD	TRIBAL ENROLLMENT		
						Year	County	No.
DP	1 Adams, John Quincey		40	M	I.W.			
13796	2 " Arabella F	Wife	26	F	1/2	1896	Blue	4359
13797	3 " Nanava M	Dau	2mo	"				
	4							
	5							
	6 No1 transferred to Chickasaw							
	7 card #1828. October 19, 1905. See							
	8 decision of October 3, 1905.							
	9							
	10							
	11 ENROLLMENT							
	12 OF NOS. 2-3- HEREON APPROVED BY THE SECRETARY							
	13 OF INTERIOR Mar 19, 1903							
	14							
	15							
	16							
	17							

TRIBAL ENROLLMENT OF PARENTS

	Name of Father	Year	County	Name of Mother	Year	County
1	Heber W Adams		non-citizen	Elizabeth Adams		Non-Citizen
2	Alfred W Folsom		Blue Co Choctaw Roll	Levina Folsom	1897	Chick residing in Choctaw N. 3rd Dist
3	No.1			No.2		
4						
5	No1 admitted as Chick by Dawes Comm #2 but by Judgement U.S.Court at Ardmore of 3/9/98 he was denied citizenship					
6	No.1 admitted as Chick by Dawes Comm but reversed by U.S. Court Nov 15" 1897 (Does not appear to be in					
7	C.C.C.C. Note: The action of the Commission and U.S. Court as to his application was as to his marriage to					
8	Mary Parker, as the time of his marriage to No2 May 25" 1897 he was in possession of a Dawes Commission					
9	Judgement and Judgement of Court was not until Nov 15" 1897)					
	No.2 On 96 Roll as "Arabella B. Folsom" On Choctaw Census Record No.2 Blue Co Page 186					
10	No.3 Affidavit of midwife to be supplied: Received Oct 31st 1898					
11	Nos 1,2 and 3 originally enrolled on Chickasaw Card No. 1172. Transferred to this card Oct. 18,					
	1902.					
12	Certified copy of divorce proceedings between Mary C. Adams and No1 filed April 10, 1903					
13						
14	No.1 Granted as Chickasaw "I.W." Oct. 3-1905					
15	P.O Antlers 7/5/05					
16	P.O. Midway I.T. 1/17/03				Date of Application for Enrollment.	
17	P.O. Antlers I.T. 12/22/03			Oct. 12"1898		

34

Choctaw By Blood Enrollment Cards 1898-1914

RESIDENCE: Choctaw Nation ~~COUNTY~~. **Choctaw Nation** Choctaw Roll CARD NO.
POST OFFICE: South Canadian Ind Ter (Not Including Freedmen) FIELD NO. **5435**

Dawes' Roll No.	NAME	Relationship to Person First Named	AGE	SEX	BLOOD	TRIBAL ENROLLMENT		
						Year	County	No.
13798	1 McLish, John E	First Named	27	M	1/8	1896	Tobucksy	9218
	2							
	3							
	4							
	5							
	6							
	7							
	8							
	9							
	10							
	11	ENROLLMENT						
	12	OF NOS. 1 HEREON APPROVED BY THE SECRETARY						
	13	OF INTERIOR Mar 19, 1903						
	14							
	15							
	16							
	17							

TRIBAL ENROLLMENT OF PARENTS

	Name of Father	Year	County	Name of Mother	Year	County
1	Ben McLish	Dead	Chickasaw Roll	Julia McLish	Dead	Pontotoc
2						
3						
4						
5						
6	No1 on 96 Roll as "Ino E McClish"					
7	" " Choctaw Census Record #2 Page 366					
8	No1 originally enrolled on Chickasaw Card No 1180 and					
9	transferred to this card October 18, 1902.					
10						
11						
12						
13						
14						
15					Date of Application for Enrollment.	
16						
17					Oct. 12" 1898	

35

Choctaw By Blood Enrollment Cards 1898-1914

RESIDENCE: Choctaw Nation ~~COUNTY.~~ **Choctaw Nation**   Choctaw Roll   CARD NO.
POST OFFICE: McAlester, Ind. Ter.   *(Not Including Freedmen)*   FIELD NO. **5436**

Dawes' Roll No.	NAME	Relationship to Person First Named	AGE	SEX	BLOOD	TRIBAL ENROLLMENT		
						Year	County	No.
13799	1 Folsom, Alfred W	Named	45	M	1/2	1896	Tobucksy	4009
DP2260	2 " Jensy N	Wife	40	F	I.W.	"	"	14523
	3							
	4							
	5							
	6							
	7							
	8							
	9							
	10							
	11							
	12							
	13							
	14							
	15							
	16							
	17							

ENROLLMENT
OF NOS. 1 HEREON
APPROVED BY THE SECRETARY
OF INTERIOR Mar. 19, 1903

TRIBAL ENROLLMENT OF PARENTS

Name of Father	Year	County	Name of Mother	Year	County
1 Alex Folsom	Dead	Choctaw Roll		Dead	Chickasaw Roll
2 Reynolds	"	Non-Citizen		"	Non-Citizen
3					
4 No1 on 96 Roll as Alfred W Fulsom, on Choctaw Census Record No2 Page 170					
5 " 2 " " " " " " " Intermarried Roll " 30					
~~Marriage Certificate to be supplied. Received Oct 31st 1898~~					
6 Nos 1 & 2 originally enrolled on Chick. Card No 2283. Transferred					
7 to this card Oct. 18, 1902					
8			13980		
9					
10			~~NOTICE OF DEPARTMENTAL ACTION~~		
11			MAILED PARTIES HEREIN Feb. 8, 1907		
12 Jan 22/07 decision of Aug 20/06 affirmed by Dept. and					
13 No.2 REFUSED Aug 20, 1906.					
~~August 20, 1906 Record forwarded Department~~					
14 Oct. 30, 1906 Motion for appeal forwarded Department					
15					
16					
17 PO Atoka IT 11/20/02			Date of Application for Enrollment.	Oct. 12"1898	

36

Choctaw By Blood Enrollment Cards 1898-1914

RESIDENCE: Chocta[sic] Nation ~~COUNTY~~.
POST OFFICE: Sans Bois, Ind. Ter.

Choctaw Nation

Choctaw Roll *(Not Including Freedmen)*

CARD NO.
FIELD NO. **5437**

Dawes' Roll No.	NAME	Relationship to Person First Named	AGE	SEX	BLOOD	TRIBAL ENROLLMENT		
						Year	County	No.
13800	₁ Noel, Ben		23	M	1/4	1896	Sans Bois	9544
13801	₂ " Edward	Son	6wks	M	1/8			
IW 1267	₃ " Chaney	Wife	24	F	I.W.			
	4							
	5							
	6							
	7							
	8							
	9	ENROLLMENT						
	10	OF NOS. 1 - 2 HEREON						
	11	APPROVED BY THE SECRETARY OF INTERIOR Mar. 19 1903						
	12							
	13	ENROLLMENT						
	14	OF NOS. 3 HEREON						
	15	APPROVED BY THE SECRETARY OF INTERIOR Dec. 30, 1904						
	16							
	17							

TRIBAL ENROLLMENT OF PARENTS

	Name of Father	Year	County	Name of Mother	Year	County
1	Peter Noel	Dead	Sans Bois Co Choctaw Roll	Lorinda Noel	Dead	Chick residing in Choctaw N. 1st Dist
2	No.1			Chaney Noel		
3	Dave Spradley		Non-Citizen	Ellen Spradley		Non-Citizen
4						
5						

No1 on Choctaw Census Record Sans Bois Co, No2 Page 316
 "   ~~Father Peter Noel full blood Choctaw; Mother Lorinda Noel half Choctaw and half~~
    Chickasaw; Maternal Grandmother full blood Chickasaw
 "   Wife of, Chaney Noel on Chickasaw Card #D.159
No.2 Enrolled March 15th 1901.

Nos 1and2 originally enrolled on Chickasaw Card No 1184 and
    transferred to this card Oct. 18, 1902.
No3 originally listed for enrollment Oct. 12/98 on Chickasaw Card #D159
~~transferred to this Card Dec 15 1904. See decision of Nov. 29, 1904.~~

Date of Application for Enrollment.
Oct. 12th 1898

37

Choctaw By Blood Enrollment Cards 1898-1914

RESIDENCE: Chocta█████████████ **Choctaw Nation** **Choctaw Roll** CARD No.
POST OFFICE: Featherston, Ind. Ter. *(Not Including Freedmen)* FIELD No. **5438**

Dawes' Roll No.	NAME	Relationship to Person First Named	AGE	SEX	BLOOD	TRIBAL ENROLLMENT		
						Year	County	No.
13802	1 Moore, Joseph	First Named	34	M	Full	1896	Sans Bois	8417
	2							
	3							
	4							
	5							
	6							
	7							
	8							
	9							
	10							
	11	ENROLLMENT						
	12	OF NOS. 1 HEREON APPROVED BY THE SECRETARY						
	13	OF INTERIOR Mar. 9, 1903						
	14							
	15							
	16							
	17							

TRIBAL ENROLLMENT OF PARENTS

	Name of Father	Year	County	Name of Mother	Year	County
1	No-ubby Moore	Dead	Chickasaw Roll	Emeline Moore	Dead	Chickasaw Roll
2						
3						
4						
5	No1 on Choctaw Census Record No2, Sans Bois Co, Page 345.					
6	" Husband of Mary Moore Choctaw Roll Card #380					
7	No1 originally enrolled on Chickasaw Card No. 1191. Transferred to this card Oct. 18, 1902.					
8						
9	For child of No1 see NB (Mar. 3rd 1905) Card #84					
10						
11						
12						
13						
14						
15						
16						
17				Date of Application for Enrollment.		Oct. 12" 1898

38

Choctaw By Blood Enrollment Cards 1898-1914

RESIDENCE: Choctaw Nation ~~COUNTY.~~ **Choctaw Na**~~tion~~...oll CARD No.
POST OFFICE: Featherston, Ind. Ter. *(Not Including Freedmen)* FIELD No. **5439**

Dawes' Roll No.	NAME	Relationship to Person First Named	AGE	SEX	BLOOD	TRIBAL ENROLLMENT		
						Year	County	No.
13803	₁ Colbert, Lily	First Named	28	F	Full	1896	Sans Bois	2104
13804	₂ Choate, Jimmie	Son	12	M	1/2	"	" "	2105
13805	₃ " Mary	Dau	9	F	1/2	"	" "	2106
13806	₄ Colbert, Willie	Son	6	M	Full	"	" "	2107
	₅							
	₆							
	₇							
	₈							
	₉							
	₁₀							
	₁₁	ENROLLMENT						
	₁₂	OF NOS. 1-2-3-4 HEREON APPROVED BY THE SECRETARY						
	₁₃	OF INTERIOR MAR 19 1903						
	₁₄							
	₁₅							
	₁₆							
	₁₇							

TRIBAL ENROLLMENT OF PARENTS

	Name of Father	Year	County	Name of Mother	Year	County
₁	Charles Wright	Dead	Chickasaw Roll	Tom-mah-ho-ye	Dead	Chickasaw Roll
₂	Albert Choate	"	Choctaw Roll	No.1		
₃	" "	"	" "	No.1		
₄	Elias Colbert	"	Chick residing in ~~Choctaw N. 1ˢᵗ Dist~~	No.1		
₅						
₆						
₇						
₈	Nos 1,2,3&4 on Choctaw Census Record, Sans Bois Co, Page 85					
₉						
₁₀	Nos 1 to 4 inclusive originally enrolled on Chickasaw Card No. 1193 and transferred to this card Oct. 18, 1902.					
₁₁						
₁₂						
₁₃						
₁₄						
₁₅						
₁₆				Date of Application for Enrollment.		
₁₇					Oct. 12"1898	

39

Choctaw By Blood Enrollment Cards 1898-1914

RESIDENCE: Choctaw Nation ~~COUNTY.~~
POST OFFICE: Featherston, Ind. Ter.

Choctaw Nation

Choctaw Roll *(Not Including Freedmen)*

CARD NO.
FIELD NO. 54

Dawes' Roll No.	NAME	Relationship to Person First Named	AGE	SEX	BLOOD	TRIBAL ENROLLMENT		
						Year	County	No.
13807	₁ Byington, Nancy	First Named	23	F	Full	1896	Sans Bois	7696
13808	₂ Lewis, Emily	Dau	2	"	"	"	" "	7697
14831	₃ Riddle, Lucinda	"	3mo	"	"			
15694	₄ " Susan	"	7mo	"	"			
	₅							
	₆	ENROLLMENT						
	₇	OF NOS. 1 - 2 HEREON APPROVED BY THE SECRETARY						
	₈	OF INTERIOR MAR 19 1903						
	₉							
	₁₀							
	₁₁	ENROLLMENT OF NOS. 3 HEREON						
	₁₂	APPROVED BY THE SECRETARY OF INTERIOR MAY 20 1903						
	₁₃	ENROLLMENT						
	₁₄	OF NOS. 4 HEREON						
	₁₅	APPROVED BY THE SECRETARY OF INTERIOR DEC -2 1904						
	₁₆							
	₁₇							

TRIBAL ENROLLMENT OF PARENTS

Name of Father	Year	County	Name of Mother	Year	County
₁ Wallace Byington	Dead	Chickasaw Roll	Phoebe Byington	Dead	Chickasaw Roll
₂ Tom Lewis	1897	Chick residing in Choctaw N. 1ˢᵗ Dist	No.1		
₃ Coleman Riddle	1896		No.1		Illegitimate
₄ " "	1896	San Bois	No.1		
₅					
₆	No1 on 96 Roll as Nancy Lewis; On Choctaw Census Record No 21 Sans Bois Co as "Nancy Lewis"				
₇	No 2 " " " ; " " " " " " " "				
₈	Nos 1,2 and 3 originally enrolled on Chick. Card #1192 and transferred to this card Oct. 18, 1902.				
₉	No3 Born May 26, 1899; proof of birth filed Feby 20, 1903				
₁₀	No1 is the wife of Coleman Riddle on Choctaw card #4723				
₁₁	No4 Born May 31, 1902. Application made Dec 22, 1902 only one affidavit being furnished. Complete affidavits of birth filed and No4 enrolled March 29, 1904				
₁₂	For child of No.1 see NB (March 3, 1905) #1381				
₁₃					
₁₄					
₁₅				Date of Application for Enrollment.	#1 to 2
₁₆					9/6/99
₁₇					Oct. 12" 1898

Choctaw By Blood Enrollment Cards 1898-1914

RESIDENCE: Choctaw Nation ~~COUNTY.~~ **Choctaw Nation** Choct[blacked out]
POST OFFICE: Hartshorn[sic], Ind Ter. *(Not Includi[ ])*

Dawes' Roll No.	NAME	Relationship to Person First Named	AGE	SEX	BLOOD	TRIBAL ENROLLMENT		
						Year	County	No.
13809	1 Pulcher, Sarah		40	F	Full	1896	Gaines	10213
13810	2 " Belle	Dau	10	"	1/2	"	"	10314
13811	3 " Alice	"	8	"	1/2	"	"	10315
13812	4 " Osborn	Son	1	M	"			
	5							
	6							
	7							
	8							
	9							
	10							
	11	ENROLLMENT						
	12	OF NOS. 1-2-3-4 HEREON APPROVED BY THE SECRETARY						
	13	OF INTERIOR MAR 19 1903						
	14							
	15							
	16							
	17							

TRIBAL ENROLLMENT OF PARENTS

	Name of Father	Year	County	Name of Mother	Year	County
1	George Johnson	Dead	Chickasaw Roll	Lucy Johnson	Dead	Chickasaw Roll
2	John Pulcher		Gaines Co Choctaw Roll	No.1		
3	" "		" "	No.1		
4	" "		" "	No.1		
5						
6						
7	No1,2,& 3 on Choctaw Census Record, Gaines Co, Page 394					
8	Nos 1 to 4 inclusive originally enrolled on Chick. Card #1201 and transferred to this card Oct. 18, 1902					
9						
10						
11						
12						
13						
14						
15						Date of Application for Enrollment.
16						
17						Oct. 12" 1898

41

Choctaw By Blood Enrollment Cards 1898-1914

RESIDENCE: Choctaw Nation   ~~COUNTY~~,   **Nation**   CARD NO.
POST OFFICE: Stigler, Ind. Ter.   FIELD NO. **5442**

Dawes' Roll No.	NAME	Relationship to Person First Named	AGE	SEX	BLOOD	TRIBAL ENROLLMENT		
						Year	County	No.
13813	₁ Palmer, Myrtle		12	F	1/4	1896	Sans Bois	10050
13814	₂ " Benjamin Cleveland	Bro	9	M	1/4	"	" "	10051
	₃							
	₄							
	₅							
	₆							
	₇							
	₈							
	₉							
	₁₀							
	₁₁	ENROLLMENT						
	₁₂	OF NOS. 1- 2- HEREON APPROVED BY THE SECRETARY						
	₁₃	OF INTERIOR MAR 19 1903						
	₁₄							
	₁₅							
	₁₆							
	₁₇							

TRIBAL ENROLLMENT OF PARENTS

	Name of Father	Year	County	Name of Mother	Year	County
₁	Benj. F. Palmer		White man	Adaline Palmer	Dead	Chick residing in Choctaw N. 1st Dist
₂	" " "		" "	" "	"	" " " "
₃						
₄	No 1		On Choctaw Census Record Sans Bois Co No2 Page 390			
₅	" 2 On 96 Roll as "Benjamin Palmer" " "		"	" "	"	" " " "
₆	as "Benjamin Palmer" 1&2 Father of, Benjamin F. Palmer on Chickasaw #D.165					
₇						
₈	Nos 1 and 2 originally enrolled on Chick. Card on No. 1204 and					
₉	transferred to this card Oct. 18, 1902. For child of No.1 see NB (March 3, 1905) #1350					
₁₀						
₁₁						
₁₂						
₁₃						
₁₄						
₁₅					Date of Application for Enrollment.	
₁₆						
₁₇					Oct. 13ʳᵈ 1898	

42

Choctaw By Blood Enrollment Cards 1898-1914

RESIDENCE: Choctaw Nation   Choctaw Roll   CARD NO.

POST OFFICE: Bennington, Ind. Ter.   (Not Including Freedmen)   FIELD NO. **5443**

Dawes' Roll No.	NAME	Relationship to Person First Named				Year	TRIBAL ENROLLMENT County	No.
IW608	1 Lloyd, John M	First Named	28	M	IW	1896	Jackson	14772
13815	2 " Ida	Wife	24	F	1/4	"	"	8168
13816	3 " Anneta	Dau	3	"	1/8	"	"	8169
13817	4 " Charley	Son	2	M	1/8	"	"	8170
13818	5 " William Gregg	"	3mo	"	1/8			
13819	6 " Russell	"	12da	"	1/8			
	7							
	8 ENROLLMENT							
	9 OF NOS. 2-3-4-5-6 HEREON APPROVED BY THE SECRETARY							
	10 OF INTERIOR MAR 19 1903							
	11 ENROLLMENT							
	12 OF NOS. 1 HEREON APPROVED BY THE SECRETARY							
	13 OF INTERIOR FEB -8 1904							
	14							
	15							
	16							
	17							

TRIBAL ENROLLMENT OF PARENTS

Name of Father	Year	County	Name of Mother	Year	County
1 W.J.B. Lloyd		Non-Citizen	Mattie Lloyd		Non-Citizen
2 Dave Watts	Dead	Choctaw Roll	Minerva Watts	Dead	Chick residing in Choctaw N. 3rd Dist
3	No.1		No.2		
4	No.1		No.2		
5	No.1		No.2		
6	No.1		No.2		
7					

8 No.1 on 96 Roll as "John Lloyd" On Choctaw Intermarried Roll Page 64

9 2 " " " " " Census Record No.2 " 338

10 3 " " " as "Arnetta Lloyd" " " " " " " "
   4 " " " " "Charlie " " " " " " " " "

11 6 Enrolled Feb. 13" 1901

12 Nos 1 to 6 inclusive originally enrolled on Chick. Card No. 1205 and

13 transferred to this card Oct. 18, 1902.
   Nos 1 and 3 admitted by Dawes Commission in 1896, Choc. Case No. 1253

14 For child of Nos 1&2 see NB (March 3, 1905) #1232

					Date of Application for Enrollment.

43

Choctaw By Blood Enrollment Cards 1898-1914

RESIDENCE: Choctaw Nation ~~COUNTY~~.
POST OFFICE: Stewart, Ind. Ter

Choctaw Nation

Choctaw Roll
(Not Including Freedmen)

Dawes' Roll No.	NAME	Relationship to Person First Named	AGE	SEX	BLOOD	TRIBAL ENROLLMENT Year	County	No.
13820	1 Wade, Alemos F		40	M	1/2	1896	Tobucksy	12997
	2							
	3							
	4							
	5							
	6							
	7							
	8							
	9							
	10							
	11	ENROLLMENT						
	12	OF NOS. 1 HEREON APPROVED BY THE SECRETARY						
	13	OF INTERIOR MAR 19 1903						
	14							
	15							
	16							
	17							

TRIBAL ENROLLMENT OF PARENTS

	Name of Father	Year	County	Name of Mother	Year	County
1	Thlock-o-fin-tubby	Dead	Choctaw Roll	Mutch-a-toi-ye	Dead	
2						
3						
4						
5	No1 Also on Choctaw Census Record No.2 Page 463					
6	" Husband of Icy Wade Choctaw Roll, Card #63					
7	No.1 originally enrolled on Chickasaw Card #32 . Transferred to this card Oct. 20, 1902.					
8						
9						
10						
11						
12						
13						
14						
15						
16						
17				Date of Application for Enrollment.	Sept 7" 1898	

44

Choctaw By Blood Enrollment Cards 1898-1914

RESIDENCE: Choctaw Nation ~~COUNTY.~~ **Choctaw Nation**   Choctaw Roll   CARD NO.

POST OFFICE: Stewart Ind. Ter.   (Not Including Freedmen)   FIELD NO. **5445**

Dawes' Roll No.	NAME	Relationship to Person First Named	AGE	SEX	BLOOD	TRIBAL ENROLLMENT		
						Year	County	No.
13821	₁ Watson, Ida		8	F	1/4	1896	Atoka	14000
14950	₂ Laflore, Bensey	Mother	30	F	1/2	1896	Tobucksey	13039
	3							
	4							
	5							
	6	ENROLLMENT						
	7	OF NOS. 2 HEREON						
	8	~~APPROVED BY THE SECRETARY~~ OF INTERIOR OCT 15 1903						
	9							
	10							
	11							
	12							
	13	ENROLLMENT						
	14	OF NOS. 1 HEREON ~~APPROVED BY THE SECRETARY~~						
	15	OF INTERIOR MAR 19 1903						
	16							
	17							

TRIBAL ENROLLMENT OF PARENTS

Name of Father	Year	County	Name of Mother	Year	County
₁ Elias Watson	Dead	Atoka Co ~~Choctaw Roll~~	Laflore, Bensey		Chick residing in ~~Choctaw N. 3ʳᵈ Dist~~
₂ Adam Laflore	Dead	Choctaw roll	Micey Sealy		
3					
4					
5					
6 No1 On Choctaw Census Record No2 Page 485					
7 " Daughter of Bensey Laflore on Chickasaw Card #315.					
8					
9 No.1 originally enrolled on Chick. Card No 315. Transferred to this					
10 card Oct. 20, 1902.					
11 No2 transferred from Chickasaw card #315 August 15, 1903. See					
~~decision of July 30, 1903.~~					
12 No2 on Choctaw 1896 census roll as Bensy[sic] L. Wade					
13					
14					
15				Date of Application for Enrollment.	
16					
17				Sept 7" 1898	

Choctaw By Blood Enrollment Cards 1898-1914

RESIDENCE: Choctaw Nation ~~COUNTY.~~ **Choctaw Nation** Choctaw Roll CARD NO.
POST OFFICE: Jeff Ind. Ter (Not Including Freedmen) FIELD NO. **5446**

Dawes' Roll No.	NAME	Relationship to Person First Named	AGE	SEX	BLOOD	TRIBAL ENROLLMENT Year	County	No.
13822	1 Scott, Phoebe	First Named	26	F	1/4	1896	Atoka	11671
~~DEAD~~	2 " ~~Andrew J~~	~~Son~~	~~6~~	~~M~~	~~1/8~~	"	"	~~11672~~
13823	3 " John	"	3	"	1/8	"	"	11673
13824	4 " Laura	Dau	1	F	1/8			
13825	5 " Lula Elizabeth	"	2mo	"	1/8			
	6							
	7							
	8 No. __2__ HEREON DISMISSED UNDER ORDER OF THE COMMISSION TO THE FIVE 9 CIVILIZED TRIBES OF MARCH 31, 1905.							
	10							
	11 ENROLLMENT OF NOS. **1-3-4-5** HEREON 12 APPROVED BY THE SECRETARY OF INTERIOR MAR 19 1903							
	13							
	14							
	15							
	16							
	17							

TRIBAL ENROLLMENT OF PARENTS

Name of Father	Year	County	Name of Mother	Year	County
1 Ben Burris	Dead	Choctaw	Salina Walton	1897	Pontotoc
2 ~~John P Scott~~		~~I.W.~~	~~No.1~~		
3 " " "		" "	No.1		
4 " " "		" "	No.1		
5 " " "		" "	No.1		
6 No1 On Choctaw Census Record No.2 Page 431					
7 " 2 " " " ~~" " " "~~ ; On '96 Roll as A.J. Scott					
8 " 4 " " " " " " " ~~Evidence of Birth received & filed Mar 25" 1902~~					
9 " 5 Enrolled Oct 16" 1900					
10 Nos 1 to 5 inclusive originally enrolled on Chick Card No 265 and transferred to this card October 20, 1902.					
11 ~~No2 Died Dec. 12, 1899; proof of death filed Nov. 12, 1902~~					
12 For child of No1 see NB (March 3, 1905) #1118					
13					
14					
15					
16					
17 P.O. Lella I.T. 6/16/03			Date of Application for Enrollment.		Sept 6" 1898

46

Choctaw By Blood Enrollment Cards 1898-1914

RESIDENCE: Choctaw Nation 3rd Dist ~~COUNTY~~

POST OFFICE: Lehigh Ind Ter

Choctaw Nation

Choctaw Roll (Not Including Freedmen)

CARD NO.
FIELD NO. **5447**

Dawes' Roll No.	NAME	Relationship to Person First Named	AGE	SEX	BLOOD	TRIBAL ENROLLMENT		
						Year	County	No.
DEAD.	1 Burris, Edmund		18	M	Full	1896	Atoka	1736
15030	2 Roberts, Josephine		4	F	1/2	"	"	10984
	3							
	4							
	5							
	6							
	7							
	8							
	9							
	10							
	11							
	12							
	13							
	14							
	15							
	16							
	17							

ENROLLMENT
OF NOS. 2 HEREON
APPROVED BY THE SECRETARY
OF INTERIOR OCT 15 1903

No. 1 HEREON DISMISSED UNDER ORDER OF THE COMMISSION TO THE FIVE CIVILIZED TRIBES OF MARCH 31, 1905.

TRIBAL ENROLLMENT ...'S

Name of Father	Year	County		f Mother	Year	County
						Chick residing in Choctaw N. 3rd Dist
1 ~~John Burris~~	Dead	~~Chickasaw Roll~~		Burris	Dead	
2 Sampson Roberts		Choctaw Roll		Roberts	"	" " " "
3						
4						
5 No1 On Choctaw Census Record No.2 Page 71						
6 " 2 " " " " " 415						
7 ~~Nos 1&2 Grandchildren of Becca Roberts on Chickasaw Roll Card #200~~						
8 Nos 1 and 2 originally enrolled on Chick. Card #200 Transferred to this card Oct. 20, 1902.						
9 No1 died in Dec. 1900; proof of death filed Nov. 26, 1902.						
10 ~~No2 " " Nov. 1900, " " " " " " Error.~~						
11 ~~Letter received from Sampson Roberts dated Feby 27, 1903 stating that No2 is not dead, filed herein March 24, 1903.~~						
12 Notations as to death of No.2 are erroneous: Nov. 5, 1903.						
13						
14						
15						
16						Date of Application for Enrollment.
17						Sept 5" 1898

47

Choctaw By Blood Enrollment Cards 1898-1914

POST OFFICE: Jackson Ind. Ter.   *(Not Including Freedmen)*   FIELD NO. **5448**

Dawes' Roll No.	NAME	Relationship to Person First Named	AGE	SEX	BLOOD	TRIBAL ENROLLMENT		
						Year	County	No.
13826	1 LeFlore, Michael W	First Named	24	M	1/8	1896	Jackson	8153
	2							
	3							
	4							
	5							
	6							
	7							
	8							
	9							
	10	ENROLLMENT						
	11	OF NOS. 1 HEREON						
	12	APPROVED BY THE SECRETARY OF INTERIOR MAR 19 1903						
	13							
	14							
	15							
	16							
	17							

TRIBAL ENROLLMENT OF PARENTS

Name of Father	Year	County	Name of Mother	Year	County
1 Wm Le Flore		Choctaw	Rosanna LeFlore		Chickasaw
2					
3					
4					
5					
6 No1 On 96 Roll also #8119 as Michael LeFlore					
7 " " " " #8153 " " "					
8 No.1 originally enrolled on Chick. Card #1524 and transferred to this card Oct. 20, 1902					
9					
10					
11					
12					
13					
14					
15					
16					
17				Date of Application for Enrollment.	Aug. 21st 99	

Choctaw By Blood Enrollment Cards 1898-1914

Dawes' Roll No.	NAME	Relationship to Person First Named	AGE	SEX	BLOOD	TRIBAL ENROLLMENT		
						Year	County	No.
13827	1 LeFlore, Rosanna	First Named	45	F	1/4	1896	Jackson	8109
13828	2 " William W	Son	21	M	1/8	"	"	8112
13829	3 " Jincey	Dau	15	F	1/8	"	"	8116
13830	4 " Jorilla	"	12	"	1/8	"	"	8114
13831	5 " Josephine	"	12	"	1/8	"	"	8115
13832	6 " David A	Son	10	M	1/8	"	"	8117
13833	7 " Thomas J	"	2	"	1/8			
IW851	8 " Daisy	Wife of N°2	22	F	I.W.			
	9							
	10							
	11							

ENROLLMENT
OF NOS. 1-2-3-4-5-6-7 HEREON
APPROVED BY THE SECRETARY
OF INTERIOR MAR 19 1903

ENROLLMENT
OF NOS. 8 HEREON
APPROVED BY THE SECRETARY
OF INTERIOR MAY 21 1904

TRIBAL ENROLLMENT OF PA___

Name of Father	Year	County	N___er		Year	County
1 William Wilson	Dead	Choctaw	Ellen ___		Dead	Chickasaw
2 William LeFlore	Choc 12-69-C.C.3599	"	No.1			
3 " "		"	No.1			
4 " "		"	No.1			
5 " "		"	No.1			
6 " "		"	No.1			
7 " "		"	No.1			
8 John Smith		noncitizen	Eliza Smith			noncitizen

9 No1 On 96 Roll as "Rose LeFlore"

10 " 2 " " " " "Willie W. LeFlore" now the Husband of Daisy LeFlore on Chickasaw Card

" 4 " " " " "Joulla LeFlore" #D358 June 26/02

11 " 5 " " " " "David " " " For children of Nos 2&8 see NB (Mar 3'05) #418

12 " 7 Affidavit of Birth to be filed. Filed Nov 4" 1899

13 Nos 1 to 7 inclusive originally enrolled on Chick. Card #1523. Transferred to this card Oct. 20, 1902.

14 For child of Nos 2&8 see NB (Apr 26-06) Card #283.

15 No 1 transferred from Chickasaw card D351 April 13, 1904.

16 See decision of March 15, 1904.

#1 to 7
Date of Application
for Enrollment.
Aug 21st '99

49

Choctaw By Blood Enrollment Cards 1898-1914

RESIDENCE: Choctaw Nation ~~COUNTY.~~ POST OFFICE: Durant Ind. Ter.

Choctaw Nation

Choctaw Roll *(Not Including Freedmen)*

CARD NO.
FIELD NO. **5450**

Dawes' Roll No.	NAME	Relationship to Person First Named	AGE	SEX	BLOOD	TRIBAL ENROLLMENT		
						Year	County	No.
13834	1 Robinson, William	First Named	18	M	1/4	1896	Blue	10895
	2							
	3							
	4							
	5							
	6							
	7							
	8							
	9							
	10							
	11	ENROLLMENT						
	12	OF NOS. 1 HEREON APPROVED BY THE SECRETARY						
	13	OF INTERIOR Mar. 9, 1903						
	14							
	15							
	16							
	17							

TRIBAL ENROLLMENT OF PARENTS

	Name of Father	Year	County	Name of Mother	Year	County
1	F.R. Robinson		I.W. Choctaw	Salina Robinson	Dead	Chick. Roll
2						
3						
4						
5	No.1 His Father F. R. Robinson is on Choctaw Card #3403, having been admitted					
6	by Dawes Com. as an Intermarried Choctaw under name of "F.R. Roberson"					
7						
8	No.1 originally enrolled on Chickasaw Card No. 1497. Transferred					
9	to this card Oct. 20, 1902					
10						
11						
12						
13						
14						
15					Date of Application for Enrollment.	
16						
17					Aug. 15, 1899	

Choctaw By Blood Enrollment Cards 1898-1914

RESIDENCE: Choctaw Nation ~~COUNTY~~ **Choctaw Nation** Choctaw Roll CARD NO.
POST OFFICE: Durant Ind. Ter (Not Including Freedmen) FIELD NO. **5451**

Dawes' Roll No.	NAME	Relationship to Person First Named	AGE	SEX	BLOOD	TRIBAL ENROLLMENT		
						Year	County	No.
13835	1 Mullens, Tempy	First Named	18	F	1/4	1896	Blue	8754
13836	2 " Lewis	Son	3	M	1/8			8755
13837	3 " Claude	"						
13838	4 " Marvin Allen	"						
	5							
	6							
	7							
	8							
	9							
	10							
	11	ENROLLMENT						
	12	OF NOS. 1-2-3-4 HEREON APPROVED BY THE SECRETARY						
	13	OF INTERIOR MAR 19 1903						
	14							
	15							
	16							
	17							

TRIBAL ENROLLMENT OF PARENTS

	Name of Father	Year	County	Name of Mother	Year	County
1	Fred Robinson		Non-Citizen	Saline Robinson	Dead	Chick. Roll
2	Jasper Mullens		" "	No.1		
3	" "		" "	No.1		
4	" "		" "	No.1		
5						
6	No1 On 96 Roll as "Tempy Mullins"					
7	" 2 " " " " "Lewis " "					
8	" 3 Affidavit of birth to be supplied Filed Nov 4" 1899					
9	" 4 ~~Enrolled Oct 15" 1901~~					
10	Nos. 1,2,3 and 4 originally enrolled on Chickasaw Card No 1496 and transferred to this card October 20, 1902.					
11	For child of No1 see NB (Mar 3'05) #405					
12						
13						
14						
15					Date of Application for Enrollment.	
16						
17				For Nos 1,2&3	Aug. 14" 1899	

RESIDENCE: Choctaw Nation ~~COUNTY.~~
POST OFFICE: Durant, Ind. Ter.

...aw **Nation**   **Choctaw Roll**   CARD No.
(Not Including Freedmen)   FIELD No.

Dawes' Roll No.	NAME	Relationship to Person First Named	AGE	SEX	BLOOD	TRIBAL ENROLLMENT Year	County	No.
13839	1 Durant, Melvina	First Named	42	F	1/2	1896	Blue Co.	3516
13840	2 " Lena	Dau	20	"	1/4	"	" "	3517
13841	3 " Ethelbert	Son	17	M	1/4	"	" "	3518
13842	4 " Martha	Dau	15	F	1/4	"	" "	3519
13843	5 " Juanita	"	12	"	1/4	"	" "	3520
13844	6 " Clint	Son	10	M	1/4	"	" "	3521
13845	7 " Florence	Dau	5	F	1/4	"	" "	3522
	8							
	9							
	10							
	11	ENROLLMENT						
	12	OF NOS. 1-2-3-4-5-6-7 HEREON APPROVED BY THE SECRETARY						
	13	OF INTERIOR MAR 19 1903						
	14							
	15					Child of No5 on NB (Apr 26-06) Card #278		
	16					" " " " (Mar 3-05) " #630		
	17							

TRIBAL ENROLLMENT OF PARENTS

	Name of Father	Year	County	Name of Mother	Year	County
1	V. D. Durant		Choctaw Roll	Kitty Durant	Dead	Chick. Roll
2	Pier Durant		" "	No.1		
3	" "		" "	No.1		
4	" "		" "	No.1		
5	" "		" "	No.1		
6	" "		" "	No.1		
7	" "		" "	No.1		
8						
9	No1 Wife of Pier Durant on Choctaw Card #3423					
10	" 3 On '96 Roll as "Bud Durant"					
11	~~Nos. 1 to 7 inclusive originally enrolled on Chickasaw Card #1502 and~~					
12	~~transferred to this card Oct. 20, 1902.~~					
13						
14						
15						
16						
17				Date of Application for Enrollment.	Aug. 18" 1899	

Choctaw By Blood Enrollment Cards 1898-1914

RESIDENCE: Choctaw Nation ~~COUNTY~~. **Choctaw Nation** **Choctaw Roll** (*Not Including Freedmen*) CARD NO.

POST OFFICE: Bennington, Ind. Ter. FIELD NO. **5453**

Dawes' Roll No.	NAME	Relationship to Person First Named	AGE	SEX	BLOOD	TRIBAL ENROLLMENT		
						Year	County	No.
13846	1 Durant, Sophia		48	F	1/4	1896	Jackson	3464
13847	2 Clark, Burnetta A	Dau	21	"	1/8	"	"	3466
13848	3 Durant, Zozare	Son	15	M	1/8	"	"	3468
13849	4 Clark, Juston T.	Gr. Son	3mo	"	1/16			
	5							
	6							
	7							
	8							
	9							
	10							
	11	ENROLLMENT OF NOS. 1-2-3-4 HEREON APPROVED BY THE SECRETARY OF INTERIOR MAR 19 1903						
	12							
	13							
	14							
	15							
	16							
	17							

TRIBAL ENROLLMENT OF PARENTS

	Name of Father	Year	County	Name of Mother	Year	County
1	David Cavender	Dead	Non-Citizen	Annie Cavender	Dead	Chick. Roll
2	Joe Durant	"	Choctaw Roll	No.1		
3	" "	"	" "	No.1		
4	T.A. Clark		Non-citizen	No.2		
5						
6	No.1 On '96 Roll as "Sophie Durant"					
7	" 2 " " " " "B. A. " " Now wife of J.A.Clark, non-citizen Evidence of marriage					
8	" 3 " " " " "Zosia " " " requested 7/22/02 Filed Aug. 14" 1902					
9	" 4 Born March 30" 1902. Enrolled July 22nd 1902 Nos 1,2,3 and 4 originally enrolled on Chickasaw Card #1517 and					
10	transferred to this card Oct. 20, 1902.					
11						
12	For child of No2 see NB (Apr 26-06) Card #277					
13	" " " " " " " (Mar 3-05) " #1028					
14						
15						
16						
17			Date of Application for Enrollment. Aug. 18"/99			

Choctaw By Blood Enrollment Cards 1898-1914

RESIDENCE: Choctaw Nation ~~COUNTY.~~ **Choctaw Nation**   Choctaw Roll   CARD NO.
POST OFFICE: Bennington, Ind. Ter.   *(Not Including Freedmen)*   FIELD NO. **5454**

Dawes' Roll No.	NAME	Relationship to Person First Named	AGE	SEX	BLOOD	TRIBAL ENROLLMENT		
						Year	County	No.
13850	1 Gray, Cordelia	First Named	19	F	1/8	1896	Jackson	3467
13851	2 " Roy	Son	2	M	1/16			
DEAD.	3 " ~~Cordelia Amelia~~	~~Dau~~	~~1mo~~	~~F~~	~~1/16~~			
13852	4 " Ellie Bernetta	"	1mo	F	1/16			
	5							
	6							
	7							
	8	ENROLLMENT						
	9	OF NOS. 1-2-4 HEREON APPROVED BY THE SECRETARY						
	10	OF INTERIOR MAR 19 1903						
	11	NO. 3 HEREON DISMISSED UNDER						
	12	ORDER OF THE COMMISSION TO THE FIVE						
	13	CIVILIZED TRIBES OF MARCH 31, 1905.						
	14							
	15							
	16							
	17							

TRIBAL ENROLLMENT OF PARENTS

	Name of Father	Year	County	Name of Mother	Year	County
1	Joe Durant	Dead	Choctaw Roll	Sophia Durant		Chickasaw
2	Ransom E. Gray		Non-Citizen	No.1		
3	" " "		" "	~~No.1~~		
4	" " "		" "	No.1		
5						
6	No1 on '96 Roll as "Cordelia Durant"					
7	" 3 Enrolled Aug. 22ᵈ 1900					
	~~" 4 Born Oct 19" 1901: Enrolled Nov. 27" 1901~~					
8	No. 1 to 4 inclusive originally enrolled on Chickasaw Card No. 1518 and					
9	transferred to this card Oct. 20, 1902.					
10						
11	~~No3 died Nov. 2, 1900: proof of death filed Dec. 5, 1902.~~					
12						
13						
14						
15						
16				Date of Application for Enrollment.		
17				Aug. 18"/99		

54

Choctaw By Blood Enrollment Cards 1898-1914

RESIDENCE: Jackson COUNTY. **Choctaw Nation** **Choctaw Roll** CARD NO.
POST OFFICE: Bennington Ind. Ter. *(Not Including Freedmen)* FIELD NO. **5455**

Dawes' Roll No.	NAME	Relationship to Person First Named	AGE	SEX	BLOOD	TRIBAL ENROLLMENT		
						Year	County	No.
13853	1 Durant, Albert P		38	M	1/8	1896	Jackson	3462
	2							
	3							
	4							
	5							
	6							
	7							
	8							
	9							
	10							
	11	ENROLLMENT OF NOS. 1 HEREON						
	12	APPROVED BY THE SECRETARY OF INTERIOR MAR 19 1903						
	13							
	14							
	15							
	16							
	17							

TRIBAL ENROLLMENT OF PARENTS

Name of Father	Year	County	Name of Mother	Year	County
1 Joe Durant	Dead	Choctaw Roll	Sophia Durant		Chickasaw
2					
3					
4					
5 No1 On 96 Roll as "A. P. Durant"					
6					
7 No.1 originally enrolled on Chickasaw Card #1519. Transferred to this card Oct. 20, 1902					
8					
9					
10					
11					
12					
13					
14					
15					
16				Date of Application for Enrollment.	Aug. 18" 1899
17					

Choctaw By Blood Enrollment Cards 1898-1914

RESIDENCE: Choctaw Nation COUNTY. **Choctaw Nation** Choctaw Roll CARD NO.
POST OFFICE: Bennington, Ind. Ter. *(Not Including Freedmen)* FIELD NO. **5456**

Dawes' Roll No.	NAME	Relationship to Person First Named	AGE	SEX	BLOOD	TRIBAL ENROLLMENT Year	County	No.
13854	1 Durant, Morgan J	First Named	27	M	1/8	1896	Jackson	3465
IW 1145	2 " Carmine	Wife	18	F	I.W.			
13855	3 " Ulmont U	Son	9mo	M	1/16			
13856	4 " Oliver H	"	2mo	M	1/16			
	5							
	6							
	7							
	8							
	9 ENROLLMENT							
	10 OF NOS. 1-3-4- HEREON							
	11 APPROVED BY THE SECRETARY OF INTERIOR MAR 19 1903							
	12							
	13 ENROLLMENT							
	14 OF NOS. 2 HEREON APPROVED BY THE SECRETARY							
	15 OF INTERIOR NOV 16 1904							
	16							
	17							

TRIBAL ENROLLMENT OF PARENTS

	Name of Father	Year	County	Name of Mother	Year	County
1	Joe Durant	Dead	Choctaw Roll	Sophia Durant		Chickasaw
2	W. M. Caruthers	"	Non-Citizen	Mollie Caruthers		Non-Citizen
3	No.1			No.2		
4	No.1			No.2		
5						
6						
7	No1 On '96 Roll as "M. J. Durant"					
8	" 2 Evidence of Marriage to No1 to be supplied. Filed Jan. 5" 1900					
9	" 3 Evidence of Birth to be supplied. Filed Nov 4" 1899					
	" 4 Enrolled Dec 3rd 1900					
10	Nos 1,2,3 and [sic] originally enrolled on Chick. Card #1520 and					
11	transferred to this card Oct. 20, 1902.					
12						
13						
14						
15						#1 to 3
16						Date of Application for Enrollment.
17						Aug. 18" 1899

56

Choctaw By Blood Enrollment Cards 1898-1914

RESIDENCE: Choctaw Nation   COUNTY. **Choctaw Nation**   **Choctaw Roll**   CARD No.
POST OFFICE: Jackson, I.T.   *(Not Including Freedmen)*   FIELD No. **5457**

Dawes' Roll No.	NAME	Relationship to Person First Named	AGE	SEX	BLOOD	TRIBAL ENROLLMENT		
						Year	County	No.
I.W. 609	1 Bills, Robert C	Named	35	M	I.W.			
13857	2 " Sarah	Wife	19	F	1/4	1896	Jackson	8111
	3							
	4							
	5							
	6							
	7	ENROLLMENT OF NOS. 1 HEREON						
	8	APPROVED BY THE SECRETARY OF INTERIOR FEB -8 1904						
	9							
	10	ENROLLMENT OF NOS. 2 HEREON						
	11	APPROVED BY THE SECRETARY						
	12	OF INTERIOR MAR 19 1903						
	13							
	14							
	15							
	16							
	17							

TRIBAL ENROLLMENT OF PARENTS

Name of Father	Year	County	Name of Mother	Year	County
1 G. C. Bills		Non-Citizen	Nannie E Bills	Dead	Non-Citizen
2 Wᵐ LeFlore		Choctaw Roll	Rosa LeFlore		Chickasaw
3					
4					
5					
6					
7 No.2 On 96 Roll as "Sarah Le Flore"					
8 Nos 1 and 2 originally enrolled on Chick. Card #1522. Transferred					
9 to this card Oct. 20, 1902					
10					
11					
12					
13					
14					
15				Date of Application for Enrollment	
16					
17				Aug. 21ˢᵗ 1899	

Choctaw By Blood Enrollment Cards 1898-1914

RESIDENCE: Tishomingo COUNTY. **Choctaw Nation** Choctaw Roll CARD No.
POST OFFICE: Dougherty, Ind. Ter. *(Not Including Freedmen)* FIELD No. **5458**

Dawes' Roll No.	NAME	Relationship to Person First Named	AGE	SEX	BLOOD	TRIBAL ENROLLMENT		
						Year	County	No.
13858	1 Hays, Thomas	First Named	43	M	1/2	1896	Chickasaw Dist	6161
I.W. 775	2 " Rose	Wife	32	F	I.W.	"	" "	14667
13859	3 " Annetta	Dau	2	"	1/4	"	" "	6170
13860	4 " Jennetta	"	8mo	"	1/4			
DEAD.	5 " Benton Orthella	Son	3mo	M	1/4			
	6							
	7	ENROLLMENT OF NOS. 1, 3 & 4 HEREON APPROVED BY THE SECRETARY OF INTERIOR MAR 19 1903						
	8							
	9							
	10							
	11							
	12							
	13	ENROLLMENT OF NOS. 2 HEREON APPROVED BY THE SECRETARY OF INTERIOR MAY -7 1904						
	14							
	15							
	16							
	17							

TRIBAL ENROLLMENT OF PARENTS

	Name of Father	Year	County	Name of Mother	Year	County
1	Alexander Hays	Dead	Choctaw Roll	Jennie Hays	Dead	Chickasaw Roll
2	B.T. Elkin		Non-Citizen	Tempy Elkin		Non-Citizen
3	No.1			No.2		
4	No.1			No.2		
5	No.1			No.2		
6						
7	No1 On 96 Roll as "Thomas Hayes" On Choctaw Census Record No2 Page 358					
8	" 2 " " " " "Rose " " " " Intermarried Roll " 47					
9	" 3 " " " " "Annetta Hays" " " Census Record No2 Paege 358					
10	" 4 Affidavit of Attending Physician to b supplied. Received Oct 5" 1898					
	" 5 Enrolled May 24" 1900					
11	Nos 1 to 5 inclusive originally enrolled on Chick. Card #658 and transferred to this Card Oct 20 1902					
12	No5 Died July 18" 1900. Proof of Death filed Nov 7" 1902					
	No2 See decision of March 2, '04.					
13						
14						
15						
16						
17					Sept 27 1898	

58

Choctaw By Blood Enrollment Cards 1898-1914

Choctaw Nation
(Not Including Freedmen)

Choctaw Roll   CARD No
FIELD N

Dawes' Roll No.	NAME	Relationship to Person First Named	AGE	SEX	BLOOD	TRIBAL ENROLLMENT Year	County	No.
13861	1 Shipman, Ella		21	F	1/2	1896	Jacks Fork	7352
DEAD.	2 Joel, Alice	Dau	2	"	3/4			
13862	3 " Lee	"	1mo	"	3/4			
13863	4 Shipman, Buck	Son	5mo	M	1/4			
DEAD.	5 " Willie Augustus	"	8da	"	1/4			
13864	6 " Kieth[sic]	"	2wks	"	1/4			
	7							
	8				No. 2&5 HEREON DISMISSED UNDER			
	9				ORDER OF THE COMMISSION TO THE FIVE			
	10				CIVILIZED TRIBES OF MARCH 31, 1905.			
	11							
	12 Nos 1 to 6 inclusive originally enrolled							
	13 on Chickasaw Card No. 521.							
	14 Transferred to this card Oct. 20, 1902							
	15				#3-"Died prior to September 25, 1902; not entitled to land			
	16				or money." See Indian Office letter May 13, 1910,			
	17				D.C #669-1910			

ENROLLMENT
OF NOS 1-3-4-6 HEREON
APPROVED BY THE SECRETARY
OF INTERIOR MAR 19 1903

TRIBAL ENROLLMENT OF PARENTS

Name of Father	Year	County	Name of Mother	Year	County
1 Willie Wauchubby		Choctaw Roll	Rhoda Watubby		Chickasaw
2 Solomon Joel		" "	No.1		
3 " "		" "	No.1		
4 D. C. Shipman		" "	No.1		
5 " " "		" "	No.1		
6 " " "		" "	No.1		
7 No1 On Choctaw census Record No2 Page 308					
8 See attached Decree of Divorce from Solomon Joel of No.1					
9 and Marriage License to D.C. Shipman Feb. 12" 1900					
10 D.C. Shipman father of No4,5 & 6 on Chickasaw Card #D.71.					
11 No4 Enrolled May 24" 1900					
12 No5 Enrolled Aug. 30" 1901					
13 No6 Born Aug 25" 1902 Enrolled Sept 4" 1902					
14				For child of No1 see NB (Mar 3'05)#409	
15 No2 Died March 7, 1899 proof of death filed Feby 20, 1903					
16 No5 Died Sept 3, 1901. proof of death filed Feby 20, 1903					
17					

Choctaw By Blood Enrollment Cards 1898-1914

RESIDENCE: Choctaw Nation ~~COUNTY.~~ **Choctaw Nation** Choctaw Roll CARD NO.
POST OFFICE: Atoka, Ind. Ter. *(Not Including Freedmen)* FIELD NO. **5460**

Dawes' Roll No.	NAME	Relationship to Person First Named	AGE	SEX	BLOOD	TRIBAL ENROLLMENT		
						Year	County	No.
	1 Tumbler, Willie		26	M	1/2	1896	Atoka	12457
	2							
	3							
	4							
	5							
	6							
	7							
	8							
	9							
	10							
	11							
	12							
	13							
	14							
	15							
	16							
	17							

CANCELLED

Re Transferred [remainder illegible.]

TRIBAL ENROLLMENT OF PARENTS

	Name of Father	Year	County	Name of Mother	Year	County
1	Jesse Tumbler	Dead	Atoka	Molsey Tumbler	Dead	Chick. Dist.
2						
3						
4						
5						
6						
7	No1 Wife and child of. On Choctaw Card #4D58 March 6" 1900					
8	No.1 originally enrolled on Chick. Card No. 4258. Transferred					
9	to Chick card No. 1570 on March 6, 1900. Transferred					
10	to this card Oct. 20, 1902					
11						
12						
13						
14						
15						
16					Date of Application for Enrollment.	
17						3/6/1900

Choctaw By Blood Enrollment Cards 1898-1914

RESIDENCE: Choctaw Nation ~~COUNTY~~ **Choctaw Nation**   **Choctaw Roll**   CARD No.
POST OFFICE: Atoka, Ind. Ter.   (Not Including Freedmen)   FIELD No. **5461**

Dawes' Roll No.	NAME	Relationship to Person First Named	AGE	SEX	BLOOD	TRIBAL ENROLLMENT		
						Year	County	No.
13866	1 Leader, Silas	First Named	19	M	3/4	1896	Atoka	8285
	2							
	3							
	4							
	5							
	6							
	7							
	8							
	9							
	10							
	11	ENROLLMENT						
	12	OF NOS. 1 HEREON APPROVED BY THE SECRETARY						
	13	OF INTERIOR MAR 19 1903						
	14							
	15							
	16							
	17							

TRIBAL ENROLLMENT OF PARENTS

	Name of Father	Year	County	Name of Mother	Year	County
1	Tecumseh Leader	Dead	Chick Roll	Bicey Leader	Dead	Chick Roll
2						
3						
4						
5						
6	No.1 originally enrolled on Chick. Card #1547; Transferred					
7	to this card Oct. 20, 1902					
8	For child of No1 see NB (Act Mar.3-05) Card #260.					
9						
10						
11						
12						
13						
14						
15						Date of Application for Enrollment.
16						
17						Sept. 2nd 1899

61

Choctaw By Blood Enrollment Cards 1898-1914

RESIDENCE: Choctaw Nation ~~COUNTY.~~ **Choctaw Nation**   **Choctaw Roll** CARD NO.
POST OFFICE: Atoka, Ind. Ter.   *(Not Including Freedmen)* FIELD NO. **5462**

Dawes' Roll No.	NAME	Relationship to Person First Named	AGE	SEX	BLOOD	TRIBAL ENROLLMENT		
						Year	County	No.
13867	1 Carnes, Amanda	First Named	17	F	1/2	1893	Atoka Pay Roll	276
	2							
	3							
	4							
	5							
	6							
	7							
	8							
	9							
	10							
	11	ENROLLMENT OF NOS. 1 HEREON APPROVED BY THE SECRETARY OF INTERIOR MAR 19 1903						
	12							
	13							
	14							
	15							
	16							
	17							

TRIBAL ENROLLMENT OF PARENTS

	Name of Father	Year	County	Name of Mother	Year	County
1	Tillis Carnes	Dead	Choctaw	Phoebe Carnes	Dead	Chick Roll
2						
3						
4						
5						
6						
7	~~No1 On 93 Roll as "Mandy Carn"~~					
8						
9	No.1 originally enrolled on Chickasaw Card No. 1545. Transferred					
10	to this card Oct. 20, 1902					
11						
12						
13						
14						
15						
16					Date of Application for Enrollment.	
17					Sept. 1st 1899	

62

Choctaw By Blood Enrollment Cards 1898-1914

RESIDENCE: Choctaw Nation ~~COUNTY.~~ **Choctaw Nation** Choctaw Roll CARD NO.
POST OFFICE: Limestone, Ind. Ter. *(Not Including Freedmen)* FIELD NO. **5463**

Dawes' Roll No.	NAME	Relationship to Person First Named	AGE	SEX	BLOOD	TRIBAL ENROLLMENT		
						Year	County	No.
IW690	1 Thurlow, Herman C	First Named	45	M	I.W.	1896	Atoka	15112
13868	2 " Joseph	Son	12	"	1/8	"	"	12462
13869	3 " Josephine	Dau	10	F	1/8	"	"	12470
13870	4 " Louisa	"	8	"	1/8	"	"	12471
13871	5 " Sylvina E	"	4	"	1/8	"	"	12472
	6							
	7 ENROLLMENT							
	8 OF NOS. 1 HEREON							
	9 APPROVED BY THE SECRETARY OF INTERIOR MAR 26 1904							
	10 ENROLLMENT							
	11 OF NOS. 2-3-4-5 HEREON							
	12 APPROVED BY THE SECRETARY OF INTERIOR MAR 19 1903							
	13							
	14							
	15							
	16							
	17							

TRIBAL ENROLLMENT OF PARENTS

	Name of Father	Year	County	Name of Mother	Year	County
1	Amos Thurlow		Non-Citizen	Sylvina Thurlow	Dead	Non-Citizen
2	No.1			Sophia Thurlow	"	Chick Roll
3	No.1			" "	"	" "
4	No.1			" "	"	" "
5	No.1			" "	"	" "
6						
7	No1 On 96 Roll as "Herman C. Thurlow"					
8	" License and Certificate exhibited found satisfactory, but not in condition to be filed.					
9	" ~~Admitted as an Intermarried Choctaw by Dawes Com in 1896. See Choctaw Case 285~~					
10	" Now the Husband of Lucinda Wade on Choctaw Card #5366: Jan 22nd 1902					
11	" 5 On '96 Roll as "Eliza Thurlow" Admitted as a Choctaw by blood by Dawes Com in 1896.					
12	See Choctaw Case #285					
	~~Nos 1 to 5 inclusive originally enrolled on Chickasaw Card No. 1543 and~~					
13	transferred to this card Oct. 20, 1902.					
14						
15						
16						
17	6/16/02 P.O. Connerville I.T.			Date of Application for Enrollment	Sept. 1st 1899	

Choctaw By Blood Enrollment Cards 1898-1914

| RESIDENCE: | | COUNTY. **Choctaw Nation** | | | | **Choctaw Roll** (Not Including Freedmen) | | CARD No. FIELD No. **5464** | |
| POST OFFICE: | | | | | | | | | |

Dawes' Roll No.	NAME	Relationship to Person First Named	AGE	SEX	BLOOD	TRIBAL ENROLLMENT		
						Year	County	No.
13872	1 Colbert, Ben	First Named	31	M	F	1896	Jacks Fork	3049
	2							
	3							
	4							
	5							
	6							
	7							
	8 ENROLLMENT							
	9 OF NOS. 1 HEREON APPROVED BY THE SECRETARY							
	10 OF INTERIOR MAR 19 1903							
	11							
	12 In case inquiry is made concerning							
	13 this man, Address William Anderson							
	14 Pontotoc Ind. Ter							
	15							
	16							
	17							

TRIBAL ENROLLMENT OF PARENTS

Name of Father	Year	County	Name of Mother	Year	County
1 Jim Colbert	Dead	Chickasaw	Wycie Colbert	Dead	Chickasaw
2					
3					
4					
5					
6 No.1 originally enrolled on Chick. Card #1560. Transferred					
7 to this card Oct. 20, 1902					
8					
9					
10 "Duplicate enrollment of Chickasaw Roll No. 3817; not entitled to land or money [illegible]					
11					
12					
13					
14					
15					
16					
17				Date of Application for Enrollment.	Nov 15"1899	

64

RESIDENCE:	Sans Bois	COUNTY.	**Choctaw Nation**		Choctaw Roll	CARD No.	
POST OFFICE:	Featherstone, Ind. Ter.			*(Not Including Freedmen)*		FIELD NO. **5465**	

Dawes' Roll No.	NAME	Relationship to Person First Named	AGE	SEX	BLOOD	TRIBAL ENROLLMENT		
						Year	County	No.
13873	1 Bascomb, Jincy		23	F	1/2	1896	Sans Bois	2089
13874	2 Carney, Morton	Bro	21	M	1/2	"	" "	2085
13875	3 " William	"	10	"	1/2	"	" "	2086
13876	4 " George	"	9	"	1/2	"	" "	2087
13877	5 " Adeline	Sister	7	F	1/2	"	" "	2090
13878	6 Bascomb, Lena	Dau	4mo	"	3/4			
	7							
	8 ENROLLMENT							
	9 OF NOS. 1-2-3-4-5-6 HEREON APPROVED BY THE SECRETARY							
	10 OF INTERIOR Mar 19 1903							
	11							
	12 For child of No1 See NB (Apr 26'06) Card #341							
	13 " " " No2 " " (Mar 3-05) " #1289							
	14 " " " No1 " " " " " #1353							
	15							
	16							
	17							

TRIBAL ENROLLMENT OF PARENTS

	Name of Father	Year	County		Name of Mother	Year	County
1	Wallace Carney		Choctaw Freedman		Susan Carney	Dead	Chickasaw
2	" "		" "		" "	"	"
3	" "		" "		Annie Carney	"	"
4	" "		" "		" "	"	"
5	" "		" "		" "	"	"
6	Charles Bascom[sic]		Choctaw Roll		No.1		
7							
8	Nos 1,2,3,4,5 Children of Wallace Carney on Choctaw Freedman Care #786						
9	No1 now the wife of Charles Bascom on Choctaw card #3730 Feb. 14th 1901.						
10	" Evidence of marriage to be supplied. Filed March 21st 1901						
11	"3 On 96 Roll as Wm Carney.						
12	" Notation as to him being 'Dead' is an error, See letter of Wallace Carney March 18th 1901						
13	" 6 Enrolled March 6th 2902						
14	Nos 1 to 6 inclusive originally enrolled on Chickasaw Card #1561 and transferred to this card Oct. 20, 1902						
15							
16						#1 to 5 inc	
17	P.O. Quinton I.T. 4/27/05				Date of Application for Enrollment.	Nov 16th 1899	

Choctaw By Blood Enrollment Cards 1898-1914

Dawes' Roll No.	NAME	Relationship to Person First Named	AGE	SEX	BLOOD	TRIBAL ENROLLMENT		
						Year	County	No.
13879	1 Colbert, Ely[sic]	First Named	31	F	Full	1893	Gaines	78
13880	2 " Emily	Dau	10	"	"	"	"	79
	3							
	4							
	5							
	6							
	7							
	8							
	9							
	10							
	11	ENROLLMENT						
	12	OF NOS. 1 - 2 - HEREON APPROVED BY THE SECRETARY						
	13	OF INTERIOR MAR 19 1903						
	14							
	15							
	16							
	17							

TRIBAL ENROLLMENT OF PARENTS

Name of Father	Year	County	Name of Mother	Year	County
1 Silas Colbert	Dead	Gaines	Julia Colbert	Dead	Sans Bois
2 Nels Thompson		Sugar Loaf	No.1		
3					
4					
5					
6					
7 No1 On Choctaw Roll as "Aly Colbert"					
8 No.1 originally enrolled on Chick. Card #1554. Transferred to this card Oct. 20, 1902					
9					
10					
11					
12					
13					
14					
15					
16					
17			Date of Application for Enrollment.	Sept. 5 1899	

Choctaw By Blood Enrollment Cards 1898-1914

RESIDENCE: Choctaw Nation   COUNTY. **Choctaw Nation**   **Choctaw Roll**   CARD No.

POST OFFICE: Atoka Ind Ter   *(Not Including Freedmen)*   FIELD No. 546

wes' No. T5881	NAME	Relationship to Person First Named	AGE	SEX	BLOOD	TRIBAL ENROLLMENT Year	County	No.
881	1 Folsom, Julia		37	F	1/2	1893	Blue	590
	2							
	3							
	4							
	5							
	6							
	7							
	8							
	9							
	10							
	11							
	12							
	13							
	14							
	15							
	16							
	17							

ENROLLMENT
OF NOS. 1 HEREON
APPROVED BY THE SECRETARY
OF INTERIOR MAR 19 1903

TRIBAL ENROLLMENT OF PARENTS

	Name of Father	Year	County	Name of Mother	Year	
1	Ellis Folsom	Dead	Choctaw	Selina Folsom	Dead	Chick
2						
3						
4						
5						
6						
7	No 1 originally enrolled on Chickasaw Card No. 541 Transferred					
8	to this card Oct. 20, 1902					
9						
10						
11						
12						
13						
14						
15						
16						
17				Date of Application for Enrollment.	Aug 31st 1899	

Choctaw By Blood Enrollment Cards 1898-1914

NAME	Relationship to Person First Named	AGE	SEX	BLOOD	TRIBAL ENROLLMENT		
					Year	County	No.
Peter, Alexander	First Named	22	M	1/2	1896	Atoka	10542
8							
9							
10							
11	ENROLLMENT						
12	OF NOS. 1 HEREON APPROVED BY THE SECRETARY						
13	OF INTERIOR MAR 19 1903						
14							
15							
16							
17							

TRIBAL ENROLLMENT OF PARENTS

Name of Father	Year	County	Name of Mother	Year	County
1 Simon Peter	Dead	Choctaw	Nancy Peter	Dead	Chick Roll
2					
3					
4					
5					
6					
7 No.1 originally enrolled on Chickasaw Card No. 1539. Transferred					
8 to this card Oct. 20, 1902					
9					
10					
11					
12					
13					
14					
15					
16				Date of Application for Enrollment.	Aug 3rd 1899
17					

Choctaw By Blood Enrollment Cards 1898-1914

RESIDENCE: Choctaw Nation   COUNTY. **Choctaw Nation**   **Choctaw Roll**   CARD No.
POST OFFICE: Atoka Ind. Ter   (Not Including Freedmen)   FIELD No. **5469**

Dawes' Roll No.	NAME	Relationship to Person First Named	AGE	SEX	BLOOD	TRIBAL ENROLLMENT		
						Year	County	No.
883	1 Wilson, John	First Named	45	M	1/4	1896	Jacks Fork	14121
	2							
	3							
	4							
	5							
	6							
	7							
	8							
	9							
	10							
	11	ENROLLMENT						
	12	OF NOS. 1 HEREON APPROVED BY THE SECRETARY						
	13	OF INTERIOR MAR 19 1903						
	14							
	15							
	16							
	17							

TRIBAL ENROLLMENT OF PARENTS

Name of Father	Year	County	Name of Mother	Year	County
1 William Wilson	Dead	Choctaw Roll	Ellen Wilson	Dead	Chick Roll
2					
3					
4					
5					
6 No.1 originally enrolled on Chick. Card No. 1538. Transferred					
7 to this card Oct. 20, 1902					
8 Wife and children on 17-1060					
9					
10					
11					
12					
13					
14					
15					
16					
17				Date of Application for Enrollment.	Aug 30" 1899	

69

Choctaw By Blood Enrollment Cards 1898-1914

Choctaw Nation

(Not Including Freedmen) FIELD NO. **5470**

Dawes' Roll No.	NAME	Relationship to Person First Named	AGE	SEX	BLOOD	TRIBAL ENROLLMENT Year	County	No.
13884	1 Belvin, Melissa	First Named	50	F	3/4	1896	Jackson	1510
13885	2 Frazier, Rosa	G.D.	9	"	3/16	1893	Cedar	169
	3							
	4							
	5							
	6							
	7							
	8							
	9							
	10							
	11	ENROLLMENT						
	12	OF NOS. 1- 2- HEREON APPROVED BY THE SECRETARY						
	13	OF INTERIOR MAR 19 1903						
	14							
	15							
	16							
	17							

TRIBAL ENROLLMENT OF PARENTS

	Name of Father	Year	County	Name of Mother	Year	
1	Tecumseh Lata	Dead	Chick Roll	Sho-pa-you-key	Dead	
2	Joe Frazier	"	Choc. Roll	Emily Frazier	"	
3						
4						
5						
6						
7	No.1 on 96 Roll as "Melissie Belvin"					
8	Nos. 1 and 2 originally enrolled on Chickasaw Card No. 1537. Transferred					
9	to this card Oct. 20, 1902.					
10	For child of No2 see NB (Apr 26-06) Card #314					
11						
12						
13						
14						
15					Date of Application for Enrollment.	
16						
17					Aug 28" 1899	

RESIDENCE: Pontotoc COUNTY. **Choctaw Nation**   **Choctaw Roll** CARD No.
POST OFFICE: Waupanucka Ind Ter   *(Not Including Freedmen)*   FIELD No. **5471**

Dawes' Roll No.	NAME	Relationship to Person First Named	AGE	SEX	BL			ROLLMENT unty	No.
13886	1 Mosely, Ida		9	F	1/2	1893	Atoka		803
	2								
	3								
	4								
	5								
	6								
	7								
	8								
	9								
	10								
	11	ENROLLMENT							
	12	OF NOS. 1 HEREON APPROVED BY THE SECRETARY							
	13	OF INTERIOR MAR 19 1903							
	14								
	15								
	16								
	17								

TRIBAL ENROLLMENT OF PARENTS

	Name of Father	Year	County	Name of Mother	Year	County
1	William Mosely		Choctaw Roll	Sarah Mosely		Chick Card #1536
2						
3						
4						
5						
6	No1 on 93 Roll as "Ida Mosly[sic]"					
7	No1 Dau of William Moseley[sic] on Choctaw Card #4014 " " " Sarah " " Chickasaw " #1536					
8						
9	No.1 originally enrolled on Chickasaw Card #1536. Transferred to this card Oct. 20, 1902					
10						
11						
12						
13						
14						
15						
16						
17			Date of Application for Enrollment.		Aug. 28" 1899	

Choctaw By Blood Enrollment Cards 1898-1914

RESIDENCE: Choctaw Nation ~~COUNTY.~~ **Choctaw Nation** Choctaw Roll CARD NO.
POST OFFICE: Antlers, Ind. Ter *(Not Including Freedmen)* FIELD NO. **5472**

Dawes' Roll No.	NAME	Relationship to Person First Named	AGE	SEX	BLOOD	TRIBAL ENROLLMENT		
						Year	County	No.
13887	1 Wade, Thomas	First Named	31	M	1/2	1896	Atoka	13985
	2							
	3							
	4							
	5							
	6							
	7							
	8							
	9							
	10							
	11	ENROLLMENT						
	12	OF NOS. 1 HEREON APPROVED BY THE SECRETARY						
	13	OF INTERIOR MAR 19 1903						
	14							
	15							
	16							
	17							

TRIBAL ENROLLMENT OF PARENTS

Name of Father	Year	County	Name of Mother	Year	County
1 Simon Wade	Dead	Choctaw	Nancy Peter	Dead	Chick. Roll
2					
3					
4					
5					
6					
7 No1 Wife and children o Choctaw Card #3990					
8					
9 No.1 originally enrolled on Chickasaw Card No. 1534. Transferred to this card Oct. 20, 1902					
10					
11					
12					
13					
14					
15					
16				Date of Application for Enrollment.		
17				Aug 28" 1899		

Choctaw By Blood Enrollment Cards 1898-1914

RESIDENCE: Choctaw Nation ~~COUNTY:~~

POST OFFICE: Owl, Ind. Ter.

Choctaw Nation

Choctaw Roll
(Not Including Freedmen)

Dawes' Roll No.	NAME	Relationship to Person First Named	AGE	SEX	BLOOD	TRIBAL ENROLLMENT		
						Year	County	No.
13888	1 Churchman, Lizzie		19	F	Full	1893	Atoka	301
DEAD	2 Bond, Unice	Dau	1	"	1/2			
13889	3 Churchman, Mertie May	"	6mo	"	1/2			
	4							
	5							
	6							
	7	ENROLLMENT OF NOS. 1 - 3 HEREON						
	8	APPROVED BY THE SECRETARY OF INTERIOR MAR 19 1903						
	9							
	10	No. 2 HEREON DISMISSED UNDER ORDER OF THE COMMISSION TO THE FIVE						
	11	CIVILIZED TRIBES OF MARCH 31, 1905.						
	12							
	13							
	14							
	15							
	16							
	17							

TRIBAL ENROLLMENT ~~PARENTS~~

	Name of Father	Year	County		ne of Mother	Year	County
1	Larsen Roberts	Dead	Chick Roll		Roberts		Chick Roll
2	Reed Bond		Chocta				
3	Thomas Churchman		Non-Ci				
4							
5							
6				For child of No1 see NB (Apr 26, 1906) #118[3 or 5]			

7 No1 On '93 Roll as Elizabeth Roberts

8 " Husband on Choctaw Card #3985

9 " Now the wife of Thomas Churchman, non citizen; Evidence of marriage filed June 28" 1902

" 2 Affidavit of Birth to be supplied.

10 " 3 Born Dec 28" 1901; Enrolled June 28" 1902

11 Nos 1,2 and 3 originally enrolled on Chickasaw Card No. 1533 and

12 transferred to this card Oct. 20, 1902.

~~No2 Died in October 1899; proof of death filed Oct 23, 1902.~~

13 No1 is now the wife of Thomas Churchman on Chickasaw card #D377 Oct. 20, 1902

14

15

16 #1&2

17 P.O. Wallville Ind Ter — Date of Application for Enrollment — Aug 28" 1899

73

Choctaw By Blood Enrollment Cards 1898-1914

RESIDENCE: Choctaw Nation   COUNTY. **Choctaw Nation**   Choctaw Roll   CARD
POST OFFICE: Owl Ind. Ter.   *(Not Including Freedmen)*   FIELD NO. 5474

Dawes' Roll No.	NAME	Relationship to Person First Named	AGE	SEX	BLOOD	TRIBAL ENROLLMENT		
						Year	County	No.
13890	1 Roberts, Sloan	First Named	13	M	Full	1893	Atoka	907
	2							
	3							
	4							
	5							
	6							
	7							
	8							
	9							
	10							
	11							
	12							
	13							
	14							
	15							
	16							
	17							

ENROLLMENT
OF NOS. 1 HEREON
APPROVED BY THE SECRETARY
OF INTERIOR MAR 19 1903

TRIBAL ENROLLMENT OF PARENTS

	Name of Father	Year	County	Name of Mother	Year	County
1	Louis Benton		Chick Roll	Alice Bond		Chick Roll
2						
3						
4						
5						
6	No.1 On '93 Roll as "Sldne[sic] Roberts"					
7						
8	No.1 originally enrolled on Chick. Card No. 1532. Transferred to this card Oct. 20, 1902					
9	Father of No.1 is Louis Benton on Chickasaw card #218					
10	Mother of No.1 is Alice Bond on Choctaw card #5382.					
11	No.1 lives with his uncle Wilson Roberts; see Chickasaw card #192 No.1 is also known as Sloan Benton.					
12						
13						
14						
15						Date
16						for
17						Aug

74

Choctaw By Blood Enrollment Cards 1898-1914

RESIDENCE: Choctaw Nation ~~COUNTY~~. **Choctaw Nation** **Choctaw Roll** CARD NO.
POST OFFICE: Caddo, Ind. Ter *(Not Including Freedmen)* FIELD NO. **5475**

Dawes' Roll No.	NAME	Relationship to Person First Named	AGE	SEX	BLOOD	TRIBAL ENROLLMENT		
						Year	County	No.
1	Robinson, Raymond	Named	9	M	1/2	1896	Blue	10901
2	" Sallie	Sister	6	F	1/2	"		10902
3								
4								
5								
6								
7								
8								
9								
10								
11								
12								
13								
14								
15								
16								
17								

CANCELLED

Re-Transferred to Choctaw Card #3763 Nov. 24ᵗʰ 1902

TRIBAL ENROLLMENT OF PARENTS

	Name of Father	Year	County	Name of Mother	Year	County
1	Loring Robinson		Choctaw Roll	Minerva Robinson	Dead	Chick Roll
2	" "		" "	" "	"	" "
3						
4						
5						
6	No1 On '96 Roll as "Raymond Roberson"					
7	" 2 " " " . " 'Sally " "					
8	Nos. 1 and 2 originally enrolled on Chickasaw Card No. 1531 and					
9	transferred to this card October 20th 1902.					
10						
11						
12						
13						
14						
15				Original Ticket issued Aug. 23ʳᵈ 1899		
16						
17				Date of Application for Enrollment.	Aug 25" 1899	

Choctaw By Blood Enrollment Cards 1898-1914

RESIDENCE: Choctaw Nation   COUNTY. **Choctaw**   ▮▮▮▮ **Roll**   CARD No.
POST OFFICE: Caddo, Ind. Ter   *reedmen)*   FIELD No. **5476**

Dawes' Roll No.		NAME	Relationship to Person First Named	AGE	SEX	BLOOD	TRIBAL ENROLLMENT		
							Year	County	No.
13891	1	Frazier, William		30	M	1/2	1896	Blue	4408
	2								
	3								
	4								
	5								
	6								
	7								
	8								
	9								
	10								
	11	ENROLLMENT							
	12	OF NOS. 1 HEREON APPROVED BY THE SECRETARY							
	13	OF INTERIOR MAR 19 1903							
	14								
	15								
	16								
	17								

TRIBAL ENROLLMENT OF PARENTS

	Name of Father	Year	County	Name of Mother	Year	County
1	Daniel Frazier	Dead	Choctaw Roll	Ho-te-a-ho-ke	Dead	Chick Roll
2						
3						
4						
5						
6	No.1 Wife and Child on Choctaw Card #3716					
7						
8	No.1 originally enrolled on Chick. Card #1530. Transferred					
9	to this card Oct. 20, 1902					
10						
11						
12						
13						
14				No Ticket Issued		
15				Original Ticket Issued 9/22/99		
16				Enrolled Aug. 25" 1899		
17				Date of Application for Enrollment.		

Choctaw By Blood Enrollment Cards 1898-1914

RESIDENCE: Choctaw Nation COUNTY. **Choctaw Nation** Choctaw ~~Roll~~ No.
POST OFFICE: Blue Ind. Ter. *(Not Including Freedmen)* FIELD NO. **5477**

Dawes' Roll No.	NAME	Relationship to Person First Named	AGE	SEX	BLOOD	TRIBAL ENROLLMENT		
						Year	County	No.
DEAD	1 Houston, Martha		40	F	Full	1896	Blue	9423
13892	2 Loring, Edmond	Son	11	M	1/2	"	"	8219
	3							
	4							
	5							
	6							
	7 No. 1 hereon dismissed under							
	order of the Commission to the							
	8 Five Civilized Tribes of March							
	9 31, 1905.							
	10							
	11 ENROLLMENT							
	OF NOS. 2 HEREON							
	12 APPROVED BY THE SECRETARY							
	13 OF INTERIOR Mar 19 1903							
	14							
	15							
	16							
	17							

TRIBAL ENROLLMENT OF PARENTS

	Name of Father	Year	County	Name of Mother	Year	County
1	Allen Tishkilia	Dead	Chick. Dist		Dead	Chickasaw
2	Louis Loring	"	Choctaw	No1		
3						
4						
5						
6	No.1 On 96 Roll as Martha "McCann"					
7	" Husband of, on Choctaw Card #3372					
8	Nos 1 and 2 originally enrolled on Chick. Card #1529. Transferred to this card Oct. 20, 1902.					
9	No.1 died Feb. 15, 1900; proof of death filed Nov. 22, 1902					
10						
11						
12						
13				No Ticket Issued for No1-2		
14				Original Ticket Issued 8/14/99		
15				Enrolled Aug. 25th 1899		
16						
17				Date of Application for Enrollment.		

Choctaw By Blood Enrollment Cards 1898-1914

RESIDENCE: Choctaw Nation   COUNTY. **Choctaw Nation**   Choctaw Roll   CARD NO.
POST OFFICE: Caddo, Ind. Ter   *(Not Including Freedmen)*   FIELD NO. **5478**

Dawes' Roll No.	NAME	Relationship to Person First Named	AGE	SEX	BLOOD	TRIBAL ENROLLMENT		
						Year	County	No.
Void	1 Jones, Betsy		39	F	Full	1896	ue	7240
	2							
	3							
	4							
	5							
	6							
	7							
	8							
	9							
	10							
	11							
	12							
	13							
	14							
	15							
	16							
	17							

Cancelled and No. 1 transferred to Choctaw card No. 3 (?) with her husband Allington Jones Nov. 19, 1902

CANCELLED

TRIBAL ENROLLMENT OF PARENTS

	Name of Father	Year	County	Name of Mother	Year	County
1	Pin-te-sh-ta-be	Dead	Chick Roll	Sha-ta-ho-ye	Dead	Chick Roll
2						
3						
4						
5						
6	No1 On '96 Roll as "Betsey[sic] Jones"					
7	No.1 originally enrolled on Chickasaw Card No. 1527. Transferred to this card Oct. 20, 1902					
8						
9						
10						
11						
12						
13						
14						
15						
16				Date of Application for Enrollment.	Aug 23rd 1899	
17						

78

Choctaw By Blood Enrollment Cards 1898-1914

RESIDENCE: Choctaw Nation ~~COUNTY.~~ **Choctaw Nation** Choctaw Roll CARD NO.
POST OFFICE: Blue Ind. Ter. (Not Including Freedmen) FIELD NO. **5479**

Dawes' Roll No.	NAME	Relationship to Person First Named	AGE	SEX	BLOOD	TRIBAL ENROLLMENT		
						Year	County	No.
13893	₁ King, Mary A	First Named	19	F	1/4	1896	Blue	7634
13894	₂ " Louisa	Dau	2	"	1/8			
	₃							
	₄							
	₅							
	₆							
	₇							
	₈							
	₉							
	10							
	11							
	12							
	13							
	14							
	15							
	16							
	17							

ENROLLMENT OF NOS. 1 & 2 HEREON APPROVED BY THE SECRETARY OF INTERIOR Mar 19 1903

TRIBAL ENROLLMENT OF PARENTS

	Name of Father	Year	County	Name of Mother	Year	County
₁	Norman Capin	Dead	Choctaw	Silwee Capin		Chickasaw
₂	Chas King	"	"	No.1		
₃						
₄						
₅						
₆						
₇	No.1 On '96 Roll as "Mary King"					
₈	Nos 1 and 2 originally enrolled on Chickasaw Card No. 1526. Transferred					
₉	to this card Oct. 20, 1902					
10						
11						
12						
13						
14						
15						Date of Application for Enrollment.
16						
17						Aug 21" 1899

Choctaw By Blood Enrollment Cards 1898-1914

RESIDENCE: Choctaw Nation ~~COUNTY.~~ **Choctaw Nation** Choctaw Roll CARD No.
POST OFFICE: Blue Ind Ter. (Not Including Freedmen) FIELD No. **5480**

Dawes' Roll No.	NAME	Relationship to Person First Named	AGE	SEX	BLOOD	TRIBAL ENROLLMENT		
						Year	County	No.
13895	1 Capin, Silwee	First Named	45	F	1/2	1896	Blue	7636
	2							
	3							
	4							
	5							
	6							
	7							
	8							
	9							
	10							
	11							
	12							
	13	ENROLLMENT OF NOS. 1 HEREON APPROVED BY THE SECRETARY OF INTERIOR Mar 19 1903						
	14							
	15							
	16							
	17							

TRIBAL ENROLLMENT OF PARENTS

	Name of Father	Year	County	Name of Mother	Year	County
1	Joel Shocubbee	Dead	Choctaw Roll	Lottie	Dead	Chickasaw
2						
3						
4						
5						
6						
7	No.1 on 96 Roll as Silay Kaper					
8	No.1 originally enrolled on Chickasaw Card No. 1525 and					
9	transferred to this card October 20, 1902.					
10						
11						
12						
13						
14						
15						Date of Application for Enrollment.
16						
17						

Choctaw By Blood Enrollment Cards 1898-1914

RESIDENCE: Choctaw Nation

POST OFFICE: Krebs, Ind. Ter

hoctaw Nation

Choctaw Roll (Not Including Freedmen)

CARD No.

FIELD No. **5481**

Dawes' Roll No.	NAME	Relationship to Person First Named	AGE	SEX	BLOOD	TRIBAL ENROLLMENT		
						Year	County	No.
13896	1 James, Lewis		6	M	1/4	1896	Skullyville	6473
	2							
	3							
	4							
	5							
	6							
	7							
	8							
	9							
	10							
	11							
	12	ENROLLMENT OF NOS. 1 HEREON APPROVED BY THE SECRETARY OF INTERIOR MAR 19 1903						
	13							
	14							
	15							
	16							
	17							

TRIBAL ENROLLMENT OF PARENTS

	Name of Father	Year	County	Name of Mother	Year	County
1	Jacob James	Dead	Choctaw Roll	Melviney James	Dead	Chick res Choctaw
2						
3						
4						
5						
6						
7		No.1 On Choctaw Census Record No2 (Skullyville Co) Page 273				
8		" " 96 Roll as "Louis James"				
9		No.1 originally enrolled on Chickasaw Card No. 1199. Transferr to this card Oct. 20, 1902				
10						
11						
12						
13						
14					Date of Application for Enrollment.	
15						Oct. 1
16						
17	Chickasha Okla					

81

Choctaw By Blood Enrollment Cards 1898-1914

RESIDENCE: **Panola**   COUNTY.   **Choctaw Nation**   **Choctaw Roll**   CARD No.

POST OFFICE: **Albany Ind. Ter.**   *(Not Including Freedmen)*   FIELD No. **5482**

Dawes' Roll No.	NAME	Relationship to Person First Named	AGE	SEX	BLOOD	TRIBAL ENROLLMENT Year	County	No.
DEAD	1 Mc Donald, Eliza J	Named	20	F	1/2	1896	Blue	8217
DEAD	2 " Margaret B	Dau	9mo	"	3/4			
	3							
	4							
	5							
	6							
	7							
	8							
	9							
	10							
	11							
	12							
	13							
	14		No. 1 and 2 HEREON DISMISSED UNDER						
	15		ORDER OF THE COMMISSION TO THE FIVE						
	16		CIVILIZED TRIBES OF MARCH 31, 1905.						
	17								

~~CANCELLED~~

Applicant died prior to ratification of Choctaw Chickasaw agreement Sept 25, 1902.

TRIBAL ENROLLMENT OF PARENTS

Name of Father	Year	County	Name of Mother	Year	County
1 Nelson Lewis	Dead	Blue Co Choctaw Roll	Martha Lewis	1897	Chick residing in Choctaw N. 3rd Dist
2 Albert S. Mc Donald	1897	Panola	No. 1		
3					
4					

5   No1 On 96 Roll as Eliza Lewis; On Choctaw Census Record No.2 (Blue Co) Page 340

6   " 2 Affidavit of Midwife to be supplied. Received Oct. 21st 1898

7   Nos. 1 and 2 originally enrolled on Chick. Card No. 1215 and transferred to this card Oct 20, 1902.

9   No.1 Died Oct. 1, 1899: Proof of death filed Nov. 11, 1902

  No.2 Died Sept. 13, 1899. Proof of death filed Nov. 11, 1902.

Date of Application for Enrollment.   Oct. 1

| RESIDENCE: Panola | COUNTY. **Choctaw Nation** | Choctaw | CARD No. |
| POST OFFICE: Mead Ind. Ter | | (Not Including Freedmen) | FIELD No. **548** |

Dawes' Roll No.	NAME	Relationship to Person First Named	AGE	SEX	BLOOD	TRIBAL ENROLLMENT		
						Year	County	No.
13897	1 Jeflow, Maulsie		18	F	Full	1896	Blue	2899
DEAD.	2 " Rena	Dau	9mo	"	"			
13898	3 " Jane	"	1m	"	"			
	4							
	5							
	6							
	7							
	8							
	9							
	10 ENROLLMENT OF NOS. 1&3 HEREON APPROVED BY THE SECRETARY OF INTERIOR MAR 19 1903							
	11							
	12 No. 2 HEREON DISMISSED UNDER ORDER OF THE COMMISSION TO THE FIVE CIVILIZED TRIBES OF MARCH 31, 1905.							
	13							
	14							
	15							
	16							
	17							

TRIBAL ENROLLMENT OF PARENTS

	Name of Father	Year	County	Name of Mother	Year	
1	Stephen Chester	Dead	Chickasaw Roll	Selvey Chester		Panol
2	Joe Jeflow	1897	Panola	No.1		
3	" "	"	"	No.1		
4						
5						
6	No1 On 96 Roll as Molsey Chester					
7	" " Choctaw Census Record No.2 Blue Co Page 118 as "Molsey Chester"					
8	3 Enrolled June 25" 1900					
9	Nos 1,2 and 3 originally enrolled on Chick. Card No. 1218 and transferred to this card Oct. 20, 1902.					
10	No2 Died June 1900; Proof of death filed Nov. 6, 1902.					
11	For child of No1 see NB (April 26-06) Chick Card #166					
12	" " " " " (Mar 3-1905) " " #511					
13						
14						
15					#1&2 Date of Application for Enrollment.
16						
17						Oct. 1

Choctaw By Blood Enrollment Cards 1898-1914

RESIDENCE: Choctaw Nation ~~COUNTY.~~ **Choctaw Nation**　Choctaw Roll
POST OFFICE: Tuskahoma, Ind. Ter.　*(Not Including Freedmen)*　FIELD No. **5484**

Dawes' Roll No.	NAME	Relationship to Person First Named	AGE	SEX	BLOOD	TRIBAL ENROLLMENT		
						Year	County	No.
13899	1 Moore, Nathaniel	First Named	2	M	1/2	1896	Jacks Fork	8893
	2							
	3							
	4							
	5							
	6							
	7							
	8							
	9							
	10							
	11	ENROLLMENT						
	12	OF NOS. 1　HEREON APPROVED BY THE SECRETARY						
	13	OF INTERIOR　Mar 19 1903						
	14							
	15							
	16							
	17							

TRIBAL ENROLLMENT OF PARENTS

	Name of Father	Year	County	Name of Mother	Year	County
1	Jonas Moore	Dead	Choctaw Roll	Katie Mackintubby		Chick Card 1239
2						
3						
4						
5						
6	No 1 on '96 Roll as "Nathaniel More"					
7	"　Enrolled May 24" 1899					
8	No. 1 originally enrolled on Chickasaw Card No. 1237 and transferred to this card Oct. 20, 1902.					
9						
10						
11						
12						
13						
14						
15						
16						
17	P.O. Redden, Okla 4/23/08				Date of Application for Enrollment.	Oct. 13" 1898

Choctaw By Blood Enrollment Cards 1898-1914

RESIDENCE: Jacks Fork   COUNTY. **Choctaw Nation**   **Choctaw Roll** CARD NO. ▓
POST OFFICE: Tuskahomma Ind. Ter   *(Not Including Freedmen)*   FIELD NO.

Dawes' Roll No.	NAME	Relationship to Person First Named	AGE	SEX	BLOOD	TRIBAL ENROLLMENT Year	TRIBAL ENROLLMENT County	No.
▓	olbert, Sallie	First Named	23	F	1/2	1896	Jacks Fork	1978
▓	enton, Willie	Son	8	M	1/4	"	" "	1980
13902	₃ " Everidge	"	5	"	1/4	"	" "	1981
13903	₄ " Margaret	Dau	2	F	1/4			
13904	₅ Allen, Adaline	S.Dau	14	"	1/4	1896	Jacks Fork	1979
13905	₆ Benton, George	Son	3mo	M	1/4			
13906	₇ Colbert, Elias	Son	5mo	M	1/4			
[?]551	₈ " Nathanael[sic]							
	₉							
	10							
	11 ENROLLMENT							
	12 OF NOS. 123456&7 HEREON							
	13 APPROVED BY THE SECRETARY OF INTERIOR MAR 19 1903							
	14							
	15 No6 born July 26, 1899							
	16							
	17							

TRIBAL ENROLLMENT OF PARENTS

	Name of Father	Year	County	Name of Mother	Year	County
₁	Allington Anderson	Dead	Choctaw Roll	Louisa Impson	1896	Chick Roll
₂	George Benton	"	" "	No.1		
₃	" "	"	" "	No.1		
₄	" "	"	" "	No.1		
₅	" "	"	" "	Sissy Benton	Dead	Chick Roll
₆	" "	"	" "	No.1		
₇	Washington Colbert	1896	Jacks Forks[sic]	No.1		
₈	" "			"	Born	Feb. 9-06
₉	No5 Enrolled May 24" 1899					
₁₀	No6 Enrolled Nov 4" 1899					
₁₁	For child of No.1 see NB (April 26, 1906) No. 551					
₁₂	~~Nos. 1 to 6 inclusive originally enrolled on Chickasaw Card #1435 and transferred to this card Oct. 20, 1902.~~					
₁₃	No1 is now the wife of Washington Colbert on Choctaw Card #1435 See letter of N.H. Morgan Oct 16, 1902 copy filed herein Oct 22, 1902 evidence requested Oct 22, 1902					
₁₄	~~No7 Born May 1, 1902 enrolled Oct 22, 1902; Evidence of marriage filed Oct 25, 1902~~					
₁₅	No5 is now the wife of Rufus Allen on Choctaw card #1897					
₁₆	Evidence of marriage filed December 15, 1902.					
₁₇	PO Mill Creek IT 4/14/02			Date of Application for Enrollment	For Nos 1 to 4 Inc	May 22"

85

Choctaw By Blood Enrollment Cards 1898-1914

RESIDENCE: Pontotoc   Co███████ ████aw Nation   **Choctaw Roll**   CARD NO.
POST OFFICE: Minco, Ind. Ter.   *(Not Including Freedmen)*   FIELD NO. **5486**

Dawes' Roll No.	NAME	Relationship to Person First Named	AGE	SEX	BLOOD	TRIBAL ENROLLMENT Year	County	No.
13907	1 Reynolds, Charles	First Named	4	M	3/8	'96	Chick. Dist	11070
	2							
	3							
	4							
	5							
	6							
	7							
	8							
	9							
	10							
	11	ENROLLMENT						
	12	OF NOS. 1 HEREON APPROVED BY THE SECRETARY						
	13	OF INTERIOR MAR 19 1903						
	14							
	15							
	16							
	17							

TRIBAL ENROLLMENT OF PARENTS

	Name of Father	Year	County	Name of Mother	Year	County
1	Jack Reynolds	1897	Pontotoc	Edna Reynolds		
2						
3						
4						
5						
6	No.1 On '96 Roll as "Charlie Raynolds[sic]"					
7	" 1 " Choctaw Census Record No.2 Page 417					
8	" 1 Son of Edna F. Henley on Choctaw Card #D97					
9	Citizenship of Edna Reynolds not determined					
10	No.1 originally enrolled on Chickasaw Card No. 1315 and transferred to this card Oct. 20, 1902.					
11						
12						
13						
14						
15						
16						
17				Date of Application for Enrollment.	Oct. 21st 1898	

Choctaw By Blood Enrollment Cards 1898-1914

RESIDENCE: Choctaw Nation ~~COUNTY.~~ **Choctaw Nation**   **Choctaw Roll**
POST OFFICE: South McAlester Ind Ter   *(Not Including Freedmen)*

Dawes' Roll No.	NAME	Relationship to Person First Named	AGE	SEX	BLOOD	TRIBAL ENROLLMENT		
						Year	County	No.
I.W. 525	1 Sittel, Fritz		36	M	I.W.	1896	Tobucksy	15031
13908	2 " Malvina	Wife	30	F	1/4	"	"	11257
13909	3 " Edward	Son	14	M	1/8	"	"	11258
13910	4 " William B	"	11	"	1/8	"	"	11259
13911	5 " Myrtle	Dau	9	F	1/8	"	"	11260
13912	6 " Lottie	"	7	"	1/8	"	"	11261
13913	7 " Josie	"	5	"	1/8	"	"	11262
13914	8 " Fritz, Jr	Son	3	M	1/8	"	"	11263
13915	9 " Farris G	"	7mo	"	1/8			
13916	10 " Melven Cornish	"	9mo	"	1/8			
	11							
	12 ENROLLMENT							
	13 OF NOS. 23456789 10 HEREON							
	APPROVED BY THE SECRETARY							
	14 OF INTERIOR MAR 19 1903							
	15 ENROLLMENT							
	OF NOS. 1 HEREON							
	16 APPROVED BY THE SECRETARY							
	OF INTERIOR DEC 24 1903							
	17							

TRIBAL ENROLLMENT OF PARENTS						
Name of Father	Year	County	Name of Mother	Year	County	
1 Edward Sittel		Non-Citizen	Lena Sittel		Non-Citizen	
2 Wᵐ B Pitchlynn	Dead	Choctaw Roll	Elsie Pitchlynn	Dead	Chick residing in Choctaw N. 1ˢᵗ Dist	
3 No.1			No.2			
4 No.1			No.2			
5 No.1			No.2			
6 No.1			No.2			
7 No.1			No.2			
8 No.1			No.2			
9 No.1			No.2			
10 No.1			No.2			
11						
12 No9 Enrolled Nov 4" 1899						
13 " 10 Born Dec 28" 1901; Enrolled Sept. 24" 1902						
14 ~~Nos 1 to 10 inclusive originally enrolled on Chickasaw Card No. 1380 and transferred to this card Oct. 20, 1902.~~						
15 For child of Nos 1 and 2 see NB (Mar 3'05) #406						
16 " " " No.3 " Chickasaw NB (March 3, 1905) #288				#1 to 8		
17				Date of Application for Enrollment.	Mar 20" 1899	

87

Choctaw By Blood Enrollment Cards 1898-1914

RESIDENCE: Choctaw Nation ~~COUNTY.~~ **Choctaw Nation** | Choctaw Roll | CARD NO.
POST OFFICE: Legal, Ind. Ter | (Not Including Freedmen) | FIELD NO. **5488**

Dawes' Roll No.	NAME	Relationship to Person First Named	AGE	SEX	BLOOD	TRIBAL ENROLLMENT		
						Year	County	No.
13917	1 King, Hayes		18	M	1/2	1896	Atoka	7644
	2							
	3							
	4							
	5							
	6							
	7							
	8							
	9							
	10							
	11	ENROLLMENT						
	12	OF NOS. 1 HEREON APPROVED BY THE SECRETARY						
	13	OF INTERIOR MAR 19 1903						
	14							
	15							
	16							
	17							

TRIBAL ENROLLMENT OF PARENTS

Name of Father	Year	County	Name of Mother	Year	County
1 Anderson King		Atoka Co Choctaw Roll	Susan King	Dead	Chick residing in Choctaw N. 1st Dist
2					
3					
4					
5					
6					
7 No.1 transferred from Chickasaw card No. 1387 October 20, 1902					
8					
9					
10					
11					
12					
13					
14					
15					
16					
17			Date of Application for Enrollment.		March 20/99

Choctaw By Blood Enrollment Cards 1898-1914

RESIDENCE:	Choctaw Nation	~~COUNTY.~~				**Choctaw Nation**	**Choctaw Roll** *(Not Including Freedmen)*	CARD No.
POST OFFICE:	Goodland Ind Ter							FIELD NO. **5489**

Dawes'	NAME	Relationship to Person First Named	AGE	SEX	BLOOD	TRIBAL ENROLLMENT		
						Year	County	No.
	, Wilson		22	M	1/4	1896	Kiamitia	8086
2	" Marion	Bro	20	"	1/4	"	"	8087
3	" Mary Jane	Sis	18	F	1/4	"	"	8088
4								
5								
6								
7								
8								
9								
10								
11	ENROLLMENT							
12	OF NOS. 1 2 & 3 HEREON APPROVED BY THE SECRETARY							
13	OF INTERIOR Mar. 19, 1903							
14								
15								
16								
17								

TRIBAL ENROLLMENT OF PARENTS

	Name of Father	Year	County	Name of Mother	Year	County
1	Benj F Locke		White Man	Hattie Locke	Dead	Chick residing in Choctaw N. 3rd Dist
2	" " "		" "	" "	"	" " " "
3	" " "		" "	" "	"	" " " "
4						
5						
6	No3 on 96 Roll as "Kithe Locke					
7	Nos 1, 2 and 3 originally enrolled on Chickasaw Card No. 1398					
8	and transferred to this card October 20, 1902.					
9	Child of No3 on NB (Apr 26-06) Card #302					
10	" " " " " (Mar 3-05) " #1132					
11	" No1 " " " " " #1407					
12						
13						
14						
15						
16						
17	PO Hugo IT 4/19/05			Date of Application for Enrollment.		Mar 21"-99

Choctaw By Blood Enrollment Cards 1898-1914

RESIDENCE: Choctaw Nation ~~COUNTY~~.

POST OFFICE: Talihina, Ind. Ter

Choctaw Nation

Choctaw Roll
(Not Including Freedmen)

CARD NO.

FIELD NO. **5490**

Dawes' Roll No.	NAME	Relationship to Person First Named	AGE	SEX	BLOOD	TRIBAL ENROLLMENT		
						Year	County	No.
13921	1 Hitcher, Harrison	First Named	40	M	Full	1896	Wade	5400
	2							
	3							
	4							
	5							
	6							
	7							
	8							
	9							
	10							
	11	ENROLLMENT						
	12	OF NOS. 1 HEREON APPROVED BY THE SECRETARY						
	13	OF INTERIOR MAR 19 1903						
	14							
	15							
	16							
	17							

TRIBAL ENROLLMENT OF PARENTS

	Name of Father	Year	County	Name of Mother	Year	County
1	Hih-cha	Dead	Chick. Roll	Siney Hih-cha	Dead	Chick. Roll
2						
3						
4						
5						
6	No.1 Wife and children of, on Choctaw Card #2128					
7	No.1 originally enrolled on Chickasaw Card No. 1441 and					
8	transferred to this card Oct. 20, 1902.					
9	For child of No.1 see NB (March 3 1905) #769.					
10						
11						
12						
13						
14						
15					~~Date of Application for Enrollment.~~	
16						
17						5/30/99

Choctaw By Blood Enrollment Cards 1898-1914

RESIDENCE: Choctaw Nation ~~COUNTY.~~ **Choctaw Nation**   Choctaw Roll   CARD NO.
POST OFFICE: Howe, Ind. Ter/   *(Not Including Freedmen)*   FIELD NO. **5491**

Dawes' Roll No.	NAME	Relationship to Person First Named	AGE	SEX	BLOOD	TRIBAL ENROLLMENT		
						Year	County	No.
13922	1 Wyatt, Celie	First Named	19	F	1/4	1896	Sugar Loaf	2240
13923	2 Wyatt, Maud Lee	Dau	3w	"	1/8			
	3							
	4							
	5							
	6							
	7							
	8							
	9							
	10							
	11	ENROLLMENT						
	12	OF NOS. 1 & 2 HEREON APPROVED BY THE SECRETARY						
	13	OF INTERIOR MAR 19 1903						
	14							
	15							
	16							
	17							

TRIBAL ENROLLMENT OF PARENTS

Name of Father	Year	County	Name of Mother	Year	County
1 Chas Church		Non Citizen	Newktie Church	1896	Chick. Roll
2 E.L. Wyatt		" "	No.1		
3					
4					
5					
6 No 1 Evidence of marriage to E.L. Wyatt to be supplied: Received & filed Jan 13" 1901					
7 " 2 Enrolled Jan. 15" 1901					
8 Nos. 1 and 2 originally enrolled on Chickasaw Card No. 1445 and transferred to this card Oct. 20, 1902.					
9 For children of No.1 see NB (March 3, 1905) #1439					
10					
11					
12					
13					
14					
15					
16				Date of Application for Enrollment.	6/5/1899
17					

Choctaw By Blood Enrollment Cards 1898-1914

RESIDENCE: Choctaw Nation ~~COUNTY.~~ **Choctaw Nation** Choctaw Roll CARD
POST OFFICE: Howe, Ind. Ter *(Not Including Freedmen)* FIELD

Dawes' Roll No.	NAME	Relationship to Person First Named	AGE	SEX	BLOOD	TRIBAL ENROLLMENT			
						Year		County	No.
13924	1 Hitcher, Henry	First Named	26	M	Full	1896	5262		
	2								
	3								
	4								
	5								
	6								
	7								
	8								
	9								
	10								
	11	ENROLLMENT							
	12	OF NOS. 1 HEREON APPROVED BY THE SECRETARY							
	13	OF INTERIOR MAR 19 1903							
	14								
	15								
	16								
	17								

TRIBAL ENROLLMENT OF PARENTS

	Name of Father	Year	County	Name of Mother	Year	County
1	Hitcher	Dead	Chick Roll	Siney Hitcher	Dead	Chick Roll
2						
3						
4						
5						
6	No1 The husband of Dicey Hitcher on Choctaw Card #2384					
7	No.1 originally enrolled on Chickasaw Card No. 1447 and transferred to this card Oct. 20, 1902					
8						
9						
10						
11						
12						
13						
14						
15					Date of Application for Enrollment.	
16						
17					6/7/99	

Choctaw By Blood Enrollment Cards 1898-1914

RESIDENCE: Choctaw Nation ~~COUNTY.~~ **Choctaw Nation** **Choctaw Roll** CARD NO.
POST OFFICE: Sans Bois, Ind. Ter *(Not Including Freedmen)* FIELD NO. **5493**

Dawes' Roll No.	NAME	Relationship to Person First Named	AGE	SEX	BLOOD	TRIBAL ENROLLMENT		
						Year	County	No.
13925	1 Cooper, Jeff D		22	M	1/2	1896	Sans Bois	2091
	2							
	3							
	4							
	5							
	6							
	7							
	8							
	9							
	10							
	11	ENROLLMENT						
	12	OF NOS. 1 HEREON APPROVED BY THE SECRETARY						
	13	OF INTERIOR MAR 19 1903						
	14							
	15							
	16							
	17							

TRIBAL ENROLLMENT OF PARENTS

	Name of Father	Year	County	Name of Mother	Year	County
1	Thompson Cooper	Dead	Choctaw	Kittie Cooper	Dead	Chickasaw
2						
3						
4						
5						
6	No.1 originally enrolled on Chickasaw Card No. 1452 and					
7	transferred to this card October 20th, 1902.					
8						
9						
10						
11						
12						
13						
14						
15						
16						
17				Date of Application for Enrollment.	6/19/99	

Choctaw By Blood Enrollment Cards 1898-1914

RESIDENCE: Blue			**Choctaw Nation**				**Choctaw Roll** (Not Including Freedmen)		CARD No	
POST OFFICE: Blue, Ind. Ter									FIELD No. 5494	

Dawes' Roll No.	NAME	Relationship to Person First Named	AGE	SEX	BLOOD	TRIBAL ENROLLMENT		
						Year	County	No.
13926	1 Wiley, Robert	First Named	20	M	Full	1893	Blue	557
	2							
	3							
	4							
	5							
	6							
	7							
	8							
	9							
	10							
	11	ENROLLMENT						
	12	OF NOS. 1 HEREON APPROVED BY THE SECRETARY						
	13	OF INTERIOR MAR 19 1903						
	14							
	15							
	16							
	17							

TRIBAL ENROLLMENT OF PARENTS

Name of Father	Year	County	Name of Mother	Year	County
1 Forbes Wiley	Dead	Chick. Nation	Bacey Wiley	Dead	Blue
2					
3					
4					
5					
6 No.1 originally enrolled on Chickasaw Card No. 1488 and transferred to this card Oct. 20, 1902.					
7 Also on 1896 Choctaw census roll page 363 #13860 as Robert Wesley					
8					
9					
10					
11					
12					
13					
14					
15				Date of Application for Enrollment.	
16					
17				8/14/99	

Choctaw By Blood Enrollment Cards 1898-1914

RESIDENCE: Choctaw Nation ~~COUNTY.~~ **Choctaw Nation** Choctaw Roll CARD NO.
POST OFFICE: Caddo, Ind. Ter. (Not Including Freedmen) FIELD NO. **5495**

Dawes' Roll No.	NAME	Relationship to Person First Named	AGE	SEX	BLOOD	TRIBAL ENROLLMENT		
						Year	County	No.
13927	1 Jones, Nat	First Named	12	M	1/4	1894	Jackson	7160
	2							
	3							
	4							
	5							
	6							
	7							
	8							
	9							
	10							
	11	ENROLLMENT						
	12	OF NOS. 1 HEREON APPROVED BY THE SECRETARY						
	13	OF INTERIOR MAR 19 1903						
	14							
	15							
	16							
	17							

TRIBAL ENROLLMENT OF PARENTS

	Name of Father	Year	County	Name of Mother	Year	County
1	William Jones	Dead	Choctaw	Amelia Jones		Chickasaw
2						
3						
4						
5						
6						
7	No.1 originally enrolled on Chickasaw Card No. 1528. Transferred					
8	to this card Oct. 20, 1902					
9						
10						
11						
12						
13						
14						
15						Date of Application for Enrollment.
16						
17						Aug. 25" 1899

95

Choctaw By Blood Enrollment Cards 1898-1914

RESIDENCE: Choctaw Nation ~~COUNTY.~~ **Choctaw Nation**   Choctaw Roll   CARD NO.
POST OFFICE: Scipio, Ind. Ter.   *(Not Including Freedmen)*   FIELD NO. **5496**

Dawes' Roll No.	NAME	Relationship to Person First Named	AGE	SEX	BLOOD	TRIBAL ENROLLMENT		
						Year	County	No.
13928	1 Folsom, Silas D	Named	26	M	1/2	1896	Tobucksy	4040
13929	2 " Levina	Sister	17	F	1/2	"	Sans Bois	3912
	3							
	4							
	5							
	6							
	7							
	8							
	9							
	10							
	11	ENROLLMENT OF NOS. **1 & 2** HEREON						
	12	APPROVED BY THE SECRETARY						
	13	OF INTERIOR **MAR** 19 1903						
	14							
	15							
	16							
	17							

TRIBAL ENROLLMENT OF PARENTS

	Name of Father	Year	County	Name of Mother	Year	County
1	Thomas Folsom	Dead	Choctaw Roll	Jennie Folsom	Dead	Chick residing in Choctaw N. 1st Dis
2	" "	"	" "	" "	"	" " " "
3						
4						
5						
6						
7	No.1 on Choctaw Census Record No.2 (Tobucksy Co) Page 171					
8	" 2 " " " " " (Sans Bois ") " 165					
9	Nos. 1 and 2 originally enrolled on Chickasaw Card No. 1155 and transferred to this card Oct. 20, 1902					
10						
11						
12						
13						
14						
15						Date of Application for Enrollment.
16						
17						Oct. 12" 1898

Choctaw By Blood Enrollment Cards 1898-1914

RESIDENCE: Choctaw Nation 3ʳᵈ Dist COUNTY.

POST OFFICE: Tuskahoma Ind. Ter.

Choctaw Nation

Choctaw Roll (Not Including Freedmen)

CARD NO.

FIELD NO. **5497**

Dawes' Roll No.	NAME	Relationship to Person First Named	AGE	SEX	BLOOD	TRIBAL ENROLLMENT		
						Year	County	No.
13930	1 Anderson, Norton	Named	25	M	1/2	1896	Jacks Fork	498
13931	2 " Missie	Sister	17	F	1/2	"	" "	496
	3							
	4							
	5							
	6							
	7							
	8							
	9							
	10							
	11	ENROLLMENT						
	12	OF NOS. 1 & 2 HEREON APPROVED BY THE SECRETARY						
	13	OF INTERIOR MAR 19 1903						
	14							
	15							
	16							
	17							

TRIBAL ENROLLMENT OF PARENTS

Name of Father	Year	County	Name of Mother	Year	County
1 Bartlett Anderson	Dead	Choctaw Roll	Elsey Anderson		Choc. Dist.
2 " "	"	" "	" "		" "
3					
4					
5 No.1 On Choctaw Census Record No. 2 Jacks Fork Page 29 as M J Anderson					
6 " On '96 Roll as M. J. Anderson					
" Husband of Mary Anderson on Choctaw Card #1932					
7 " 2 On Choctaw Census Record No 2 Jacks Fork, Page 20					
8 Nos 1 and 2 originally enrolled on Chickasaw Card No. 1081 and					
transferred to this card Oct. 20, 1902.					
9 For child of No.1 see NB (March 3, 1905) #859					
10 " " " " " " (April 26, 1906) #512					
11					
12					
13					
14					
15				Date of Application for Enrollment.	
16					
17				Oct. 10" 1898	

Choctaw By Blood Enrollment Cards 1898-1914

RESIDENCE: Choctaw Nation COUNTY. **Choctaw Nation** **Choctaw Roll** CARD NO.
POST OFFICE: Damon, Ind. Ter (Not Including Freedmen) FIELD NO. **5498**

Dawes' Roll No.	NAME	Relationship to Person First Named	AGE	SEX	BLOOD	TRIBAL ENROLLMENT		
						Year	County	No.
13932	1 Reed, George		8	M	1/2	1896	Gaines	10751
	2							
	3							
	4							
	5							
	6							
	7							
	8							
	9							
	10							
	11	ENROLLMENT						
	12	OF NOS. 1 HEREON APPROVED BY THE SECRETARY						
	13	OF INTERIOR MAR 19 1903						
	14							
	15							
	16							
	17							

TRIBAL ENROLLMENT OF PARENTS

	Name of Father	Year	County	Name of Mother	Year	County
1	Josiah Reed		Choctaw	Mollie Reed	Dead	Chickasaw
2						
3						
4						
5						
6	No1 Father of, on Choctaw Card #3148					
7						
8	No.1 originally enrolled on Chickasaw Card No. 1474. Transferred					
9	to this card Oct. 21, 1902					
10						
11						
12						
13						
14						
15						
16						
17						Aug 2" '99

98

Choctaw By Blood Enrollment Cards 1898-1914

RESIDENCE: Gaines　COUNTY **Choct** ation Choctaw Roll　CARD No.
POST OFFICE: Hartshorne, Ind. Ter.　*(Not Including Freedmen)*　FIELD No. **5499**

Dawes' Roll No.	NAME	Relationship to Person First Named	AGE	SEX	BLOOD	TRIBAL ENROLLME	
						Year	County
13933	1 Hahklotubbe, Adeline		21	F	Full	1896	Gaines
13934	2 " Garrett	Son	7mo	M	1/2		
	3						
	4						
	5						
	6						
	7						
	8						
	9						
	10						
	11	ENROLLMENT					
	12	OF NOS. 1 & 2 HEREON					
	13	APPROVED BY THE SECRETARY					
		OF INTERIOR Mar. 19, 1903					
	14						
	15						
	16						
	17						

TRIBAL ENROLLMENT OF PARENTS

Name of Father	Year	County	Name of Mother	Year	County
1 Joseph Haklotubbe[sic]	Dead	Gaines	Losina Haklotubbe	Dead	Gaines
2 Illegitimate Child			No.1		
3					
4					
5					
6 No.1 on 96 Roll as Adeline Baldwin					
7 " 2 Enrolled May 25" 1900					
8 Nos 1 and 2 originally enrolled on Chickasaw Card No. 1415 and transferred to this card Oct. 21, 1902.					
9					
10					
11					
12					
13					
14					
15				Date of Application for Enrollment.	
16				May 25/1900	
17					

Choctaw By Blood Enrollment Cards 1898-1914

Dawes' Roll No.	NAME	Relationship to Person First Named	AGE	SEX	BLOOD	TRIBAL ENROLLMENT		
						Year	County	No.
13935	1 Bell, Malena	First Named	21	F	1/4	1896	Jacks Fork	4994
DEAD.	2 " Melissa S	Dau	1	"	1/8			
13936	3 " Alice Vagina	"	2mo	"	1/8			
13937	4 " Henry Stephen	Son	5mo	M	1/8			
	5							
	6							
	7							
	8							
	9							
	10							
	11	ENROLLMENT						
	12	OF NOS. 1 3 & 4 HEREON APPROVED BY THE SECRETARY						
	13	OF INTERIOR MAR 19 1903						
	14	No. 2 HEREON DISMISSED UNDER						
	15	ORDER OF THE COMMISSION TO THE FIVE CIVILIZED TRIBES OF MARCH 31, 1905.						
	16							
	17							

TRIBAL ENROLLMENT OF PARENTS

	Name of Father	Year	County	Name of Mother	Year	County
1	Reuben Gipson		Choctaw Roll	Nicey Gipson		Chick. Roll
2	W M Bell		Non-Citizen	No.1		
3	" " "		" "	No.1		
4	" " "		" "	No.1		
5						
6						
7	No.1 On '96 Roll as Melinda Gibson					
8	" 2 Affidavit of Birth to be supplied: Recd Aug. 9" 1899					
9	" 3 Enrolled July 3rd 1900					
	" 4 Born Jan. 15" 1902; Enrolled June 21st 1902					
10	Nos. 1 to 4 inclusive originally enrolled on Chick. card #1480 and					
11	transferred to this card Oct. 21, 1902.					
	No.2 Died Sept. 1899; Proof of death filed Dec. 23, 1902.					
12	For child of No.2 see NB (Apr 26-06) no. 785					
13						
14						
15						
16				Date of Application for Enrollment.	#1 & 2	
17					Aug. 7. 1899	

Choctaw By Blood Enrollment Cards 1898-1914

RESIDENCE: Choctaw Nation   COUNTY. **Choctaw Nation**   **Choctaw Roll**   CARD NO.
POST OFFICE: Guertie, Ind. Ter.   (Not Including Freedmen)   FIELD NO. **5501**

Dawes' Roll No.	NAME	Relationship to Person First Named	AGE	SEX	BLOOD	TRIBAL ENROLLMENT Year	County	No.
DEAD	1 Dunford, Sarah	Named	23	F	1/2	1896	Atoka	3628
13938	2 " Turner	Son	10mo	M	1/2			
	3							
	4							
	5							
	6							
	7							
	8							
	9							
	10							
	11	ENROLLMENT						
	12	OF NOS. 2 HEREON APPROVED BY THE SECRETARY						
	13	OF INTERIOR Mar 19 1902						
	14	No. 1 hereon dismissed under order						
	15	of the Commission to the Five Civilized						
	16	Tribes of March 31, 1905.						
	17							

TRIBAL ENROLLMENT OF PARENTS

	Name of Father	Year	County	Name of Mother	Year	County
1	John Dunford	Dead	Choctaw Roll	Susan Dunford	Dead	Chick Roll
2	Unknown			No. 1		
3						
4						
5						
6	No. 1 lives with Jack Pusley at Guertie, Ind. Ter					
7	" 2 An Illegitimate child					
8	" " Born Jan. 15" 1901: Enrolled Nov. 20" 1901.					
9	Nos. 1 and 2 originally enrolled on Chickasaw Card No. 1482 and transferred to this card Oct. 21, 1902.					
10	No.1 died July 11, 1902: proof of death filed Nov. 28, 1902.					
11						
12						
13						
14						
15						
16						#1
17				Date of Application for Enrollment.		Aug. 9" 1899

Choctaw By Blood Enrollment Cards 1898-1914

RESIDENCE: Atoka   COUNTY. **Choctaw Nation**   Choctaw Roll *(Not Including Freedmen)*   CARD NO. FIELD NO. **5502**
POST OFFICE: Stewart Ind. Ter

Dawes' Roll No.	NAME	Relationship to Person First Named	AGE	SEX	BLOOD	TRIBAL ENROLLMENT		
						Year	County	No.
13939	1 Homer, Ellen	Named	22	F	1/2	1896	Atoka	8346
13940	2 Lewis, Mulbert	son	8mo	M	1/4			
14832	3 Homer, Isaac	son	11mo	M	3/4			
	4							
	5							
	6							
	7	ENROLLMENT						
	8	OF NOS. 1 & 2 HEREON APPROVED BY THE SECRETARY						
	9	OF INTERIOR Mar 19 1903						
	10							
	11	ENROLLMENT						
	12	OF NOS. 3 HEREON APPROVED BY THE SECRETARY						
	13	OF INTERIOR May 20 1903						
	14							
	15							
	16							
	17							

TRIBAL ENROLLMENT OF PARENTS

Name of Father	Year	County	Name of Mother	Year	County
1 John Lewis		Choctaw Roll	Ha-lis che		Chick Roll
2 Peter Hoktey		" "	No.1		
3 Enoch Homer	1896	Blue	No.1		
4					
5					
6		8/7/02			

7 No.1 Surname is now Homer. She is wife of Enoch Homer Choctaw Card #4178
8 " 2 Affidavit of Birth to be supplied; Received and filed Aug 7" 1902
9 Nos 1 and 2 originally enrolled on Chickasaw Card #1483 transferred to this card Oct. 21, 1902.
10 No.3 Born Jany. 15, 1902, enrolled Dec. 24, 1902.
11
12 For child of No.1 see NB (Apr 26 '06) Card #1173
   " " " " " (Mar 3 '05) " #539
13
14   # 1&2
15 Date of Application for Enrollment.
16
17 P.O. Non I.T. 3/28/05   Aug 9"/99

102

Choctaw By Blood Enrollment Cards 1898-1914

RESIDENCE: Choctaw Nation
POST OFFICE: Utica Ind. Ter

~~COUNTY:~~
Choctaw Nation

Choctaw Roll
(Not Including Freedmen)

Dawes' Roll No.	NAME	Relationship to Person First Named	AGE	SEX	BLOOD	TRIBAL ENROLLMENT Year	County	No.
DEAD. 1	Hillhouse, Ellen	Named	16	F	1/2	1896	Blue	8218
2								
3								
4								
5								
6								
	No. 1 HEREON DISMISSED UNDER ORDER OF THE COMMISSION TO THE FIVE CIVILIZED TRIBES OF MARCH 31, 1905.							
9								
10								
11								
12								
13								
14								
15								
16								
17								

CANCELLED

Applicant died prior to ratification of Choctaw-Chickasaw agreement Sept 25, 1902.

TRIBAL ENROLLMENT OF PARENTS

Name of Father	Year	County	Name of Mother	Year	County
1 Nelson Lewis	Dead	Choctaw Roll	Martha Lewis		Chick Roll
2					
3					
4					
5					
6					
7 No 1 On 96 Roll as "Ellen Lewis"					
8 No.1 originally enrolled on Chickasaw Card #1485. Transferred to this card Oct. 21, 1902					
9 No.1 Died July, 1899; Proof of death filed Nov. 6, 1902					
10					
11					
12					
13					
14					
15					
16					
17			Date of Application for Enrollment.	Aug 14/99	

Choctaw By Blood Enrollment Cards 1898-1914

RESIDENCE: Choctaw Nation ~~COUNTY.~~ **Choctaw Nation**   Choctaw Roll   CARD No.
POST OFFICE: Durant, Ind. Ter.   *(Not Including Freedmen)*   FIELD No. **5504**

Dawes' Roll No.	NAME	Relationship to Person First Named	AGE	SEX	BLOOD	TRIBAL ENROLLMENT Year	County	No.
13941	1 Cobb, Frances	Named	19	F	1/2	1896	Blue	2847
13942	2 " Annie	Dau	1	"	1/4			
13943	3 " Clarance	Son	1mo	M	1/4			
13944	4 " Edward	Son	1mo	M	1/4			
	5							
	6							
	7							
	8							
	9							
	10							
	11							
	12	ENROLLMENT OF NOS. 1 2 3 & 4 HEREON APPROVED BY THE SECRETARY OF INTERIOR MAR 19 1903						
	13							
	14							
	15							
	16							
	17							

TRIBAL ENROLLMENT OF PARENTS

Name of Father	Year	County	Name of Mother	Year	County
1 Fred Robinson		U.S.	Salina Robinson		Chick Roll
2 Charley Cobb		"	No.1		
3 " "		"	No.1		
4 " "		"	No.1		
5					
6					
7 No.1 on 1896 roll as Francis Cobb					
8 No.3 Enrolled Sept 18" 1900					
9 Nos 1,2 and 3 originally enrolled on Chickasaw Card #1493 and transferred to this card Oct. 21, 1902.					
10 No4 Born Sept 25, 1902, Enrolled Oct. 29, 1902					
11					
12					
13					
14					
15					
16			Date of Application for Enrollment.	For Nos. 1&2	
17				8/15/99	

Choctaw By Blood Enrollment Cards 1898-1914

RESIDENCE: Choctaw Nation COUNTY.	**Choctaw Nation**				**Choctaw Roll**		CARD NO.	
POST OFFICE: Stringtown, Ind. Ter.					(Not Including Freedmen)		FIELD NO. **5505**	

Dawes' Roll No.	NAME	Relationship to Person First Named	AGE	SEX	BLOOD	TRIBAL ENROLLMENT		
						Year	County	No.
13945	1 Moore, Christopher D	First Named	32	M	1/2	1896	Jacks Fork	8861
	2							
	3							
	4							
	5							
	6							
	7							
	8	ENROLLMENT OF NOS. 1 HEREON APPROVED BY THE SECRETARY OF INTERIOR MAR 19 1903						
	9							
	10							
	11							
	12							
	13							
	14							
	15							
	16							
	17							

TRIBAL ENROLLMENT OF PARENTS

Name of Father	Year	County	Name of Mother	Year	County
1 Dallas Moore	Dead	Choctaw Roll	Mary Bond Moore	1897	Chick residing in Choctaw N. 3rd Dist
2					
3					
4					
5					
6					
7 No.1 Husband of Tennessee Moore, Choctaw Roll, Card #300					
8 " 1 On Choctaw Census Record No.2 Page 357 as C. D. Moore					
" 1 Now the Husband of Ida Bob on Choctaw Care #1834. April 19" 1902					
9 " " On 96 Roll as C.D. Moore					
10 No.1 originally enrolled on Chickasaw Card No. 706. Transferred					
11 to this card Oct. 21, 1902					
12					
13					
14					
					Date of Application for Enrollment.
					Sept. 28"/98

Choctaw By Blood Enrollment Cards 1898-1914

POST OFFICE: Waupaunuka Ind. Ter		**Choctaw Nation**		**Choctaw Roll** *(Not Including Freedmen)*			CARD NO. FIELD NO. **5506**	

Dawes' Roll No.	NAME	Relationship to Person First Named	AGE	SEX	BLOOD	TRIBAL ENROLLMENT		
						Year	County	No.
13946	1 Dick, Sampson	First Named	22	M	1/2	1896	Atoka	3616
13947	2 " Taylor	Bro.	15	"	1/2	"	"	3617
13948	3 " Malina	Sis.	14	F	1/2	"	"	36[?]9
	4							
	5							
	6							
	7							
	8							
	9							
	10							
	11							
	12	ENROLLMENT OF NOS. 1 2 & 3 HEREON APPROVED BY THE SECRETARY OF INTERIOR MAR 19 1903						
	13							
	14							
	15							
	16							
	17							

TRIBAL ENROLLMENT OF PARENTS

Name of Father	Year	County	Name of Mother	Year	County
1 Martin Dick		Atoka Co Choctaw Roll	Jemima Dick	Dead	Chick residing in Choctaw N. 3rd Dist
2 " "		" "	" "		" " " "
3 " "		" "	" "		" " " "
4					
5					
6 No1, 2 & 3 Father of, Martin Dick on Choctaw Card #4315					
7 " 3 On '96 Roll as "Melina Dick"					
8 Nos. 1,2,3 originally enrolled on Chickasaw Card No. 824 and transferred to this card Oct. 21, 1902.					
9 No2 is husband of Josephine Monroe Chickasaw care #253					
10 For child of No.3 see NB (March 3, 1905) #1247					
11 " " " No.2 see Chickasaw NB (March 3, 1905) #258					
12					
13					
14					
15					
16					
17 PO Olney I.T.				Date of Application for Enrollment	Sept 29" '98

Choctaw By Blood Enrollment Cards 1898-1914

RESIDENCE: Choctaw Nation ~~COUNTY.~~ **Choctaw Nation** Choctaw Roll CARD NO.
POST OFFICE: Iron Bridge, Ind Ter (Not Including Freedmen) FIELD NO. **5507**

Dawes' Roll No.	NAME	Relationship to Person First Named	AGE	SEX	BLOOD	TRIBAL ENROLLMENT		
						Year	County	No.
13949	1 Billy, Susan	First Named	18	F	1/2	1896	Sans Bois	643
13950	2 Jackson, Jonas	Son	1	M	1/4	1896	Sans Bois	
DEAD	3 ~~Billy, James~~ DEAD	~~Bro.~~	~~14~~	"	~~1/2~~	~~1896~~	~~Sans Bois~~	~~644~~
	4							
	5							
	6							
	7							
	8							
	9	ENROLLMENT						
	10	OF NOS. 1 & 2 HEREON APPROVED BY THE SECRETARY						
	11	OF INTERIOR MAR 19 1903						
	12							
	13	No. 3 HEREON DISMISSED UNDER ORDER OF THE COMMISSION TO THE FIVE						
	14	CIVILIZED TRIBES OF MARCH 31, 1905.						
	15							
	16							
	17							

TRIBAL ENROLLMENT OF PARENTS

Name of Father	Year	County	Name of Mother	Year	County
1 Dixon Billy	1896	Choctaw Roll	Sally Billy	Dead	Chicasaw[sic]
2 Ben Jackson	"	" "	No.1		
3 ~~Dixon Billy~~	"	" "	~~Sally Billy~~	Dead	Chickasaw
4					
5					
6					
7 ~~Nos. 1,2 and 3 originally enrolled on Chickasaw Card No. 1462 and~~					
8 ~~transferred to this card Oct. 21, 1902.~~					
9					
10 ~~No.3 Died Dec. 12, 1899; Proof of death received and filed Dec. 30, 1902.~~					
11					
12					
13					
14					
15					
16			Date of Application for Enrollment	6/20/99	
17					

Choctaw By Blood Enrollment Cards 1898-1914

RESIDENCE: Choctaw Nation ~~COUNTY.~~ **Choctaw Nation** Choctaw Roll CARD NO.
POST OFFICE: Le Flore, Ind. Ter _(Not Including Freedmen)_ FIELD NO. **5508**

Dawes' Roll No.	NAME	Relationship to Person First Named	AGE	SEX	BLOOD	TRIBAL ENROLLMENT		
						Year	County	No.
13951	1 LeFlore, Joseph	First Named	53	M	1/2	1896	Sugar Loaf	7786
	2							
	3							
	4							
	5							
	6							
	7							
	8							
	9							
	10							
	11							
	12							
	13							
	14							
	15							
	16							
	17							

ENROLLMENT
OF NOS. 1 HEREON
APPROVED BY THE SECRETARY
OF INTERIOR Mar 19 1903

TRIBAL ENROLLMENT OF PARENTS

	Name of Father	Year	County	Name of Mother	Year	County
1	Wallace LeFlore	Dead	Wade	Pollea LeFlore	Dead	Chick. Roll
2						
3						
4						
5						
6	~~No.1 wife and children of on Choctaw Card #2908~~					
7	No.1 originally enrolled on Chickasaw Card No. 1463. Transferred					
8	to this card Oct. 21, 1902.					
9	~~For child of No.1 see NB (Apr. 26-06) card #409~~					
10	" " " " " " (Mar 3-05) " #220					
11						
12						
13						
14						
15						
16						
17			Date of Application for Enrollment. 6/20/99			

Choctaw By Blood Enrollment Cards 1898-1914

RESIDENCE: Choctaw Nation ~~COUNTY~~
POST OFFICE: Red Oak, Ind. Ter
Choctaw Nation
Choctaw Roll
(Not Including Freedmen)
CARD NO.
FIELD NO. **5509**

Dawes' Roll No.	NAME	Relationship to Person First Named	AGE	SEX	BLOOD	TRIBAL ENROLLMENT		
						Year	County	No.
13952	1 Colbert. Malissa	First Named	40	F	1/2	1896	Sugar Loaf	2235
13953	2 " Sukey	Dau	6	"	1/4	"	" "	2237
13954	3 " Annie	"	5	"	1/4	"	" "	2238
13955	4 " Agnes	"	3	"	1/4	"	" "	2239
13956	5 " Joe	Son	8mo	M	1/4			
13957	6 " Gill	"	1	"	1/4			
	7							
	8							
	9							
	10							
	11							
	12							
	13							
	14							
	15							
	16							
	17							

ENROLLMENT
OF NOS. 1,2,3,4,5 & 6 HEREON
APPROVED BY THE SECRETARY
OF INTERIOR Mar 19 1903

TRIBAL ENROLLMENT OF PARENTS

	Name of Father	Year	County	Name of Mother	Year	County
1	William McCurtain	Dead	Sugar Loaf	Sa-wi-cha	Dead	Sugar Loaf
2	Nat Colbert	1896	" "	No.1		
3	" "	"	" "	No.1		
4	" "	"	" "	No.1		
5	" "	"	" "	No.1		
6	" "	"	" "	No.1		
7						
8						
9	No.1 On 96 Roll as "Malissie"					
10	No.1 Husband on Choctaw Card #2943					
	" 6 Born August 24" 1901. Enrolled Sept 9" 1902					
11	" 2 On 96 Roll as "Sukie"					
12	Nos 1 to 6 originally enrolled on Chickasaw Card No. 1464. Transferred					
13	to this card Oct. 21, 1902.					
14						# 1 to 5
15						~~Date of Application~~
16						~~for Enrollment.~~
17						6/20/99

109

Choctaw By Blood Enrollment Cards 1898-1914

RESIDENCE: Choctaw Nation ~~COUNTY~~.   **Choctaw Nation**   Choctaw Roll   CARD NO.

POST OFFICE: Red Oak, Ind. Ter.   *(Not Including Freedmen)*   FIELD NO. **5510**

Dawes' Roll No.	NAME	Relationship to Person First Named	AGE	SEX	BLOOD	TRIBAL ENROLLMENT		
						Year	County	No.
DEAD	1 Jefferson, Nicholas		56	M	1/2	1896	Sans Bois	6411
	2							
	3							
	4							
	5 No. 1 HEREON DISMISSED UNDER							
	6 ORDER OF THE COMMISSION TO THE FIVE							
	7 CIVILIZED TRIBES OF MARCH 31, 1905.							
	8							
	9							
	10							
	11							
	12							
	13							
	14							
	15							
	16							
	17							

CANCELLED

Applicant died prior to ratification of Choctaw-Chickasaw agreement Sept 25, 1902.

TRIBAL ENROLLMENT OF PARENTS

Name of Father	Year	County	Name of Mother	Year	County
1 En-lo-man-tubbe	Dead	Choctaw Roll	Hot-ie-a-ky	Dead	Chick Roll
2					
3					
4					
5					
6					
7					
8 No.1 originally enrolled on Chickasaw Card #1468. Transferred					
to this card Oct. 21, 1902.					
9 No.1 Died in Aug. 1900, proof of death filed Nov. 13, 1902.					
10					
11					
12					
13					
14					
15					
16					
17			Date of Application for Enrollment.		6/20/99

Choctaw By Blood Enrollment Cards 1898-1914

RESIDENCE: Choctaw Nation ~~COUNTY.~~ **Choctaw Nation**   Choctaw Roll   CARD NO.
POST OFFICE: Red Oak, Ind. Ter.   *(Not Including Freedmen)*   FIELD NO. **5511**

Dawes' Roll No.	NAME	Relationship to Person First Named	AGE	SEX	BLOOD	TRIBAL ENROLLMENT		
						Year	County	No.
13958	1 Jesse, Eastman		22	M	1/2	1896	Sugar Loaf	6562
	2							
	3							
	4							
	5							
	6							
	7							
	8							
	9							
	10							
	11	ENROLLMENT OF NOS. 1 HEREON						
	12	APPROVED BY THE SECRETARY						
	13	OF INTERIOR MAR 19 1903						
	14							
	15							
	16							
	17							

TRIBAL ENROLLMENT OF PARENTS

Name of Father	Year	County	Name of Mother	Year	County
1 John Jesse	Dead	Choctaw Roll	Malissa Jesse		Chick. Dist.
2					
3					
4					
5					
6					
7 No.1 On 1893 Pay Roll Sugar Loaf Page 53, No 533 as "Esmond Jessee"					
8					
9 No.1 originally enrolled on Chickasaw Card #1465. Transferred to this card Oct. 21, 1902					
10					
11					
12					
13					
14					
15					
16					
17				Date of Application for Enrollment.	6/20/99	

111

Choctaw By Blood Enrollment Cards 1898-1914

RESIDENCE: ~~COUNTY.~~ **Choctaw Nation**   **Choctaw Roll**   CARD No.
POST OFFICE: *(Not Including Freedmen)*   FIELD No. **5512**

Dawes' Roll No.	NAME	Relationship to Person First Named	AGE	SEX	BLOOD	TRIBAL ENROLLMENT		
						Year	County	No.
DEAD	1 Noel, Moses	Named	18	M	1/4	1896	Sans Bois	9546
IW610	2 " Ida	wife	17	F	I.W.			
	3							
	4							
	5							
	6							
	7							
	8							
	9							
	10							
	11	ENROLLMENT						
	12	OF NOS. 2 HEREON APPROVED BY THE SECRETARY						
	13	OF INTERIOR Feb. 8 1904						
	14 ~~No. 1 hereon dismissed under order of~~							
	15 the Commission to the Five Civilized							
	16 Tribes of March 31, 1905.							
	17							

TRIBAL ENROLLMENT OF PARENTS

	Name of Father	Year	County	Name of Mother	Year	County
1	Peter Noel	Dead	Sans Bois	Lorinda Noel	Dead	Sans Bois
2	John Deason		non-citizen	Alice Deason		non citizen
3						
4						
5						
6	No.1 Brother on Chick Card #1455					
7	Nos. 1 and 2 originally enrolled on Chickasaw Card #1467 and transferred to this card Oct. 21, 1902.					
8	No 1 Died October 29 1900; Proof of death filed Dec. 30, 1902					
9						
10						
11						
12						
13						
14					Date of Application for Enrollment.	
15						
16					No.1	6/19/99
17	Dec. 22-1902 - P.O. Mt Curtain, I.T.				No.2	6/22/99

Choctaw By Blood Enrollment Cards 1898-1914

RESIDENCE: Choctaw Nation ~~COUNTY~~. **Choctaw Nation** Choctaw Roll CARD No.
POST OFFICE: Red Oak, Ind. Ter. (Not Including Freedmen) FIELD No. **5513**

Dawes' Roll No.	NAME	Relationship to Person First Named	AGE	SEX	BLOOD	TRIBAL ENROLLMENT		
						Year	County	No.
13959	1 Harlen, Sila		30	F	Full	1896	Gaines	5320
13960	2 " Edmund	Son	5	M	1/2	"	"	5321
13961	3 " Daniel	"	2	"	1/2			
	4							
	5							
	6							
	7							
	8							
	9							
	10							
	11							
	12							
	13							
	14							
	15							
	16							
	17							

ENROLLMENT OF NOS. 1, 2 & 3 HEREON APPROVED BY THE SECRETARY OF INTERIOR Mar 19 1903

TRIBAL ENROLLMENT OF PARENTS

	Name of Father	Year	County	Name of Mother	Year	County
1	Willis Thompson	1896	Chickasaw	Charlotte Thompson	Dead	Chickasaw
2	Logan Harlan	1896	Choctaw	No.1		
3	" "	1896	"	No.1		
4						
5						
6						
7	No.1 Husband on Choctaw Card #2923.					
8	" On '96 Roll as "Sally Harlen"					
9	Nos. 1,2 and 3 originally enrolled on Chickasaw Card No. 1469. Transferred to this card Oct. 21, 1902.					
10						
11	For child of No.1 see NB (Mar 3 '05) #407					
12						
13						
14					Date of Application for Enrollment.	
15						
16					Date of Application for Enrollment.	
17	P.O. Wilburton, I.T. 4/19/05				6/20/99	

Choctaw By Blood Enrollment Cards 1898-1914

RESIDENCE: Choctaw Nation ~~COUNTY.~~ **Choctaw Nation** Choctaw Roll CARD NO.
POST OFFICE: Red Oak, Ind. Ter. (Not Including Freedmen) FIELD NO. **5514**

Dawes' Roll No.	NAME	Relationship to Person First Named	AGE	SEX	BLOOD	TRIBAL ENROLLMENT		
						Year	County	No.
13962	1 James, Watkins		16	M	Full	1896	Sans Bois	6415
	2							
	3							
	4							
	5							
	6							
	7							
	8							
	9							
	10							
	11	ENROLLMENT						
	12	OF NOS. 1 HEREON APPROVED BY THE SECRETARY						
	13	OF INTERIOR MAR 19 1903						
	14							
	15							
	16							
	17							

TRIBAL ENROLLMENT OF PARENTS

	Name of Father	Year	County	Name of Mother	Year	County
1	Jacob James	Dead	Chick. Roll	Lady James	Dead	Chick. Roll
2						
3						
4						
5						
6						
7	No.1 originally enrolled on Chickasaw Card No. 1470. Transferred					
8	to this card Oct. 21, 1902					
9						
10						
11						
12						
13						
14						
15						Date of Application for Enrollment.
16						
17						6/20/99

114

Choctaw By Blood Enrollment Cards 1898-1914

RESIDENCE: Choctaw Nation   COUNTY. **Choctaw Nation**   **Choctaw Roll**   CARD NO.
POST OFFICE: Lodi, Ind. Ter.   *(Not Including Freedmen)*   FIELD NO. **5515**

Dawes' Roll No.	NAME	Relationship to Person First Named	AGE	SEX	BLOOD	TRIBAL ENROLLMENT		
						Year	County	No.
13963	1 Jefferson, Thomas		64	M	1/2	1896	Skullyville	6429
	2							
	3							
	4							
	5							
	6							
	7							
	8							
	9							
	10							
	11							
	12							
	13							
	14							
	15							
	16							
	17							

ENROLLMENT OF NOS. 1 APPROVED BY THE SECRETARY OF INTERIOR MAR 19 1903 HEREON

TRIBAL ENROLLMENT OF PARENTS

Name of Father	Year	County	Name of Mother	Year	County
1 En-lo-ma-tubbee	Dead	Choctaw Roll	Ho-ti-aka	Dead	Chick. Roll
2					
3					
4					
5					
6					
7					
8 No. 1 originally enrolled on Chickasaw Card # 471. Transferred					
9 to this card Oct. 21, 1902					
10					
11					
12					
13					
14					
15					
16					
17				Date of Application for Enrollment.	6/12/99	

Choctaw By Blood Enrollment Cards 1898-1914

RESIDENCE: Choctaw Nation COUNTY. **Choctaw Nation** Choctaw Roll CARD No.
POST OFFICE: Le Flore, Ind. Ter *(Not Including Freedmen)* FIELD No. **5516**

Dawes' Roll No.	NAME	Relationship to Person First Named	AGE	SEX	BLOOD	TRIBAL ENROLLMENT		
						Year	County	No.
13964	1 Atohko, Simon	First Named	26	M	1/2	1896	Sugar Loaf	72
13965	2 " Sarphin	Bro	24	"	1/2	"	" "	74
	3							
	4							
	5							
	6							
	7							
	8							
	9							
	10							
	11	ENROLLMENT						
	12	OF NOS. 1 & 2 HEREON APPROVED BY THE SECRETARY						
	13	OF INTERIOR MAR 19 1903						
	14							
	15							
	16							
	17							

TRIBAL ENROLLMENT OF PARENTS

	Name of Father	Year	County	Name of Mother	Year	County
1	Simeon Atohko	Dead	Choctaw	Sophia Atohko	Dead	Chickasaw
2	" "	"	"	" "	"	"
3						
4						
5						
6	No1 On '96 Roll as "Simus[sic] Atohko"					
7	Nos. 1 and 2 originally enrolled on Chickasaw Card No. 1472 and					
8	transferred to this card Oct. 21, 1902.					
9						
10						
11						
12						
13						
14						
15						
16						
17					Date of Application for Enrollment.	6/22/99

Choctaw By Blood Enrollment Cards 1898-1914

RESIDENCE: Choctaw Nation ~~COUNTY.~~   **Choctaw Nation**   Choctaw Roll   CARD NO.
POST OFFICE: Coalgate, Ind. Ter.   *(Not Including Freedmen)*   FIELD NO. **5517**

Dawes' Roll No.	NAME	Relationship to Person First Named	AGE	SEX	BLOOD	TRIBAL ENROLLMENT		
						Year	County	No.
13966	1 Harrison, Benj. F	First Named	23	M	1/4	1896	Tobucksy	5360
13967	2 " Joseph Colbert	Bro	22	"	1/4	"	"	5361
13968	3 " Charles Colbert	"	22	"	1/4	"	"	5362
	4							
	5							
	6							
	7							
	8							
	9							
	10							
	11	ENROLLMENT OF NOS. 1 2 & 3 HEREON APPROVED BY THE SECRETARY OF INTERIOR MAR 19 1903						
	12							
	13							
	14							
	15							
	16							
	17							

TRIBAL ENROLLMENT OF PARENTS

Name of Father	Year	County	Name of Mother	Year	County
1 Hilburn Harrison		Tobucksy Co Choctaw Roll	Sarah Harrison	Dead	Chick residing in Choctaw N. 3rd Dist
2 " "		" "	" "	"	" " " "
3 " "		" "	" "	"	" " " "
4					
5					

6 No1 On 96 Roll as "Ben F. Harrison" On Choctaw Census Record No 21 (Tobucksy Co) Page 228
7 " 2 " " " " "Joseph C " " " " " " " " " " " "
   " 3 " " " " "Charlie C " " " " " " " " " " " "
8 " 3 Also on 96 Roll Atoka Co #6041 as Charley Harrison
9 Nos. 1,2 and 3 originally enrolled on Chickasaw Card No. 1206
10   and transferred to this card Oct. 21, 1902.
11
12 For child of No2 see NB (Apr 26-06) Card #307
13 " " " " " " (Mar 3-05) " #734
14
15
16   Date of Application for Enrollment.
17   No3 PO Elmore IT 6/10/03   Oct. 13" 1898

117

Choctaw By Blood Enrollment Cards 1898-1914

RESIDENCE: Choctaw Nation COUNTY. **Choctaw Nation** Choctaw Roll CARD NO.
POST OFFICE: Hartshorn, Ind. Ter (Not Including Freedmen) FIELD NO. **5518**

Dawes' Roll No.	NAME	Relationship to Person First Named	AGE	SEX	BLOOD	TRIBAL ENROLLMENT		
						Year	County	No.
13969	1 James, Elizabeth	First Named	28	F	1/2	1896	Gaines	10,203
13970	2 " DIED PRIOR TO SEPTEMBER 25, 1902 Son		1	M	1/4			
15992	3 " Minnie	Dau	1	F	1/4			
	4							
	5							
	6							
	7	ENROLLMENT						
	8	OF NOS. 1 & 2 HEREON						
	9	APPROVED BY THE SECRETARY OF INTERIOR MAR 19 1903						
	10	No 3						
	11	GRANTED						
	12	JAN 19 1906						
	13					ENROLLMENT		
	14					OF NOS. 3 HEREON		
	15					APPROVED BY THE SECRETARY OF INTERIOR JUN 16 1906		
	16							
	17							

TRIBAL ENROLLMENT OF PARENTS

	Name of Father	Year	County	Name of Mother	Year	County
1	Williston Ward		Tobucksy Co Choctaw Roll	Patsey Ward	Dead	Chick residing in Choctaw N. 1st Dist
2	Israel Hancock		James Co Choctaw Roll	No.1		
3	Alex James		Chickasaw	No.1		
4						
5						
6	No1 On 96 Roll as "Elizabeth Pearson"					
7	" On Choctaw Census Record No2 Gaines Co Page 394 as Elizabeth Pearson					
8	No2 on Colored Card Oct 31st 1898					
9	Nos. 1 and 2 originally enrolled on Chickasaw Card No. 1213 and transferred to this card Oct. 21, 1902.					
10	No.2 died April 1, 1901: Enrollment Cancelled by Department July 8, 1904					
11	No3 was born Sept. 10, 1901: application received March 4, 1905,					
12	under Act of Congress approved March 3, 1905. Father is on Chickasaw card No. 1213, final Chick roll No 3561					
13						
14						
15						
16						
17	P.O. Coalgate 9/6/05			Date of Application for Enrollment. Oct. 1		

118

Choctaw By Blood Enrollment Cards 1898-1914

RESIDENCE: Choctaw Nation ~~COUNTY.~~ **Choctaw Nation** Choctaw Roll CARD NO.

POST OFFICE: Sans Bois, Ind. Ter (Not Including Freedmen) FIELD NO. **5519**

Dawes' Roll No.	NAME	Relationship to Person First Named	AGE	SEX	BLOOD	TRIBAL ENROLLMENT		
						Year	County	No.
13971	1 Burris, Sydney		40	M	Full	1896	Sans Bois	686
13972	2 Carnes, Lewis	nephew	13	"	1/2	1896	" "	2160
	3							
	4							
	5							
	6							
	7							
	8							
	9							
	10							
	11	ENROLLMENT						
	12	OF NOS. 1 & 2 HEREON APPROVED BY THE SECRETARY						
	13	OF INTERIOR Mar 19 1903						
	14							
	15							
	16							
	17							

TRIBAL ENROLLMENT OF PARENTS

	Name of Father	Year	County	Name of Mother	Year	County
1	Jim Homer	Dead	Chickasaw Roll	Stum-ma-hi-ye	Dead	Chick Roll
2	Lewis Carnes	"	Choctaw "	Wincey Carnes		Chick residing in Choctaw N. 1st Dist
3						
4						
5						
6	No.1 On Choctaw Census Record No2 Page 28 On 96 Roll as Lidney Burris					
7	" 2 " " " " " " " 87					
8	Nos. 1 and 2 originally enrolled on Chickasaw Card No. 1223. Transferred to this card Oct. 21, 1902					
9	For child of No.2 see NB (March 3, 1905) #1324					
10	No.1- "Died prior to September 25, 1902; not entitled to land or money"					
11	(See Indian Office letter of June 20, 1910. D.C. #834-1910).					
12						
13						
14						
15					Date of Application for Enrollment.	
16						
17					Oct. 13" 1898	

Choctaw By Blood Enrollment Cards 1898-1914

RESIDENCE: Choctaw Nation ~~COUNTY.~~ **Choctaw Nation**   Choctaw Roll
POST OFFICE: Atoka, Ind. Ter   *(Not Including Freedmen)*

Dawes' Roll No.	NAME	Relationship to Person First Named	AGE	SEX	BLOOD	TRIBAL ENROLLMENT		
						Year	County	No.
13973	1 Sexton, Annie	First Named	32	F	Full	1896	Atoka	11645
13974	2 " Mandy	Dau	3	"	1/2	"	"	11647
	3							
	4							
	5							
	6							
	7							
	8							
	9							
	10							
	11	ENROLLMENT						
	12	OF NOS. 1 & 2 HEREON APPROVED BY THE SECRETARY						
	13	OF INTERIOR MAR 19 1903						
	14							
	15							
	16							
	17							

TRIBAL ENROLLMENT OF PARENTS

Name of Father	Year	County	Name of Mother	Year	County
1 Newt Pierson	Dead	Pickens	Lucinda Pierson	Dead	Pickens
2 Emmerson Sexton		Atoka Co ~~Choctaw Roll~~	No.1		
3					
4					
5					
6 No1 Wife of Emmerson Sexton, Choctaw Roll, Card #391					
7 " On Choctaw Census Record No2 Atoka Co, Page 431 "2" " " " " "					
8 Nos. 1 and 2 originally enrolled on Chickasaw Card #1225 and					
9 transferred to this card Oct. 21, 1902.					
10					
11					
12					
13					
14					
15				Date of Application for Enrollment.	
16					
17				Oct. 13" 1898	

Choctaw By Blood Enrollment Cards 1898-1914

RESIDENCE: Choctaw Nation ~~COUNTY.~~ **Choctaw Nation**   **Choctaw Roll** CARD NO.

POST OFFICE: Tuskahoma, Ind. Ter.   *(Not Including Freedmen)* FIELD NO. **5521**

Dawes' Roll No.	NAME	Relationship to Person First Named	AGE	SEX	BLOOD	TRIBAL ENROLLMENT		
						Year	County	No.
DEAD	1 ~~Bohanon, Liney~~		22	F	3/4	1896	Jacks Fork	1969
13975	2 " Sam	Son	2	M	5/8	"	" "	1970
13976	3 " Vina	Dau	5mo	F	5/8			
13977	4 " Elsie	"	3mo	"	5/8			
	5							
	6							
	7							
	8							
	9							
	10							
	11 ENROLLMENT							
	12 OF NOS. **2, 3 & 4** HEREON							
	13 APPROVED BY THE SECRETARY							
	14 OF INTERIOR Mar 19 1903							
	No. 1 hereon dismissed under order							
	of the Commission to the Five Civilized							
	15 Tribes of March 31, 1905							
	16							
	17							

TRIBAL ENROLLMENT OF PARENTS

Name of Father	Year	County	Name of Mother	Year	County
1 Solomon Anderson	Dead	Chickasaw Roll	Lena Anderson	Dead	Chickasaw Roll
2 Robert Bohanon	1896	Jacks Fork Choctaw Roll	No.1		
3 " "	"	" "	No.1		
4 " "	"	" "	No.1		
5					
6					
7 No.1 On Choctaw Census Record No2 Jacks Fork Page 79 Wife of Robert Bohanon Choctaw Roll					
8 " 2 " " ' " " " " "				Card #393	
" 3 Enrolled March 27" 1899					
9 " 4 Born Jan. 23rd 1901: Enrolled May 14th 1901					
10 Nos. 1 to 4 inclusive originally enrolled on Chick. Card #1228 and					
transferred to this card Oct. 21, 1902.					
11					
12 No.1 Died July 6, 1901: proof of death filed Dec. 12, 1902.					
13					
14					
15					
16			Date of Application #1 & 2 inc.		
17			for Enrollment. Oct. 13th 1898		

Choctaw By Blood Enrollment Cards 1898-1914

RESIDENCE: Choctaw Nation 3rd Dist COUNTY.
POST OFFICE: Durant, Ind. Ter.

Choctaw Nation

Choctaw Roll
(Not Including Freedmen)

CARD No.
FIELD No. 5522

Dawes' Roll No.		NAME	Relationship to Person First Named	AGE	SEX	BLOOD	TRIBAL ENROLLMENT		
							Year	County	No.
I.W. 526	1	Busby, Smith Jefferson	First Named	37	M	I.W.	1896	Blue	14340
13978	2	" Biddie Caroline	Wife	20	F	1/8	"	"	1539
	3								
	4								
	5								
	6								
	7								
	8	ENROLLMENT							
	9	OF NOS. 2 HEREON APPROVED BY THE SECRETARY							
	10	OF INTERIOR MAR 19 1903							
	11								
	12	ENROLLMENT							
	13	OF NOS. 1 HEREON APPROVED BY THE SECRETARY							
	14	OF INTERIOR DEC 13 1903							
	15								
	16								
	17								

TRIBAL ENROLLMENT OF PARENTS

	Name of Father	Year	County	Name of Mother	Year	County
1	John Busby	Dead	Non-Citizen	Eliza Busby	Dead	Non-Citizen
2	Henry Thompson	"	" "	Caroline Spears	1897	Chick residing in Choctaw N. 3rd Dist
3						
4						
5						
6	No1 On Choctaw Intermarried Roll Page 10; On 96 Roll as "J.S. Busbey"					
7	" 2 " " Census Record No1 " 38 " " " " "Biddie Busby"					
8	Nos. 1 and 2 originally enrolled on Chickasaw Card #1229 and					
9	transferred to this card Oct. 21, 1902.					
10						
11						
12						
13						
14						
15						
16						
17	Oct. 27 1902 PO Oscar I.T.			Date of Application for Enrollment.	Oct. 13" 1898	

Choctaw By Blood Enrollment Cards 1898-1914

RESIDENCE: Choctaw Nation   COUNTY. **Choctaw Nation**   **Choctaw Roll**   CARD NO.
POST OFFICE: Red Oak, Ind. Ter.   *(Not Including Freedmen)*   FIELD NO. **5523**

Dawes' Roll No.	NAME	Relationship to Person First Named	AGE	SEX	BLOOD	TRIBAL ENROLLMENT Year	Count	No.
1	Welch, Robert C	Named	31	M	1/8	1896		12886
DEAD 2	" Minnie S	Wife	30	F	I.W.	"	"	15156
3	" Alice	Dau	9	"	1/16	"	"	12887
4	" Joe	Son	7	M	1/16	"	"	12888
5	" Frank	"	5	"	1/16	"	"	12889
6	" John H	"	2	"	1/16	"	"	12890
7	" Mildred B	Dau	6mo	F				
8								
9	No. 2 HEREON DISMISSED UNDER							
10	ORDER OF THE COMMISSION TO THE FIVE							
11	CIVILIZED TRIBES OF MARCH 31, 1905.							
12								
13								
14								
15								
16								
17								

CANCELLED

Cancelled and transferred to Chickasaw Card #1666 March 12th 1903

TRIBAL ENROLLMENT OF PARENTS

	Name of Father	Year	County	Name of Mother	Year	County
1	Wm A Welch I.W.		Chick residing in Choctaw N. 3rd Dist	Alice Welch	Dead	Chick residing in Choctaw N. 3rd Dist
2	James Carter	Dead	Non-Citizen	Rebecca Carter		Non-Citizen
3	No.1			No.2		
4	No.1			No.2		
5	No.1			No.2		
6	No.1			No.2		
7	No.1			No.2		
8						
9	No 1, 3, 4, 5 & 6 On Choctaw Census Record No.2 Page 461					
10	" 2 " " Intermarried " 112					
11	" 2 Enrolled as "Minnie L Welch"					
12	" 2 Died Sept 11" 1901. Proof of Dead[sic] filed June 9" 1902					
13	" 7 Enrolled Nov 4" 1899					
	Nos. 1 to 7 inclusive originally enrolled on Chickasaw Card No. 1230. Transferred					
	to this card October 21, 1902					
14	No.1 elects to have himself and family enrolled as Chickasaws Feby. 13, 1903.					
15	Nos. 1,2,3 and 4 on 1898 Ieshatubby Pay Roll {Chicasaw[sic]}					
16						
17			Date of Application for Enrollment.		Oct. 13" 1898	

123

Choctaw By Blood Enrollment Cards 1898-1914

Dawes' Roll No.	NAME	Relationship to Person First Named	AGE	SEX	BLOOD	TRIBAL ENROLLMENT		
						Year	County	No.
1	Welch, Charles A	First Named	27	M	1/16	1896	Sugar Loaf	12881
2	" Adelia	Wife	28		I.W.	"		15155
3	" Maney	Son	8	M	1/16	"		12882
4	" Earl	"			1/16	"		12883
DEAD. 5	" Paul	"	3		1/16	" "	" "	12884
6	" Fitzhugh Lee	"	5mo		1/16			
7	" Lucile Matilda	Dau		F	1/16			
8								
9	No. 5 HEREON DISMISSED UNDER							
10	ORDER OF THE COMMISSION TO THE FIVE							
11	CIVILIZED TRIBES OF MAR. 31, 1905.							
12								
13								
14								
15								
16	See testimony of No2 as to her status as an							
17	intermarried citizen Feby 13, 190?							

TRIBAL ENROLLMENT OF PARENTS

	Name of Father	Year	County	Name of Mother	Year	County
1	Wm A Welch I.W.		Chick residing in Choctaw N. 3rd Dist	Alice Welch	Dead	Chick residing in Choctaw N. 3rd Dist
2	C. G[?] Morton	Dead	Non-Citizen	Mary G. Morton		Non-Citizen
3	No.1			No.2		
4	No.1			No.2		
5	No.1			No.2		
6	No.1			No.2		
7	No.1			No.2		
8	Nos 1,3,4 & 5 on Choctaw Census Record No2 Page 460					
9	No1 on '96 Roll as Charley Welch also on the Choctaw Roll as such.					
10	" 2 On Choctaw Intermarried Roll Page 112					
11	" 2 On '96 Roll as "Adelia N. Welch"					
	" 7 Enrolled May 10, 1901					
12	Nos 1 to 7 inclusive originally enrolled on Chickasaw Card No. 1231					
13	and transferred to this card Oct. 21, 1902					
	No5 died February 1899. Proof of death filed Dec 24, 1902.					
14	No1 elected to have himself and family enrolled as Chickasaws Feby. 13, 1903					
15	Nos 1,2,3 and 4 on 1893 Ieshatubby Pay Roll {Chickasaw}					
16						
17				Date of Application for Enrollment.		Oct. 13" 1898

124

Choctaw By Blood Enrollment Cards 1898-1914

RESIDENCE:								
POST OFFICE:		**Choctaw Nation**		**Choctaw Roll** *(Not Including Freedmen)*		CARD No. FIELD No. **5525**		

Dawes' Roll No.	NAME	Relationship to Person First Named	AGE	SEX	BLOOD	TRIBAL ENROLLMENT		
						Year	County	No.
13999	1 Colbert, Martha	First Named	22	F	3/4	1896	Jacks Fork	3047
DEAD	2 " Frances	Dau	4mo	"	3/8			
14913	3 " Aaron	Son	1	M	3/8			
	4							
	5							
	6	ENROLLMENT						
	7	OF NOS. 1 HEREON APPROVED BY THE SECRETARY						
	8	OF INTERIOR MAR 19 1903						
	9	ENROLLMENT						
	10	OF NOS. 3 HEREON APPROVED BY THE SECRETARY						
	11	OF INTERIOR MAR 19 1903						
	12							
	13							
	14	No. 2 hereon dismissed under						
	15	order of the Commission to the Five Civilized Tribes of March 31, 1905.						
	16							
	17							

TRIBAL ENROLLMENT OF PARENTS

	Name of Father	Year	County	Name of Mother	Year	County
1	Calvin Gibson	Dead	Choctaw Roll Jacks Fork Co	Nancy Gibson	Dead	Chickasaw Roll
2	Alexander Colbert	1896	Choctaw Roll	No.1		
3	" "	"	" "	No.1		
4						
5						
6	No.1 On Choctaw Census Record No.2 Jacks Fork Co. Page 124					
7	" Wife of Alexander Colbert, Choctaw Roll, Card #395					
8	" 2 Affidavit of mother to be supplied. 3/21/99 " Enrolled March 21" 1899					
9	" 3 Born Sept 3rd 1901: Enrolled Sept 4" 1902					
10	Nos 1,2 and 3 originally enrolled on Chickasaw Card No.1235 and transferred to this card Oct. 21, 1902.					
11	No.2 died March, 1899: proof of death filed Dec. 15, 1902.					
12	No.3 died Nov. 24, 1902: " " " " " " "					
13	For child of No.1 see NB (March 3, 1905) #1122.					
14						
15						
16				Date of Application for Enrollment.	Oct. 13" 1898	
17						

Choctaw By Blood Enrollment Cards 1898-1914

RESIDENCE: Choctaw Nation COUNTY: **Choctaw Nation** POST OFFICE: Bennington, Ind. Ter.

Choctaw Roll *(Not Including Freedmen)*

CARD NO. FIELD NO. **5526**

Dawes' Roll No.	NAME	Relationship to Person First Named	AGE	SEX	BLOOD	TRIBAL ENROLLMENT		
						Year	County	No.
13980	1 Jackson, Louisa E. F.		32	F	1/2	1896	Blue	7197
	2							
	3							
	4							
	5							
	6							
	7							
	8							
	9							
	10							
	11	ENROLLMENT OF NOS. 1 HEREON APPROVED BY THE SECRETARY OF INTERIOR Mar 19 1903						
	12							
	13							
	14							
	15							
	16							
	17							

TRIBAL ENROLLMENT OF PARENTS

Name of Father	Year	County	Name of Mother	Year	County
1 Alfred R. Folsom		Blue Co Choctaw Roll	Levina Folsom	1897	Chick residing in Choctaw N. 3rd Dis
2					
3					
4					
5					
6					
7 No.1 On Choctaw Census Record No.1 Blue Co Page 177.					
8 No.1 originally enrolled on Chickasaw Card No. 1244 and					
9 transferred to this card Oct. 21, 1902.					
10					
11					
12					
13					
14					Date of Application for Enrollment.
15					Oct. 14. 1898
16					Date of Application for Enrollment.
17 P.O. Nail I.T. 2/24/05					

P.O. Kenefic, Okla. 12/22/11

126

Choctaw By Blood Enrollment Cards 1898-1914

Dawes' Roll No.	NAME	Relationship to Person First Named	AGE	SEX	BLOOD	TRIBAL ENROLLMENT		
						Year	County	No.
13981	₁ Mᶜ Murtrey, Amelia	Named	38	F	1/2	1896	Atoka	4448
13982	₂ Frinzell, John	Son	22	M	1/4	"	"	4449
13983	₃ " Lena	Dau	7	F	1/4	"	"	4451
13984	₄ Mᶜ Murtrey, Irene	Niece	12	"	1/4	"	"	4450
ᴵᵂ1223	₅ Mᶜ Murtrey, John	Hus	45	M	I.W.			
13985	₆ " " Clyde	son	2mo	"	1/4			
13986	₇ " " Glenn	Gr Nephew	1mo	"	1/8			
	₈							
	₉							
	₁₀							
	₁₁							
	₁₂							
	₁₃							
	₁₄							
	₁₅							
	₁₆							
	₁₇ For child of No.4 see NB (March 3 1905) #1323							

ENROLLMENT OF NOS. 1234 6&7 HEREON APPROVED BY THE SECRETARY OF INTERIOR Mar 19 1903

ENROLLMENT OF NOS. 5 HEREON APPROVED BY THE SECRETARY OF INTERIOR Dec 13 1904

TRIBAL ENROLLMENT OF PARENTS

	Name of Father	Year	County	Name of Mother	Year	County
₁	Benj. Smallwood	Dead	Choctaw Roll	Annie Smallwood	Dead	Chickasaw Roll
₂	John Frinzell	"	non-citizen	No.1		
₃	" "	"	" "	No.1		
₄	Harry Cox		" "	Elmira Cox	Dead	Chick residing in Choctaw N. 3ʳᵈ Dist
₅	Joe Mᶜ Murtrey	Dead	" "	Martha Mᶜ Murtrey		Non-Citizen
₆	No.5			No.1		
₇	Lora Mᶜ Murtrey		Non-Citizen	No.4		
₈						

₉ Nos 1,2,3 & 4 on Choctaw Census Record No.2 Atoka Co Page 190
₁₀ No.4 Now the wife of Lora Mᶜ Murtrey non-citizen Jan 23ʳᵈ 1902
   " 5 Enrolled Aug. 29ᵗʰ 1899
₁₁ " 6 Enrolled Decʳ 15" 1900
₁₂ " 7 Born Decʳ 12" 1901: Enrolled Jan 23ʳᵈ 1902
₁₃ Nos. 1 to 7 originally enrolled on Chickasaw Card No. 1247 and
   transferred to this card Oct 21, 1902.
₁₄ Affidavits of William MᶜBride and Nancy Emmet relative to her divorce from No.5
₁₅ also copy of divorce proceedings between Mary E and John Mᶜ Murtrey filed July 10, 1903.

	Date of Application for Enrollment.
₁₆	
₁₇	Oct. 14" 1898

127

Choctaw By Blood Enrollment Cards 1898-1914

RESIDENCE: Choctaw Nation   COUNTY. **Choctaw Nation**   **Choctaw Roll**   CARD NO.
POST OFFICE: Caddo, Ind. Ter.   (Not Including Freedmen)   FIELD NO. **5528**

Dawes' Roll No.	NAME	Relationship to Person First Named	AGE	SEX	BLOOD	TRIBAL ENROLLMENT		
						Year	County	No.
IW611	1 Long, LeRoy	First Named	30	M	I.W.	1896	Blue	14774
13987	2 " Martha	Wife	24	F	1/4	"	"	8209
13988	3 " LeRoy D	Son	1 1/2	M	1/8			
13989	4 " Wendell McLean	"	3mo	"	1/8			
	5							
	6							
	7	ENROLLMENT OF NOS. 1 HEREON						
	8	APPROVED BY THE SECRETARY						
	9	OF INTERIOR FEB -8 1904						
	10	ENROLLMENT						
	11	OF NOS. 2 3 & 4 HEREON APPROVED BY THE SECRETARY						
	12	OF INTERIOR MAR 19 1903						
	13							
	14							
	15							
	16							
	17							

TRIBAL ENROLLMENT OF PARENTS

	Name of Father	Year	County	Name of Mother	Year	County
1	W.T. Long		Non-Citizen	Mary E. Long		Non-Citizen
2	George Downing (I.W.)	Dead	Chickasaw Roll	Malissa Downing	Dead	Chick residing in Choctaw N. 3rd Dist
3	No.1			No.3		
4	No.1			No.2		
5						
6						
7	No. 1 admitted as intermarried citizen by Commission in 1896 Choctaw case #854					
8	No1 On 96 Roll as "Dr. Leroy Long" On Choctaw Intermarried Roll Page 64					
9	" 2 " " " " "Mrs Martha " " " " Census Record No2 " 339					
10	" 3 Evidence of Birth filed Jan 29" 1902 " 3 On Choctaw Census Record No 2 Page 339					
11	" 4 Affidavit of Birth filed April 29" 1890					
12	Nos. 1 to 4 inclusive originally enrolled on Chickasaw Card No. 1253 and transferred to this roll[sic] Oct. 21, 1902.					
13						
14						
15						
16						
17	~~South~~ McAlester, Ok 1/15/08			Date of Application for Enrollment.	Oct. 14" 1898	

Choctaw By Blood Enrollment Cards 1898-1914

RESIDENCE: Choctaw Nation   COUNTY.   **Choctaw Nation**   **Choctaw Roll**   CARD NO.
POST OFFICE: Atoka Ind. Ter.   *(Not Including Freedmen)*   FIELD NO. **5529**

Dawes' Roll No.	NAME	Relationship to Person First Named	AGE	SEX	BLOOD	TRIBAL ENROLLMENT		
						Year	County	No.
13990	1 Folsom, Ida	First Named	20	F	1/8	1896	Atoka	4438
13991	2 " Nellie	sister	15	"	1/8	"	"	4439
	3							
	4							
	5							
	6							
	7							
	8	ENROLLMENT						
	9	OF NOS. 1 & 2 HEREON APPROVED BY THE SECRETARY						
	10	OF INTERIOR MAR 19 1903						
	11							
	12							
	13							
	14							
	15							
	16							
	17							

TRIBAL ENROLLMENT OF PARENTS

	Name of Father	Year	County	Name of Mother	Year	County
1	Alfred E. Folsom		Atoka Co Choctaw Roll	Margaret Folsom	Dead	Chick residing in Choctaw N. 3rd Dist
2	" " "		" "	" "	"	" " " "
3						
4						
5						
6	Nos 1 & 2 On Choctaw Census Record No.2 Atoka Co Page 189					
7	No 1 & 2 Father of, Alfred Emerson Folsom, On Choctaw Card #400					
8	Nos. 1 and 2 originally enrolled on Chickasaw Card #1255. Transferred to this card Oct. 21, 1902					
9	For child of No.2 see NB (Apr 26-06) Card #433					
10						
11						
12						
13						
14						
15						
16						
17	P.O. Caddo, I.T. 3/28/03			Date of Application for Enrollment.	Oct. 14" 1898	

129

Choctaw By Blood Enrollment Cards 1898-1914

RESIDENCE: Choctaw Nation COUNTY. **Choctaw Nation** Choctaw Roll CARD NO.
POST OFFICE: Atoka, Ind. Ter. (Not Including Freedmen) FIELD NO. **5530**

Dawes' Roll No.		NAME	Relationship to Person	AGE	SEX	BLOOD	TRIBAL ENROLLMENT		
							Year	County	No.
13992	1	Armstrong, Wallace	First Named	60	M	1/2	1896	Atoka	427
13993	2	Carnes, Jackson	Step Gr. Son	14	"	1/2	"	Blue	2907
	3								
	4								
	5								
	6								
	7								
	8	ENROLLMENT OF NOS. **1 & 2** HEREON							
	9	APPROVED BY THE SECRETARY							
	10	OF INTERIOR **MAR 19 1903**							
	11								
	12								
	13								
	14								
	15								
	16								
	17								

TRIBAL ENROLLMENT OF PARENTS

	Name of Father	Year	County	Name of Mother	Year	County
1	Wm Armstrong	Dead	Choctaw Roll	Oh-ko-wi-ke	Dead	Chickasaw Roll
2	Tillis Carnes	"	" "	Phoebe Carnes	"	Chick residing in Choctaw N. 3rd Dist
3						
4						
5						
6						
7						
8	Nos[sic] 1 on Choctaw Census Record No2 Atoka Co Page 18					
9	2 " " " " " " " " 118					
10	Nos. 1 and 2 originally enrolled on Chickasaw Card No. 1256 and transferred to this card Oct. 21, 1902.					
11						
12						
13						
14						
15					Date of Application for Enrollment.	
16						
17					Oct. 14" 1898	

Choctaw By Blood Enrollment Cards 1898-1914

Dawes' Roll No.	NAME	Relationship to Person First Named	AGE	SEX	BLOOD	TRIBAL ENROLLMENT Year	County	No.
13994	1 Jones, Ellen		50	F	1/4	1896	Jackson	7128
13995	2 " Osborne	Son	21	M	1/8	"	"	7129
13996	3 " Billy	"	18	"	1/8	"	"	7130
13997	4 " Minnie	Dau	10	F	1/8	"	"	7131
13998	5 " John	Son	9	M	1/8	"	"	7132
13999	6 " Pearl	Dau	7	F	1/8	"	"	7133
IW 1632	7 " Ruthie	Wife of No 3	15	"	I.W.			
	8							
	9	ENROLLMENT OF NOS. 1-2-3-4-5-6 HEREON APPROVED BY THE SECRETARY						
	10	OF INTERIOR Mar 19 1903						
	11							
	12	ENROLLMENT						
	13	OF NOS. 7 HEREON APPROVED BY THE SECRETARY						
	14	OF INTERIOR Feb 19 1907						
	15 For children of No.2 see NB (March 3, 1905) #1318							
	16 " child " " " " (April 26, 1906) #329							
	17							

TRIBAL ENROLLMENT OF PARENTS

Name of Father	Year	County	Name of Mother	Year	County
1	Dead	Choctaw Roll	Eliza Impson	1897	Chick residing in Choctaw N. 1st Dist
2 Jacob Jones		" "	No.1		
3 " "		" "	No.1		
4 " "		" "	No.1		
5 " "		" "	No.1		
6 " "		" "	No.1		
7 Jim Everett			Callie Everett		

8 Nos. 1,2,3,4,5&6 On Choctaw Census Record No 2 Jackson Co Page 299

9 Nos. 1 to 6 inclusive originally enrolled on Chickasaw Card #1257 and transferred to this card Oct. 21, 1902.

10 No.2 is the Husband of Virginia Goode on Choctaw Card #3859.

11 For child of No.3 see NB (Apr. 26-06) No. 573

12 Foe child of No.4 see NB (Apr 26-06) Card #442

13 No.7 placed hereon under order of the Commissioner to the Five Civilized Tribes of Jan 7,'07 holding application was made for her enrollment within the time provided by the Act of

14 Congress approved April 26, 1906.

15 No.7 Granted Jan 9, 1907. For child of No.4 see NB (Mar. 3, 1905) #547.

16

17 P.O. Nos 3 and 7 Burris, I.T. | 12/29/06 | Date of Application for Enrollment. | Oct. 14" 1898

131

Choctaw By Blood Enrollment Cards 1898-1914

RESIDENCE: Choctaw Nation ~~COUNTY.~~
POST OFFICE: South McAlester, Ind. Ter

Choctaw Nation

Choctaw Roll
(Not Including Freedmen)

CARD NO.
FIELD NO. 5532

Dawes' Roll No.	NAME	Relationship to Person First Named	AGE	SEX	BLOOD	TRIBAL ENROLLMENT		
						Year	County	No.
14000	1 McLish, Israel DIED PRIOR TO SEPTEMBER 25, 1902	First Named	44	M	1/2	1896	Tobucksy	9184
	2							
	3							
	4							
	5							
	6							
	7							
	8	ENROLLMENT OF NOS. 1 HEREON						
	9	APPROVED BY THE SECRETARY						
	10	OF INTERIOR MAR 19 1903						
	11							
	12							
	13							
	14							
	15							
	16							
	17							

TRIBAL ENROLLMENT OF PARENTS

	Name of Father	Year	County	Name of Mother	Year	County
1	John McLish	Dead	Choctaw Roll	Shim-o-te-cha	Dead	Chickasaw Roll
2						
3						
4						
5						
6	No1 On Choctaw Census Record No2 Tobucksy Co, Page 365					
7	No1 On '96 Roll as "Israel McClish[sic]"					
8	No.1 originally enrolled on Chickasaw Card No. 1259. Transferred to this card Oct. 22, 1902					
9						
10						
11						
12						
13						
14						
15						
16				Date of Application for Enrollment.		
17						Oct. 14" 1898

Choctaw By Blood Enrollment Cards 1898-1914

RESIDENCE: Choctaw Nation	COUNTY.	Choctaw Nation		Choctaw Roll	CARD No.	
POST OFFICE: Tucker, Ind. Ter.				(Not Including Freedmen)	FIELD No. 5533	

Dawes' Roll No.	NAME	Relationship to Person First Named	AGE	SEX	BLOOD	TRIBAL ENROLLMENT		
						Year	County	No.
14001	1 Osborne, Nancy	First Named	53	F	1/4	1896	Skullyville	9898
	2							
	3							
	4							
	5							
	6	ENROLLMENT OF NOS. 1 HEREON						
	7	APPROVED BY THE SECRETARY OF INTERIOR MAR 19 1903						
	8							
	9							
	10							
	11							
	12							
	13							
	14							
	15							
	16							
	17							

TRIBAL ENRO

	Name of Father	Year	County	Name of Mother		County
1	Stephen Krebs	Dead	Non-Citizen	Peggy Krebs	Dead	Chickasaw Roll
2						
3						
4						
5						
6	No1 on Choctaw Census Record No 2, Skullyville, Page 389					
7	No.1 originally enrolled on Chickasaw Card No. 1264 and					
8	transferred to this card Oct. 22, 1902.					
9						
10						
11						
12						
13						
14						
15						
16				Date of Application for Enrollment.	Oct. 14" 1898	
17						

Choctaw By Blood Enrollment Cards 1898-1914

RESIDENCE: Choctaw Nation COUNTY.
POST OFFICE: Cameron, Ind. Ter. **Choctaw Nation** **Choctaw Roll** *(Not Including Freedmen)* CARD NO. FIELD NO. **5534**

Dawes' Roll No.	NAME	Relationship to Person First Named	AGE	SEX	BLOOD	TRIBAL ENROLLMENT		
						Year	County	No.
I.W. 612	1 Coffee, I.B.	First Named	44	M	I.W.	1896	Skullyville	14,374
14454	2 " Laura	Wife	30	F	1/8	"	"	2,175
14455	3 " Edwin	Son	10	M	1/16	"	"	2,176
14456	4 " Ada	Dau	6	F	1/16	"	"	2,177
14457	5 " Ruby Addie	"	5mo	"	1/16			
	6							
	7							
	8	ENROLLMENT						
	9	OF NOS. 2,3,4 and 5 HEREON APPROVED BY THE SECRETARY						
	10	OF INTERIOR APR 11 1903						
	11							
	12	ENROLLMENT						
	13	OF NOS. 1 HEREON APPROVED BY THE SECRETARY						
	14	OF INTERIOR FEB -8 1904						
	15							
	16							
	17							

TRIBAL ENROLLMENT OF PARENTS

	Name of Father	Year	County	Name of Mother	Year	County
1	Iley Coffee		Non-Citizen		Dead	Non-Citizen
2	John Pierson	Dead	" "	Nancy Osborne	1897	Chick residing in Choctaw N. 1st Dist
3	No.1			No.2		
4	No.1			No.2		
5	No.1			No.2		
6						
7	No1 On Choctaw Intermarried Roll Page 12					
8	Nos 1,2,3 and 4 Admitted by Dawes Commission Case #960 as a Choctaw and No Appeal					
	taken: Marriage papers on file in office of Dawes Com. Muskogee Ind. Ter					
9	Nos 2,3 & 4 on Choctaw Census Record No2 Page 88					
10	No5 Enrolled May 24" 1900					
11	Nos 1 to 5 inclusive originally enrolled on Chickasaw Card					
	No. 1265. Transferred to this card Oct. 24, 1902					
12						
13						
14						
15					#1 to 4	
16					Date of Application for Enrollment.	
17						

Choctaw By Blood Enrollment Cards 1898-1914

RESIDENCE: Choctaw Nation ~~COUNTY.~~ **Choctaw Nation** Choctaw Roll CARD NO.
POST OFFICE: Boggy Depot, Ind. Ter *(Not Including Freedmen)* FIELD NO. **5535**

Dawes' Roll No.	NAME	Relationship to Person First Named	AGE	SEX	BLOOD	TRIBAL ENROLLMENT		
						Year	County	No.
14002	1 Byington, Joel		32	M	Full	1896	Blue	1591
	2							
	3							
	4							
	5							
	6							
	7	ENROLLMENT						
	8	OF NOS. 1 HEREON						
	9	APPROVED BY THE SECRETARY OF INTERIOR MAR 19 1903						
	10							
	11							
	12							
	13							
	14							
	15							
	16							
	17							

TRIBAL ENROLLMENT OF PARENTS

	Name of Father	Year	County	Name of Mother	Year	County
1	Wallace Byington	Dead	Chickasaw Roll	Sibbey Byington	Dead	Chickasaw Roll
2						
3						
4						
5						
6						
7						
8	No1 On Choctaw Census Record No2 Blue Co, Page 66					
9	" 1 Husband of Emma Byington, Choctaw Roll Care #403					
10	No1 originally enrolled on Chick. Card No. 1270. Transferred this card Oct. 22nd, 1902					
11	For child of No.1 see NB (Mar. 3-05) #471					
12	" " " " " " (Apr 26-06) #669					
13						
14						
15						
16						
17	P.O. Caddo I.T. 10/14/03					

135

Choctaw By Blood Enrollment Cards 1898-1914

RESIDENCE: Choctaw Nation Towson COUNTY. **Choctaw Nation** Choctaw Roll CARD NO.
POST OFFICE: Garvin, Ind. Ter *(Not Including Freedmen)* FIELD NO. **5536**

Dawes' Roll No.	NAME	Relationship to Person First Named	AGE	SEX	BLOOD	TRIBAL ENROLLMENT		
						Year	County	No.
14003	1 Wilson, Edward H	First Named	30	M	1/4	1896	Towson	13183
	2							
	3							
	4							
	5							
	6							
	7							
	8							
	9							
	10							
	11							
	12							
	13							
	14							
	15							
	16							
	17							

ENROLLMENT OF NOS. 1 APPROVED BY THE SECRETARY OF INTERIOR HEREON Mar 19 1903

TRIBAL ENROLLMENT OF PARENTS

Name of Father	Year	County	Name of Mother	Year	County
1 John Wilson	Dead	Choctaw Roll	Jane Wilson	1896	Chick residing in Choctaw Nation
2					
3					
4					
5					
6 No.1 Wife and children on Choctaw Card #1287					
7 No.1 originally enrolled on Chickasaw Card #1413. Transferred					
8 to this card Oct. 22, 1902					
9 For child of No.1 see NB (Mar 3'05) #439					
10 " " " " " " (Apr 26'06) #459					
11					
12					
13					
14					
15					
16					
17				Date of Application for Enrollment.	May 1st 1899	

Choctaw By Blood Enrollment Cards 1898-1914

RESIDENCE: Choctaw Nation **Red River** COUNTY.

POST OFFICE: Shawneetown Ind. Ter.

Choctaw Nation

Choctaw Roll
(Not Including Freedmen)

CARD

FIELD NO. 3337

Dawes' Roll No.	NAME	Relationship to Person First Named	AGE	SEX	BLOOD	TRIBAL ENROLLMENT		
						Year	County	No.
14458	1 Love, Robert M		38	M	1/8	1896	Red River	8057
I.W. 613	2 " Kate D	Wife	32	F	I.W.	"	" "	14,768
14459	3 " Elma E.	Dau	10	"	1/16	"	" "	8.058
14460	4 " Arthur	Son	7	M	1/16	"	" "	8,059
14461	5 " Sidney	"	5	"	1/16	"	" "	8.060
14462	6 " Harry	"	2	"	1/16			
14463	7 " Robert M. Jr.	"	5m	"	1/16			
	8							
	9	ENROLLMENT						
	10	OF NOS. 1 3 4 5 6 and 7 HEREON APPROVED BY THE SECRETARY						
	11	OF INTERIOR APR 11 1903						
	12	ENROLLMENT						
	13	OF NOS. 2 HEREON						
	14	APPROVED BY THE SECRETARY OF INTERIOR FEB -8 1904						
	15							
	16							
	17							

TRIBAL ENROLLMENT OF PARENTS

	Name of Father	Year	County	Name of Mother	Year	County
1	Samuel Love	Dad	Non-Citizen	Frances Love	Dead	Chick. Roll
2	Thomas De Vor	"	" " "	Ellen De Vor	1896	Non-Citizen
3	No.1			No.2		
4	No.1			No.2		
5	No.1			No.2		
6	No.1			No.2		
7	No.1			No.2		

8 No.1 Admitted by the Dawes Commission as a Choctaw by blood Case #125. No Appeal

9 " 2 " " " " " " an Intermarried citizen " #125 " "

10 3,4&5 [sic]

No.6 Affidavit of birth to be supplied: Rec'd May 12: 1899

11 " 7 Affidavit received but irregular & returned for correction Dec 14/99:

12 Received and filed Jan 17" 1900

13 Nos. 1 to 7 inclusive originally enrolled on Chick. Card #1414 and transferred to this card Oct. 22, 1902.

14

15

16 *Date of Application for Enrollment*

17 PO Clarksville Tex 2/3/02   May 2nd 1899

137

Choctaw By Blood Enrollment Cards 1898-1914

RESIDENCE: Choctaw Nation Towson COUNTY.
POST OFFICE: Garvin, Ind. Ter

Choctaw Nation

Choctaw Roll
(Not Including Freedmen)

CARD NO.
FIELD NO. **5538**

Dawes' Roll No.	NAME	Relationship to Person First Named	AGE	SEX	BLOOD	TRIBAL ENROLLMENT		
						Year	County	No.
14004	1 Austin, Lena	First Named	18	F	1/2	1896	Towson	186
	2							
	3							
	4							
	5							
	6							
	7							
	8	ENROLLMENT OF NOS. 1 HEREON						
	9	APPROVED BY THE SECRETARY						
	10	OF INTERIOR MAR 19 1903						
	11							
	12							
	13							
	14							
	15							
	16							
	17							

TRIBAL ENROLLMENT OF PARENTS

	Name of Father	Year	County	Name of Mother	
1	Tobias Austin	Dead	Choctaw Roll	Becky Austin	
2					
3					
4					
5					
6					
7					
8	No.1 originally enrolled on Chickasaw Card No. 1415. Transferred to				
9	this card Oct. 22, 1902				
10					
11					
12					
13					
14					
15					
16				Date of Application for Enrollment.	5/8/99
17					

138

RESIDENCE: Choctaw Nation, Kiamitia COUNTY.
POST OFFICE: Goodland, Ind. Ter.

Choctaw Nation

Choctaw Roll
(Not Including Freedmen)

CARD No.
FIELD No. **5539**

Dawes' Roll No.	NAME	Relationship to Person First Named	AGE	SEX	BLOOD	TRIBAL ENROLLMENT		
						Year	County	No.
14005	1 Miller, Sinie DIED PRIOR TO SEPTEMBER 25, 1902		68	F	3/4	1896	Kiamitia	8730
	2							
	3							
	4							
	5							
	6							
	7							
	8							
	9							
	10							
	11							
	12							
	13							
	14							
	15							
	16							
	17							

ENROLLMENT OF NOS. 1 HEREON APPROVED BY THE SECRETARY OF INTERIOR MAR 19 1903

TRIBAL ENROLLMENT OF PARENTS

	Name of Father	Year	County	Name of Mother	Year	County
1	William Homma	Dead	Choctaw Roll	Lisa Homma	Dead	Chick Roll
2						
3						
4						
5						
6	No 1 originally enrolled on Chickasaw Card No. 1416. Transferred					
7	to this card Oct. 22, 1902					
8	No. 1 died ------, 1901. Enrollment cancelled by Department July 8, 1902					
9						
10						
11						
12						
13						
14						
15						
16				Date of Application for Enrollment.		5/8/99
17						

Choctaw By Blood Enrollment Cards 1898-1914

RESIDENCE: ▮▮▮ Nation, Towson COUNTY. **Choctaw Nation** Choctaw Roll CARD ▮▮▮
POST OFFICE: ▮▮▮lle Ind. Ter *(Not Including Freedmen)* FIELD ▮▮▮

Dawes' Roll No.		ME	Relationship to Person First Named	AGE	SEX	BLOOD	TRIBAL ENROLLMENT		
							Year	County	No.
14006	1	Wilso▮ D.	First Named	35	M	1/4	1896	Towson	13,179
	2								
	3								
	4								
	7	APPROVED BY THE SECRETARY							
	8	OF INTERIOR MAR 19 1903							
	9								
	10								
	11								
	12								
	13								
	14								
	15								
	16								
	17								

TRIBAL ENROLLMENT OF PARENTS

	Name of Father	Year	County	Name of Mother	Year	County
1	John Wilson	Dead	Choctaw Roll	Jane Wilson	1896	Chick residing in Choctaw Nation
2						
3						
4						
5						
6	No1 Wife and children on Choctaw Card #1426					
7						
8	No.1 originally enrolled on Chickasaw Card No. 1417. Transferred to this card Oct. 22, 1902					
9	For child of No1 see N.B. (Apr 26, 1906) Card No. 77.					
10						
11						
12						
13						
14						
15						Date of Application for Enrollment.
16						
17						▮8/99

Choctaw By Blood Enrollment Cards 1898-1914

	Choctaw Nation, Kiamitia COUNTY.							
	CE: Goodland, Ind. Ter	**Choctaw Nation**				Choctaw Roll (Not Including Freedmen)	CARD NO. FIELD NO. **5541**	

Dawes Roll No.	NAME	Relationship to Person First Named	AGE	SEX	BLOOD	TRIBAL ENROLLMENT		
						Year	County	No.
DEAD	1 Locke, Benjamin F	Named	45	M	I.W.	1896	Kiamitia	14,771
14007	2 Kelly, Mary	Ward	14	F	1/2	"	Cedar	7523
14008	3 " Dovey	"	10	"	1/2	1893	Kiamitia	389
14009	4 " Mahala	"	8	"	1/2	1896	Cedar	7524
	5							
	6							
	7							
	8							
	9	ENROLLMENT						
	10	OF NOS. 2 3 & 4 HEREON APPROVED BY THE SECRETARY						
	11	OF INTERIOR MAR 19 1903						
	12	No. 1 hereon dismissed under order						
	13	of the Commission to the Five Civilized						
	14	Tribes of March 31, 1905.						
	15							
	16							
	17							

TRIBAL ENROLLMENT OF PARENTS

Name of Father	Year	County	Name of Mother	Year	County
1 B.F. Locke	Dead	Non-Citizen	Mary Locke	Dead	Non-Citizen
2 John Kelly	"	" "	Sarah Kelly	"	Chick Roll
3 " "	"	" "	" "	"	" "
4 " "	"	" "	" "	"	" "
5					

6 No1 On 96 Roll as "B.F. Locke"

7 " was married to Hattie Wilson, Chick citizen, under Choctaw Laws, in 1875, lived with her

8 until she died in 1887. Then married a Choctaw citizen who has since died. He is now a widower License lost or destroyed with Records of Towson Co. which were destroyed by fire in

9 1897. See testimony of No.1 Henry Williams and E.W. Timms hereto attached.

10 No.3 also on 96 Roll #7663 as E. Kelly Novr 15" 1899

11 " 4 On 96 Roll as "Mahale[sic] Kelly"

12 Nos 1 to 4 inclusive originally enrolled on Chickasaw Card No. 1418 and transferred to this card Oct. 22, 1902.

13 No1 died March 1899: proof of death filed Dec. 9, 1902.

14 For child of No.2 see NB (April 26, 1906) No. 530.

15 " " " " " (March 3, 1905) " 1252.

16

17 P.O. Finley I.T. 4/25/05			Date of Application for Enrollment.	5/8/99

141

Choctaw By Blood Enrollment Cards 1898-1914

RESIDENCE Choctaw Nation, Kiamitia COUNTY.
POST OFFICE: Nelson, I.T.

Choctaw Nation

Choctaw Roll CA
(Not Including Freedmen) FIELD NO. **5542**

Dawes' Roll No.	NAME	Relationship to Person First Named	AGE	SEX	BLOOD	TRIBAL ENROLLMENT Year	County	No.
14010	1 Griggs, Willy	First Named	27	M	1/4	1896	Kiamitia	4814
14011	2 " Mary	Wife	25	F	1/4			4833
14012	3 " Joel	Son	1	M	1/4			
14013	4 " Wilson N	"	4mo	"	1/4			
14014	5 " Pate J	"	1mo	"	1/4			
	6							
	7							
	8							
	9							
	10							
	11	ENROLLMENT						
	12	OF NOS. 1-2-3-4-5 HEREON APPROVED BY THE SECRETARY						
	13	OF INTERIOR MAR 19 1903						
	14							
	15							
	16							
	17							

TRIBAL ENROLLMENT OF PARENTS

	Name of Father	Year	County	Name of Mother	Year	County
1	Thos Griggs	1896	Choctaw Roll	Mary Griggs	Dead	Chick Roll
2	Wᵐ Le Flore	"	" "	Roseana Le Flore	1896	" "
3	No.1			No.2		
4	No.1			No.2		
5	No.1			No.2		

6 No2 Also on 96 Roll #8110 (Jacks Co) as Mary LeFlore
7 " 3 Affidavit of Birth to be supplied. Received May 17" 1899
8 " 4 Enrolled June 23ʳᵈ 1900
   " 5 Enrolled Oct 15" 1901
9 Nos 1 to 5 inclusive originally enrolled on Chick Card #1420 and
10 transferred to this card Oct. 22, 1902.
11 For child of No.1 and 2 see NB *Mar 3'05) #408

12						
13						
14						
15						
16					#1 to 3 inc	
17				Date of Application for Enrollment.	5/10/99	

142

Choctaw By Blood Enrollment Cards 1898-1914

RESIDENCE: Choctaw Nation, Kiamitia COUNTY.
POST OFFICE: Nelson, Ind. Ter.

Choctaw Nation

Choctaw Roll
(Not Including Freedmen)

CARD NO.
FIELD NO. **5543**

Dawes' Roll No.	NAME	Relationship to Person First Named	AGE	SEX	BLOOD	TRIBAL ENROLLMENT		
						Year	County	No.
14015	1 Harrison, Rutha		25	F	3/8	1896	Kiamitia	5767
14016	2 " Solomon	Bro	20	M	3/8	"	"	5768
14017	3 " Sinie	Sis	15	F	3/8	"	"	5769
	4							
	5							
	6							
	7							
	8	ENROLLMENT						
	9	OF NOS. 1-2-3 HEREON APPROVED BY THE SECRETARY						
	10	OF INTERIOR Mar 19 1903						
	11							
	12							
	13							
	14							
	15							
	16							
	17							

TRIBAL ENROLLMENT OF PARENTS

	Name of Father	Year	County	Name of Mother	Year	County
1	Sim Harrison	1896	Choctaw Roll	Phoebe Harrison	Dead	Chick. Roll
2	" "	"	" "	" "	"	" "
3	" "	"	" "	" "	"	" "
4						
5						
6	No. 3 on Choctaw 96 Roll as Sinie Harrison, Jr.					
7	Nos 1,2 & 3: Father of Sim Harrison on Choctaw Care #1589					
8	Nos. 1,2 and 3 originally enrolled on Chickasaw Card No. 1421 and transferred to this card Oct. 22, 1902.					
9						
10						
11						
12						
13						
14						
15						
16						Date of Application for Enrollment.
17			Date of application for enrollment			5/11/99

Choctaw By Blood Enrollment Cards 1898-1914

RESIDENCE: Choctaw Nation, Kiamitia COUNTY. **Choctaw Nation**   **Choctaw Roll** *(Not Including Freedmen)*   CARD NO. FIELD NO. **5544**

POST OFFICE: Goodland, Ind. Ter.

Dawes' Roll No.	NAME DEAD	Relationship to Person First Named	AGE	SEX	BLOOD	TRIBAL ENROLLMENT		
						Year	County	No.
DEAD	1 Ward, Phoebe		40	F	1/2	1896	Kiamitia	13744
14018	2 " Ida	Dau	15	"	1/4	"	"	13746
14019	3 " Eastman	Son	8	M	1/4	"	"	13747
14020	4 " Sampson	"	6	"	1/4	"	"	13748
14021	5 " Samuel	"	3	"	1/4			
14022	6 " Harvey	"	6mo	"	1/4			
	7							
	8 ENROLLMENT							
	9 OF NOS. 2-3-4-5-6 HEREON APPROVED BY THE SECRETARY							
	10 OF INTERIOR Mar 19 1903							
	11 No. 1 hereon dismissed under order of							
	12 the Commission to the Five Civilized							
	13 Tribes of March 31, 1905.							
	14							
	15							
	16							
	17							

TRIBAL ENROLLMENT OF PARENTS

Name of Father	Year	County		Name of Mother	Year	County
1 William Billis	Dead	Choctaw Roll		Winey Goforth	Dead	Chick Roll
2 Allington Ward	1896	"	"	No.1		
3 " "	"	"	"	No.1		
4 " "	"	"	"	No.1		
5 " "	"	"	"	No.1		
6 " "	"	"	"	No.1		
7						
8 No.1 Husband of, on Choctaw Card #1605						
9 " Died April 22nd 1901: Evidence of Death filed July 16th 1902						
10 Nos. 1 to 5 inclusive originally enrolled on Chickasaw Card #1422 and						
11 transferred to this card Oct. 22, 1902.						
12 For child of No.2 see NB (March 3, 1905) #1532						
13						
14						
15						
16						Date of Application for Enrollment.
17 P.O. Hugo Ok.						5/11/99

Choctaw By Blood Enrollment Cards 1898-1914

RESIDENCE: Choctaw Nation, Kiamitia COUNTY.
POST OFFICE: Nelson, Ind. Ter.

Choctaw Nation

Choctaw Roll *(Not Including Freedmen)*

CARD NO.
FIELD NO. **5545**

Dawes' Roll No.	NAME	Relationship to Person First Named	AGE	SEX	BLOOD	TRIBAL ENROLLMENT		
						Year	County	No.
IW614	1 Smith, Bird Q.	First Named	48	M	I.W.	1896	Kiamitia	15,052
DEAD	2 " Delilah DEAD	Wife	28	F	1/4	"	"	11,530
14023	3 " Sim	Son	10	M	1/8	"	"	11,531
14024	4 " Fred	"	8	"	1/8	"	"	11,532
14025	5 " Ray	"	6	"	1/8	"	"	11,533
14026	6 " Eric	"	4	"	1/8	"	"	11,534
14027	7 " Pearl	Dau	2	F	1/8			
14028	8 " Annie	"	3wks	"	1/8			
14029	9 " Phoebe	"	3mo	"	1/8			
	10							
	11 ENROLLMENT OF NOS. 3 4 5 6 7 8 & 9 HEREON							
	12 APPROVED BY THE SECRETARY							
	13 OF INTERIOR Mar 19 1903							
	14 Nos 1 to 9 inclusive originally enrolled on							
	15 Chickasaw Card #1424. Transferred							
	to this card Oct. 22, 1902							
	16							
	17							

TRIBAL ENROLLMENT OF PARENTS

	Name of Father	Year	County	Name of Mother	Year	County
1	E.L. Smith	Dead	Non-Citizen	Rhoda R. Smith	Dead	Non-Citizen
2	Sim Harrison	1896	Choctaw Roll	Phoebe Harrison	"	Chick Roll
3	No.1			No.2		
4	No.1			No.2		
5	No.1			No.2		
6	No.1			No.2		
7	No.1			No.2		
8	No.1			No.2		
9	No.1			No.2		

10 No1 on 96 Roll as "Quincy Smith"
11 " 2 " " " " "Lilie" "; Died Decr 4th 1901: Evidence of Death filed Feb. 7th 1902
12 " 4 " " " " "Fred" " "
13 " 5 " " " " "Roy" " "   ENROLLMENT OF NOS. 1 HEREON
" 6 " " " " "Erick" " "   APPROVED BY THE SECRETARY
14 " 9 Born Novr 18th 1901: Enrolled Feb 7th 1902   OF INTERIOR Feb 8 1904   #1 to 8 inc
15 No. 2 hereon dismissed under order
16 of the Commission to the Five Civilized   Date of Application for Enrollment.
Tribes of March 31, 1905.
17   5/11/98[sic]

145

Choctaw By Blood Enrollment Cards 1898-1914

Choctaw Nation

Choctaw Roll *(Not Including Freedmen)*

CARD No. FIELD NO. **5546**

Dawes' Roll No.	NAME	Relationship to Person First Named	AGE	SEX	BLOOD	TRIBAL ENROLLMENT Year	County	No.
14040	1 Frazier, Joanna		17	F	1/4	1896	Kiamitia	13,745
14031	2 " Clara	Dau	4mo	"	1/2			
	3							
	4							
	5							
	6							
	7							
	8							
	9							
	10							
	11							
	12							
	13							
	14							
	15							
	16							
	17							

ENROLLMENT
OF NOS. - 1 - 2 - HEREON
APPROVED BY THE SECRETARY
OF INTERIOR MAR 19 1903

TRIBAL ENROLLMENT OF PARENTS

	Name of Father	Year	County	Name of Mother	Year	County
1	Allington Ward	1896	Choctaw Roll	Phoebe Ward	1896	Chickasaw
2	Harris Frazier	"	" "	No.1		
3						
4						
5						

6 No1 On '96 Roll as "Joanna Ward"
7 " Husband on Choctaw Card No. 1675
8 " 2 Enrolled Feb. 26th 1900
9 Nos. 1 and 2 originally enrolled on Chickasaw Card No. 1426. Transferred to this card Oct. 22, 1902
10 No.1 is divorced from Harris Frazier: see copy of letter filed Dec. 23, 1902

#1

Date of Application for Enrollment.

5/12/99

146

Choctaw By Blood Enrollment Cards 1898-1914

RESIDENCE: Choctaw Nation, Kiamitia COUNTY.

POST OFFICE: Antlers, Ind. Ter

Choctaw Nation

Choctaw Roll *(Not Including Freedmen)*

CARD NO.

FIELD NO. **5547**

Dawes' Roll No.	NAME	Relationship to Person First Named	AGE	SEX	BLOOD	TRIBAL ENROLLMENT Year	County	No.
14032	1 Locke, Sina J	First Named	24	F	1/2	1896	Jacks Fork	8365
14033	2 " Mattie P	Dau	5	"	1/4	"	" "	8366
14034	3 " Victor B.	Son	7mo	M	1/4			
	4							
	5							
	6							
	7							
	8							
	9							
	10							
	11	ENROLLMENT						
	12	OF NOS. 1-2-3 HEREON APPROVED BY THE SECRETARY						
	13	OF INTERIOR MAR 19 1903						
	14							
	15							
	16							
	17							

TRIBAL ENROLLMENT OF PARENTS

Name of Father	Year	County	Name of Mother	Year	County
1 Jim Miller	Dead	Choctaw Roll	Mahaley Miller	Dead	Chick Roll
2 James L. Locke	1896	" "	No.1		
3 " " "	"	" "	No.1		
4					
5					
6 No1 On '96 Roll as "S. Locke"					
7 " 2 " " " " "M.P. "					
8 No.1 Husband of, on Choctaw Card #1750					
9 Nos 1,2 and 3 originally enrolled on Chickasaw Card No. 1428 and transferred to this card Oct. 22, 1902.					
10					
11					
12					
13					
14					
15					
16				Date of Application for Enrollment.	
17				5/15/99	

147

Choctaw By Blood Enrollment Cards 1898-1914

RESIDENCE: Choctaw Nation, Cedar COUNTY. **Choctaw Nation** Choctaw Roll CARD NO.
POST OFFICE: Kosoma[sic], Ind. Ter (Not Including Freedmen) FIELD NO. **5548**

Dawes' Roll No.	NAME	Relationship to Person First Named	AGE	SEX	BLOOD	TRIBAL ENROLLMENT		
						Year	County	No.
14035	1 Sherred, Emma	First Named	28	F	1/2	1896	Cedar	11,358
DEAD	2 " McKennon	Son	2wk	M	1/4			
14036	3 Miller, Rena P	Dau	8	F	1/4	1896	Cedar	8598
14037	4 " Myrtle	"	6	"	1/4	"	"	8599
	Sherred, Shub	Son	3mo	M	1/4			
	8							
	9 ENROLLMENT							
	10 OF NOS. 1-3-4-5 HEREON							
	11 APPROVED BY THE SECRETARY OF INTERIOR MAR 19 1903							
	12 No. 2 HEREON DISMISSED UNDER							
	13 ORDER OF THE COMMISSION TO THE FIVE							
	14 CIVILIZED TRIBES OF MARCH 31, 1905.							
	15							
	16							
	17							

TRIBAL ENROLLMENT OF PARENTS

	Name of Father	Year	County	Name of Mother	Year	County
1	James Miller	Dead	Choctaw Roll	Mahale Miller	Dead	Chick Roll
2	Josephus Sherred	1896	" "	No.1		
3	Mike Ervin	Dead	Non-Citizen	No.1		
4	Henry John	1896	Choctaw Roll	No.1		
5	Josephus Sherred	"	" "	No.1		
6						
7	No1 Josephus Sherred (Husband) on Choctaw Care #1790					
8	" 3 on '96 Roll as "Rena Miller"					
9	" 5 Enrolled April 16"-1901					
	Nos. 1 to 5 inclusive originally enrolled on Chickasaw Card No. 1429 and					
10	transferred to this card Oct. 22, 1902.					
11	No2 Died Nov. 1, 1900; proof of death filed Dec. 24, 1902.					
12						
13						
14						
15					Date of Application for Enrollment.	
16						
17	P.O. [Illegible] I.T. 2/24/[??]			Nos. 1 to 4 -	5/16/99	

148

Choctaw By Blood Enrollment Cards 1898-1914

RESIDENCE: Jacks Fork   COUNTY. **Choctaw Nation**   **Choctaw Roll**   CARD NO.
POST OFFICE: Kosoma[sic], Ind. Ter   (Not Including Freedmen)   FIELD NO. **5549**

Dawes' Roll No.	NAME	Relationship to Person First Named	AGE	SEX	BLOOD	TRIBAL ENROLLMENT Year	County	No.
14039	1 Cooper, Sina	First Named	28	F	1/2	1896	Jacks For,	3008
14040	2 Wilson, Jeff	Ward	3	M	1/4			
	3							
	4							
	5							
	6							
	7							
	8							
	9							
	10							
	11	ENROLLMENT						
	12	OF NOS. 1 - 2 HEREON APPROVED BY THE SECRETARY						
	13	OF INTERIOR MAR 19 1903						
	14							
	15							
	16							
	17							

TRIBAL ENROLLMENT OF PARENTS

	Name of Father	Year	County	Name of Mother	Year	County
1	Kaniotabe	Dead	Jacks Fork	Silis Kaniotabe	Dead	Jacks Fork
2	Craven Wilson	1896	Nashoba	Clestie Wilson	"	Nashoba
3						
4						
5						
6	No1 On 96 Roll as Sane Cooper					
7	No1 Wife of Columbus Cooper on Choctaw Roll No. 1813					
8	Nos. 1 and 2 originally enrolled on Chickasaw Card #1430 and transferred to this card Oct. 22, 1902.					
9						
10						
11						
12						
13						
14						
15						Date of Application for Enrollment.
16						
17	P.O. Miller, Okla 6/23/08					5/16/99

149

Choctaw By Blood Enrollment Cards 1898-1914

RESIDENCE Choctaw Nation, JacksFork COUNTY.
POST OFFICE: Tuskhahomma, Ind. Ter **Choctaw Nation**   **Choctaw Roll** *(Not Including Freedmen)*   CARD NO.   FIELD NO. **5550**

Dawes' Roll No.	NAME	Relationship to Person First Named	AGE	SEX	BLOOD	TRIBAL ENROLLMENT Year	County	No.
1	Moore, Gilbert	Named	65	M	1/2	1893	Jacks Fork	528
2								
3								
4								
5								
6								
7								
8								
9	No. 1 HEREON DISMISSED UNDER							
10	ORDER OF THE COMMISSION TO THE FIVE CIVILIZED TRIBES OF MARCH 31, 1905.							
11								
12								
13								
14								
15								
16								
17								

TRIBAL ENROLLMENT OF PARENTS

	Name of Father	Year	County	Name of Mother	Year	County
1	Gilbert Moore	Dead	Chick Roll	Hettie Underwood	Dead	Chick Roll
2						
3						
4						
5						
6	No.1 Wife on Chickasaw Card #D 236					
7	No.1 originally enrolled on Chickasaw Card No. 1439. Transferred					
8	to this card Oct. 22, 1902					
9						
10						
11						
12						
13						
14						
15						
16						
17				Date of Application for Enrollment.		5/24/99

150

Choctaw By Blood Enrollment Cards 1898-1914

RESIDENCE: Choctaw Nation, Gaines COUNTY.   **Choctaw Nation**   **Choctaw Roll**   CARD No.
POST OFFICE: Hartshorne, Ind. Ter   (Not Including Freedmen)   FIELD No. **5551**

Dawes' Roll No.	NAME	Relationship to Person First Named	AGE	SEX	BLOOD	TRIBAL ENROLLMENT Year	TRIBAL ENROLLMENT County	TRIBAL ENROLLMENT No.
14041	1 Thomas, Jimmie	First Named	7	M	1/2	1896	Gaines	11,991
	2							
	3							
	4							
	5							
	6							
	7							
	8							
	9							
	10							
	11	ENROLLMENT						
	12	OF NOS. 1 HEREON APPROVED BY THE SECRETARY						
	13	OF INTERIOR MAR 19 1903						
	14							
	15							
	16							
	17							

TRIBAL ENROLLMENT OF PARENTS

Name of Father	Year	County	Name of Mother	Year	
1 Dave Thomas	1896	Choctaw Roll	Becky Thomas	Dead	
2					
3					
4					
5					
6 No1 Son of Dave Thomas on Choctaw Card #2008					
7 No.1 originally enrolled on Chickasaw Card No. 1440. Transferred					
8 to this card Oct. 22, 1902					
9					
10					
11					
12					
13					
14					
15				Date of Application for Enrollment.	
16					
17				5/24/99	

151

Choctaw By Blood Enrollment Cards 1898-1914

RESIDENCE: Choctaw Nation   COUNTY.

POST OFFICE: Lenox, Ind. Ter

Choctaw Nation

Choctaw Roll (Not Including Freedmen)

CARD No. FIELD No. 5552

Dawes' Roll No.		NAME	Relationship to Person First Named	AGE	SEX	BLOOD	TRIBAL ENROLLMENT		
							Year	County	No.
DEAD	1	Potts, Bessie		45	F	Full	1896	Wade	10,303
14042	2	Pitchlynn, Williamson	Son	13	M	1/2	"	"	10,304
14043	3	" Louisa	Dau	9	F	1/2	"	"	10,305
14044	4	" Livingston	Son	7	M	1/2	"	"	10,306
	5								
	6								
	7								
	8								
	9								
	10	ENROLLMENT							
	11	OF NOS. 2-3-4 HEREON							
	12	APPROVED BY THE SECRETARY OF INTERIOR MAR 19 1903							
	13								
	14	No. one HEREON DISMISSED UNDER							
	15	ORDER OF THE COMMISSIONER TO THE FIVE CIVILIZED TRIBES OF JULY 18, 1905.							
	16								
	17								

DIED PRIOR TO SEPTEMBER 25, 1902

TRIBAL ENROLLMENT OF PARENTS

		Year	County	Name of Mother	Year	County
1	Hch-	Dead	Chick Roll	Siney Hch-cha	Dead	Chick Citizen
2	Tom P	"	Choc. Roll	No.1		
3	"	"	" "	No.1		
4	" "	"	" "	No.1		
5						
6	No1 Husband of, on Choctaw Card #2129					
7	" 2 on 96 Roll as "Wm Pitchlynn"					
8	" 3 " " " "Levicey " "					
	" 4 " " " "Levinson" "					
9	Nos. 1 to 4 originally enrolled on Chickasaw Card #1442. Transferred					
10	to this card Oct. 22, 1902.					
11						
12	No.1 died about March 15, 1899. Proof of death filed Nov. 15, 1905.					
13	No.2 died Oct, 1900: Enrollment cancelled by Department May 2, 1906					
14						
15						
16						
17				Date of Application for Enrollment. 5/30/99		

Choctaw By Blood Enrollment Cards 1898-1914

RESIDENCE: Choctaw Nation ~~COUNTY.~~ **Choctaw Nation**   **Choctaw Roll**   CARD No.

POST OFFICE: Talihina, Ind. Ter.   *(Not Including Freedmen)*   FIELD No. **5553**

Dawes' Roll No.	NAME	Relationship to Person First Named	AGE	SEX	BLOOD	TRIBAL ENROLLMENT		
						Year	County	No.
14045	1 King, Robert		37	M	1/2	1896	Wade	7510
I.W. 615	2 " Emma	Wife	24	F	I.W.	"	"	14721
14046	3 " Osie	Dau	7	"	1/4	"	"	7512
14047	4 " Willis	Son	5	M	1/4	"	"	7513
14048	5 " Gilbert	"	2	"	1/4			
14049	6 " Oscar	"	3m	"	1/4			
	7							
	8 ENROLLMENT OF NOS. 1-3-4-5-6 HEREON APPROVED BY THE SECRETARY OF INTERIOR Mar 19 1903							
	9							
	10							
	11							
	12 ENROLLMENT OF NOS. 2 HEREON APPROVED BY THE SECRETARY OF INTERIOR Feb 8, 1904							
	13							
	14							
	15							
	16							
	17							

TRIBAL ENROLLMENT OF PARENTS

	Name of Father	Year	County	Name of Mother	Year	County
1	William King	Dead	Choctaw Roll	Wiona[sic] King	Dead	Chick. Roll
2	Ransom Parrs	"	Non-Citizen	Ann Lolley	1896	Non-Citizen
3	No.1			No.2		
4	No.1			No.2		
5	No.1			No.2		
6	No.1			No.2		
7						
8	No2 On 96 Roll as "Amanda King"					
9	No1 as to marriage to No.2 see testimony of G.W. Dukes					
10	" 5 Affidavit of Birth to be supplied. Received May 30, 1899 ~~" 6 Born Oct. 16" 1901: Enrolled Jan 24" 1902.~~					
11	Nos. 1 to 6 inclusive originally enrolled on Chickasaw Card #1443					
12	and transferred to this card Oct. 22nd 1902.					
13	For chi,d of Nos. 1 and 2 see NB (Mar 3, 1905) #512.					
14						#1 to 5
15				Date of application for Enrollment. 5/30/99		
16						
17				Date of Application for Enrollment		

153

Choctaw By Blood Enrollment Cards 1898-1914

POST OFFICE: Lenon, Ind. Ter.

Choctaw Nation

Choctaw Roll (Not Including Freedmen)

CARD NO. FIELD NO. **5554**

Dawes' Roll No.	NAME	Relationship to Person First Named	AGE	SEX	BLOOD	TRIBAL ENROLLMENT Year	County	No.
14050	1 Hitcher, Jackson	First Named	31	M	Full	1896	Wade	5405
	2							
	3							
	4							
	5							
	6							
	7							
	8							
	9							
	10							
	11	ENROLLMENT						
	12	OF NOS. 1 HEREON APPROVED BY THE SECRETARY						
	13	OF INTERIOR MAR 19 1903						
	14							
	15							
	16							
	17							

TRIBAL ENROLLMENT OF PARENTS

	Name of Father	Year	County	Name of Mother	Year	County
1	Hitcher	Dead	Chick Roll	Siney Hitcher	Dead	Chick Roll
2						
3						
4						
5						
6	No. 1 originally enrolled on Chickasaw Card No. 1444. Transferred					
7	to this card Oct. 22, 1902					
8						
9						
10						
11						
12						
13						
14						
15						
16						
17				Date of Application for Enrollment.	6/1/99	

154

Choctaw By Blood Enrollment Cards 1898-1914

		Relationship to Person	AGE	SEX	BLOOD	TRIBAL ENROLLMENT		
NAME						Year	County	No.
...rson, Jane		First Named	66	F	1/2	1896	Sans Bois	6410
	2							
	3							
	4							
	5							
	6							
	7							
	8							
	9							
	10							
	11	ENROLLMENT OF NOS. 1 HEREON						
	12	APPROVED BY THE SECRETARY						
	13	OF INTERIOR MAR 19 1903						
	14							
	15							
	16							
	17							

Choctaw Nation COUNTY. **Choctaw Nation** Red Oak, Ind. Ter.

Choctaw Roll (Not Including Freedmen)

CARD No. FIELD No. **5555**

TRIBAL ENROLLMENT OF PARENTS

	Name of Father	Year	County	Name of Mother	Year	County
1	W^m Mc Curtain	Dead	Choctaw	Polly Mc Curtain	Dead	Chickasaw
2						
3						
4						
5						
6	No.1 originally enrolled on Chickasaw Card No. 1453 and					
7	transferred to this card Oct. 22, 1902.					
8						
9						
10						
11						
12						
13						
14						
15						
16					Date of Application	
17					for Enrollment. 6/20/99	

Choctaw By Blood Enrollment Cards 1898-1914

RESIDENCE: Choctaw Nation ~~COUNTY~~. **Choctaw Nation** Choctaw Roll CARD NO.
POST OFFICE: Red Oak, Ind. Ter. *(Not Including Freedmen)* FIELD NO. **5556**

Dawes' Roll No.	NAME	Relationship to Person First Named	AGE	SEX	BLOOD	TRIBAL ENROLLMENT		
						Year	County	No.
14052	1 Jefferson, Wallace	First Named	37	M	1/2	1896	Sans Bois	6406
	2							
	3							
	4							
	5							
	6							
	7							
	8							
	9							
	10							
	11	ENROLLMENT OF NOS. 1 HEREON						
	12	APPROVED BY THE SECRETARY						
	13	OF INTERIOR MAR 19 1903						
	14							
	15							
	16							
	17							

TRIBAL ENROLLMENT OF PARENTS

	Name of Father	Year	County	Name of Mother	Year	County
1	Soben Jefferson	Dead	Choctaw	Jennie Jefferson	1896	Chickasaw
2						
3						
4						
5						
6	No.1 Wife and children on Choctaw Card #2904.					
7	No.1 originally enrolled on Chickasaw Card No. 1457.					
8	Transferred to this card Oct. 22, 1902					
9						
10						
11						
12						
13						
14						
15						
16						
17						6/20/99

Choctaw By Blood Enrollment Cards 1898-1914

RESIDENCE: Choctaw Nation ~~COUNTY~~ **Choctaw Nation**   **Choctaw Roll** CARD NO.
POST OFFICE: Red Oak, Ind. Ter.   (Not Including Freedmen)   FIELD NO. **5557**

Dawes' Roll No.	NAME	Relationship to Person	AGE	SEX	BLOOD	TRIBAL ENROLLMENT		
						Year	County	No.
14053	1 Hancock, Jincey	First Named	30	F	1/2	1896	Sans Bois	5148
14054	2 " Amanda	Dau	9	"	1/4	"	" "	5150
14055	3 " Aaron	Son	4	M	1/4	"	" "	5149
14056	4 " Rhoda	Dau	3	F	1/4	"	" "	5151
14057	5 " Bazada	"	1 1/2	"	1/4			
14058	6 " Corah[sic]	"	8mo	"	1/4			
	7							
	8							
	9							
	10							
	11	ENROLLMENT						
	12	OF NOS. 1 2 3 4 5 & 6 HEREON APPROVED BY THE SECRETARY						
	13	OF INTERIOR MAR 19 1903						
	14							
	15							
	16							
	17							

TRIBAL ENROLLMENT OF PARENTS

Name of Father	Year	County	Name of Mother	Year	County
1 Soben Jefferson	Dead	Choctaw	Jinnie Jefferson	1896	Chickasaw
2 Simon Hancock	"	"	No.1		
3 Willis Hancock	1896	"	No.1		
4 " "	"	"	No.1		
5 " "	"	"	No.1		
6 " "	"	"	No.1		
7					
8 No1 Husband, Willis Hancock, on Choctaw Card #2905.					
9 No2 On 96 Roll as "Maud Hancock"					
10 No6 Born Jan. 17" 1901: Enrolled Nov 8" 1901					
~~Nos. 1 to 6 inclusive originally enrolled on Chickasaw Card No. 1459 and~~					
11 ~~transferred to this card Oct. 22, 1902~~					
12					
13					
14 For child of No1 see NB (Apr 26-06) Card #818					
15 " " " " " " (Mar 3-05) " #549				#1 to 5
16					Date of Application for Enrollment.
17					6/20/99

157

Choctaw By Blood Enrollment Cards 1898-1914

RESIDENCE: Choctaw Nation ~~COUNTY~~

POST OFFICE: Red Oak, Ind. Ter.

Choctaw Nation

Choctaw Roll
(Not Including Freedmen)

Dawes' Roll No.	NAME	Relationship to Person First Named	AGE	SEX	BLOOD	TRIBAL ENROLLMENT Year	County	No.
14059	1 Hancock, Isaac	First Named	58	M	1/2	1896	Sans Bois	5146
	2							
	3							
	4							
	5							
	6							
	7							
	8							
	9							
	10							
	11							
	12							
	13							
	14							
	15							
	16							
	17							

ENROLLMENT
OF NOS. 1 HEREON
~~APPROVED BY THE SECRETARY~~
OF INTERIOR MAR 19 1903

TRIBAL ENROLLMENT OF PARENTS

	Name of Father	Year	County	Name of Mother	Year	County
1	Yarlis Hancock	Dead	Choctaw	Un-te-ni-ge	Dead	Chickasaw
2						
3						
4						
5						
6						
7						
8		No.1 originally enrolled on Chickasaw Card No. 1460 and				
9		transferred to this card Oct. 22, 1902.				
10						
11						
12						
13						
14						
15						
16						
17	So Mᶜ Alester IT 11/1/04					

158

Choctaw By Blood Enrollment Cards 1898-1914

RESIDENCE: Pickens COUNTY. ████████ CARD No.
POST OFFICE: Ardmore Ind. Ter Choctaw Nation (Not Including Freedmen) FIELD No. 5559

Dawes' Roll No.	NAME	Relationship to Person First Named	AGE	SEX	BLOOD	TRIBAL ENROLLMENT		
						Year	County	No.
15505	1 Chivers, Maud A	First Named	22	F	1/16	1896	Atoka	8289
15506	2 " Jennie A	Dau	8mo	"	1/32			
15507	3 " Charles Eynon	Son	2wks	M	1/32			
IW 1046	4 " Edgar E	Husband	27	M	I.W.			
	5							
	6							
	7							
	8							
	9	ENROLLMENT OF NOS. 1-2-3 HEREON APPROVED BY THE SECRETARY OF INTERIOR May 9 1904						
	10							
	11							
	12	ENROLLMENT OF NOS. 4 HEREON APPROVED BY THE SECRETARY OF INTERIOR Oct 21 1904						
	13							
	14							
	15							
	16							
	17							

TRIBAL ENROLLMENT OF PARENTS

	Name of Father	Year	County	Name of Mother	Year	County
1	Charles LeFlore		Choctaw Roll	Angie G. LeFlore	Dead	Chick. Roll
2	Edgar E. Chivers		Intermarried	No.1		
3	" " "		"	No.1		
4	Elijah E. Chivers		non-citz	Jane E. Chivers		non-citz
5						
6	No.1 on 96 Roll as "Maud A. LeFlore"					
7	" Husband on Card #D 246 (Chickasaw)					
8	No2 Affidavit of birth to be supplied; Filed Nov 4th 1899 No3 Enrolled April 17th 1901					
9	Nos. 1,2 and 3 originally enrolled on Chick. Card No. 1487 and					
10	transferred to this card Oct. 22, 1902.					
11						
12	No.4 transferred from Chickasaw Card #D246. See decision of September 9, 1904 Sept 24 1904					
13	For child of nos 1 & 4 see NB (Apr 26-06) Card #620					
14	" " " " " " " (Mar 3-05) " #410					
15						#1 & 2
16						Date of Application for Enrollment
17	P.O. Mannsville I.T. 5/29/03					Aug 14" 1899

159

Choctaw By Blood Enrollment Cards 1898-1914

RESIDENCE: Choctaw Nation ~~COUNTY~~.
POST OFFICE: Lehigh, Ind. Ter

Choctaw Nation

Choctaw Roll
(Not Including Freedmen)

CARD No.
FIELD No. **5560**

Dawes' Roll No.	NAME	Relationship to Person	AGE	SEX	BLOOD	TRIBAL ENROLLMENT		
						Year	County	No.
14060	1 McIntosh, Thomas _DIED PRIOR TO SEPTEMBER 25, 1902_	First Named	15	M	1/4	1896	Blue	9,429
14061	2 Robinson, Lee	1/2 Bro	13	"	1/4	"	"	10m955
	3							
	4							
	5							
	6							
	7							
	8							
	9							
	10							
	11	ENROLLMENT						
	12	OF NOS. 1 & 2 HEREON APPROVED BY THE SECRETARY						
	13	OF INTERIOR MAR 19 1903						
	14							
	15							
	16							
	17							

TRIBAL ENROLLMENT OF PARENTS

Name of Father	Year	County	Name of Mother	Year	County
1 Roach McIntosh		Creek Citizen	Mary Robinson	Dead	Chick residing in Choctaw N. 3rd Dist
2 Jim Robinson		Kiamitia Co Choctaw Roll	" "	"	" " " "
3					
4					
5					
6 No1 On Choctaw Census Record #2, Page 372; lives with H.C. Wilson					
7 " 2 " " " " " 414 " " " " "					
8 Nos. 1 and 2 originally enrolled on Chick. Card #1343. Transferred to this card Oct. 22, 1902					
9					
10 No.1 died Oct. 29, 1901; Enrollment cancelled by the Department May 8, 1904.					
11					
12					
13					
14					
15					
16					
17		Date of Application for Enrollment	Novr 24"1898		

Choctaw By Blood Enrollment Cards 1898-1914

RESIDENCE: Blue COUNTY. **Choctaw Nation** **Choctaw Roll** CARD NO.
POST OFFICE: Durant, Ind. Ter (Not Including Freedmen) FIELD NO. **5561**

Dawes' Roll No.	NAME	Relationship to Person First Named	AGE	SEX	BLOOD	TRIBAL ENROLLMENT		
						Year	County	No.
14662	1 Conn, Minnie J	First Named	24	F	1/2	1896	Blue	10894
14663	2 " Agnes	Dau	2	"	1/4			
14664	3 Robinson, James	Son	7	M	1/4	1896	Blue	10896
14665	4 " Billy	"	4	"	1/4	"	"	10897
14666	5 Conn, Edna	Dau	2mo	F	1/4			
14667	6 " Mary E	"	1mo	"	1/4			
	7							
	8							
	9							
	10							
	11	ENROLLMENT OF NOS. 1-2-3-4-5-6 HEREON						
	12	APPROVED BY THE SECRETARY						
	13	OF INTERIOR MAR 19 1903						
	14							
	15							
	16							
	17							

TRIBAL ENROLLMENT OF PARENTS

	Name of Father	Year	County	Name of Mother	Year	County
1	Fred Robinson		Non-Citizen	Salena Robinson	Dead	Chickasaw Roll
2	John Conn		" "	No.1		
3	Jake Robinson		" "	No.1		
4	" "		" "	No.1		
5	John Conn		" "	No.1		
6	" "		" "	No.1		
7						
8	No1 On '96 Roll as "Janie Roberson"					
9	" 3 " " " " "James " "					
10	" 4 " " " " "Billy " "					
11	" 5 Enrolled May 24th 1900					
12	" 6 " July 10" 1901					
13	Nos. 1 to 6 inclusive originally enrolled on Chickasaw Card No. 1494 and transferred to this card Oct. 22, 1902.					
14	For child of No1 see NB (Apr 26-06) Card #829					
15	" children " " " " (Mar 3'05) " #411					
16						Date of Application for Enrollment.
17	P.O. Roberta I.T. 3/23/05					Aug 15 1899

161

Choctaw By Blood Enrollment Cards 1898-1914

RESIDENCE: Choctaw Nation ~~COUNTY.~~ **Choctaw Nation** Ch█████ CARD NO.
POST OFFICE: Atoka, Ind. Ter. *(Not Including Freedmen)* FIELD NO. **5562**

Dawes' Roll No.	NAME	Relationship to Person First Named	AGE	SEX	BLOOD	TRIBAL ENROLLMENT		
						Year	County	No.
14068	1 Downing, Sam	First Named	26	M	1/4	1896	Atoka	3586
~~Granted~~	2 " Mose	Bro	21	"	1/4	"	"	3587
I.W. 527	3 " Maud	Wife	27	F	I.W.			
DEAD.	4 " ~~Gordon S~~	~~Son~~	3wks	M	1/8			
~~Granted~~	5 " ~~Mary Mozella~~	Dau of Nº2	1mo	F	1/8			
14069	6 " George Todd	Son	6mo	M	1/8			
	7							
	8	ENROLLMENT			No. 4 HEREON DISMISSED UNDER			
	9	OF NOS. 3 HEREON			ORDER OF THE COMMISSION TO THE FIVE			
	10	APPROVED BY THE SECRETARY OF INTERIOR DEC 24 1903			CIVILIZED TRIBES OF MARCH 31, 1905.			
	11 No2 also on 1896 Chickasaw roll Page 38				DECISION PREPARED			
	12							
	13 ENROLLMENT							
	14 OF NOS. -1-6- HEREON APPROVED BY THE SECRETARY							
	15 OF INTERIOR MAR 19 1903							
	16 No2 and 5 transferred to Chic card #1714							
	17							

(Left margin: NB (Mar 3-05) #994 see 1 and 3 of Nos. 1 and 3 NB For child of Nos. 1 and 3)

TRIBAL ENROLLMENT O█████

	Name of Father	Year	County				Year	
1	George Downing	Dead	Non-Citizen	Ma█		█ing	Dea█	
2	" "	"	" "	"		"	"	█
3	D.M. Miller		" "	Wi█		█iller		Non-Citizen
4	~~No.1~~							
5	~~No.2~~			Ma█		█ing on	Chick Card #D261	
6	No.1			[illegible]				

7 Wife Of No2 Mattie Downing in Chickasaw Card D361

8 No2 filed Dec 31"03 Affidavit of Election on behalf of himself No5 and his wife electing to be enrolled as Chickasaws.

No1 On Choctaw Census Record No2 Page 148

9 " 2 " " " " " " " ; wife on Chick #D361 July 17" 1902

10 " 3 Evidence of marriage to be supplied. Filed Nov 3" 1899

11 " 3 Enrolled Sept 1st 1899

" 4 Enrolled Jan 2nd 1901

12 ~~" 5 Born June 5" 1902: Enrolled July 17" 1902~~

13 " 6 Born March 29" 1902: Enrolled Oct 2nd 1902.

14 Nos. 1 to 6 inclusive originally enrolled on Chickasaw Card No. 1271 and transferred to this card Oct. 22, 1902.

15 ~~No.4 died Sept 23, 1902, proof of death filed Nov. 26, 1902~~

16

17 No2 P.O. Lehigh I.T. | Date of Application for Enrollment. | Oct. 14" 1898

Choctaw By Blood Enrollment Cards 1898-1914

RESIDENCE: Choctaw Nation ~~COUNTY.~~ **Choctaw Nation** Choctaw Roll CARD NO.
ICE: Atoka, Ind. Ter. *(Not Including Freedmen)* FIELD NO. **5563**

NAME	Relationship to Person	AGE	SEX	BLOOD	TRIBAL ENROLLMENT		
					Year	County	No.
1 Fronterhouse, William	First Named	41	M	I.W.	1896	Atoka	14544
2 " Dick	Son	20	"	1/4	"	"	4497
3 Scroggins, Lucinda	Dau	17	F	1/4	"	"	4498
4 Fronterhouse, Addie	"	14	"	1/4	"	"	4499
5 " Willie	Son	12	M	1/4	"	"	4501
6 " Ward	"	7	"	1/4	1893		283
7 Scroggins, Alvin	Gr. Son	6wks	"	1/8			
8							
9 No1 is now married to Nellie James							
10 on Choctaw card #5595							

11
12 **ENROLLMENT**
OF NOS. **2-3-4-5-6-7** HEREON
13 APPROVED BY THE SECRETARY
OF INTERIOR **MAR 19 1903**

ENROLLMENT
OF NOS **1** HEREON
APPROVED BY THE SECRETARY
OF INTERIOR **MAR 14 1905**

14 No.1 formerly husband of Lucy
15 Fronterhouse (nee Folsom) 1893 Atoka
No 278, who died Nov. 4, 1897.
16
17

TRIBAL ENROLLMENT OF PARENTS

Name of Father	Year	County	Name of Mother	Year	County
1 John T. Fronterhouse	Dead	Non Citizen	Cynda Fronterhouse		Non-Citizen
2 No.1			Lucy "	Dead	~~Chick residing in Choctaw N. 3rd Dist~~
3 No.1			" "	"	" " " "
4 No.1			" "	"	" " " "
5 No.1			" "	"	" " " "
6 No.1			" "	"	" " " "
7 G.W. Scroggins		Non-Citizen	No.3		

8 No1 On Choctaw Intermarried Roll Atoka Co Page 32
9 " 2 " " Census Record No2 " " ' 191: On 96 Roll is Fronterhouse
10 " 3 " " " " " " " wife G.W. Scroggins non-citizen Evidence of
" 4 " " " " " " " marriage filed Oct. 16" 1901
11 " 5 " " " " " " " "
12 " 6 " " " " " " " "
13 " 7 Born Aug. 28, 1901, Enrolled Oct. 16" 1901
14 Nos. 1 to 7 originally enrolled on Chickasaw Card No. 1267. Transferred
to this card Oct. 22, 1902.
15 For child of No.3 see NB (March 3, 1905) #1373

16 " " " No.4 " " " " " #1483	Date of Application for Enrollment.	for #1 to 6 Oct 14" 1898

17 P.O. Caney I.T. 12/12/02

163

Choctaw By Blood Enrollment Cards 1898-1914

RESIDENCE: Choctaw Nation ~~COUNTY.~~ **Choctaw Nation**   Choctaw Roll   CARD No.
POST OFFICE: Antlers, Ind. Ter   *(Not Including Freedmen)*   FIELD No. **5564**

Dawes' Roll No.	NAME	Relationship to Person First Named	AGE	SEX	BLOOD	TRIBAL ENROLLMENT		
						Year	County	No.
14076	1 Sharp, Elba		29	F	3/16	1896	Jacks Fork	11699
14077	2 " Leo C	Son	6	M	3/32	"	" "	11700
	3							
	4							
	5							
	6							
	7							
	8							
	9							
	10							
	11	ENROLLMENT						
	12	OF NOS. 1 - 2 HEREON APPROVED BY THE SECRETARY						
	13	OF INTERIOR MAR 19 1903						
	14							
	15							
	16							
	17							

TRIBAL ENROLLMENT OF PARENTS

Name of Father	Year	County	Name of Mother	Year	County
1 Geo. W. Colbert	1897	Chick residing in Choctaw N. 2nd Dist	Lizzie Colbert	Dead	Non-Citizen
2 John Sharp	Dead	Non-Citizen	No.1		
3					
4					
5					
6 No 1 On 96 Roll as "Elbie Sharp"; on Choctaw Census Record No2 Jacks Fork Co Page 432					
7 " 2 " " " " "Leo B. " "; " " " " " " " " " as					
8					"Leo B. Sharp"
9 Nos. 1 and 2 originally enrolled on Chickasaw Card No. 1329. Transferred					
10 to this card Oct. 22, 1902					
11					
12					
13					
14					
15					
16				Date of Application for Enrollment.	Nov 21st 1898
17					

RESIDENCE: Pickens   COUNTY.   **Choctaw Nation**   **Choctaw Roll**   CARD NO.
POST OFFICE: Burdy, Ind. Ter   *(Not Including Freedmen)*   FIELD NO. **5565**

Dawes' Roll No.	NAME	Relationship to Person First Named	AGE	SEX	BLOOD	TRIBAL ENROLLMENT Year	County	No.
14078	1 Gibson, Thomas	First Named	26	M	1/2	1896	Jacks Fork	4990
IW 1224	2 " Laura	Wife	20	F	I.W.	"	" "	14,583
14079	3 " Ada	Dau	3	"	1/4	"	" "	4991
14080	DIED PRIOR TO ~~Verda~~BER 25, 1902 "	1	"	1/4		C. C. R.		
14081	5 " Jesse	Son	3mo	M	1/4			
14082	6 " Etta	Dau	7mo	F	1/4			
	7							
	8	ENROLLMENT OF NOS. 1-3-4-5-6 HEREON						
	9	APPROVED BY THE SECRETARY						
	10	OF INTERIOR MAR 19 1903						
	11							
	12	ENROLLMENT OF NOS. 2 HEREON						
	13	APPROVED BY THE SECRETARY						
	14	OF INTERIOR DEC 13 1904						
	15							
	16							
	17							

TRIBAL ENROLLMENT OF PARENTS

	Name of Father	Year	County	Name of Mother	Year	County
1	Reuben Gibson		Choctaw residing in Chickasaw Dist	Nicey Gibson	1897	Pickens
2	Newt Hale	Dead	Non-Citizen	Mollie Hale		Non-Citizen
3	No.1			No.2		
4	No.1			No.2		
5	No.1			No.2		
6	No.1			No.2		

7 No1 On Choctaw Census Record No2 Page 213
8 " 2 " " Intermarried Roll " 39
9 " 3 " " Census Record No2 Page 213; on 96 Roll as Eda Gibson
" 4 " " " " " " "
10 " 5 Enrolled Aug. 6" 1900
11 " 6 Born Jan 8" 1902 Enrolled Aug 23rd 1902
12 Nos. 1 to 6 inclusive originally enrolled on Chickasaw Card No. 1306 and transferred to this card Oct. 22, 1902.
13 No4 Died about March 19, 1900, proof of death filed Jany 29, 1903.
14 No4 died March 19, 1900: Enrollment cancelled by Department July 8, 1904

15						
16						1 to 4 inc
17	P.O. Foster Aug 12/04			Date of Application for Enrollment.		Oct 20" 1898

Choctaw By Blood Enrollment Cards 1898-1914

RESIDENCE: Choctaw Nation ~~COUNTY.~~ **Choctaw Nation** Choctaw Roll (Not Including Freedmen) CARD No.
POST OFFICE: Antlers, Ind. Ter FIELD No. **5566**

Dawes' Roll No.		NAME	Relationship to Person First Named	AGE	SEX	BLOOD	TRIBAL ENROLLMENT		
							Year	County	No.
14083	1	Stevens, Ellen	First Named	38	F	3/8	1896	Kiamitia	11535
14084	2	" Samuel	Son	16	M	3/16	"	"	11536
14085	3	" Eva	Dau	13	F	3/16	"	"	11537
14086	4	" Mary	"	8	"	3/16	"	"	11538
14087	5	" Martha	"	6	"	3/16	"	"	11539
14088	6	" John D.	Son	5	M	3/16	"	"	11540
	7								
	8								
	9								
	10								
	11	ENROLLMENT OF NOS. 1-2-3-4-5-6 HEREON							
	12	APPROVED BY THE SECRETARY							
	13	OF INTERIOR MAR 19 1903							
	14								
	15								
	16								
	17								

TRIBAL ENROLLMENT OF PARENTS

	Name of Father	Year	County	Name of Mother	Year	County
1	Samuel Colbert	Dead	Chickasaw Roll	Loucina Colbert	Dead	Chick Roll
2	Alexander Stevens	"	Non-Citizen	No.1		
3	" "	"	" "	No.1		
4	" "	"	" "	No.1		
5	" "	"	" "	No.1		
6	" "	"	" "	No.1		
7						
8						
9	1,2,3,4,5 & 6 on Choctaw Census Record No.2 Kiamitia Co Page 428					
10	No1 On Choctaw Roll as Ella Stevens					
11	" 2 " " " " Dan "					
12	" 6 " " " " Dexter "					
13	Nos. 1 to 6 inclusive originally enrolled on Chickasaw Card #1330 and transferred to this card Oct. 22, 1902.					
14						
15					Date of Application for Enrollment.	
16						
17					Nov 21st 98	

166

Choctaw By Blood Enrollment Cards 1898-1914

		Relationship to Person	AGE	SEX	BLOOD	TRIBAL ENROLLMENT		
ENCE: Choctaw Nation ~~COUNTY~~ **Choctaw Nation** **Choctaw Roll** (Not Including Freedmen) CARD NO. FIELD NO. **5567**						Year	County	No.
OFFICE: Nelson, Ind. Ter.								
es' No.	NAME							
89	₁ Griggs, Thomas	First Named	20	M	3/8	1896	Kiamitia	4829
	2							
	3							
	4							
	5							
	6							
	7							
	8							
	9							
	10							
	11	ENROLLMENT OF NOS. **1** HEREON						
	12	APPROVED BY THE SECRETARY						
	13	OF INTERIOR **MAR 19 1903**						
	14							
	15							
	16							
	17							

TRIBAL ENROLLMENT OF PARENTS

	Name of Father	Year	County	Name of Mother	Year	County
1	Thomas L. Griggs		Kiamitia Co Choctaw Roll	Mary Griggs	Dead	Chickasaw Roll
2						
3						
4						
5						
6	No1 on 96 Roll as "Thomas L Griggs Jr"					
7	" 1 on Choctaw Census Record No2, Page 207					
8	No.1 originally enrolled on Chickasaw Card No. 1335. Transferred to this card Oct. 22, 1902					
9						
10						
11						
12						
13						
14						
15						
16						
17					Date of Application for Enrollment.	Nov 22nd 1898

Choctaw By Blood Enrollment Cards 1898-1914

RESIDENCE: Choctaw Nation ~~COUNTY.~~   **Choctaw Nation**   Choctaw Roll   CARD NO.
POST OFFICE: Nelson, Ind. Ter.   *(Not Including Freedmen)*   FIELD NO. **5568**

Dawes' Roll No.	NAME	Relationship to Person First Named	AGE	SEX	BLOOD	TRIBAL ENROLLMENT Year	County	No.
DEAD	1 Thompson, George W ~~DEAD~~		40	M	I.W.	1896	Kiamitia	15108
14090	2 " Mattie	Wife	30	F	3/8	"	"	12365
14091	3 " Juanita	Dau	13	"	3/16	"	"	12366
14092	4 " Eugene	"	12	"	3/16	"	"	12367
14093	5 " Edgar	Son	10	M	3/16	"	"	12368
14094	6 " Daisy	Dau	7	F	3/16	"	"	12369
14095	7 " Grace	"	5	"	3/16	"	"	12370
14096	8 " Atwood	Son	3	M	3/16	"	"	12371
14097	9 " Georgie	Dau	2mo	F	3/16			
	10							
	11 ENROLLMENT OF NOS. 23456789 HEREON							
	12 APPROVED BY THE SECRETARY							
	13 OF INTERIOR Mar 19 1903							
	14 No.1 hereon dismissed under order of							
	15 the Commission to the Five Civilized							
	16 Tribes of March 31, 1905.							
	17							

TRIBAL ENROLLMENT OF PARENTS

	Name of Father	Year	County	Name of Mother	Year	County
1	Alfred Thompson	Dead	Non-Citizen	Eliza Thompson		Non-Citizen
2	George Colbert	1897	Chick residing in Choctaw N. 3rd Dist	Elizabeth Colbert	Dead	" "
3	No.1			No.2		
4	No.1			No.2		
5	No.1			No.2		
6	No.1			No.2		
7	No.1			No.2		
8	No.1			No.2		
9	No.1			No.2		

10 No1 On Choctaw Intermarried Roll Page 106. Died Apr 24th 1899 Proof of death filed Aug 5th
11 Nos 2,3,4,5,6,7,& 8 on Choctaw Census Record No.2 Page 448
12 No1 On 96 Roll as "George Thompson"
13 " 3 " " " " "Netta " " " "
13 " 8 " " " " "Etwood " " " "
14 " 9 Enrolled Nov 4th 1899
15 Nos. 1 to 9 inclusive originally enrolled on Chickasaw Card No. 1336 and transferred to this card Oct. 22, 1902.
16 For child of No2 see NB *Apr 26 '06) Card #187

#1 to 8 i[n]

Date of Application for Enrollment. Nov

168

Choctaw By Blood Enrollment Cards 1898-1914

RESIDENCE: Towson COUNTY.
POST OFFICE: Doaksville Ind. Ter

Choctaw Nation

Choctaw Roll
(Not Including Freedmen)

CARD No.
FIELD No. **5569**

Dawes' Roll No.	NAME	Relationship to Person	AGE	SEX	BLOOD	TRIBAL ENROLLMENT		
						Year	County	No.
14098	1 Wilson, Jane	First Named	62	F	1/2	1896	Towson	13187
	2							
	3							
	4							
	5							
	6							
	7							
	8							
	9							
	10							
	11	ENROLLMENT						
	12	OF NOS. 1 HEREON APPROVED BY THE SECRETARY						
	13	OF INTERIOR Mar 19 1903						
	14							
	15							
	16							
	17							

TRIBAL ENROLLMENT OF PARENTS

Name of Father	Year	County	Name of Mother	Year	County
1 James	Dead	non citizen	Ruthie James	Dead	Chickasaw Descen
2					
3					
4					
5					
6 No. 1 originally enrolled on Chickasaw Card No. 1411. Transferred					
7 to this card Oct. 22, 1902					
8					
9					
10					
11					
12					
13					
14					
15					
16			Date of Application for Enrollment.	April 20' 99	
17					

169

Choctaw By Blood Enrollment Cards 1898-1914

RESIDENCE: Choctaw Nation, Towson COUNTY.
POST OFFICE: Clear Creek, Ind. Ter

Choctaw Nation

Choctaw Roll
(Not Including Freedmen)

CARD NO.
FIELD NO. **5570**

Dawes' Roll No.	NAME	Relationship to Person First Named	AGE	SEX	BLOOD	TRIBAL ENROLLMENT		
						Year	County	No.
14099	1 Wilson, Raphael F		28	M	1/4	1896	Towson	13219
	2							
	3							
	4							
	5							
	6							
	7							
	8							
	9							
	10							
	11	ENROLLMENT						
	12	OF NOS. 1 HEREON APPROVED BY THE SECRETARY						
	13	OF INTERIOR MAR 19 1903						
	14							
	15							
	16							
	17							

TRIBAL ENROLLMENT OF PARENTS

Name of Father	Year	County	Name of Mother	Year	County
1 John Wilson	Dead	Choctaw Roll	Jane Wilson	1896	Chick residing in Choctaw Nation
2					
3					
4					
5					
6 No1 On 96 Roll as Raphael Wilson					
7 " 1 Husband of Emma J Wilson on Choctaw Card No 992					
8 No.1 originally enrolled on Chickasaw Card No. 1412. Transferred to this card Oct. 22, 1902					
9 For child of No1 see NB (March 3 1905) #701					
10					
11					
12					
13					
14					
15					
16					
17			Date of Application for Enrollment.	April 27" 99	

170

Choctaw By Blood Enrollment Cards 1898-1914

RESIDENCE: Choctaw Nation, Towson COUNTY. **Choctaw Nation** Choctaw (Not Including Fr CARD No.

POST OFFICE: Doaksville Ind Ter FIELD NO. **5571**

Dawes' Roll No.	NAME	Relationship to Person First Named	AGE	SEX	BLOOD	TRIBAL ENROLLMENT		
						Year	County	No.
14100	1 Wilson, W. W.	First Named	42	M	1/4	1896	Towson	13204
	2							
	3							
	4							
	5							
	6							
	7							
	8							
	9							
	10							
	11	ENROLLMENT OF NOS. 1 HEREON						
	12	APPROVED BY THE SECRETARY						
	13	OF INTERIOR MAR 19 1903						
	14							
	15							
	16							
	17							

TRIBAL ENROLLMENT OF PARENTS

	Name of Father	Year	County	Name of Mother	Year	County
1	John Wilson	Dead	Choc Descent	Jane Wilson	1896	Chick residing in Choctaw Nation
2						
3						
4						
5	No1 Wife and family on Choctaw Card #587					
6						
7	No.1 originally enrolled on Chickasaw Card No. 1410. Transferred					
8	to this card Oct. 22, 1902					
9						
10						
11						
12						
13						
14						
15						
16						
17				Date of Application for Enrollment.		April 20 '99

171

Choctaw By Blood Enrollment Cards 1898-1914

RESIDENCE: Choctaw Nation ~~COUNTY~~.
POST OFFICE: Red Oak, Ind. Ter.

Choctaw Nation

Choctaw Roll (Not Including Freedmen)

CARD NO.
FIELD NO. **5572**

Dawes' Roll No.	NAME	Relationship to Person First Named	AGE	SEX	BLOOD	TRIBAL ENROLLMENT Year	County	No.
IW528	1 Witt, Marion	First Named	33	M	I.W.			
14101	2 " Peggy	Wife	33	F	1/2	1896	Sugar Loaf	12856
14102	3 " Mary A	Dau	2	"	1/4			
14103	4 " John	Son	1mo	M	1/4			
14104	5 Darden, William	S.Son	7	"	1/4	1896	Sugar Loaf	3248
14105	6 " Minnie	" Dau	6	F	1/4	"	" "	3250
14106	7 " Charley	S.Son	3	M	1/4	"	" "	3249
14107	8 Witt, Fannie	Dau	3mo	F	1/4			
	9							
	10 ENROLLMENT							
	11 OF NOS. 2-3-4-5-6-7-8 HEREON APPROVED BY THE SECRETARY							
	12 OF INTERIOR Mar 19 1903							
	13							
	14 ENROLLMENT							
	15 OF NOS. 1 HEREON APPROVED BY THE SECRETARY							
	16 OF INTERIOR Dec 24 1903							
	17							

TRIBAL ENROLLMENT OF PARENTS

	Name of Father	Year	County	Name of Mother	Year	County
1	Jesse Witt		non-citizen	Polly A. Witt	Dead	Non-Citizen
2	Wm Mc Curtain	Dead	Choctaw	Swega Mc Curtain	"	Chick Roll
3	No.1			No.2		
4	No.1			No.2		
5	James Darden	Dead	non-citizen	No.2		
6	" "	"	" "	No.2		
7	" "	"	" "	No.2		
8	No.1			No.2		

9 No.2 on 96 Roll as "Pikie Witt"
10 3 Affidavit of birth to be supplied. Received July 27" 1899
11 4 " " " " " " " "
~~8 Enrolled Sept 4: 1901~~
12 Nos. 1 to 8 inclusive originally enrolled on Chickasaw Card #1466 and
13 transferred to this card Oct. 22, 1902.
14 ~~For child of Nos 1 and 2 see NB (March 3, 1905) #1244~~
15
16 #1 to 7
17 P.O. Nashoba I.T. 4/22/05 | Date of Application for Enrollment 6/21/99

172

Choctaw By Blood Enrollment Cards 1898-1914

RESIDENCE: Tobucksy   COUNTY.
POST OFFICE: Calvin Ind. Ter.

Choctaw Nation

Choctaw Roll *(Not Including Freedmen)*
CARD NO.
FIELD NO. **5573**

Dawes' Roll No.	NAME	Relationship to Person First Named	AGE	SEX	BLOOD	TRIBAL ENROLLMENT Year	County	No.
IW529	1 Wall, Chris	First Named	55	M	I.W.	1896	Tobucksy	15160
14108	2 " Delilah	Wife	30	F	1/4	"	"	13009
14109	3 " Sarah C	Dau	10	"	1/8	"	"	13010
14110	4 " Pearl	"	8	"	1/8	"	"	13011
14111	5 " James H	Son	7	M	1/8	"	"	13012
14112	6 " Benjamin F	"	3	"	1/8	"	"	13013
14113	7 " Mary D	Dau	1/2	F	1/8			
14114	8 " Charles C	Son	3mo	M	1/8			
	9							
	10							
	11	ENROLLMENT OF NOS. 2-3-4-5-6-7-8 HEREON						
	12	APPROVED BY THE SECRETARY						
	13	OF INTERIOR Mar 19 1903						
	14	ENROLLMENT						
	15	OF NOS. 1 HEREON						
	16	APPROVED BY THE SECRETARY OF INTERIOR Dec 24 1903						
	17							

TRIBAL ENROLLMENT OF PARENTS

	Name of Father	Year	County	Name of Mother	Year	County
1	James Wall		Non-citizen	Catherine Wall		Non-citizen
2	Hilburn Harrison	1896	Tobucksy	Sarah Harrison	Dead	Kiamitia
3	No.1			No.2		
4	No.1			No.2		
5	No.1			No.2		
6	No.1			No.2		
7	No.1			No.2		
8	No.1			No.2		
9	No2 On 96 Roll as Delila Wall					
10	" 3 " " " " Sarah K " " 5 " " " " Jas H "					
11	" 6 " " " "Benj F. "					
12	" 7 Affidavit of birth to be supplied					
13	" 8 Born Nov 29: 1901. Enrolled Feb 21st 1902					
14	Nos. 1 to 8 inclusive originally enrolled on Chick. Card No. 1481. Transferred to this card Oct. 22, 1902					
15	For child of Nos 1&2 see NB (March 3, 1905) #1150					
16					Date of Application for Enrollment.	8/8/99
17						1 to 7

173

Choctaw By Blood Enrollment Cards 1898-1914

RESIDENCE: Choctaw Nation   ~~COUNTY.~~   **Choctaw Nation**   Choctaw Roll   CARD NO.
POST OFFICE: Atoka, Ind. Ter.   *(Not Including Freedmen)*   FIELD NO. **5574**

Dawes' Roll No.	NAME	Relationship to Person First Named	AGE	SEX	BLOOD	TRIBAL ENROLLMENT		
						Year	County	No.
I.W. 616	1 Anglin, Charles Robert		48	M	I.W.	1896	Atoka	14264
14115	2 " Mary	Wife	27	F	1/4	"	"	426
	3							
	4							
	5							
	6							
	7							
	8	ENROLLMENT						
	9	OF NOS. 2 HEREON						
	10	APPROVED BY THE SECRETARY OF INTERIOR Mar 19 1903						
	11							
	12	ENROLLMENT						
	13	OF NOS. 1 HEREON						
	14	APPROVED BY THE SECRETARY OF INTERIOR Feb 8, 1904						
	15							
	16							
	17							

TRIBAL ENROLLMENT OF PARENTS

Name of Father	Year	County	Name of Mother	Year	County
1 Hezekiah Anglin	Dead	Non-Citizen	Kate Anglin	Dead	Non-Citizen
2 George Downing (I.W.)	"	Chick Roll	Melissa Downing	"	Chick residing in Choctaw N. 3rd Dist
3					
4					
5					
6					
7 No 1 On Choctaw Intermarried roll Page 3, on 96 Roll as C. R. Anglin					
8 " 2 " " Census Record No. 2 " 18					
9 ~~Nos. 1 and 2 originally enrolled on Chickasaw Card No. 1254 and transferred to this card Oct. 23, 1902.~~					
10					
11					
12					
13					
14					
15					
16					
17			Date of Application for Enrollment.	Oct. 14"/98	

174

Choctaw By Blood Enrollment Cards 1898-1914

RESIDENCE: Choctaw Nation ~~COUNTY.~~ **Choctaw Nation**   Choctaw Roll   CARD No.

POST OFFICE: Red Oak Ind. Ter   *(Not Including Freedmen)*   FIELD NO. **5575**

Dawes' Roll No.	NAME	Relationship to Person First Named	AGE	SEX	BLOOD	TRIBAL ENROLLMENT		
						Year	County	No.
DEAD.	~~₁ Mc Curtain, Sampson~~	~~Named~~	~~39~~	~~M~~	~~1/2~~	~~1896~~	~~Gaines~~	~~9165~~
14116	₂ Jessie, Buster	Neph	14	"	1/2	"	Sugar Loaf	6502
	₃							
	₄							
	₅							
	₆							
	₇							
	₈							
	₉							
	10							
	11	ENROLLMENT						
	12	OF NOS. 2 HEREON APPROVED BY THE SECRETARY						
	13	OF INTERIOR MAR 19 1903						
	14	No. 1 HEREON DISMISSED UNDER						
	15	ORDER OF THE COMMISSION TO THE FIVE CIVILIZED TRIBES OF MARCH 31, 1905.						
	16							
	17							

TRIBAL ENROLLMENT OF PARENTS

Name of Father	Year	County	Name of Mother	Year	County
₁ ~~Wᵐ Mc Curtain~~	~~Dead~~	~~Choctaw~~	~~Sa-ni-cho~~	~~Dead~~	~~Chickasaw~~
₂ Joshua Jessie	"	"	Melissa Jessie		"
₃					
₄					
₅					
₆ No1 Wife on Choctaw Card #2852					
₇ Nos. 1 and 2 originally enrolled on Chickasaw Card No. 1450 and					
₈ transferred to this card Oct. 23, 1902.					
₉ No1 died May 1901; proof of death filed Dec. 15, 1902.					
10					
11					
12					
13					
14					
15					
16				Date of Application for Enrollment.	6/19/99
17					

Choctaw By Blood Enrollment Cards 1898-1914

RESIDENCE: Choctaw Nation ~~COUNTY.~~ **Choctaw Nation** Choctaw Roll CARD No.
POST OFFICE: Wilburton, Ind. Ter. *(Not Including Freedmen)* FIELD NO. **5576**

Dawes' Roll No.	NAME	Relationship to Person First Named	AGE	SEX	BLOOD	TRIBAL ENROLLMENT Year	County	No.
14117	1 Ward, John Harris	First Named	26	M	1/2	1896	Gaines	12937
	2							
	3							
	4							
	5							
	6							
	7							
	8							
	9							
	10							
	11	ENROLLMENT						
	12	OF NOS. 1 HEREON APPROVED BY THE SECRETARY						
	13	OF INTERIOR Mar 19 1903						
	14							
	15							
	16							
	17							

TRIBAL ENROLLMENT OF PARENTS

	Name of Father	Year	County	Name of Mother	Year	County
1	Williston Ward	Dead	Choctaw Roll	Betsey Ward	Dead	Chick residing in Choctaw N 1st Dist
2						
3						
4						
5						
6	No 1 originally enrolled on Chickasaw Card No. 1399 and					
7	transferred to this card Oct. 23, 1902.					
8	No 1 died prior to September 25, 1902: not entitled to land or money ~~(See Indian office letter September 20, 1910. D.C. 1289-1910).~~					
9						
10						
11						
12						
13						
14						
15						
16						
17					Date of Application for Enrollment.	Mar. 21st 1899

176

Choctaw By Blood Enrollment Cards 1898-1914

Cd #5577

RESIDENCE: Sugar Loaf

POST OFFICE: Fanshaw, Ind. Ter.

Choctaw Nation

Choctaw Roll CARD 1
(Not Including Freedmen) FIELD NO.

Dawes' Roll No.	NAME	Relationship to Person First Named	AGE	SEX	BLOOD	TRIBAL ENROLLMENT		
						Year	County	No.
14118	1 Mc Curtain, Joshua	First Named	38	M	1/2	1896	Sugar Loaf	9118
14119	2 Adams, Jincy	Niece	22	F	1/2	"	" "	58
	3							
	4							
	5							
	6							
	7							
	8							
	9							
	10							
	11	ENROLLMENT						
	12	OF NOS. 1-2 HEREON APPROVED BY THE SECRETARY						
	13	OF INTERIOR MAR 19 1903						
	14							
	15							
	16							
	17							

TRIBAL ENROLLMENT OF PARENTS

Name of Father	Year	County	Name of Mother	Year	County
1 W^m Mc Curtain	Dead	Sugar Loaf	Sa-w-e-cha McCurtain	Dead	Sugar Loaf
2 William Adams	"	" "	Fannie Adams	"	" "
3					
4					
5					
6 No1 Children of, on Choctaw Card #2887					
7 No2 On 96 Roll as "Winnie Adams"					
8 Nos. 1 and 2 originally enrolled on Chickasaw Card No. 1454 and transferred to this card Oct. 23, 1902.					
9					
10					
11 Is not No.1 husband of Charlotta A. McCurtain: father of child on card # [???]8					
12					
13					
14					
15					
16					
17					6/19/99

Choctaw By Blood Enrollment Cards 1898-1914

RESIDENCE: Choctaw Nation ~~COUNTY.~~
POST OFFICE: Red Oak, Ind. Ter.

Choctaw Nation

Choctaw Roll
(Not Including Freedmen)

CARD NO.
FIELD NO. **5578**

Dawes' Roll No.	NAME	Relationship to Person First Named	AGE	SEX	BLOOD	TRIBAL ENROLLMENT		
						Year	County	No.
14120	1 Pope, Gilbert	First Named	21	M	1/2	1896	Skullyville	10106
	2							
	3							
	4							
	5							
	6							
	7							
	8							
	9							
	10							
	11	ENROLLMENT						
	12	OF NOS. 1 HEREON APPROVED BY THE SECRETARY						
	13	OF INTERIOR MAR 19 1903						
	14							
	15							
	16							
	17							

TRIBAL ENROLLMENT OF PARENTS

Name of Father	Year	County	Name of Mother	Year	County
1 Sampson Pope	Dead	Gaines	Liney Pope	Dead	Gaines
2					
3					
4					
5					
6 No1 Wife & child of, on Choctaw Card #2933					
7 No.1 originally enrolled on Chickasaw Card No. 1458 and					
8 transferred to this card Oct. 23, 1902.					
9					
10 For child of No1 see NB (Mar 3rd 1905) Card #221.					
11					
12					
13					
14					
15					
16				Date of Application	
17 P.O. Krebs I.T. 1/[?]/05				for Enrollment.	6/20/99

178

Choctaw By Blood Enrollment Cards 1898-1914

RESIDENCE: Choctaw Nation ~~COUNTY~~.
POST OFFICE: Sans Bois Ind Ter

Choctaw Nation

Choctaw Roll
(Not Including Freedmen)

CARD No.
FIELD No. **5579**

Dawes' Roll No.		NAME	Relationship to Person First Named	AGE	SEX	BLOOD	TRIBAL ENROLLMENT		
							Year	County	No.
14121	1	Noel, Robert	First Named	20	M	1/4	1896	Sans Bois	9545
14122	2	" Edmund	Bro.	11	"	1/4	1896	" "	9547
I.W. 852	3	" Mary	Wife	26	F	I.W.			
	4								
	5								
	6								
	7								
	8								
	9								
	10								
	11								
	12		ENROLLMENT OF NOS. HEREON APPROVED BY THE SECRETARY OF INTERIOR MAR 19 1903						
	13								
	14								
	15		ENROLLMENT OF NOS. HEREON APPROVED BY THE SECRETARY OF INTERIOR MAR 19 1903						
	16								
	17								

TRIBAL ENROLLMENT OF PARENTS

	Name of Father	Year	County	Name of Mother	Year	County
1	Peter Noel	Dead	Sans Bois	Corinda Noel	Dead	Sans Bois
2	" "	"	" " "	" "	"	" " "
3	David Spradley	"	noncitizen	Elizabeth Spradley		noncitizen
4						
5						
6	Nos 1 and 2 are brothers of Moses Noel on Chickasaw card #1467 now transferred to					
7	Choctaw card #5512					
8	No.1 now Husband of Mary Cole, Choctaw Card #D.956					
9	Nos. 1 and 2 originally enrolled on Chickasaw Card No. 1455 and transferred to this card Oct. 23, 1902.					
10						
11	No3 transferred from Choctaw card D 956 April 15, 1904. See decision of March 15, 1904					
12						
13						
14						
15						
16						
17					Date of Application for Enrollment.	6/19/99

179

Choctaw By Blood Enrollment Cards 1898-1914

RESIDENCE: Choctaw Nation ~~COUNTY.~~ **Choctaw Nation** Choctaw Roll CARD NO.
POST OFFICE: Red Oak, Ind. Ter. (Not Including Freedmen) FIELD NO. **5580**

Dawes' Roll No.	NAME	Relationship to Person First Named	AGE	SEX	BLOOD	TRIBAL ENROLLMENT		
						Year	County	No.
14123	1 James, John	First Named	9	M	1/2	1896	Sans Bois	6419
	2							
	3							
	4							
	5							
	6							
	7							
	8							
	9							
	10							
	11	ENROLLMENT						
	12	OF NOS. 1 HEREON APPROVED BY THE SECRETARY						
	13	OF INTERIOR MAR 19 1903						
	14							
	15							
	16							
	17							

TRIBAL ENROLLMENT OF PARENTS

	Name of Father	Year	County	Name of Mother	Year	County
1	Joseph James	1896	Sans Bois	Patsy James	Dead	Sans Bois
2						
3						
4						
5						
6	No 1 Father and brothers on Choctaw Card #2937					
7	No.1 originally enrolled on Chickasaw Card No. 1461. Transferred					
8	to this card Oct. 23, 1902					
9						
10						
11						
12						
13						
14						
15						
16				Date of Application for Enrollment.		6/20/99
17						

Choctaw By Blood Enrollment Cards 1898-1914

RESIDENCE: Choctaw Nation, Jacks Fork COUNTY. POST OFFICE: Hartshorne, Ind. Ter. **Choctaw Nation** CARD NO. FIELD NO. **5581**

Dawes' Roll No.	NAME	Relationship to Person First Named	AGE	SEX	BLOOD	TRIBAL ENROLLMENT		
						Year	County	No.
14124	1 Ward, Charles	First Named	21	M	1/2	1896	Jacks Fork	14087
	2							
	3							
	4							
	5							
	6							
	7							
	8							
	9							
	10							
	11	ENROLLMENT						
	12	OF NOS. 1 HEREON APPROVED BY THE SECRETARY						
	13	OF INTERIOR MAR 19 1903						
	14							
	15							
	16							
	17							

TRIBAL ENROLLMENT OF PARENTS

	Name of Father	Year	County	Name of Mother	Year	County
1	Williston Ward	Dead	Choctaw Roll	Patsy Ward	Dead	Chick. Roll
2						
3						
4						
5						
6	No 1 originally enrolled on Chickasaw Card No. 1432. And					
7	transferred to this card Oct. 23, 1902.					
8						
9						
10						
11						
12						
13						
14						
15						
16				Date of Application for Enrollment.		5/22/99
17						

Choctaw By Blood Enrollment Cards 1898-1914

RESIDENCE: Choctaw, Sans Bois COUNTY.
POST OFFICE: Sans Bois, Ind. Ter.

Choctaw Nation

Choctaw Roll
(Not Including Freedmen)

CARD No.
FIELD No. **5582**

Dawes' Roll No.	NAME	Relationship to Person First Named	AGE	SEX	BLOOD	TRIBAL ENROLLMENT Year	TRIBAL ENROLLMENT County	TRIBAL ENROLLMENT No.
14125	1 Woods, Jane	First Named	42	F	Full	1896	Sans Bois	3831
14126	2 Frazier, Edmund	Son	20	M	3/4	"	" "	3827
	3							
	4							
	5							
	6							
	7							
	8							
	9							
	10							
	11 ENROLLMENT OF NOS. 1 & 2 HEREON							
	12 APPROVED BY THE SECRETARY							
	13 OF INTERIOR Mar 19 1903							
	14							
	15							
	16							
	17							

TRIBAL ENROLLMENT OF PARENTS

	Name of Father	Year	County	Name of Mother	Year	County
1	Garland William	Dead	Chickasaw Roll	Eliza William	Dead	Chick. Roll
2	Campbell Frazier	"	Gaines	No.1		
3						
4						
5						
6	Nos 1 and 2 originally enrolled on Chickasaw Card No. 1434 and					
7	transferred to this card Oct. 23, 1902.					
8	No.1 is now wife of Wesley Woods on Choctaw card #2140 Evidence of marriage filed December 20, 1902.					
9	No.1 dead - see G.F. #31965-1911 9/29/11					
10						
11						
12						
13						
14						
15					Date of Application for Enrollment.	
16						
17	#2 P.O. Wauchula, De Soto Co, Florida 9/29/11					5/22/99

182

Choctaw By Blood Enrollment Cards 1898-1914

RESIDENCE: Choctaw Nation, Jacks Fork COUNTY.
POST OFFICE: Tuskhahomma, Ind. Ter. **Choctaw Nation** Choctaw Roll (Not Including Freedmen) CARD NO. FIELD NO. **5583**

Dawes' Roll No.	NAME	Relationship to Person First Named	AGE	SEX	BLOOD	TRIBAL ENROLLMENT		
						Year	County	No.
14127	1 Moore, Gertie		12	F	1/2	1896	Jacks Fork	8892
	2							
	3							
	4							
	5							
	6							
	7							
	8							
	9							
	10							
	11	ENROLLMENT						
	12	OF NOS. 1 HEREON APPROVED BY THE SECRETARY						
	13	OF INTERIOR MAR 19 1903						
	14							
	15							
	16							
	17							

TRIBAL ENROLLMENT OF PARENTS

Name of Father	Year	County	Name of Mother	Year	County
1 Isaac Gibson	Dead	Choctaw Roll	Nancy Moore	Dead	Chick. Fork
2					
3					
4					
5					
6 No.1 On 96 Roll as "Gurdie[sic] Moore"					
7 No.1 originally enrolled on Chickasaw Card No. 1438. Transferred					
8 to this card Oct. 23, 1902					
9					
10					
11					
12					
13					
14					
15					
16					
17			Date of Application for Enrollment.		5/23/99

Choctaw By Blood Enrollment Cards 1898-1914

RESIDENCE: Chickasaw Nation ~~COUNTY~~. **Choctaw Nation** Choctaw Roll CARD No.
POST OFFICE: Pocola, Ind. Ter. *(Not Including Freedmen)* FIELD No. **5584**

Dawes' Roll No.	NAME	Relationship to Person First Named	AGE	SEX	BLOOD	TRIBAL ENROLLMENT		
						Year	County	No.
IW530	1 Brown, Henry	First Named	23	M	IW			
14128	2 " Eliza	Wife	24	F	1/2	1896	Sans Bois	588
	3							
	4							
	5							
	6							
	7	ENROLLMENT						
	8	OF NOS. 2 HEREON APPROVED BY THE SECRETARY						
	9	OF INTERIOR MAR 19 1903						
	10							
	11							
	12	ENROLLMENT						
	13	OF NOS. 1 HEREON APPROVED BY THE SECRETARY						
	14	OF INTERIOR DEC 24 1903						
	15							
	16							
	17							

TRIBAL ENROLLMENT OF PARENTS

	Name of Father	Year	County	Name of Mother	Year	County
1	George Brown	Dead	Non-Citizen	Rose Brown	Dead	Non-Citizen
2	Moses Riddle	"	Choctaw Roll	Easter Riddle	"	Chick. Roll
3						
4						
5						
6	Nos. 1 and 2 originally enrolled on Chickasaw Card No. 1446 and					
7	transferred to this card Oct. 23, 1902.					
8						
9						
10						
11						
12						
13						
14						
15						
16						
17	10/16/1902 P.O. Mc Curtain IT			Date of Application for Enrollment.		6/6/99

Choctaw By Blood Enrollment Cards 1898-1914

| | | Choctaw Nation Starr, Ind. Ter. | COUNTY. **Choctaw Nation** | | | Choctaw Roll (Not Including Freedmen) | CARD NO. FIELD NO. **5585** | |

Dawes' Roll No.	NAME	Relationship to Person First Named	AGE	SEX	BLOOD	TRIBAL ENROLLMENT		
						Year	County	No.
14129	1 Mc Cann, Austin		41	M	1/2	1896	Sans Bois	9026
IW617	2 " Alice	Wife	22	F	I.W.			
14130	3 " Julia	Dau	1	"	1/4			
	4							
	5							
	6							
	7							
	8							
	9	ENROLLMENT						
	10	OF NOS. 1 - 3 HEREON APPROVED BY THE SECRETARY						
	11	OF INTERIOR MAR 19 1903						
	12							
	13	ENROLLMENT						
	14	OF NOS. 2 HEREON APPROVED BY THE SECRETARY						
	15	OF INTERIOR FEB -8 1904						
	16							
	17							

TRIBAL ENROLLMENT OF PARENTS

	Name of Father	Year	County	Name of Mother	Year	County
1	Alen Mc Cann	Dead	Choctaw	Ho-ya-ho-ke	Dead	Chickasaw
2	Hampton	"	Non-Citizen	Emeline Mantis	1896	Non-Citizen
3	No.1			No.2		
4						
5						
6	No.3 Affidavit of Birth to be supplied: Received 7/1/99					
7	Nos. 1,2 and 3 originally enrolled on Chickasaw Card No. 1449.					
8	Transferred to this card Oct. 23, 1902.					
9	For child of Nos 1 and 2 see NB (Mar. 3 1905) #712					
10						
11						
12						
13						
14						
15						
16					Date of Application for Enrollment	
17	Dec. 18-02 PO Cowlington IT				6/15/99	

185

Choctaw By Blood Enrollment Cards 1898-1914

Dawes' Roll No.	NAME	Relationship to Person First Named	AGE	SEX	BLOOD	TRIBAL ENROLLMENT Year	County	No.
14131	1 Garland, Harriet	First Named	30	F	Full	1896	Sans Bois	4602
14132	2 " Louisa	Dau	8	"	1/2	"	" "	4603
14133	3 " Louena	"	5	"	1/2	"	" "	4604
14134	4 " Henry	Son	3	M	1/2	"	" "	4605
14135	5 Kaniotubbe, Mitchell	Son	13	M	1/2	"	" "	7446
	6							
	7							
	8							
	9							
	10							
	11	ENROLLMENT						
	12	OF NOS. 1-2-3-4-5 HEREON APPROVED BY THE SECRETARY						
	13	OF INTERIOR MAR 19 1903						
	14							
	15							
	16							
	17							

TRIBAL ENROLLMENT OF PARENTS

	Name of Father	Year	County	Name of Mother	Year	County
1	Charius Wright	Dead	Gaines	Sha-ho-yeh-cha	Dead	G
2	Joel Garland	1896	Sans Bois	No.1		
3	" "	"	" "	No.1		
4	" "	"	" "	No.1		
5	Kaniotubbe	Dead	Gaines	No.1		
6						
7	No1 Husband on Choctaw Card #2854					
8	Nos. 1 to 5 inclusive originally enrolled on Chickasaw Card No. 1451. Transferred to this card Oct. 23, 1902					
9						
10						
11						
12						
13						
14						
15						
16					Date of Application for Enrollment.	
17						6/15/99

Choctaw By Blood Enrollment Cards 1898-1914

RESIDENCE: Choctaw Nation COUNTY.
POST OFFICE: Red Oak, Ind. Ter.

Choctaw Nation

Choctaw Roll
(Not Including Freedmen)

CARD NO.
FIELD NO. **5587**

Dawes' Roll No.	NAME	Relationship to Person First Named	AGE	SEX	BLOOD	TRIBAL ENROLLMENT		
						Year	County	No.
6 ₁ Luke, David			52	M	1/2	1896	Sans Bois	7694
2								
3								
4								
5								
6								
7								
8								
9								
10								
11	ENROLLMENT							
12	OF NOS. 1 HEREON APPROVED BY THE SECRETARY							
13	OF INTERIOR MAR 19 1903							
14								
15								
16								
17								

TRIBAL ENROLLMENT OF PARENTS

Name of Father	Year	County	Name of Mother	Year	County
₁ Anderson Luke	Dead	Sans Bois	On-ti-ma-ye	Dead	Sans Bois
2					
3					
4					
5					
6 No1 On '96 Roll as "Dave Luke"					
7 No1 Wife and child of, on Choctaw Card #2890					
8 No.1 originally enrolled on Chickasaw Card No. 1456. Transferred to this card Oct. 23, 1902					
9					
10					
11					
12					
13					
14					
15					
16					
17			Date of Application for Enrollment.		6/19/99

Choctaw By Blood Enrollment Cards 1898-1914

RESIDENCE: Choctaw Nation   COUNTY.   **Choctaw Nation**   **Choctaw Roll**   CARD NO.
POST OFFICE: Durant, Ind. Ter.   (Not Including Freedmen)   FIELD NO. **5588**

Dawes' Roll No.	NAME	Relationship to Person First Named	AGE	SEX	BLOOD	TRIBAL ENROLLMENT		
						Year	County	No.
14137	₁ Wilkinson, Ada		16	F	1/2	1896	Blue	12606
14138	₂ Died prior to September 25, 1902 Albert L	Son	3mo	M	1/4			
14139	₃ " Durward Arthur	"	3wks	"	1/4			
	₄							
	₅							
	₆							
	₇							
	₈							
	₉							
	₁₀							
	₁₁	ENROLLMENT OF NOS. 1-2-3 HEREON APPROVED BY THE SECRETARY OF INTERIOR Mar 19 1903						
	₁₂							
	₁₃							
	₁₄							
	₁₅							
	₁₆							
	₁₇							

TRIBAL ENROLLMENT OF PARENTS

	Name of Father	Year	County	Name of Mother	Year	County
₁	John Vails		non-citizen	Louvina Vails	dead	
₂	Henry Wilkinson		" "	No.1		
₃	" "		" "	No.1		
₄						
₅						

₆ No.1 on Choctaw Census Record no.1 Blue Co, Page 331
₇ No.1 on 96 Roll as "Ada Vail[sic]"
₈ No2 Enrolled Nov. 4ᵗʰ 1899
   "3 Enrolled Oct 1ˢᵗ 1901
₉ Nos. 1,2 and 3 originally enrolled on Chickasaw Card No. 1251 and
₁₀   transferred to this card Oct. 23, 1902.
₁₁
₁₂ No.2 died Dec 4, 1899: Enrollment cancelled by Department July 8, 1904.
₁₃
₁₄   For child of No.1 see NB (Apr 26 '06) Card #167
₁₅   " " " " " (Mar 3 '05) " #413
₁₆

				Date of Application for Enrollment.	Oct 14-1898
₁₇					

Choctaw By Blood Enrollment Cards 1898-1914

RESIDENCE: Choctaw Nation ~~COUNTY.~~ **Choctaw Nation**   Choctaw Roll   CARD NO.
POST OFFICE: Caddo, Ind. Ter.   *(Not Including Freedmen)*   FIELD NO. **5589**

Dawes' Roll No.	NAME	Relationship to Person First Named	AGE	SEX	BLOOD	TRIBAL ENROLLMENT		
						Year	County	No.
13458	1 Nail, David Oscar	First Named	26	M	1/8	1896	Blue	9793
IW618	2 " Pearl E	Wife	20	F	I.W.			
13459	3 " Claud B	Son	6mo	M	1/16			
DEAD	4 ~~" Haskell E~~	~~"~~	~~6wks~~	~~"~~	~~1/16~~			
	5							
	6 No. 4 hereon dismissed under order of							
	7 the Commission to the Five Civilized							
	Tribes of March 31, 1905.							
	8							
	9 ~~ENROLLMENT~~							
	10 OF NOS. 1&3 HEREON							
	11 APPROVED BY THE SECRETARY OF INTERIOR Mar 19, 1903							
	12							
	13 ~~ENROLLMENT~~							
	14 OF NOS. 2 HEREON							
	15 APPROVED BY THE SECRETARY OF INTERIOR Feb 8, 1904							
	16							
	17							

TRIBAL ENROLLMENT OF PARENTS

Name of Father	Year	County	Name of Mother	Year	County
1 Joel H. Nail		Chick residing in Choctaw Nation	Nettie Nail	Dead	Non-Citizen
2 Ben Brewer		Non-Citiz	Tennie Brewer		" "
3 No1			No2		
4 ~~No2~~			~~No2~~		
5					
6 No1 on 96 Roll as "Oscar H Nail"					
7 No3 Enrolled March 27" 1899					
" 4 Enrolled March 9" 1901					
8 ~~Nos 1 to 4 inclusive originally enrolled on Chickasaw Card #1396 and~~					
9 ~~transferred to this card Oct 23, 1902~~					
10 No.4 died July 12, 1902: Proof of death filed Nov. 28, 1902					
11					
12 For child of Nos 1 and 2 see NB (Mar 3, 1905) #429					
13					
14					
15					
16				#1&2	
17			Date of Application for Enrollment.	March 21st/99	

189

Choctaw By Blood Enrollment Cards 1898-1914

RESIDENCE: Choctaw Nation ~~COUNTY.~~ **Choctaw Nation**   Choctaw Roll   CARD NO. 5590

POST OFFICE: Kosome[sic], Ind. Ter.   *(Not Including Freedmen)*   FIELD NO. 55.

Dawes' Roll No.	NAME	Relationship to Person First Named	AGE	SEX	BLOOD	TRIBAL ENROLLMENT Year	County	No.
	on, Melvina	First Named	36	F	1/2	1896	Jacks Fork	6334
	Harriet	Dau	13	"	1/4	"	" "	6335
	Ammizon B	Son	10	M	1/4	"	" "	6336
4								
5								
6								
7								
8								
9								
10								
11	ENROLLMENT							
12	OF NOS. 1-2-3 HEREON APPROVED BY THE SECRETARY							
13	OF INTERIOR MAR 19 1903							
14								
15								
16								
17								

TRIBAL ENROLLMENT OF PARENTS

	Name of Father	Year	County	Name of Mother	Year	County
1	Allendon Anderson	Dead	Choctaw Roll	Louisa Impson		Chick residing in Choctaw N. 3rd Dist
2	Isaac J Impson		Jacks Fork Co Choctaw Roll	No.1		
3	" " "		" "	No.1		
4						
5						
6	No1 Wife of Isaac J Impson, Choctaw Card #463					
7	Nos. 1,2 and 3 originally enrolled on Chickasaw Card #1393 and					
8	transferred to this card Oct. 23, 1902.					
9						
10						
11						
12						
13						
14						
15						
16				Date of Application for Enrollment.	March 20" '99	
17						

Choctaw By Blood Enrollment Cards 1898-1914

RESIDENCE: Choctaw Nation ~~COUNTY.~~ **Choctaw Nation**   **Choctaw Roll** 5591   CARD NO.

POST OFFICE: Savannah, Ind. Ter   *(Not Including Freedmen)*   FIELD NO. 5

Dawes' Roll No.	NAME	Relationship to Person First Named	AGE	SEX	BLOOD	TRIBAL ENROLLMENT		
						Year	County	No.
13379	1 Carney, Norris	First Named	32	M	Full	1896	Atoka	2944
	2							
	3							
	4							
	5							
	6							
	7							
	8							
	9							
	10							
	11	ENROLLMENT						
	12	OF NOS. 1 HEREON APPROVED BY THE SECRETARY						
	13	OF INTERIOR MAR 19 1903						
	14							
	15							
	16							
	17							

TRIBAL ENROLLMENT OF PARENTS

	Name of Father	Year	County	Name of Mother	Year	County
1	Tombey Carney	Dead	Chickasaw Roll	Kitsey Alberson		Chick residing in Choctaw N. 1st Dist
2						
3						
4						
5						
6	No1 Wife and Children on Choctaw Card #460					
7	No1 originally enrolled on Chickasaw Card No. 1391. Transferred					
8	to this card Oct. 23, 1902					
9	For child of No1 see NB (Mar 3rd 1905) Card #96.					
10						
11						
12						
13						
14						
15						
16					Date of Application for Enrollment.	March 20" 99
17						

191

Choctaw By Blood Enrollment Cards 1898-1914

RESIDENCE: Choctaw Nation ~~COUNTY.~~ **Choctaw Nation** Choctaw Roll CARD NO.
POST OFFICE: Wilburton, Ind. Ter. *(Not Including Freedmen)* FIELD NO. **5592**

Dawes' Roll No.	NAME	Relationship to Person First Named	AGE	SEX	BLOOD	TRIBAL ENROLLMENT		
						Year	County	No.
13400	1 Ward, Henry		32	M	1/2	1896	Gaines	12979
	2							
	3							
	4							
	5							
	6							
	7							
	8							
	9							
	10							
	11	ENROLLMENT						
	12	OF NOS. 1 HEREON APPROVED BY THE SECRETARY						
	13	OF INTERIOR MAR 19 1903						
	14							
	15							
	16							
	17							

TRIBAL ENROLLMENT OF PARENTS

Name of Father	Year	County	Name of Mother	Year	County
1 Williston Ward	Dead	Choctaw Roll	Patsy Ward	Dead	Chickasaw Roll
2					
3					
4					
5					
6 No1 Child of, Plenna Ward on Choctaw Card #459					
7 No.1 originally enrolled on Chickasaw Card No. 1389. Transferred					
8 to this card Oct. 23, 1902					
9					
10					
11					
12					
13					
14					
15					
16				Date of Application for Enrollment.	March 20 '99
17					

192

Choctaw By Blood Enrollment Cards 1898-1914

RESIDENCE: Choctaw Nation COUNTY. **Choctaw Nation** Choctaw Roll ▓▓▓
POST OFFICE: Lehigh, Ind. Ter (Not Including Freedmen) FIELD NO. **5593**

Dawes' Roll No.	NAME	Relationship to Person First Named	AGE	SEX	BLOOD	TRIBAL ENROLLMENT Year	County	No.
13433	1 Battiest, Cain		18	M	1/2	1896	Atoka	1796
13434	2 " Allen	Bro	9	"	1/2	"	"	1804
	3							
	4							
	5							
	6							
	7							
	8							
	9							
	10							
	11							
	12							
	13							
	14							
	15							
	16							
	17							

ENROLLMENT
OF NOS. 1 & 2 HEREON
APPROVED BY THE SECRETARY
OF INTERIOR MAR 19 1903

TRIBAL ENROLLMENT OF PARENTS

	Name of Father	Year	County		Name of Mother		Year	County
1	Allen Battiest	Dead	Choctaw Roll		Wisey Battiest		Dead	Chick residing in Choctaw N. 1st Dist
2	" "	"	" "		"	"	"	" " " "
3								
4								
5								
6	Nos.1 and 2 originally enrolled on Chickasaw Card No. 1388 and							
7	transferred to this card Oct. 23, 1902.							
8								
9								
10								
11								
12								
13								
14								
15								Date of Application for Enrollment.
16								
17	No.1 P.O. Garvin Okla 11/11/11							March 20" 1899

193

Choctaw By Blood Enrollment Cards 1898-1914

RESIDENCE: Choctaw Nation COUNTY. **Choctaw Nation** **Choctaw Roll** CARD NO.
POST OFFICE: Stringtown, Ind. Ter. *(Not Including Freedmen)* FIELD NO. **5594**

Dawes' Roll No.	NAME	Relationship to Person First Named	AGE	SEX	BLOOD	TRIBAL ENROLLMENT		
						Year	County	No.
13402	1 Folota, Martin	First Named	45	M	1/2	1896	Jacks Ford	4548
	2							
	3							
	4							
	5							
	6							
	7							
	8							
	9							
	10							
	11							
	12	ENROLLMENT OF NOS. HEREON APPROVED BY THE SECRETARY OF INTERIOR Mar. 19, 1903						
	13							
	14							
	15							
	16							
	17							

TRIBAL ENROLLMENT OF PARENTS

Name of Father	Year	County	Name of Mother	Year	County
1 Folota	Dead	Choctaw Roll	Siney Folota	Dead	Chick Roll
2					
3					
4					
5					
6 No1 originally enrolled on Chickasaw Card No. 1383. Transferred					
7 to this card Oct. 23, 1902					
8					
9					
10					
11					
12					
13					
14					
15					
16					
17			Date of Application for Enrollment.		March 22/99

Choctaw By Blood Enrollment Cards 1898-1914

RESIDENCE: Choctaw Nation   COUNTY. **Choctaw Nation**   Choctaw Roll
POST OFFICE: Phillips, Ind. Ter.   I.W 5592 *(Not Including Freedmen)* Fr.

Dawes' Roll No.	NAME	Relationship to Person First Named	AGE	SEX	BLOOD	TRIBAL ENROLLMENT		
						Year	County	No.
I.W 1357	1 Fronterhouse, Nellie		25	F	I.W	1896	Atoka	14708
	2							
	3							
	4							
	5							
	6							
	7							
	8							
	9							
	10							
	11	ENROLLMENT OF NOS. 1 HEREON						
	12	APPROVED BY THE SECRETARY						
	13	OF INTERIOR MAR 19 1903						
	14							
	15							
	16							
	17							

TRIBAL ENROLLMENT OF PARENTS

Name of Father	Year	County	Name of Mother	Year	County
1 Abner Hill		Non-Citizen	Mary E Hill		Non-Citiz
2					
3					
4					
5					
6 No1 On Choctaw Intermarried Roll, Atoka Co, Page 53;					
7 No1 Married as a Choctaw					
8 No1 Widow of Thomas James 1/4 Chickasaw Indian					
No1 now wife of William Fronterhouse on Choctaw card #5563					
9 Evidence of marriage filed Dec. 6, 1902					
10 No.1 originally enrolled on Chick. Card No. 1327: Transferred					
11 to this card Nov. 7, 1902					
No.1 formerly wife of Thomas James, 1893 Atoka, No 606.					
12 who died about 1896					
13					
14					
15					
16					
17 Caney I.T. 12/2/02				Date of Application for Enrollment.	Oct. 14" 1898

Choctaw By Blood Enrollment Cards 1898-1914

RESIDENCE: Choctaw Nation ~~COUNTY.~~ **Choctaw Nation**   Choctaw Roll   CARD NO.
POST OFFICE: Caddo, Ind. Ter.   (Not Including Freedmen)   FIELD NO. **5596**

Dawes' Roll No.	NAME	Relationship to Person First Named	AGE	SEX	BLOOD	TRIBAL ENROLLMENT		
						Year	County	No.
13439	1 Nail, Joel H	First Named	49	M	1/4	1896	Blue	9791
IW531	2 " Lou	Wife	24	F	I.W.			
13440	3 Robertson, Vivia	Dau	23	"	1/8	1896	Blue	9794
13441	4 Perkins, Ethel	"	21	"	1/8	"	"	9795
13442	5 Nail, Ishtoyapi	Som	18	M	1/8	"	"	9796
13443	6 Fulsom, Catherine	Mother	65	F	1/2	"	"	4406
13444	7 Robertson, Wesley L	Gr. Son	6m	M	1/16			
IW853	8 " Albert M	Hus of No3	28	M	I.W.			
IW1358	9 Perkins, Ormal H	Husband of No4	25	M	I.W.			
	10 Nos 4 and 9 married Sept 3, 1902							
	11							
	12	ENROLLMENT OF NOS. 1-3456&7 HEREON APPROVED BY THE SECRETARY OF INTERIOR MAR 19 1903			ENROLLMENT OF NOS. 9 HEREON APPROVED BY THE SECRETARY OF INTERIOR MAR 14 1905			
	13							
	14							
	15	ENROLLMENT OF NOS. 2 HEREON APPROVED BY THE SECRETARY OF INTERIOR DEC 24 1903			ENROLLMENT OF NOS. 8 HEREON APPROVED BY THE SECRETARY OF INTERIOR MAY 21 1904			
	16							
	17							

TRIBAL ENROLLMENT OF PARENTS

	Name of Father	Year	County	Name of Mother	Year	County
1	Jonathan Nail	Dead	Choctaw Roll	Catherine Nail Now Fulsom		Chick residing in Choctaw N. 1st Dist
2	Daily	"	non-citizen	A. M. Daily		non-citizen
3	No.1			Nettie Nail	Dead	" "
4	No.1			" "	"	" "
5	No.1			" "	"	" "
6	Jim Perry	Dead	Choctaw Roll		"	Chickasaw Roll
7	Albert M Robertson		White Man	No.3		
8	W.L. Robertson		noncitizen	Mattie Robertson	Dead	noncitizen
9	T.J. Perkins		noncitizen	Ophelia Perkins		noncitizen

10	No1 transferred from Chickasaw card D348 April 13 1904. See decision of March 15, 1904
11	No.3 now the wife of Albert M Robertson on Chickasaw Card #D.348. Aug 29" 1901
12	4 now the wife of Ormal H Perkins on Chickasaw #D364 Evidence of marriage filed Sept 4" 1902 " 7 Born Nov 6 1901; Enrolled May 13" 1902
13	Nos. 1 to 7 inclusive originally enrolled on Chickasaw Card No. 1395 and transferred to this
14	card Oct. 23, 1902.
15	No9 originally listed for enrollment on Chickasaw card D364 Sept 4 1902; transferred to this card Jan 29, 1905. See decision of Jan. 13, 1905
16	Record as to enrollment of No9 forwarded to Department Mar 14, 1906. Record returned.
17	No9 P.O. Durant, I.T. See opinion of Assistant Attorney General of Mar. 21st 1899

March 15, 1906 in case of Omer R. Nicholson

RESIDENCE: Choctaw Nation	COUNTY. **Choctaw Nation**					CARD No.
POST OFFICE: Stringtown, Ind. Ter						FIELD No. **5597**

Dawes' Roll No.	NAME	Relationship to Person First Named	AGE	SEX	BLOOD	TRIBAL ENROLLMENT		
						Year	County	No.
13435	1 Billie, Simon	First Named	40	M	1/2	1896	Jacks Fork	1892
13436	2 " Nancy	Wife	26	F	1/2	1893	" "	733
	3							
	4							
	5							
	6							
	7							
	8							
	9							
	10							
	11	ENROLLMENT						
	12	OF NOS. **1 - 2** HEREON APPROVED BY THE SECRETARY						
	13	OF INTERIOR **MAR 19 1903**						
	14							
	15							
	16							
	17							

TRIBAL ENROLLMENT OF PARENTS

	Name of Father	Year	County	Name of Mother	Year	County
1	Alexander Billie	Dead	Choctaw Roll	Ah-lo-wi-che	Dead	Chickasaw Roll
2	Thomas Noah	1896	" "	Asey Noah	"	" "
3						
4						
5						
6	No1 On 96 Roll as "Simon Billy"; On Choctaw Census Record No2 Page 76 Jacks Fork Co.					
7	No1 Has a child by former Choctaw wife, on Choctaw card #1963					
8	No2 On '93 Roll as "Nancy Watson"					
	" Enrolled May 23rd 1899					
9	Nos1 and 2 originally enrolled on Chickasaw Card No. 707 and					
10	transferred to this card Oct. 23, 1902.					
11						
12						
13						
14						
15					Date of Application for Enrollment.	
16						
17					For No. 1 Sept 28" 1898	

Choctaw By Blood Enrollment Cards 1898-1914

RESIDENCE: Blue   COUNTY. **Choctaw** ion   Choctaw Roll

POST OFFICE: Durant Ind. Ter   *(Not Including Freedmen)*   FIELD NO. **5598**

Dawes' Roll No.	NAME		Relationship to Person First Named	AGE	SEX	BLOOD	TRIBAL ENROLLMENT	
							Year	County
13445	1	Robinson, Jesse	First Named	21	M	1/2	1896	Blue	8
IW532	2	" Sarah	Wife	19	F	I.W.	"	"	88
13446	3	" Finnie	Dau	9mo	"	1/4		
13447	4	" Walter	Son	1mo	M	1/4		
	8							
		ENROLLMENT OF NOS. 1 3 & 4 HEREON APPROVED BY THE SECRETARY OF INTERIOR MAR 19 1903						
	12							
	13	ENROLLMENT OF NOS. 2 HEREON APPROVED BY THE SECRETARY OF INTERIOR DEC 24 1903						
	14							
	15							
	16							
	17							

TRIBAL ENROLLMENT OF PARENTS

	Name of Father	Year	County	Name of Mother	Year	County
1	Fred Robinson		U.S.	Salina Robinson	Dead	Ch
2	C. C. Mullens		U.S.	Julia Mullens		
3	No.1			No.2		
4	No.1			No.2		
5						
6	No1 On 96 Roll as "Jesse Roberson"					
7	" 2 Admitted by Dawes Commission No. 684					
8	" 4 Enrolled Jan. 15" 1901					
	Nos. 1 to 4 inclusive originally enrolled on Chickasaw Card #1495					
9	and transferred to this card Oct. 23, 1902					
10						
11	Child of Nos 1&2 on NB (Apr 26 '06) Card #305					
	" " " " " " " (Mar 3 '05) " #430					
12						
13						
14						
15						
16				Date of Application for Enrollment.	8/15/99	

Choctaw By Blood Enrollment Cards 1898-1914

RESIDENCE:	Choctaw Nation	~~COUNTY.~~		**Choctaw Nation**			**Choctaw Roll**	CARD No.	
POST OFFICE:	Goodland, Ind. Ter						*(Not Including Freedmen)*	FIELD No. **5599**	

Dawes' Roll No.	NAME	Relationship to Person First Named	AGE	SEX	BLOOD	TRIBAL ENROLLMENT		
						Year	County	No.
13448	1 Roberts, Betsey		6	F	1/2	1896	Kiamitia	10835
13449	2 Wachubbe, Lewis	Uncle	14	M	1/2	1893	"	865
	3							
	4							
	5							
	6							
	7							
	8							
	9							
	10							
	11	ENROLLMENT						
	12	OF NOS. 1 & 2 HEREON APPROVED BY THE SECRETARY						
	13	OF INTERIOR MAR 19 1903						
	14							
	15							
	16							
	17							

	TRIBAL ENROLLMENT OF PARENTS				Name of Mother			
1 Eastman Roberts			Roll		Mollie Roberts			
2 Wilke Wachubbe		"	"		Rhoda Wachubbe		Chickasaw Card #1337	
3								
4								
5								
6 No 1 on Choctaw Census Record No.2 Page 411								
7 " 2 Enrolled March 21st 1899								
8 " 2 On '93 Roll as "Lee Wachubbee[sic]"								
9 Nos. 1 and 2 originally enrolled on Chickasaw Card No. 1337 and transferred to this card Oct. 23, 1902.								
10								
11								
12								
13								
14								
15						Date of Application for Enrollment.		
16								
17						Nov 23" 1898		

199

Choctaw By Blood Enrollment Cards 1898-1914

RESIDENCE: Pickens COUNTY. **Choctaw Nation** ~~Choctaw Roll~~ CARD NO.
POST OFFICE: Brownsville, Ind. Ter. *(Not Including Freedmen)* FIELD NO. **5600**

Dawes' Roll No.	NAME	Relationship to Person First Named	AGE	SEX	BLOOD	TRIBAL ENROLLMENT		
						Year	County	No.
13415	1 King, Elie		47	F	Full	1896	Blue	7632
	2							
	3							
	4							
	5							
	6							
	7							
	8							
	9							
	10							
	11	ENROLLMENT OF NOS. 1 HEREON APPROVED BY THE SECRETARY OF INTERIOR Mar. 19, 1903						
	12							
	13							
	14							
	15							
	16							
	17							

TRIBAL ENROLLMENT OF PARENTS

	Name of Father	Year	County		Name of Mother	Year	County
1	Hotumbby	Dead	Panola	[??]	bota Hotumbby	1897	Pickens
2							
3							
4							
5							
6	No1 On Choctaw Census Record No. 2 Blue Co. Page 322						
7	No1 originally enrolled on Chickasaw Card #970. Transferred						
8	to this card Oct. 24, 1902						
9							
10							
11							
12							
13							
14							
15							
16							
17					Date of Application for Enrollment.	Oct 3rd 1898	

200

Choctaw By Blood Enrollment Cards 1898-1914

RESIDENCE: Choctaw Nation ~~COUNTY~~ **Choctaw Nation**
POST OFFICE: South McAlester, Ind Ter

Choctaw Roll (Not Including Freedmen) **CARD NO.** **FIELD NO. 5601**

Dawes' Roll No.	NAME	Relationship to Person First Named	AGE	SEX	BLOOD	TRIBAL ENROLLMENT Year	County	No.
13796	1 Lester, Preston S *	First Named	38	M	I.W.	1896	Tobucksy	14759
14140	2 " Alice	Wife	25	F	1/2	"	"	7880
14141	3 " McCurtain	Son	5	M	1/4	"	"	7881
14142	4 " Lucile	Dau	3	F	1/4	"	"	7882
14143	5 " Wynema	"	10mo	"	1/4			
14144	6 Jones, Josephine	Sister in law	20	"	1/2	1896	Tobucksy	10264
14145	7 Lester, Louise A	Dau	6mo	"	1/4			
14146	8 " Preston S, Jr	Son	2mo	M	1/4			
14147	9 Jones, William B	Son of No6	8days	"	1/4			
14148	10 " Capitola	Dau of No6	2	F	1/4			
	11 now Kyser							

12 No1 on Choctaw Intermarried Roll page 61
13 " 2 " " Census Record No2 " 331 as "Alice P Lester"
14 " 3 " " " " 331 as "Green McCurtain"
14 " 4 " " " " 331
15 " 5 affidavit of attending physician to be supplied. Received Oct 21st 1898
16 " 6 on Choctaw census Record No2 Tobucksy Co Page 395
" 6 Now the wife of John W Jones Choctaw Card #4727 June 3rd 1902
17 " " Evidence of marriage filed Oct 18" 1902

TRIBAL ENROLLMENT OF PARENTS

	Name of Father	Year	County	Name of Mother	Year	County
1	Preston Lester		Non-Citizen	Carrie Lester		Non-Citizen
2	Wm Pitchlynn	Dead	Choctaw Roll	Elsie Pitchlynn	Dead	Chick residing in Choctaw N. 1st Dist
3	No.1			No.2		
4	No.1			No.2		
5	No.1			No.2		
6	Wm Pitchlynn	Dead	Choctaw Roll	Elsie Pitchlynn	Dead	Chick residing in Choctaw N. 1st Dist
7	No.1			No.2		
8	No.1			No.2		
9	John W. Jones		Choctaw Card 4727	No.6		
10	" " "		" " "	No.6		
11						

For child of Nos 1&2 see NB (Mar 3'05)#1032 *Decision of U.S.Court Central District July 13, 1897
12 No7 Enrolled Nov 4" 1899 vacated and set aside by decree of Choctaw-Chickasaw
" 8 Enrolled July 12" 1901 Citizenship Court Nov term 1902; Case No 15.
13 " 9 Born Aug 4" 1902 Enrolled Aug 7" 1902 No1 was admitted by U.S.Court Central Dist Case
14 " 10 Born June 2"1900 Enrolled Oct 18" 1902 No 14
15 Nos 1 to 10 inclusive originally enrolled on Chick Card #1248 and
transferred to this card Oct. 24, 1902
16 No8 Died Oct 28, 1902; Proof of death filed Dec. 15, 1902
17 Additional Proof filed Dec 24-1902 For child of No6 see NB (Apr 26-06) Card #333

Date of Application for Enrollment. 1 to 5 **For Nos** Oct 14" 1898

Choctaw By Blood Enrollment Cards 1898-1914

RESIDENCE: Choctaw Nation ~~COUNTY~~. **Choctaw Nation** Choctaw Roll CARD NO.
POST OFFICE: Tuskahoma, Ind. Ter. *(Not Including Freedmen)* FIELD NO. **5602**

Dawes' Roll No.	NAME	Relationship to Person First Named	AGE	SEX	BLOOD	TRIBAL ENROLLMENT		
						Year	County	No.
14157	1 Potts, Judy		38	F	1/2	1896	Wade	10312
14158	2 " Sarah	Dau	17	"	1/4	"	"	10313
14159	3 " Joshua	Son	12	M	1/4	"	"	10314
14160	4 " Allie	Dau	10	F	1/4	"	"	10315
14161	5 " Willie	Son	8	M	1/4	"	"	10316
14162	6 " Lillie	Dau	6	F	1/4	"	"	10317
14163	7 " Eli	Son	5	M	1/4	"	"	10318
14164	8 " Horace, Jr	"	3	"	1/4	"	"	10319
14165	9 " Laura	Dau	1	F	1/4			
14166	10 " Rebecca	"	5mo	"	1/4			
14167	11 " Margaret Susan	Dau of No2	2 1/2	"	1/4			
	12 Nos 1 to 11 originally enrolled on							
	13 Chickasaw Card #1240 and transferred							
	to this card Oct. 24, 1902.							
	14							
	15 For child of No4 see NB (Mar 3-05) Card #112							
	16 " " " No2 " " " " " " #431							
	" " " No2 " " " " " " #981							
	17							

ENROLLMENT
OF NOS. 1,2,3,4,5,6,7,8,9,10,11 HEREON
APPROVED BY THE SECRETARY
OF INTERIOR Mar 19, 1903

TRIBAL ENROLLMENT OF PARENTS

	Name of Father	Year	County	Name of Mother	Year	County
1	Billie King	Dead	Choctaw Roll	Lith-lo-ke	Dead	Chickasaw Roll
2	Horace Potts		Wade Co Choctaw Roll	No.1		
3	" "			No.1		
4	" "			No.1		
5	" "			No.1		
6	" "			No.1		
7	" "			No.1		
8	" "			No.1		
9	" "			No.1		
10	" "			No.1		
11	(Illegit) Archie Heath on Choctaw Card #2059			No.2		
12	No1 on Choctaw 96 Roll as Julia Potts: Wife of Horace Potts, Choctaw Roll Card #396					
13	"4 " " " " " Alice "					
14	"10 Enrolled Nov 4" 1899					
	"11 Illegitimate (Born Feb 7" 1900; Enrolled July 22nd 1902					
15	Nos 1,2,3,4,5,6,7,8 on Choctaw Census Record No2 Wade Co Page 397				1 to 9 inc	
16					Date of Application for Enrollment.	
17	No2 PO Talihina IT 4/10/05		Date of application for enrollment	Oct 13-1898		

RESIDENCE: Choctaw Nation, Kiamitia COUNTY.
POST OFFICE: Antlers, Ind. Ter.

Choctaw Nation

Choctaw Roll
(Not Including Freedmen)

CARD NO.
FIELD NO. **5603**

Dawes' Roll No.	NAME	Relationship to Person First Named	AGE	SEX	BLOOD	TRIBAL ENROLLMENT Year	County	No.
IW936	1 Locke, Elisha S		40	M	I.W.			
13406	2 " Jane	Wife	36	F	1/2	1893	Cedar	113
14833	3 " Elisha	Son	5	M	1/4			
14834	4 " Mary	Dau	3	F	1/4			
13407	5 " Bertie	"	6mo	"	1/4			
13408	6 Hampton, Susan	S.Dau	11	"	1/4	1893	Cedar	114
13409	7 Locke, Jesse	Son	7wks	M	1/4			
	8							
	9							
	10							
	11	ENROLLMENT						
	12	OF NOS. 2,5,6 & 7 HEREON APPROVED BY THE SECRETARY						
	13	OF INTERIOR Mar. 19, 1903						
	14							
	15	ENROLLMENT						
	16	OF NOS. 3 & 4 HEREON APPROVED BY THE SECRETARY						
	17	OF INTERIOR May 20 1903						

TRIBAL ENROLLMENT OF PARENTS

	Name of Father	Year	County	Name of Mother	Year	County
1	Frank Locke	Dead	Non-Citizen	Mary Locke	Dead	Non-Citizen
2	Barney Davenport	"	Choctaw Roll	Saleney Yakambe	"	Chick. Roll
3	No.1			No.2		
4	No.1			No.2		
5	No.1			No.2		
6	Julius Hampton	1896	Choctaw Roll			
7	No.1			No.2		
8						
9	No2 on 93 Roll as "Jane Davenport"					
10	" 5 affidavit of Birth to be supplied, Recd May 18" 1899 " 7 Born November 16"1901. Enrolled Jan 3rd 1902					
11	No 1 to 7 inclusive originally enrolled on Chick Card No. 1425					
12	and transferred to this card Oct. 24, 1902.					
13	No3 Born Feby 8, 1895. Proof of birth filed Feby 27, 1903.					
14	No4 Born Jany 26, 1897. Proof of birth filed Feby 27, 1903.					
15				ENROLLMENT		#1 to 6
16				OF NOS. 1 HEREON APPROVED BY THE SECRETARY		Date of Application for Enrollment.
17				OF INTERIOR Aug. 3, 1904		5/12/99

Choctaw By Blood Enrollment Cards 1898-1914

RESIDENCE: Tobucksy   COUNTY.   **Choctaw Nation**   **Choctaw Roll**   CARD No.

POST OFFICE: Legal IT   *(Not Including Freedmen)*   FIELD No. 5

Dawes' Roll No.	NAME	Relationship to Person First Named	AGE	SEX	BLOOD	TRIBAL ENROLLMENT		
						Year	County	No.
1	Clark, George A	Named	32	M	I.W.			
2								
3								
4								
5								
6								
7								
8								
9								
10								
11								
12								
13								
14								
15								
16								
17								

DENIED CITIZENSHIP BY THE CHOCTAW AND CHICKASAW CITIZENSHIP COURT

TRIBAL ENROLLMENT OF PARENTS

	Name of Father	Year	County	Name of Mother	Year
1					
2					
3					
4					
5					
6	No 1 is husband of No1 on Choctaw card #3297				
7	No1 is placed on this card November 1, 1902 having been				
8	transferred from Choctaw card R#352 by order of the Secretary of the Interior of July 5, 1902.				
9					
10					
11					
12					
13					
14					
15					
16					
17				Date of Application for Enrollment.	NOV -1 1902

204

Choctaw By Blood Enrollment Cards 1898-1914

RESIDENCE: Chickasaw Nation ~~COUNTY.~~ **Choctaw Nation**   **Choctaw Roll** CARD NO.
POST OFFICE: McMillan, Ind. Ter.   *(Not Including Freedmen)* FIELD NO. **5605**

Dawes' Roll No.	NAME	Relationship to Person First Named	AGE	SEX	BLOOD	TRIBAL ENROLLMENT		
						Year	County	No.
13426	1 Pickens, Grilbert[sic]		25	M	Full	1896	Gaines	10166
	2							
	3							
	4							
	5							
	6							
	7							
	8							
	9							
	10							
	11	ENROLLMENT						
	12	OF NOS. 1 HEREON APPROVED BY THE SECRETARY						
	13	OF INTERIOR MAR 19 1903						
	14							
	15							
	16							
	17							

TRIBAL ENROLLMENT OF PARENTS

Name of Father	Year	County	Name of Mother	Year	County
1 Thompson Pickens			Bessie Pickens		
2					
3					
4					
5					
6 No 1 on Tobucksy Co pay roll page 20 #196					
7 Also on 1896 Choctaw census roll page 258 #10166					
8 No 2 is the husband of Leona Pickens on Chickasaw card #972 Nov. 12, 1902					
9 For child of No.1 see Chickasaw NB (March 3, 1905) #451					
10					
11					
12					
13					
14					
15				Date of Application for Enrollment.	
16					
17				Oct 30, 1902	

Choctaw By Blood Enrollment Cards 1898-1914

RESIDENCE:
COUNTY. **Choctaw Nation**
POST OFFICE: Legal, I.T.

Roll
CARD No.
FIELD No. 5606

Dawes' Roll No.	NAME	Relationship to Person First Named	AGE	SEX	BLOOD	TRIBAL ENROLLMENT		
						Year	County	No.
13430	1 King, Levenia	First Named	24	F	3/4	1896	Sans Bois	2124
13431	2 Lucas, Susan	Dau	6	F	3/8	1896	" "	7768
	3							
	4							
	5							
	6							
	7							
	8							
	9							
	10							
	11	ENROLLMENT						
	12	OF NOS. 1 - 2 HEREON APPROVED BY THE SECRETARY						
	13	OF INTERIOR MAR 19 1903						
	14							
	15							
	16							
	17							

TRIBAL ENROLLMENT OF PARENTS

	Name of Father	Year	County	Name of Mother	Year	County
1	Louie Leflore	Dead		Susan Hancock	Dead	
2				No.1		
3						
4						
5						
6	No1 is wife of Charles King Choctaw card #4953 and mother					
7	of No.2 thereon.					
8	No1 appears on 1896 Choctaw roll Sans Bois County No 2124 as Louvina Chubbs					
9	No2 appears on 1896 Choctaw roll Sans Bois County No 7708 as Susan Lucas.					
10						
11						
12						
13						
14						
15					Date of Appl for Enrollr	
16						
17					NOV	

Choctaw By Blood Enrollment Cards 1898-1914

RESIDENCE: Atoka	COUNTY.	Choctaw Nation	Choctaw Roll	CARD No.
POST OFFICE: Atoka, I.T.			(Not Including Freedmen)	FIELD No. **5607**

Dawes' Roll No.	NAME	Relationship to Person First Named	AGE	SEX	BLOOD	TRIBAL ENROLLMENT		
						Year	County	No.
13470	1 Jacob, Harriet	First Named	23	F	Full	1896	Blue	1700
15508	2 " Johnson	Hus	28	M	Full	1893	Atoka	639
	3							
	4							
	5							
	6							
	7	ENROLLMENT						
	8	OF NOS. 1 HEREON						
	9	APPROVED BY THE SECRETARY OF INTERIOR Mar. 19, 1903						
	10							
	11							
	12	ENROLLMENT						
	13	OF NOS. 2 HEREON APPROVED BY THE SECRETARY						
	14	OF INTERIOR May 9, 1904						
	15							
	16							
	17							

TRIBAL ENROLLMENT OF PARENTS

	Name of Father	Year	County	Name of Mother	Year	County
1	Blinchee	Dead		Kasey Homer		
2	Caleb Jacob	"		Sealy Jacob	Dead	
3						
4						
5						
6	No 1 on Choctaw roll Blue County No 1700 a Harriet Bleache					
7						
8						
9	Is not No 1 wife of Johnson Jacob on Choctaw card D#826					
10	No 2 transferred from Choctaw Card D/826 April 13, 1904;					
11	See decision of March 15, 1904.					
12						
13						
14						
15						
16						
17			Date of Application for Enrollment.		Nov. 19, 1902	

Choctaw By Blood Enrollment Cards 1898-1914

RESIDENCE:	COUNTY.		Choctaw Roll	CARD No.
POST OFFICE: Legal I.T.	**Choctaw Nation**		*(Not Including Freedmen)*	FIELD No. **5608**

Dawes' Roll No.	NAME	Relationship to Person First Named	AGE	SEX	BLOOD	TRIBAL ENROLLMENT		
						Year	County	No.
13473	1 Bohannan, Lucy	First Named	70	F	Full	1896	Sans Bois	651
	2							
	3							
	4							
	5							
	6							
	7							
	8							
	9							
	10							
	11	ENROLLMENT OF NOS. 1 HEREON APPROVED BY THE SECRETARY OF INTERIOR Mar. 19, 1903						
	12							
	13							
	14							
	15							
	16							
	17							

TRIBAL ENROLLMENT OF PARENTS

	Name of Father	Year	County	Name of Mother	Year	County
1	Charles King	Dead		Wisey King	Dead	
2						
3						
4						
5						
6	No1 on Choctaw roll 1896 Sans Bois Co as Lucy Bohanan					
7						
8						
9						
10						
11						
12						
13						
14						
15						
16						Date of Application for Enrollment.
17						Nov 18 1902

P.O. Stratford Okla 4/15/09
RESIDENCE: Chickasaw Nation COUNTY.
POST OFFICE: Mᶜ Gee, I.T.

Choctaw Nation

Choctaw Roll
(Not Including Freedmen)

CARD No.
FIELD NO. **5609**

Dawes' Roll No.	NAME	Relationship to Person First Named	AGE	SEX	BLOOD	TRIBAL ENROLLMENT		
						Year	County	No.
14149	1 Hyden, Whit W	First Named	57	M	1/8	1896	Chickasaw Dist	6145
14150	2 " Leonard	son	23	M	1/16	1896	" "	6147
14151	3 Mitchell, Ida	Dau	21	F	1/16	1896	" "	6148
14152	4 Hyden, Whit	son	19	M	1/16	1896	" "	6149
14153	5 " Ella	Dau	17	F	1/16	1896	" "	6150
14154	6 " Cleveland	son	15	M	1/16	1896	" "	6151
14155	7 " Benjamin	son	13	M	1/16	1896	" "	6152
14156	8 " Ruth	Dau	10	F	1/16	1896	" "	6153
IW 1609	9 " Martha	wife	51	F	IW	1896	" "	14665

Enrollment of No9 cancelled by order of Department of March 4, 1907
No.9 restored to roll by Departmental authority of August 9, 1909. (File 5-5)

12 ENROLLMENT
13 OF NOS. 1 2 3 4 5 6 7 & 8 HEREON APPROVED BY THE SECRETARY
14 OF INTERIOR Mar 19, 1903

15 No.9 Granted October 1, 1906
Oct. 20, 1906 Record forwarded Department
16 Nov. 17, 1906 Affirmed by Dept.
17 Nov. 30, 1906 Partied herein notified

TRIBAL ENROLLMENT OF PARENTS

Name of Father	Year	County	Name of Mother	Year	County
1 Sam Hyden	Dead	Choctaw Roll	Nancy Hyden		Non Citizen
2 No.1			Martha Hyden		
3 No.1			" "		
4 No.1		ENROLLMENT	" "		
5 No.1		OF NOS. 9 HEREON APPROVED BY THE SECRETARY	" "		
6 No.1		OF INTERIOR Feb. 12, 1907	" "		
7 No.1			" "		
8 No.1			" "		
9		dead	non citizen		dead	non citizen

10 Nos 1-8 inclusive on C C. R #2 Page 258
11 No2 on 1896 Choctaw roll as Lorenda Hyden
No1 is husband of Martha Hyden on Choctaw card #5182
12 No3 is now wife of W.B. Mitchell a non citizen; evidence of marriage filed Nov. 24, 1902
13 Nos 1 to 8 inclusive transferred from Choctaw Card #D16 Nov. 29, 1902   Sept. 13/98
14 Nos 1-8 inclusive admitted by act of Choctaw Council of Oct 31, 1895   Date of Application for Enrollment.
For child of No4 see NB (Apr 26, 1906) Card No 169
15 No 9 transferred from Choctaw card #5182 Oct. 15, 1906; see decision of Oct 1/06   Date of Transfer
16   to this card
17   Nov 29-1902

209

Choctaw By Blood Enrollment Cards 1898-1914

RESIDENCE:	COUNTY.				Choctaw Roll	CARD NO.
POST OFFICE: Eagletown, I.T.	**Choctaw Nation**				(Not Including Freedmen)	FIELD NO. **5610**

Dawes' Roll No.	NAME	Relationship to Person First Named	AGE	SEX	BLOOD	TRIBAL ENROLLMENT		
						Year	County	No.
13477	1 Tonihka, Waston[sic]		16	M	Full	1896	Eagle	12213
	2							
	3							
	4							
	5							
	6							
	7							
	8							
	9							
	10							
	11	ENROLLMENT						
	12	OF NOS. 1 HEREON APPROVED BY THE SECRETARY						
	13	OF INTERIOR Mar 9, 1903						
	14							
	15							
	16							
	17							

TRIBAL ENROLLMENT OF PARENTS

Name of Father	Year	County	Name of Mother	Year	County
1 Solomon Tonihka	Dead		Susan Tonihka		Eagle
2					
3					
4					
5					
6 No1 probable duplicate of Sylvester Tonihka A-2409					
7					
8					
9					
10					
11					
12					
13					
14					
15					
16				Date of Application for Enrollment.	Nov. 27, 1902	
17					

Choctaw By Blood Enrollment Cards 1898-1914

RESIDENCE: Jackson COUNTY.
POST OFFICE: Matoy, I.T.

Choctaw Nation

Choctaw Roll
(Not Including Freedmen)

CA.
FIELD NO. **5611**

Dawes' Roll No.	NAME	Relationship to Person First Named	AGE	SEX	BLOOD	TRIBAL ENROLLMENT		
						Year	County	No.
13478	1 Jones, Willis	First Named	28	M	Full	1896	Jackson	7117
	2							
	3							
	4							
	5							
	6							
	7							
	8							
	9							
	10							
	11	ENROLLMENT OF NOS. 1 HEREON APPROVED BY THE SECRETARY OF INTERIOR MAR 19 1903						
	12							
	13							
	14							
	15							
	16							
	17							

TRIBAL ENROLLMENT OF PARENTS

	Name of Father	Year	County	Name of Mother	Year	
1	Thomas Jones	Dead		Seana Jones	Dead	
2						
3						
4						
5						
6	No1 is husband of Phoebe Le Flore on Choctaw card #3676					
7						
8						
9						
10						
11						
12						
13						
14						
15						
16						
17				Date of Application for Enrollment.	Nov. 20, 1902	

Choctaw By Blood Enrollment Cards 1898-1914

RESIDENCE: Nashoba   COUNTY. **Choctaw Nation**   **Choctaw Roll**   CARD NO.
POST OFFICE: Alikchi I.T.   (Not Including Freedmen)   FIELD NO. **5612**

Dawes' Roll No.	NAME	Relationship to Person First Named	AGE	SEX	BLOOD	TRIBAL ENROLLMENT Year	County	No.
13428	1 Miashintubi, Silvina	First Named	11	F	1/2	1896	Nashoba	8616
13429	2 " Martha	Sister	9	F	1/2	1896	"	8617
IW 1504	3 " Mary	Mother	59	F	IW	1896	"	14821
	4							
	5							
	6							
	7							
	8	ENROLLMENT OF NOS. 1-2 HEREON						
	9	APPROVED BY THE SECRETARY						
	10	OF INTERIOR Mar. 19, 1903						
	11							
	12	ENROLLMENT OF NOS. 3 HEREON						
	13	APPROVED BY THE SECRETARY						
	14	OF INTERIOR Nov. 27, 1905						
	15							
	16							
	17							

TRIBAL ENROLLMENT OF PARENTS

	Name of Father	Year	County	Name of Mother	Year	County
1	Barnes Miashintubi	Dead	Wade	Mary Miashintubi		Non citizen
2	" "		"	" "		
3						
4						

5   No.3 placed on this card Jany 6, 1905 in accordance with decision of Commission of that
6   date holding application was made within time prescribed by Act of Congress of July 1, 1902
7   No1 on 1893 Pay Roll Wade County No 390
   No2 " " " " " " 391
8
9   No1 on 1896 roll Nashoba County No 8616 as Fannie Miashintubbi[sic]
   No2 " " " " " 8617 " Martha "
10   For child of No1 see NB (Apr 26-06) Card #706 - No1 died Apr 10' 1906 see proof in
11   Jacket NB #706
12   Notify Apple & Franklin of approval by   No. 3 Granted
13   Dept of No3 hereon   Oct. 2-1905
14   2/9/16 This notation in error,
15   Dec. 17, 02 is not date of Apple
16   for enrollment. see enrollment Record   Date of Application
   WHA   for Enrollment.
17   December 17, 1902

Choctaw By Blood Enrollment Cards 1898-1914

RESIDENCE: Cherokee COUNTY. **Choctaw Nation** **Choctaw Roll** CARD NO.
POST OFFICE: Sallisaw, I.T. (Not Including Freedmen) FIELD NO. **5613**

Dawes' Roll No.	NAME	Relationship to Person First Named	AGE	SEX	BLOOD	TRIBAL ENROLLMENT Year	County	No.
14464	1 Agent, Annie G	First Named	34	F	3/16			
14465	2 " Ruby G	Dau	11	F	3/32			
14466	3 " Charles C	Son	9	M	3/32			
	4							
	5							
	6							
	7	ENROLLMENT						
	8	OF NOS. 1 2 and 3 HEREON APPROVED BY THE SECRETARY						
	9	OF INTERIOR APR 11 1903						
	10							
	11							
	12							
	13							
	14							
	15							
	16							
	17							

TRIBAL ENROLLMENT OF PARENTS

Name of Father	Year	County	Name of Mother	Year	County
1 Chas. A. Fargo		Cherokee	Narcissa Fargo	Dead	Choctaw
2 Henry C. Agent		noncitizen	No.1		
3 " " "		" "	No.1		
4					
5					
6 No1 admitted by Dawes Commission in Choctaw case #489 as Annie Agent					
7 No2 " " "	" " "	" " " " Ruby G. "			
8 No3 " " "	" " "	" " " " Charlie C "			
9 For child of No1 see NB (Mar 3 '05) #437.					
10					
11					
12					
13					
14					
15					
16					
17				December 17, 1902		

213

Choctaw By Blood Enrollment Cards 1898-1914

RESIDENCE: Cherokee COUNTY. **Choctaw Nation** **Choctaw Roll** CARD No.
POST OFFICE: Muldrow, I.T. *(Not Including Freedmen)* FIELD No. **5614**

Dawes' Roll No.	NAME	Relationship to Person First Named	AGE	SEX	BLOOD	TRIBAL ENROLLMENT		
						Year	County	No.
14467	1 Goodman, Ida	First Named	32	F	3/16			
14468	2 " Clyde	Son	11	M	3/32			
14469	3 " Willis O	Son	7	M	3/32			
14470	4 " Ruth	Dau	2	F	3/32			
	5							
	6							
	7							
	8							
	9							
	10							
	11	ENROLLMENT						
	12	OF NOS. 1 2 3 and 4 HEREON APPROVED BY THE SECRETARY						
	13	OF INTERIOR APR 11 1903						
	14							
	15							
	16							
	17							

TRIBAL ENROLLMENT OF PARENTS

	Name of Father	Year	County	Name of Mother	Year	County
1	Chas A. Fargo		Cherokee	Narcissa Fargo	dead	Choctaw
2	Joe W. Goodman		noncitizen	No1		
3	" " "		" "	No1		
4	" " "		" "	No1		
5						
6	Nos 1,2 and 3 admitted by Dawes Commission in 1896, Choctaw case #489, Ann Agent et al					
7	vs Choctaw Nation, No appeal					
8	For child of No.1 see NB (March 3, 1905) #918					
9						
10	9/11/1916- Nos. 1 to 4 inclusive transferred from Choctaw Census Card No D-572					
11						WHA
12						
13						
14						
15						
16			Nov. 4, 1901			
17			Date of Application for Enrollment.			December 17, 1902

214

Choctaw By Blood Enrollment Cards 1898-1914

RESIDENCE: Cherokee   COUNTY. **Choctaw Nation**   **Choctaw Roll**   CARD NO.
POST OFFICE: Muldrow, I.T.   *(Not Including Freedmen)*   FIELD NO. **5615**

Dawes' Roll No.	NAME	Relationship to Person First Named	AGE	SEX	BLOOD	TRIBAL ENROLLMENT		
						Year	County	No.
14386	1 Fargo, Emily	First Named	24	F	1/4			
	2							
	3							
	4							
	5	ENROLLMENT						
	6	OF NOS. 1 HEREON APPROVED BY THE SECRETARY						
	7	OF INTERIOR APR 11 1903						
	8							
	9							
	10							
	11							
	12							
	13							
	14							
	15							
	16							
	17							

TRIBAL ENROLLMENT OF PARENTS

	Name of Father	Year	County	Name of Mother	Year	County
1	Charlie Fargo		Cherokee	Narcissa Taylor	dead	Choctaw
2						
3						
4						
5						
6	No1 admitted to Choctaw citizenship by Dawes Commission in 1896.					
7	Choctaw case #489 Annie Agent, et al No appeal.					
8	For child of No.1 see NB (Apr 26 '06) Card No. 262					
9	" " " " " " (Mar 3 '05) " " 417					
10						
11						
12						
13						
14						
15					Date of Application for Enrollment.	
16						
17	P.O. Sallisaw IT 43/25/05				Date of Application for Enrollment. December 17, 1902	

Choctaw By Blood Enrollment Cards 1898-1914

RESIDENCE: Sans Bois   COUNTY. **Choctaw Nation**   **Choctaw Roll** *(Not Including Freedmen)*   CARD No.
POST OFFICE: Ironbridge   FIELD No. **5616**

Dawes' Roll No.	NAME	Relationship to Person First Named	AGE	SEX	BLOOD	TRIBAL ENROLLMENT Year	County	No.
15993	1 Stallaby, Thomas	First Named	27	M	Full	1893	Skullyville	Page 56 540
	2							
	3							
	4							
	5							
	6	ENROLLMENT						
	7	OF NOS. 1 HEREON						
	8	APPROVED BY THE SECRETARY OF INTERIOR June 16 1906						
	9							
	10							
	11							
	12							
	13	Atty						
	14	Notify T Mitchell Mc Curtain						
	15	I.T. of decision 5/11/05						
	16							
	17							

TRIBAL ENROLLMENT OF PARENTS

	Name of Father	Year	County	Name of Mother	Year	County
1	Anderson Stallaby		Miss. Choc.	Eliza Stallaby	Dead	
2						
3						
4						
5						
6						
7						

8 For child of No1 see NB (March 3, 1905) #1448
9 No1 on 1893 Leased Dist payroll Skullyville Co page 56 No 540 as Thos. Starlobley
10 First made application for enrollment June 21, 1899 and was placed on Choctaw Card #D262
July 23-1902 Choctaw Card #D262 cancelled and name of applicant transferred to M.C.R. Card
11 #563 to be considered as Miss Choc Case July 23 M.C.R. Card cancelled and No1 transferred to
12 Fullblood Miss Choc Card #R6100
January 2, 1903 Miss Choc Card #R6100 cancelled and record transferred to
13 Choctaw #5616
14 See Choc card #D262 M.C.R. card #563 M.C. Card#R6100.
15 See testimony of Dec. 16, 1902.

Date of Application for Enrollment.
17 Granted Oct 27' 1905   6/21/99   Date of Application for Enrollment.   Dec. 16, 1902

Choctaw By Blood Enrollment Cards 1898-1914

RESIDENCE:	Boktuklo	COUNTY.						CARD NO.	
POST OFFICE:	Lukfata Ind. Ter.	**Choctaw Nation**				Choctaw Roll (Not Including Freedmen)		FIELD NO. **5617**	

Dawes' Roll No.	NAME	Relationship to Person	AGE	SEX	BLOOD	TRIBAL ENROLLMENT		
						Year	County	No.
13478	1 Hicks, Simeon	First Named	12	M	Full	1896	Nashoba	5528
	2							
	3							
	4							
	5							
	6							
	7							
	8							
	9							
	10							
	11	ENROLLMENT						
	12	OF NOS. 1 HEREON APPROVED BY THE SECRETARY						
	13	OF INTERIOR MAR 19 1903						
	14							
	15							
	16							
	17							

TRIBAL ENROLLMENT OF PARENTS

	Name of Father	Year	County	Name of Mother	Year	County
1	Cephus Hicks	1896	Nashoba	Elsie Hicks	Dead	Choctaw
2						
3						
4						
5						
6	No1 also on 1896 Choctaw census roll page 135 #5528 as Simeon Hayes					
7	No1 lives near Lukfata I.T. with his grandfather Madison E. Jefferson					
8						
9						
10						
11						
12						
13						
14						
15					Date of Application for Enrollment.	
16						
17					NOV 28 1902	

Choctaw By Blood Enrollment Cards 1898-1914

RESIDENCE: Wade COUNTY.
POST OFFICE: Tushkahomma Ind Ter

Choctaw Nation

Choctaw Roll
(Not Including Freedmen)

CARD NO.
FIELD NO. **5618**

Dawes' Roll No.	NAME	Relationship to Person First Named	AGE	SEX	BLOOD	TRIBAL ENROLLMENT Year	County	No.
13505	1 Choate, Roberson	First Named	31	M	Full	1896	Wade	11334
	2							
	3							
	4							
	5							
	6							
	7							
	8							
	9							
	10							
	11	ENROLLMENT						
	12	OF NOS. 1 HEREON APPROVED BY THE SECRETARY						
	13	OF INTERIOR Mar 19, 1903						
	14							
	15							
	16							
	17							

TRIBAL ENROLLMENT OF PARENTS

	Name of Father	Year	County	Name of Mother	Year	County
1	Lyman Choate	1896	Wade	Betsy Choate	Dead	Choctaw
2						
3						
4						
5						
6	No1 also on 1893 Leased Dist pay roll Wade Co pager 19 #184 as Robinson Choate					
7	No1 also on 1896 Choctaw census roll page 282 #11334 as Robertson Choate					
8	No1 is husband of Elizabeth Battiest Choctaw card #1965					
9						
10						
11						
12						
13						
14						
15						
16						
17					Date of Application for Enrollment.	Dec. 10, 1902

218

Choctaw By Blood Enrollment Cards 1898-1914

RESIDENCE: Choctaw Nation	COUNTY.	**Choctaw Nation**				**Choctaw Roll** (Not Including Freedmen)	CARD NO.	
POST OFFICE: Goodland, I.T.							FIELD NO. **5619**	

Dawes' Roll No.	NAME	Relationship to Person First Named	AGE	SEX	BLOOD	TRIBAL ENROLLMENT		
						Year	County	No.
14835 ₁	Lawechubbe, Rhoda	Named	49	F	Full	1896	Kiamitia Co	8101
14836 ₂	" Lewes	Son	16	M	"	1896	" "	8102
₃								
₄								
₅								
₆								
₇								
₈								
₉								
₁₀								
₁₁	ENROLLMENT							
₁₂	OF NOS. 1 and 2 HEREON APPROVED BY THE SECRETARY							
₁₃	OF INTERIOR May 20, 1903							
₁₄								
₁₅								
₁₆								
₁₇								

TRIBAL ENROLLMENT OF PARENTS

	Name of Father	Year	County	Name of Mother	Year	County
₁	Garland		Unknown	Liza Garland	Dead	Chickasaw
₂	Lawechubbe, W^m	1896	Kiamitia	No.1		
₃						
₄						
₅	William Lawechubbi, husband of No.1 and father of No.2					
₆	Enrolled on Choctaw card #5322					
₇	Nos.1&2 Transferred from Chickasaw Card #1571 to this card Jan. 16' 1903					
₈	No.2 is duplicate of Lewis Wachubbe, No2 on Choctaw card #5599. Enrollment cancelled					
₉	under Departmental authority of September 11, 1906 I.T.D. #15622-1906/DC 40078-1906					
₁₀	No.1 died May 31, 1900. Enrollment cancelled by Department Dec. 12, 1906.					
₁₁						
₁₂						
₁₃						
₁₄						
₁₅						
₁₆					Date of Application for Enrollment.	
₁₇						March 1" 1900

Choctaw By Blood Enrollment Cards 1898-1914

RESIDENCE: Cedar
POST OFFICE: Antlers, I.T.
COUNTY. **Choctaw Nation**
Choctaw Roll (Not Including Freedmen)
CARD No.
FIELD No. **5620**

Dawes' Roll No.	NAME	Relationship to Person First Named	AGE	SEX	BLOOD	TRIBAL ENROLLMENT Year	County	No.
14837	1 Tupper, Bartemus		21	M	1/2	1893	Cedar	137
	2							
	3							
	4							
	5							
	6							
	7							
	8							
	9							
	10							
	11	ENROLLMENT						
	12	OF NOS. 1 HEREON APPROVED BY THE SECRETARY						
	13	OF INTERIOR MAY 20 1903						
	14							
	15							
	16							
	17							

TRIBAL ENROLLMENT OF PARENTS

	Name of Father	Year	County	Name of Mother	Year	County
1	Thomas Tupper		Choc. Roll	Elsie Tupper	Dead	Chick Roll
2						
3						
4						
5						
6	No1 is on 1893 Leased District Payment Roll. Cedar Co Page 12 No 137					
7	as Bartimus[sic] Topa					
8	No1 originally on Chickasaw card #D235. transferred to this card January 13, 1903					
9						
10						
11						
12						
13						
14						
15				Date of Application for Enrollment. 5/23/99		
16						
17					JAN 13 1903	

220

Choctaw By Blood Enrollment Cards 1898-1914

RESIDENCE: Cedar COUNTY.	POST OFFICE: Kosoma, Ind. Ter.	**Choctaw Nation** *(Not Including Freedmen)*	**Choctaw Roll**	CARD NO. FIELD NO. **5621**

Dawes' Roll No.	NAME	Relationship to Person First Named	AGE	SEX	BLOOD	TRIBAL ENROLLMENT Year	County	No.
13480	1 Pisomotubby, Frances	First Named	57	F	Full	1893	Cedar	35/377
	2							
	3							
	4							
	5							
	6							
	7							
	8							
	9							
	10							
	11	ENROLLMENT						
	12	OF NOS. 1 HEREON APPROVED BY THE SECRETARY						
	13	OF INTERIOR MAR 19 1903						
	14							
	15							
	16							
	17							

TRIBAL ENROLLMENT OF PARENTS

	Name of Father	Year	County	Name of Mother	Year	County
1	Mishia	dead		Meely Ann	dead	
2						
3						
4						
5						
6	No1 Claims to have appeared before the Commission at Antlers Ind. Ter. in					
7	1890, but there is no record that application was made for her enrollment.					
8	It is said No1 has also been known as Frances Charles. See testimony of Dec. 5, 1902.					
9						
10						
11						
12						
13						
14						
15						
16						
17				Date of Application for Enrollment.	DEC 5	

221

Choctaw By Blood Enrollment Cards 1898-1914

RESIDENCE: Jacks Forks[sic] COUNTY. **Choctaw Nation**   **Choctaw Roll** CARD NO.
POST OFFICE: Dexter Ind. Ter.   (Not Including Freedmen) FIELD NO. **5622**

Dawes' Roll No.	NAME	Relationship to Person First Named	AGE	SEX	BLOOD	TRIBAL ENROLLMENT		
						Year	County	No.
14838	1 Bohanan, Emiziah		19	M	Full	1893	Wade	14 #140
	2							
	3							
	4							
	5							
	6							
	7							
	8							
	9							
	10							
	11	ENROLLMENT						
	12	OF NOS. 1 HEREON APPROVED BY THE SECRETARY						
	13	OF INTERIOR MAY 20 1903						
	14							
	15							
	16							
	17							

TRIBAL ENROLLMENT OF PARENTS

	Name of Father	Year	County	Name of Mother	Year	County
1	Amos Bohanan	dead	Wade	Lista Bohanan	dead	Nashoba
2						
3						
4						
5						
6	Brother of Emily Hardy Choctaw card #1936 also brother of					
7	Catherine Bohanan Choctaw card #1940 and of Emma Bohanan Choctaw card #5623					
8	For child of No1 see NB (March 3, 1905) #981.					
9						
10						
11						
12						
13						
14						
15						
16						
17	Talihina				DEC 12 1902	

Choctaw By Blood Enrollment Cards 1898-1914

RESIDENCE: Jacksforks[sic] COUNTY. **Choctaw Nation** **Choctaw Roll** CARD NO.
POST OFFICE: Tushkahomma Ind. Ter. (Not Including Freedmen) FIELD NO. **5623**

Dawes' Roll No.	NAME	Relationship to Person First Named	AGE	SEX	BLOOD	TRIBAL ENROLLMENT Year	County	No.
	Bohanan, Emma		14	F	Full	1893	Wade	14 #142
3								
4	ENROLLMENT OF NOS. HEREON APPROVED BY THE SECRETARY OF INTERIOR MAY 20 1903							
5								
6								
7								
8								
9								
10								
11								
12								
13								
14								
15								
16								
17								

TRIBAL ENROLLMENT OF PARENTS

	Name of Father	Year	County	Name of Mother	Year	County
1	Amos Bohanan	dead	Wade	Lista Bohanan	dead	Nashoba
2						
3						
4						
5						
6	Sister of Emiziah Bohanan on Choctaw card #5622, also sister of					
7	Emily Hardy on Choctaw card #1936, and of Catherine Bohanan on Choctaw card #1940.					
8	Lives with Silas McKinney Tushkahomma, I.T.					
9						
10						
11						
12						
13						
14						
15						
16						
17						DEC 12 1902

Choctaw By Blood Enrollment Cards 1898-1914

Choctaw Nation

Choctaw Roll ████
(Not Including Freedmen)

Dawes' Roll No.	NAME	Relationship to Person First Named	AGE	SEX	BLOOD	TRIBAL ENROLLMENT Year	TRIBAL ENROLLMENT County	TRIBAL ENROLLMENT No.
14840	1 Noel, Natsy	First Named	23	F	Full	1896	Tobucksy	9607
15062	2 " Ellen	Dau	3 1/2	F	"			
	3							
	4							
	5							
	6							
	7	ENROLLMENT						
	8	OF NOS. 1 HEREON APPROVED BY THE SECRETARY						
	9	OF INTERIOR MAY 20 1903						
	10							
	11							
	12	ENROLLMENT						
	13	OF NOS. 2 HEREON APPROVED BY THE SECRETARY						
	14	OF INTERIOR FEB 16 1904						
	15							
	16							
	17							

TRIBAL ENROLLMEN████████NTS

Name of Father	Year	County		of Mother	Year	County
1 Forbis Noel	dead		████	Noel	dead	
2 Gilbert Pickens				No1		
3						
4						
5						
6	No1 also on 1893 payroll Tobucksy Co page 54 #486 as Nancy Noel					
7	No2 born June 28, 1899: Proof of birth filed Oct. 24, 1903.					
8	For child of No.1 see NB (March 3, 1905) #1314					
9						
10						
11						
12						
13						
14						
15						
16					Date of Application for Enrollment.	
17					DEC 22 1902	

Choctaw By Blood Enrollment Cards 1898-1914

RESIDENCE: Tobucksy COUNTY.
POST OFFICE: Blanco, Ind. Ter.

Choctaw Nation (Not Including Freedmen)

Choctaw Roll

CARD N
FIELD N

Dawes' Roll No.	NAME	Relationship to Person First Named	AGE	SEX	BLOOD	TRIBAL ENROLLMENT		
						Year	County	No.
14841	1 Noel, Georgia Ann		14	F	Full	1893	Gaines	17/158
	2							
	3							
	4							
	5							
	6							
	7							
	8							
	9							
	10							
	11	ENROLLMENT						
	12	OF NOS. 1 HEREON APPROVED BY THE SECRETARY						
	13	OF INTERIOR MAY 20 1903						
	14							
	15							
	16							
	17							

TRIBAL ENROLLMENT OF PARENTS

	Name of Father	Year	County	Name of Mother		
1	Johnson Noel	dead	Choctaw	Lucy Frazier		
2						
3						
4						
5						
6	No 1 on 1893 Tobucksy County pay roll as Jenny Noel page 17 #158					
7	No 1 is daughter of Lucy Frazier Choctaw card #4910.					
8	See testimony of Wilson Frazier of Dec. 24. 1902					
	For child of No.1 see NB (March 3, 1905) #1292					
9						
10						
11						
12						
13						
14						
15						
16						
17					DEC 24 1902	

Choctaw By Blood Enrollment Cards 1898-1914

RESIDENCE: Choctaw Nation COUNTY. **Choctaw Nation** Choctaw Roll CARD NO.
POST OFFICE: Hartshorn, Ind. Ter. *(Not Including Freedmen)* FIELD NO. **5626**

Dawes' Roll No.	NAME	Relationship to Person First Named	AGE	SEX	BLOOD	TRIBAL ENROLLMENT		
						Year	County	No.
14842	1 Anderson, Tom	First Named	25	M	3/4	1896	Jacks Fork	497
IW 1536	2 " Alice	Wife	18	F	I.W			
14843	3 " Lena (DIED PRIOR TO SEPTEMBER 25, 1902)	Dau	3mo	"	3/8			
14844	4 " Mary Jane	"	3mo	"	3/8			
14845	5 " Graham	Son	7wks	M	3/8			
	6							
	7							
	8 ENROLLMENT OF NOS. 1,3,4 and 5 HEREON							
	9 APPROVED BY THE SECRETARY							
	10 OF INTERIOR May 20 1903							
	11							
	12 ENROLLMENT OF NOS 2 HEREON							
	13 APPROVED BY THE SECRETARY OF INTERIOR Mar 14, 1906							
	14							
	15 No.2 Granted							
	16 Nov 11-1905							
	17							

TRIBAL ENROLLMENT OF PARENTS

	Name of Father	Year	County	Name of Mother	Year	County
1	Wm Anderson	1897	Chick residing in Choctaw N. 3rd Dist	Lizzie Anderson	Dead	Chickasaw Roll
2	Wm Ridge	Dead	non citizen	Mary Ridge		Non-Citizen
3	No.1			No.2		
4	No.1			No.2		
5	No.1			No.2		

6 No1 On Choctaw Census record No2 Jack's Fork Co Page 20
7 No1 On 1896 Choctaw Roll as Thomas Anderson
8 No2 Marriage certificate to be supplied. Received Nov. 1/98.
No4 Enrolled June 23rd 1900
9 No5 Born Aug. 6, 1902: Enrolled Sept 30, 1902
10 No1,2,3,4 and 5 transferred from Chickasaw Card #1146 to this card Jan. 16-1903
No.3 died Nov -, 1898: Enrollment cancelled by Department July 8, 1904
11 For child of Nos 1&2 see NB (Apr 26 06) Card #703
12
13
14
15
16   Date of Application #1 to 3 inc
17 Buck I.T. 9/30/02   for Enrollment Feb 11/98

226

Choctaw By Blood Enrollment Cards 1898-1914

RESIDENCE:		COUNTY.	**Choctaw Nation**			**Choctaw Roll**	CARD NO.	
POST OFFICE: Hartshorne, I.T.						*(Not Including Freedmen)*	FIELD NO. **5627**	

Dawes' Roll No.	NAME	Relationship to Person First Named	AGE	SEX	BLOOD	TRIBAL ENROLLMENT		
						Year	County	No.
13456	1 Watkins, Sallie		38	F	Full	1896	Tobucksy	42
	2							
	3							
	4							
	5							
	6							
	7							
	8							
	9							
	10							
	11	ENROLLMENT OF NOS. HEREON APPROVED BY THE SECRETARY OF INTERIOR MAR 19 1903						
	12							
	13							
	14							
	15							
	16							
	17							

TRIBAL ENROLLMENT OF PARENTS

	Name of Father	Year	County	Name of Mother	Year	
1	Mastatubbee	Dd	Tobucksy	Lucy	Dd	
2						
3						
4						
5						
6	No1 On 1896 Choctaw Roll Page 98 No 4052 Tobucksy Co as Sallie Frazier					
7	No1 Transferred from Chickasaw Card #1550 to this card January 16, 1903.					
8						
9						
10						
11						
12						
13						
14						
15						
16					Date of Application for Enrollment.	
17					9/11/99	

Choctaw By Blood Enrollment Cards 1898-1914

RESIDENCE: Gaines COUNTY. **Choctaw Nation** CARD i

POST OFFICE: Bower *(Non-residing Precinct)* FIELD NO. **5628**

Dawes' Roll No.	NAME	Relationship to Person First Named	AGE	SEX	BLOOD	TRIBAL ENROLLMENT		
						Year	County	No.
13467	1 Jennings, Nathaniel F	First Named	17	M	Full	1896	Gaines	6620
IW 1482	2 " Crotia A	Wife	21	F	I.W.			
	3							
	4							
	5							
	6							
	7	ENROLLMENT						
	8	OF NOS. I HEREON APPROVED BY THE SECRETARY						
	9	OF INTERIOR MAR 19 1903						
	10							
	11							
	12	ENROLLMENT						
	13	OF NOS. Two HEREON APPROVED BY THE SECRETARY						
	14	OF INTERIOR AUG 22 1905						
	15							
	16							
	17							

TRIBAL ENROLLMENT OF PARENTS

	Name of Father	Year	County	Name of Mother	Year	County
1	Richard P Jenning[sic]		Gaines	Suckey Jennings	Dead	Gaines
2	W.P. Trower		non citizen	Nancy C. Trower		non citizen
3						
4						

5 No1 On 1896 Choctaw Roll as Nathaniel F Jenning

6 No1 is now the husband of Crotia Jennings on Chickasaw Card #D382 Sept 24-1902

7 No1 Transferred from Chickasaw Card #1555 to this card Jan 16 1903

8 No2 originally listed for enrollment on Chickasaw card #D-372 Sept 24, 1902, transf. to this July 17, 1905. See decision of June 27, 1905

9 For children of Nos 1&2 see NB (March 3, 1905) #1049

10 Nos 1 and 2 were married September 23, 1902

11 Record as to enrollment of No.s forwarded Department March 14, 1906

12 Record returned. See opinion of Assistant Attorney General of March 15, 1906 in case of Omer [?] Nicholson.

13

14

15

16 P.O. Watonga Okla 2/10/10

17 P.O. [Illegible] IT 4/10/05

Choctaw By Blood Enrollment Cards 1898-1914

Tobucksy   COUNTY. **Choctaw Nation**   **Choctaw Roll**   CARD NO.
Savanna Ind Ter   *(Not Including Freedmen)*   FIELD NO. **5629**

ROLL NO.		NAME	Relationship to Person First Named	AGE	SEX	BLOOD	TRIBAL ENROLLMENT		
							Year	County	No.
15803	1	Cann, George		21	M	Full	1893	Tobucksy	97 / 809
	2								
	3								
	4								
	5								
	6								
	7								
	8								
	9								
	10								
	11	ENROLLMENT							
	12	OF NOS. 1 HEREON APPROVED BY THE SECRETARY							
	13	OF INTERIOR MAR 15 1905							
	14								
	15								
	16								
	17								

TRIBAL ENROLLMENT OF PARENTS

	Name of Father	Year	County	Name of Mother	Year	County
1	Sampson Payne	Dead		Wikey Wilson	1893	Tobucksy
2						
3						
4						
5	Enrolled on statement of Wilson S James made Dec. 24, 1902.					
6	No1 is also known by the surname of Cann also M° Cann					
7	It is not believed that any member of this family has been enrolled by the Commission. They are said to belong to					
8	the "Snakes"					
9	Correct name of No1 is George Cann. See					
10	testimony taken Jan 12, 1905. No.1 originally listed on this card as George Kaen, Dec. 24, 1902					
11	No.1 is half brother of Nos 1,2 and 3 on Choctaw card No. 5701					
12	For child of No.1 see NB (Mar; 3'05) card #357.					
13						
14						
15						
16						
17				Date of Application for Enrollment	DEC. 24 1902	

Choctaw By Blood Enrollment Cards 1898-1914

RESIDENCE: Jackson COUNTY.
POST OFFICE: Bennington I.T.

Choctaw Nation

Choctaw Roll *(Not Including Freedmen)*

CARD NO. FIELD NO. **5630**

Dawes' Roll No.	NAME	Relationship to Person First Named	AGE	SEX	BLOOD	TRIBAL ENROLLMENT Year	TRIBAL ENROLLMENT County	TRIBAL ENROLLMENT No.
14846	1 Murray, Belle	First Named	38	F	1/4	1896	Jackson	8742
14847	2 Coy, Milton	Son	19	M	1/8	1896	"	2796
14848	3 " Nora	Dau	17	F	1/8	1896	"	2797
14849	4 " Frank	Son	15	M	1/8	1896	"	2798
14850	5 " Oscar	Son	13	M	1/8	1896	"	2799
14851	6 Murray, Arthur	Son	8	M	1/8	1896	"	8743
14852	7 " Howard	Son	4	M	1/8			
14853	8 " Liddie	Dau	3	F	1/8			
14854	9 " Aldie L	Dau	6mo	F	1/8			
	10							
	11							
	12							
	13							
	14							
	15							
	16							
	17							

ENROLLMENT
OF NOS. 1.2.3.4.5.6.7.8 & 9 HEREON
APPROVED BY THE SECRETARY
OF INTERIOR MAY 20 1903

TRIBAL ENROLLMENT OF PARENTS

	Name of Father	Year	County	Name of Mother	Year	
1	John Ward	Dead	Choctaw Roll	Rebecca Ward	Dead	Non-
2	Allen Coy	"	Noncitizen	No.1		
3	" "	"	"	No.1		
4	" "	"	"	No.1		
5	" "	"	"	No.1		
6	Marion Murray	1896	"	No.1		
7	" "	1896	"	No.1		
8	" "		"	No.1		
9	" "		"	No.1		
10						
11						
12						
13						
14						
15						
16						
17						

D-16

Date of Application for Enrollment. 5/15/99

Date of Transfer to this Card.

Choctaw By Blood Enrollment Cards 1898-1914

RESIDENCE: Wade   COUNTY. **Choctaw Nation**   Choctaw Roll   CARD No.

POST OFFICE: Tuskahoma IT   (Not Including Freedmen)   FIELD No. **5631**

Dawes' Roll No.	NAME	Relationship to Person First Named	AGE	SEX	BLOOD	TRIBAL ENROLLMENT		
						Year	County	No.
13371	1 Spring, Ida		21	F	1/2	1896	Skullyville	694
13372	2 " Fatie	Son	3	M	5/8			
	3							
	4							
	5							
	6							
	7							
	8							
	9							
	10							
	11	ENROLLMENT OF NOS. HEREON						
	12	APPROVED BY THE SECRETARY OF INTERIOR MAR 19 1903						
	13							
	14							
	15							
	16							
	17							

TRIBAL ENROLLMENT OF PARENTS

	Name of Father	Year	County	Name of Mother	Year	County
1	John Bond	Dead	Wade	Creasy Bond	1896	Noncitizen
2	Solomon Spring		"	No.1		
3						
4						
5						
6	No.1 is now wife of Solomon Spring on Choctaw card #7898					
7						
8						
9						
10						
11						
12						
13						
14						
15						
16				5/22/99		
17				Date of Application for Enrollment.	DEC 24 1902	

Choctaw By Blood Enrollment Cards 1898-1914

RESIDENCE: Sugar Loaf COUNTY. **Choctaw Nation** **Choctaw Roll** CARD No.
POST OFFICE: Gilmore I.T. *(Not Including Freedmen)* FIELD No. **5632**

Dawes' Roll No.	NAME	Relationship to Person First Named	AGE	SEX	BLOOD	TRIBAL ENROLLMENT		
						Year	County	No.
14855	1 Durant, Walter N	First Named	19	M	1/2	1896	Sugar Loaf	3266
14856	2 " Rina J	Sister	18	F	1/2	1896	" "	3265
14857	3 " John K	Brother	15	M	1/2	1896	" "	3267
	4							
	5							
	6							
	7							
	8							
	9							
	10							
	11	ENROLLMENT OF NOS. 1 2 and 3 HEREON APPROVED BY THE SECRETARY OF INTERIOR May 20 1903						
	12							
	13							
	14							
	15							
	16							
	17							

TRIBAL ENROLLMENT OF PARENTS

	Name of Father	Year	County	Name of Mother	Year	County
1	John H Durant	Dead	Sugar Loaf	Sarah C. Griffiths		noncitizen
2	" "	"	" "	" "	1896	"
3	" "	"	" "	" "	1896	"
4						
5						
6	No2 on 1896 roll as Rena J Durant					
7	No3 on 1896 roll as Jno H. Durant					
8						
9	For child of No1 see N.B. (Apr 26-06) Card #497					
10	" " " No2 " " (Mar 3-05) " #1156					
11						
12	6/7/15 Nos 1,2 and 3 transferred from Choctaw card D-190					
13	6/7/1915 Ages hereon calculated to Sept 25, 1902					
14						
15						
16				6/5/99 Date of Application for Enrollment.		Date of Transfer to this Card.
17	P.O. Gilmore I.T. 7/25/04					Dec 24-1902

Choctaw By Blood Enrollment Cards 1898-1914

RESIDENCE: Nashoba
POST OFFICE: Smithville I.T.

COUNTY. **Choctaw Nation**

Choctaw Roll
(Not Including Freedmen)

CARD No.
FIELD No. **5633**

Dawes' Roll No.	NAME	Relationship to Person First Named	AGE	SEX	BLOOD	TRIBAL ENROLLMENT		
						Year	County	No.
13865	1 Watson, Thomas	First Named	21	M	1/4	1896	Nashoba	13391
	2							
	3							
	4							
	5							
	6							
	7							
	8							
	9							
	10							
	11	ENROLLMENT						
	12	OF NOS. 1 HEREON APPROVED BY THE SECRETARY						
	13	OF INTERIOR Mar 9 1903						
	14							
	15							
	16							
	17							

TRIBAL ENROLLMENT OF PARENTS

	Name of Father	Year	County	Name of Mother	Year	County
1	Joseph Watson	Dead	Nashoba	Rosanna Watson	Dead	Non citizen
2						
3						
4						
5						
6	No1 is husband of Podenie Watson on Choctaw card #2151					
7	For child of No1 see N.B. (Mar 3-1905) Card #59					
8						
9						
10						
11						
12						
13						
14						
15						
16						Date of Application for Enrollment.
17						Dec 24 1902

Choctaw By Blood Enrollment Cards 1898-1914

Dawes' Roll No.	NAME	Relationship to Person First Named	AGE	SEX	BLOOD	TRIBAL ENROLLMENT		
						Year	County	No.
14858	1 Collins, Joseph	First Named	21	M	1/4	1896	Kiamitia	2726
14859	2 " Charles	Bro	17	M	1/4	1896	"	2725
	3							
	4							
	5							
	6							
	7	ENROLLMENT OF NOS. 1 and 2 HEREON						
	8	APPROVED BY THE SECRETARY						
	9	OF INTERIOR MAY 20 1903						
	10							
	11							
	12							
	13							
	14							
	15							
	16							
	17							

TRIBAL ENROLLMENT OF PARENTS

	Name of Father	Year	County	Name of Mother	Year	County
1	Charley Collins	Dead	Kiamitia	Mary J Collins	Dead	Noncitizen
2	" "	"	"	" "	"	"
3						
4						
5						
6	No1 on 1896 roll as Josephus C Collins					
7	No1 is now husband of Mattie Oakes on Choctaw card #1460					
8	For child of No.1 see NB (March 3, 1905) #1157					
9						
10						
11						
12						
13						
14						
15			Date of Application for Enrollment.			
16			5/8/99		Date of Transfer to this Card.	
17					DEC 24 1902	

Choctaw By Blood Enrollment Cards 1898-1914

RESIDENCE: Nashoba
POST OFFICE: Alikchi I.T.

COUNTY. **Choctaw Nation**

Choctaw Roll
(Not Including Freedmen)

CARD No.
FIELD No. **5635**

Dawes' Roll No.	NAME	Relationship to Person First Named	AGE	SEX	BLOOD	TRIBAL ENROLLMENT		
						Year	County	No.
13452	1 Winship, Isaac	First Named	27	M	1/2	1896	Nashoba	13350
	2							
	3							
	4							
	5							
	6							
	7							
	8 ENROLLMENT							
	9 OF NOS. 1 HEREON APPROVED BY THE SECRETARY OF INTERIOR MAR 19 1903							
	11							
	12							
	13							
	14							
	15							
	16							
	17							

TRIBAL ENROLLMENT OF PARENTS

	Name of Father	Year	County	Name of Mother	Year	County
1	Tobias Winship	Dead	Nashoba	Mary Winship	1896	Noncitizen
2						
3						
4						
5						
6	No1 is now husband of Ennettie Noah on Choctaw card #681 Nov. 25, 1901					
7	For children of No.1 see NB (March 3, 1905) #925					
8						
9						
10						
11						
12						
13						
14						
15				Date of Application for Enrollment.	11/25/01	
16						
17				on this card	DEC 24 1902	

Choctaw By Blood Enrollment Cards 1898-1914

RESIDENCE: Atoka
POST OFFICE: Guertie, I.T.

COUNTY. **Choctaw Nation**

Choctaw Roll
(Not Including Freedmen)

CARD NO.
FIELD NO. **5636**

Dawes' Roll No.	NAME	Relationship to Person	AGE	SEX	BLOOD	TRIBAL ENROLLMENT		
						Year	County	No.
12161	1 Leader, J. M.	First Named	46	M	1/2	1896	Atoka	8295
	2							
	3							
	4							
	5							
	6							
	7							
	8							
	9							
	10							
	11	ENROLLMENT						
	12	OF NOS. 1 HEREON APPROVED BY THE SECRETARY						
	13	OF INTERIOR MAR 6 1903						
	14							
	15							
	16							
	17							

TRIBAL ENROLLMENT OF PARENTS

	Name of Father	Year	County	Name of Mother	Year	County
1	Ed Leader	1897	Chick residing in Choctaw N. 3rd Dist	Mary Leader		Cherokee roll
2						
3						
4						
5						
6	No.1 is husband of Isabinda Leader on Choctaw card #5379.					
7						
8						
9						
10						
11						
12						
13						
14						
15						Date of Transfer to this Card.
16						
17						DEC 24 1902

Choctaw By Blood Enrollment Cards 1898-1914

RESIDENCE: Towson COUNTY. **Choctaw Nation** **Choctaw Roll** *(Not Including Freedmen)*
POST OFFICE: Nelson(?) IT

Dawes' Roll No.	NAME	Relationship to Person First Named	AGE	SEX	BLOOD	TRIBAL ENROLLMENT		
						Year	County	No.
14860	1 Lemon, Ida	First Named	23	F	1/4	1896	Towson	4138
14861	2 Fowler, Emma	Dau	7	F	1/8	1896	"	4139
14862	3 " Charlie	Son	4	M	1/8			
	4							
	5							
	6							
	7							
	8							
	9							
	10							
	11	ENROLLMENT						
	12	OF NOS. 1,2 and 3 HEREON APPROVED BY THE SECRETARY						
	13	OF INTERIOR MAY 20 1903						
	14							
	15							
	16							
	17							

TRIBAL ENROLLMENT OF PARENTS

	Name of Father	Year	County	Name of Mother	Year	County
1	Nathan Stewart	Dead	Eagle	Jane Stewart	Dead	Noncitizen
2	George Fowler	1896	Noncitizen	No.1		
3	" "	1896	"	No.1		
4						
5						

6 No.1 is now wife of John Lemon on Choctaw card #474; evidence of marriage filed
7 December 11, 1902 (This notation is in error)★
8 Nos. 1-3 inclusive transferred from Choctaw card D #126. See decision of December 8, 1902.
★ See letter of Ida Lemon of July 26, 1906 stating that her husband is noncitizen
9 For child of No1 see NB (Apr 26-06) Care #912

		Date of Application for Enrollment. 4/24/99
17	[Illegible] I.T. 4/12/05	DEC 24 1902

237

Choctaw By Blood Enrollment Cards 1898-1914

RESIDENCE: Eagle COUNTY. **Choctaw Nation** Choctaw Roll NO.
POST OFFICE: Eagletown Ind. Ter *(Not Including Freedmen)* FIELD NO. **5638**

Dawes' Roll No.	NAME	Relationship to Person First Named	AGE	SEX	BLOOD	TRIBAL ENROLLMENT		
						Year	County	No.
14863	1 Ebahotubbi, Nancy	First Named	24	F	Full	1893	Wade	Page 71 #530
	2							
	3							
	4							
	5							
	6							
	7							
	8							
	9							
	10							
	11							
	12							
	13							
	14							
	15							
	16							
	17							

ENROLLMENT
OF NOS. 1 HEREON
APPROVED BY THE SECRETARY
OF INTERIOR MAY 20 1903

TRIBAL ENROLLMENT OF PARENTS

	Name of Father	Year	County	Name of Mother	Year	County
1	Davis Potts	1896	Wade	Liney Potts	Dead	Wade
2						
3						
4						
5						
6	Transferred from Choctaw card #D140, Jany 31, 1903					
7	No1 is wife of Davis Ebahotubbi Choctaw card #849					
8						
9						
10						
11						
12						
13						
14						
15					Date of Application for Enrollment.	5/1/99
16						
17						JAN 31 1903

Choctaw By Blood Enrollment Cards 1898-1914

RESIDENCE: Choctaw Nation ~~COUNTY.~~ **Choctaw Nation**   Choctaw Roll   CARD NO.
POST OFFICE: Stringtown, Ind. Ter   (Not Including Freedmen)   FIELD NO. **5639**

Dawes' Roll No.	NAME	Relationship to Person First Named	AGE	SEX	BLOOD	TRIBAL ENROLLMENT		
						Year	County	No.
14864	1 Tupper, Louvicey	First Named	24	F	1/2	1893	Cedar	136
14865	2 " Hobson	Son	4	M	1/4			
	3							
	4							
	5							
	6							
	7							
	8							
	9							
	10							
	11	ENROLLMENT						
	12	OF NOS. 1 and 2 HEREON APPROVED BY THE SECRETARY						
	13	OF INTERIOR MAY 20 1903						
	14							
	15							
	16							
	17							

TRIBAL ENROLLMENT OF PARENTS

	Name of Father	Year	County	Name of Mother	Year	County
1	Thomas Tupper		Choctaw	Leona Brown	Dead	Chickasaw
2	Dick Locke			No.1		
3						
4						
5						
6	Nos 1 & 2 Originally enrolled on Chickasaw #D 387. Transferred to this card Feb. 16, 1903					
7						
8						
9						
10						
11						
12						
13						
14						
15				Date of Application for Enrollment.	8/30/99	
16						
17				on this card	Nov 21, 1902	

239

Choctaw By Blood Enrollment Cards 1898-1914

Dawes' Roll No.	NAME	Relationship to Person First Named	AGE	SEX	BLOOD	TRIBAL ENROLLMENT		
						Year	County	No.
14866	1 Bennett, Walter Lee	First Named	21	M	1/16	1893	Chick. Dist.	Page 1 #6
	2							
	3							
	4							
	5							
	6	ENROLLMENT						
	7	OF NOS. 1 HEREON APPROVED BY THE SECRETARY						
	8	OF INTERIOR MAY 20 1903						
	9							
	10							
	11							
	12							
	13							
	14							
	15							
	16							
	17							

TRIBAL ENROLLMENT OF PARENTS

	Name of Father	Year	County	Name of Mother	Year	County
1	Bennett	dead	non-citizen	Margaret Anderson	1896	Choctaw residing in Chickasaw Dist
2						
3						
4						
5						
6	No1 on 1893 Leased Dist pay roll Chickasaw District page 1 No6. as Walter L Anderson					
7	See sworn statement of A. Telle Dec. 24, 1902					
8	Son of Margaret Anderson, Choctaw card #437.					
9						
10						
11						
12						
13						
14						
15						
16						
17				Date of Application for Enrollment.	Dec. 24, 1902	

Choctaw By Blood Enrollment Cards 1898-1914

RESIDENCE: Tobucksy   COUNTY. **Choctaw Nation**   **Choctaw Roll** *(Not Including Freedmen)*   CARD NO.
POST OFFICE: Canadian, I.T.   FIELD NO. **5641**

Dawes' Roll No.	NAME	Relationship to Person First Named	AGE	SEX	BLOOD	TRIBAL ENROLLMENT		
						Year	County	No.
15027	1 Adams, Wiley	First Named	61	M	[?] W	1896	Tobucksy	14203
	2							
	3							
	4							
	5							
	6							
	7							
	8							
	9 ENROLLMENT							
	10 OF NOS. 1 HEREON							
	11 APPROVED BY THE SECRETARY OF INTERIOR Oct 15 1903							
	12							
	13 Enrollment of No.1							
	14 cancelled by order of department of March 1, 1907							
	15 No.1 restored to roll by							
	16 departmental authority of							
	17 January 19, 1909 (File 5-51)							

TRIBAL ENROLLMENT OF PARENTS						
Name of Father	Year	County	Name of Mother	Year	County	
1 Riley Adams	Dead	Non-citizen	Eliza Adams	Dead	noncitizen	
2						
3						
4						
5						
6 No.1 Denied by Dawes Commission in 1896 Choctaw Case #1128. No appeal.						
7						
8 No1 transferred from Choctaw card R#2. See decision of February 21, 1903. On May 21, 1903						
9 the Secretary of the Interior affirmed the decision of the Commission admitting No1 of February 21, 1903.						
10						
11 No1 admitted by Act of Choctaw Council of Nov. 6, 1884						
12						
13						
14						
15			Date of Application for Enrollment.			
16			Oct 29/1902			
17			on this card	Mar 9, 1903		

241

Choctaw By Blood Enrollment Cards 1898-1914

RESIDENCE:		COUNTY.	**Choctaw Nation**			**Choctaw Roll**	CARD No.	
POST OFFICE: Enterprise, I.T.						(Not Including Freedmen)	FIELD NO. **5642**	

Dawes' Roll No.	NAME	Relationship to Person First Named	AGE	SEX	BLOOD	TRIBAL ENROLLMENT Year	County	No.
IW 53	1 Dyer, Joseph E	First Named	38	M	I.W.			
14867	2 " Lorena A	Wife	33	F	1/2	1896	Blue	3508
14868	3 " Joseph A	Son	14	M	1/4	1896	"	3509
14869	4 " Mary	Dau	11	F	1/4	1896	"	3510
14870	5 " Jessie	Dau	9	F	1/4	1896	"	3511
14871	6 " James R	Son	5 6	M	1/4			
14872	7 " Fannie	Dau	3 4	F	1/4			
14873	8 " Mammie	Dau	3 4	F	1/4			
14784	9 " Susana	Dau	1	F	1/4			
	10							
	11	ENROLLMENT						
	12	OF NOS. 2,3,4,5,6,7,8,9 HEREON APPROVED BY THE SECRETARY						
	13	OF INTERIOR May 20 1903						
	14	ENROLLMENT						
	15	OF NOS. 1 HEREON APPROVED BY THE SECRETARY						
	16	OF INTERIOR June 3 1903						
	17							

	TRIBAL ENROLLMENT OF PARENTS					
Name of Father	Year	County	Name of Mother	Year	County	
1 James L Dyer	Dead	Non citizen	Susana F Dyer		noncitizen	
2 Daniel Graves		Blue	Jenny Graves	1896	Blue	
3 No.1			No.2			
4 No.1			No.2			
5 No.1			No.2			
6 No.1			No.2			
7 No.1			No.2			
8 No.1			No.2			
9 No.1			No.2			
10 No 3 on 1896 roll as Joe Dye						
11 No.5 on 1896 roll as Jesse Dye						
12 No.1 transferred from Choctaw Card D#522 Nos 2-9 inclusive transferred from Choctaw D266. See decision of February 25, 1903.						
13						
14						
15						
16						on this card
17 P.O. Quinton, Okla 9/6/08			11/14/99	Date of Application for Enrollment.	Mar 13, 1903	

242

Choctaw By Blood Enrollment Cards 1898-1914

RESIDENCE:		COUNTY.	**Choctaw Nation**				**Choctaw Roll** *(Not Including Freedmen)*		CARD NO.
POST OFFICE: Hatfield Arkansas									FIELD NO. **5643**

Dawes' Roll No.	NAME	Relationship to Person First Named	AGE	SEX	BLOOD	TRIBAL ENROLLMENT		
						Year	County	No.
14811	1 Wilson, Edmund	First Named	20	M	1/2	1896	Nashoba	13225
	2							
	3							
	4							
	5	ENROLLMENT OF NOS. 1 HEREON APPROVED BY THE SECRETARY OF INTERIOR May 20 1903						
	6							
	7							
	8							
	9							
	10							
	11							
	12							
	13							
	14							
	15							
	16							
	17							

TRIBAL ENROLLMENT OF PARENTS

Name of Father	Year	County	Name of Mother	Year	County
1 Rayburn Wilson	1896	Nashoba	Martha Cusher		noncitizen
2					
3					
4					
5					
6 No1 also on 1893 Pay Roll Nashoba County page 35 No. 415					
7 as Edmon Wilson					
8 No1 transferred from Choctaw D#141 See decision of February 25, 1903.					
9					
10					
11					
12					
13					
14			Date of Application for Enrollment. 5/2/99		Date of Transfer to this Card
15					
16					
17					Mar 13, 1903

Choctaw By Blood Enrollment Cards 1898-1914

RESIDENCE: Tobucksy   COUNTY. **Choctaw Nation**   **Choctaw Roll**   CARD NO.
POST OFFICE: McAlester, I.T.   (Not Including Freedmen)   FIELD NO. **5644**

Dawes' Roll No.	NAME	Relationship to Person First Named	AGE	SEX	BLOOD	TRIBAL ENROLLMENT		
						Year	County	No.
15804	1 Cannedy, Georgia	First Named	42	F	Full	1893	Tobucksy	177
15805	2 Thompson, Charles	son	23	M	1/2	1893	"	178
15806	3 " Beulah	Dau	21	F	1/2	1893	"	181
15807	4 Cannedy, Earl	Son	14	M	1/2	1893	"	179
15808	5 " Roy	son	11	M	1/2	1893	"	180
15809	6 " Irma	Dau	8	F	1/2			
	7							
	8							
	9							
	10 For child of no2 see NB (Apr 26-06) Card #812							
	11 " " " No3 " " (Mar 3'05) " #1524							
	12							
	13							
	14 ENROLLMENT OF NOS. 1,2,3,4,5 and 6 HEREON							
	15 APPROVED BY THE SECRETARY OF INTERIOR Mar 15 1905							
	16							
	17							

TRIBAL ENROLLMENT OF PARENTS

	Name of Father	Year	County	Name of Mother	Year	County
1	Augustus Wallace	Dead	Choctaw	Tennessee Wallace	Dead	Choctaw
2	Jim Thompson	"	non citizen	No1		
3	" "	"	"	No1		
4	Lin Cannedy		"	No1		
5	" "		"	No1		
6	" "		"	No1		
7						
8	No1 on 1893 Pay Roll Tobucksy County No. 177 as Georgia Cannady					
9	No2 " 1893 " " " " " 178 as Charles T "					
10	No3 " 1893 " " " " " 181 " Beulah "					
11	No4 " 1893 " " " " " 179 " Earl "					
12	No5 " 1893 " " " " " 180 " Ray "					
13	Nos1-6 inclusive transferred from Choctaw D181 See decision of February 25, 1903					
	Protest of Choctaw Nation filed April 15, 1903					
14	Record forwarded Secretary of the Interior Aug 6, 1903			5/23/99 Date of Application for Enrollment.		
15	Decision of Commission to Five Civilized Tribes of Feby 25, 1903 enrolling					
	Nos 1 to 6 incl. affirmed by Secty of Interior Dec 6, 1904 (I.T.D 6490-1904)					
16				Mar 13, 1903		
17				on this card		

244

Choctaw By Blood Enrollment Cards 1898-1914

RESIDENCE: Chickasaw Nation COUNTY. **Choctaw Nation** **Choctaw Roll** CARD NO.
POST OFFICE: Purcell, I.T. (Not Including Freedmen) FIELD NO. **5645**

Dawes' Roll No.	NAME	Relationship to Person First Named	AGE	SEX	BLOOD	TRIBAL ENROLLMENT		
						Year	County	No.
IW 54	1 Bowles, John	First Named	52	M	IW	1876	Chickasaw Dist	14356
	2							
	3							
	4							
	5							
	6							
	7							
	8							
	9							
	10							
	11	ENROLLMENT						
	12	OF NOS. 1 HEREON APPROVED BY THE SECRETARY						
	13	OF INTERIOR JUN 13 1903						
	14							
	15							
	16							
	17							

TRIBAL ENROLLMENT OF PARENTS

	Name of Father	Year	County	Name of Mother	Year	County
1	Michael Bowles	Dead	Noncitizen	Mary Bowles	Dead	Noncitizen
2						
3						
4						
5						
6	June 28 1905 Original record and decision returned by Department for reconsideration and					
7	re-adjudication in conformity with opinion of Assistant Attorney General of June 19, 1905 in Cherokee enrollment case of Thomas J. Lasley					
8	Sept 28, 1905: Report to Department Feb. 13, 1907. Department affirms former [illegible]					
9	No.1 admitted by Dawes Commission in 1896 Choctaw case No. 893					
10	No.1 was formerly husband of Catherine C. Burnett Roll No. 216					
11						
12						
13						
14						
15				Date of Application for Enrollment.		
16				Sept 16/98		
17						MAR 19, 1903

245

Choctaw By Blood Enrollment Cards 1898-1914

Dawes' Roll No.	NAME	Relationship to Person First Named	AGE	SEX	BLOOD	TRIBAL ENROLLMENT		
						Year	County	No.
IW 55	1 Cloud, H.D.		31	M	IW	1896	Chick Dist	14430
	2							
	3							
	4							
	5							
	6							
	7							
	8							
	9							
	10							
	11	ENROLLMENT						
	12	OF NOS. 1 HEREON APPROVED BY THE SECRETARY						
	13	OF INTERIOR JUN 13 1903						
	14							
	15							
	16							
	17							

TRIBAL ENROLLMENT OF PARENTS

Name of Father	Year	County	Name of Mother	Year	County
1 Isaac Cloud		Non citizen	Lookey J Cloud		non citizen
2					
3					
4					
5 [Illegible entry - too light to read]					
6 Protest overruled by Department March 21, 1903.					
7 Admitted by Dawes Com Case No 717 and no appeal taken					
8 Marriage license and certificate on file in office of Dawes Com, Muskogee					
9					
10 No1 transferred from Choctaw card #D 113 See decision of March 13, 1903.					
11					
12					
13					
14				Date of Application for Enrollment.	
15				Nov 26/98	
16					
17 See Choctaw card #231					MAR 29, 1903

Choctaw By Blood Enrollment Cards 1898-1914

RESIDENCE: Towson County COUNTY. **Choctaw Nation** **Choctaw Roll** CARD No.
POST OFFICE: Valliant, I.T. *(Not Including Freedmen)* FIELD No. **5647**

Dawes' Roll No.	NAME	Relationship to Person First Named	AGE	SEX	BLOOD	TRIBAL ENROLLMENT		
						Year	County	No.
IW 56	1 Lucas, Thomas L		52	M	I.W.	1896	Towson	14763
	2							
	3							
	4							
	5							
	6							
	7							
	8							
	9							
	10							
	11	ENROLLMENT OF NOS. 1 HEREON						
	12	APPROVED BY THE SECRETARY						
	13	OF INTERIOR JUN 13 1903						
	14							
	15							
	16							
	17							

TRIBAL ENROLLMENT OF PARENTS

	Name of Father	Year	County	Name of Mother	Year	County
1	Le Flaniel Lucas	Dead	Non Citz	Ann Lucas	Dead	Non Citz
2						
3						
4						
5	No1 is husband of Luvicey Lucas on Choctaw card #535					
6						
7	On 1896 roll as Thos L Lucas					
8	Married Mrs. Vicey Austin about three years ago without license.					
9	Remarried under Choctaw license May 23/99/					
10	See testimony of himself.					
11						
12	No1 transferred from Choctaw card #D260. See decision of March 13, 1903.					
13						
14						
15				6/20/99		
16				Date of Application for Enrollment.		
17					MAR **29**, 1903 transfer date	

247

Choctaw By Blood Enrollment Cards 1898-1914

RESIDENCE: Atoka County
POST OFFICE: Kiowa, I.T.

COUNTY.

Choctaw Nation

Choctaw Roll
(Not Including Freedmen)

CARD NO.
FIELD NO. **5648**

Dawes' Roll No.	NAME	Relationship to Person First Named	AGE	SEX	BLOOD	TRIBAL ENROLLMENT		
						Year	County	No.
IW484	1 Fortson, Josiah R	First Named	70	M	I.W.			
	2							
	3							
	4							
	5							
	6							
	7							
	8							
	9							
	10							
	11	ENROLLMENT						
	12	OF NOS. 1 HEREON APPROVED BY THE SECRETARY						
	13	OF INTERIOR SEP 12 1903						
	14							
	15							
	16							
	17							

TRIBAL ENROLLMENT OF PARENTS

Name of Father	Year	County	Name of Mother	Year	County
1 Roderick Fortson	Dead	Non Citz	Harriet Fortson	Dead	Non Citz
2					
3					
4					
5					
6 Admitted by Dawes Com as J.R. Fortson					
7 as an Intermarried Citizen Case No 435					
8 Married in 1884, separated in about four months.					
9 Married a U.S. Citizen about four or five years ago.					
10 No.1 transferred from Choctaw card #D270: See decision of Mach 13, 1903.					
11					
12					
13					
14					
15					
16			Aug 1/99		MAR 29 1903
17			Date of Application for Enrollment.		

248

Choctaw By Blood Enrollment Cards 1898-1914

RESIDENCE: Atoka County	COUNTY. **Choctaw Nation**	**Choctaw Roll** *(Not Including Freedmen)*	CARD No.
POST OFFICE: Kiowa, I.T.			FIELD No. **5649**

Dawes' Roll No.	NAME	Relationship to Person First Named	AGE	SEX	BLOOD	TRIBAL ENROLLMENT		
						Year	County	No.
IW 57	1 Doyle, James G		63	M	I.W.			
	2							
	3							
	4							
	5							
	6							
	7							
	8	ENROLLMENT						
	9	OF NOS. HEREON APPROVED BY THE SECRETARY						
	10	OF INTERIOR Jan 13, 1903 20						
	11							
	12							
	13							
	14							
	15							
	16							
	17							

TRIBAL ENROLLMENT OF PARENTS

	Name of Father	Year	County	Name of Mother	Year	County
1	Burton Doyle	Dead	Non Citz	Dulcenia Doyle	Dead	Non Citz
2						
3						
4						
5	Further action in connection with allotment to No1 suspended under protest of					
6	attorneys for Choctaw and Chickasaw Nations Jan 23, 1904 Protest overruled by Department March 31, 1904.					
7	Admitted by Dawes Com as an intermarried citizen. Case No. 334 under name of					
8	J.G. Doyle. No appeal.					
9	Married in 1880 separated from wife after about two months. Has never lived					
10	with her since. See his testimony					
11	No1 transferred from Choctaw card D#268. See decision of March 14, 1903					
12						
13						
14						
15				Date of Application for Enrollment.	transfer date to this card	
16						
17				Aug 1/99	Mar 30, 1903	

249

Choctaw By Blood Enrollment Cards 1898-1914

RESIDENCE: Jackson COUNTY. **Choctaw Nation** **Choctaw Roll** CARD NO.
POST OFFICE: Crowder, Ind Ter *(Not Including Freedmen)* FIELD NO. **5650**

Dawes' Roll No.		NAME	Relationship to Person First Named	AGE	SEX	BLOOD	TRIBAL ENROLLMENT		
							Year	County	No.
14951	1	Wallace, Fannie		31	F	1/8	1896	Jackson	13814
14952	2	" Dora	Dau	10	"	1/16	1896	"	13815
14953	3	" Caldonia	"	7	"	1/16	1896	"	13816
14954	4	" Leona	"	14mo	"	1/16			
	5								
	6								
	7								
	8								
	9								
	10								
	11	ENROLLMENT							
	12	OF NOS. 1,2,3 and 4 HEREON APPROVED BY THE SECRETARY							
	13	OF INTERIOR OCT 15 1903							
	14								
	15								
	16								
	17								

TRIBAL ENROLLMENT OF PARENTS

	Name of Father	Year	County	Name of Mother	Year	County
1	Thos. C. Crowder	1896	Jackson	Flora Crowder	Dead	Cherokee rolls
2	Jesse H. Wallace	1896	Non-citizen	No.1		
3	" "	"	" "	No.1		
4	" "	"	" "	No.1		
5						
6	Nos 1-2-3 admitted by Dawes Commission in 1896 as citizens by blood					
7	Choctaw case #1162 1/2. No appeal.					
8	No1 is daughter of Thomas C. Crowder on Choctaw card #1456					
	No2 on 1896 Choctaw Census roll as Laura Wallace.					
9	No3 " 1896 " " " Cardonia[sic] "					
10	No4 Born Jany 20, 1902 enrolled March 19, 1902					
11	Nos 1 to 4 inclusive transferred from Choctaw card #D166. See decision of March 26, 1903.					
12	For child of No.1 see NB (Apr 26, 1906) Card No. 17.					
13						
14						
15						
16						
17		Date of Application for Enrollment. 5/9/99			Date of Transfer to this Card.	APR 10 1903

250

Choctaw By Blood Enrollment Cards 1898-1914

RESIDENCE: Chickasaw Nation ~~COUNTY.~~   **Choctaw Nation**   **Choctaw Roll** (Not Including Freedmen)   CARD NO.

POST OFFICE: Emet Ind Ter   FIELD NO. **5651**

Dawes' Roll No.	NAME	Relationship to Person First Named	AGE	SEX	BLOOD	TRIBAL ENROLLMENT		
						Year	County	No.
	...ith, Nathaniel W	First Named	51	M	I.W			
3								
4								
5								
6								
7								
8								
9								
10								
11	ENROLLMENT							
12	OF NOS. 1 HEREON APPROVED BY THE SECRETARY							
13	OF INTERIOR JUN 13 1903							
14								
15								
16								
17								

TRIBAL ENROLLMENT OF PARENTS

	Name of Father	Year	County	Name of Mother	Year	County
1	Asa M. Smith	Dead	non-citz	Henrietta Smith	Dead	non-citz
2						
3						
4						
5						
6	~~No1 was admitted by Dawes Commission in 1896 as an~~					
7	intermarried citizen in Choctaw citizenship case #825. No appeal.					
8	No1 transferred from Choctaw card #D327. See decision					
9	of April 22, 1903.					
10						
11						
12						
13						
14						
15					Date of transfer to this card.	
16				Aug 16/99 ~~Date of Application~~		
17				~~for Enrollment.~~	MAY 7 1903	

Choctaw By Blood Enrollment Cards 1898-1914

RESIDENCE: Blue ▮▮▮▮▮ COUNTY.
POST OFFICE: Caddo Ind Ter

Choctaw Nation

Choctaw Roll ▮▮▮▮
(Not Including Freedmen) FIELD NO. **5652**

Dawes' Roll No.	NAME	Relationship to Person First Named	AGE	SEX	BLOOD	TRIBAL ENROLLMENT		
						Year	County	No.
14955	1 Hampton, Walton	First Named	14	M	1/4	1896	Blue	5843
14956	2 " Jene	Bro	12	M	1/4	1896	"	5844
	3							
	4							
	5							
	6							
	7							
	8							
	9							
	10							
	11	ENROLLMENT						
	12	OF NOS. 1 and 2 HEREON APPROVED BY THE SECRETARY						
	13	OF INTERIOR OCT 15 1903						
	14							
	15							
	16							
	17							

TRIBAL ENROLLMENT OF PARENTS

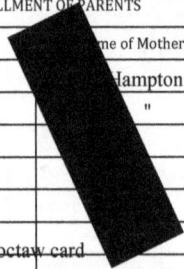

	Name of Father	Year	County	Name of Mother	Year	County
1	Julius C. Hampton		Blues	▮ Hampton	Dead	Cherokee
2	" " "		"	"	"	"
3						
4						
5						
6	Nos 1 and 2 inclusive transferred from Choctaw card					
7	#D339. See decision of March 26, 1903.					
8						
9						
10						
11						
12						
13						
14						
15						
16				Aug 21/99 Date of Application for Enrollment.		Date of transfer to this card.
17						APR 10 1903

Choctaw By Blood Enrollment Cards 1898-1914

RESIDENCE: Blue
POST OFFICE: Caddo Ind. Ter.

COUNTY **Choctaw Nation**

Choctaw Roll CARD NO
(Not Including Freedmen) FIELD NO

Dawes' Roll No.	NAME	Relationship to Person First Named	AGE	SEX	BLOOD	TRIBAL ENROLLMENT		
						Year	County	No.
IW 462	1 Smith, William T.	First Named	48	M	I.W.	1896	Blue	15054
	2							
	3							
	4							
	5							
	6							
	7							
	8							
	9							
	10							
	11	ENROLLMENT						
	12	OF NOS. 1 HEREON APPROVED BY THE SECRETARY						
	13	OF INTERIOR JUN 13 1903						
	14							
	15							
	16							
	17							

TRIBAL ENROLLMENT OF PARENTS

	Name of Father	Year	County	Name of Mother	Year	County
1	George Smith	Dead	non-citz	Elvira Smith		non-citz
2						
3						
4						
5						
6	No1 was admitted in 1896 by Dawes Commission as an					
7	intermarried citizen Choctaw citizenship case #784. No appeal.					
8	No1 Transferred from Choctaw card #D.346. See decision of April 22, 1903.					
9	No1 is husband of Louvina Smith on Choctaw card #3710.					
10						
11						
12						
13						
14						
15				Date of Application for Enrollment. 8/22/99		Date of transfer to this card.
16						
17						MAY 7 1903

Choctaw By Blood Enrollment Cards 1898-1914

RESIDENCE: Blue   COUNTY. **Choctaw Nation**   Choctaw Roll   CARD NO.
POST OFFICE: Caddo Ind. Ter.   *(Not Including Freedmen)*   FIELD NO. **5654**

Dawes' Roll No.	NAME	Relationship to Person First Named	AGE	SEX	BLOOD	TRIBAL ENROLLMENT Year	County	No.
IW533	1 Seago, Charles W	First Named	36	M	I.W.	1896	Blue	15057
14957	2 " Addie A	Wife	33	F	1/4	1896	"	11609
14958	3 " John T	Son	13	M	1/8	1896	"	11610
14959	4 " David E	"	10	"	1/8	1896	"	11611
14960	5 " Charles W Jr	"	8	"	1/8	1896	"	11612
14961	6 " William F	"	6	"	1/8	1896	"	11613
14962	7 " Ramsey D	"	4	"	1/8			
14963	8 Betts, James D	Bro in Law	13	"	1/8	1896	Blue	1581
14964	9 " Selina E	Sister in Law	12	F	1/8	1896	"	1582
14965	10 Seago, Ida May	Dau	3	"	1/8			
	No1 on 1896 Choctaw Census Roll as Chas W Sigo[sic]					ENROLLMENT		
	No2 12 " 1896 " " " " Adie E Sego[sic]					OF NOS.2,3,4,5,6,7,8,9 and 10 HEREON		
	No3 " 1896 " " " " John T "					APPROVED BY THE SECRETARY		
	No4 13 " 1896 " " " " David E "					OF INTERIOR Oct 15 1903		
	No5 " 1896 " " " " Chas W "							
	No6 15 " 1896 " " " " Wm T "					ENROLLMENT		
	No8 " 1896 " " " " Jas D Betts					OF NOS. 1 HEREON		
	16					APPROVED BY THE SECRETARY		
						OF INTERIOR Dec 24 1903		
	17							

TRIBAL ENROLLMENT OF PARENTS

Name of Father	Year	County	Name of Mother	Year	County
1 Chas W Seago	Dead	non-citz	Mary Seago	Dead	non-citz
2 Chas E Betts	"	Blue	Katie Betts	"	Cherokee
3 No1			No2		
4 No1			No2		
5 No1			No2		
6 No1			No2		
7 No1			No2		
8 Chas E Betts	Dead	Blue	Mollie Betts	Dead	non-citz
9 " " "	"	"	" "	"	" " "
10 No1			No2		
11 No10 enrolled May 24, 1900					
12 Nos 1 to 10 inclusive transferred from Choctaw card #D365 see decision of March 26, 1903 No7 Born April 17-1898, enrolled Aug. 21, 1899					
13 No10 Born Feb 22, 1900, enrolled April 13, 1900					
14 For child of nos 1&2 see NB (Mar 3'05) #417					
15					
16			Date of Application for Enrollment. Aug 24/99		
17			Listed on this card	Apr 10 1903	

Choctaw By Blood Enrollment Cards 1898-1914

RESIDENCE: Blue	COUNTY.	**Choctaw Nation**	**Choctaw Roll** (Not Including Freedmen)	CARD NO.
POST OFFICE: Caddo Ind Ter				FIELD NO. **5655**

Dawes' Roll No.		NAME	Relationship to Person First Named	AGE	SEX	BLOOD	TRIBAL ENROLLMENT		
							Year	County	No.
14966	1	Tolbert, Rufus	First Named	28	M	1/2	1896	Blue	12429
	2								
	3								
	4								
	5								
	6								
	7								
	8								
	9								
	10								
	11	ENROLLMENT							
	12	OF NOS. 1 HEREON APPROVED BY THE SECRETARY							
	13	OF INTERIOR OCT 15 1903							
	14								
	15								
	16								
	17								

TRIBAL ENROLLMENT OF PARENTS

	Name of Father	Year	County	Name of Mother	Year	County
1	John Tolbert	Dead	Blue	Mary Tolbert	Dead	Cherokee
2						
3						
4						
5						
6	No 1 transferred from Choctaw card #D375					
7	See decision of March 26, 1903.					
8						
9						
10						
11						
12						
13						
14						
15				Date of Application for Enrollment.		Date of transfer to this card.
16				Aug 25/99		APR 11 1903
17						

Choctaw By Blood Enrollment Cards 1898-1914

RESIDENCE: Jacks Fork   COUNTY. **Choctaw Nation**   **Choctaw Roll**   CARD NO.

POST OFFICE: Stringtown Ind Ter   *(Not Including Freedmen)*   FIELD NO. **5656**

Dawes' Roll No.	NAME	Relationship to Person First Named	AGE	SEX	BLOOD	TRIBAL ENROLLMENT Year	County	No.
14967	1 Rogers, George	First Named	24	M	1/4	1896	Jacks Fork	11012
14968	2 " Coowee	Bro	18	M	14	1896	" "	11013
	3							
	4							
	5							
	6							
	7							
	8							
	9							
	10							
	11	ENROLLMENT						
	12	OF NOS. 1 and 2 HEREON APPROVED BY THE SECRETARY						
	13	OF INTERIOR OCT 15 1903						
	14							
	15							
	16							
	17							

TRIBAL ENROLLMENT OF PARENTS

	Name of Father	Year	County	Name of Mother	Year	County
1	Lawega Rogers		Cherokee	Isabelle Rogers	Dead	Jacks Fork
2	" "		"	" "	"	" "
3						
4						
5						
6	Nos1 and 2 transferred from Choctaw card #D.395					
7	See decision of March 26, 1903.					
8						
9						
10						
11						
12						
13						
14						
15					Date of transfer to this card.	
16				Date of Application for Enrollment.		
17				Aug 31/99	APR 11 1903	

256

Choctaw By Blood Enrollment Cards 1898-1914

RESIDENCE:	Atoka	COUNTY.							CARD No	
POST OFFICE:	Atoka, Ind. Ter.		**Choctaw Nation**				*(Not Including Freedmen)*	**Choctaw Roll**	FIELD No	

Dawes' Roll No.	NAME	Relationship to Person First Named	AGE	SEX	BLOOD	TRIBAL ENROLLMENT		
						Year	County	No.
14969	1 Lee, Thomas D	First Named	31	M	1/4	1896	Atoka	8322
IW534	2 " Leila C	Wife	29	F	I.W.	1896	"	14790
14970	3 " Willie H	Son	7	M	1/8	1896	"	8323
14971	4 " Mamie A	Dau		F	1/8			
	5							
	6	ENROLLMENT						
	7	OF NOS. 1, 3 and 4 HEREON						
	8	APPROVED BY THE SECRETARY						
	9	OF INTERIOR OCT 15 1903						
	10							
	11							
	12	ENROLLMENT						
	13	OF NOS. 2 HEREON						
	14	APPROVED BY THE SECRETARY OF INTERIOR DEC 24 1903						
	15							
	16							
	17							

TRIBAL ENROLLMENT OF PARENTS

	Name of Father	Year	County	Name of Mother	Year	County
1	James Lee	Dead	Cherokee	Elizabeth Lee	Dead	Choctaw
2	James Gleason	"	non-citz	Elizabeth Gleason	"	non-citz
3	No1			No2		
4	No1			No2		
5						
6	No1 on 1896 Choctaw census roll as Thos. D. Lee					
7	No2 " 1896 " " " " Lula "					
8	No3 " 1896 " " " " Willie "					
9	No4 Enrolled Feby 18, 1901. Nos 1 to 4 inclusive transferred from Choctaw card #D396					
10	See decision of March 26, 1903.					
11						
12						
13						
14						
15						
16				Date of Application for Enrollment.		Date of transfer to this card.
17				Aug 31/99		APR 11 1903

Choctaw By Blood Enrollment Cards 1898-1914

RESIDENCE: Atoka   COUNTY.   **Choctaw Nation**   Choctaw Roll   CARD No.

POST OFFICE: Atoka Ind Ter   *(Not Including Freedmen)*   FIELD No. **5658**

Dawes' Roll No.	NAME	Relationship to Person First Named	AGE	SEX	BLOOD	TRIBAL ENROLLMENT Year	County	No.
14972	1 Dunn, Annie	First Named	29	F	1/16	1896	Atoka	3572
14973	2 " Lillian G	Dau	10	"	3/32	1896	"	3573
14974	3 " Emma Brazelia	"	8	"	3/32	1896	"	3574
14975	4 " William Alfred	Son	6	M	3/32	1896	"	3575
14976	5 " Arthur Ward	"	3	"	3/32			
14977	6 " Allen Yates	"	1	"	3/32			
	7							
	8							
	9							
	10							
	11							
	12							
	13							
	14							
	15							
	16							
	17							

ENROLLMENT
OF NOS. 1,2,3,4,5 and 6 HEREON
APPROVED BY THE SECRETARY
OF INTERIOR OCT 15 1903

TRIBAL ENROLLMENT OF PARENTS

	Name of Father	Year	County	Name of Mother	Year	County
1	W. G. Ward		Blue	Eliza Ward		Cherokee
2	W. M. Dunn		Atoka	No 1		
3	" " "		"	No 1		
4	" " "		"	No 1		
5	" " "		"	No 1		
6	" " "		"	No 1		
7						
8	No4 on 1896 Choctaw census roll as Alfred W Dunn					
9	No5 Affidavits of birth filed Oct. 31, 1899					
10	No6 Born Feby 21, 1902. Enrolled April 9, 1902					
	~~Husband of No1 is W.M. Dunn on Choctaw card #4350~~					
11	Nos 1 to 6 inclusive transferred from Choctaw Card #D399					
12	See decision of March 21, 1903.					
13						
14						
15			Date of Application for Enrollment.	9/1/99		
16				Date of Transfer to this Card.		
17				APR 6 1903		

258

Choctaw By Blood Enrollment Cards 1898-1914

RESIDENCE: Jacks Fork   COUNTY.   **Choctaw Nation**   Date of ~~Choctaw Ro~~ to this Card ~~(Freedmen)~~   FIELD 5659
POST OFFICE: Stringtown, Ind. Ter

Dawes' Roll No.	NAME	Relationship to Person First Named	AGE	SEX	BLOOD	TRIBAL ENROLLMENT		
						Year	County	No.
14978	1 Beck, Nannie	First Named	26	F	1/4	1896	Jacks Fork	1986
14979	2 " Sutt	Son	4	M	1/8	1896	" "	1988
14980	3 " Benjamin	"	1	M	1/8			
14981	4 " Barton	"	1wk	M	1/8			
14982	5 " Pheoba[sic] A	Dau	4mo	F	1/8			
	6							
	7							
	8							
	9							
	10							
	11	ENROLLMENT						
	12	OF NOS. 1,2,3,4 and 5 HEREON APPROVED BY THE SECRETARY						
	13	OF INTERIOR OCT 15 1903						
	14							
	15							
	16							
	17							

TRIBAL ENROLLMENT OF PARENTS

	Name of Father	Year	County	Name of Mother	Year	County
1	James Lee	Dead	Cherokee	Elizabeth Lee	Dead	Choctaw
2	Lycurgus C Beck	Dead	intermarried	No1		
3	" "	"	"	No1		
4	" "	"	"	No1		
5	" "	"	"	No1		
6	No2 on 1896 Choctaw census roll as Sudd Beck					
7	No5 Born Dec. 20, 1901. Enrolled April 11, 1902.					
8	Nos 1 to 5 inclusive transferred from Choctaw card #D403 ~~See decision of March 21, 1903.~~					
9	No3 Born April 13, 1897 ~~enrolled Sept 9, 1897~~ 7/12/15 The foregoing notation in error,					
10	Nos 4 & 5 Proof of birth filed Oct. 31, 1899 date should be Sept 1, 1899					
11	7/12/1915 The ages given hereon are as given at date of application for enrollment which was Sept 1, 1899. R.S.					
12						
13						
14						
15						
16		Date of Application for Enrollment. 9/1/99				
17				Date of Transfer to this Card. APR 6 1903		

Choctaw By Blood Enrollment Cards 1898-1914

RESIDENCE: Tobucksy   COUNTY. **Choctaw N**   CARD No.

POST OFFICE: Celestine Ind. Ter.   FIELD No. **5660**

Dawes' Roll No.	NAME	Relationship to Person First Named	AGE	SEX	BLOOD	TRIBAL ENROLLMENT Year	County	No.
14983	1 Jones, Alexander	First Named	33	M	1/8	1893	Atoka	614
IW535	2 " Mattie	Wife	33	F	I.W.			
14984	3 " Vergia Ellen	Dau	1	"	1/16			
	4							
	5							
	6							
	7							
	8	ENROLLMENT OF NOS. 1 and 3 HEREON						
	9	APPROVED BY THE SECRETARY OF INTERIOR OCT 15 1903						
	10							
	11							
	12	ENROLLMENT OF NOS. 2 HEREON						
	13	APPROVED BY THE SECRETARY OF INTERIOR DEC 24 1903						
	14							
	15							
	16							
	17							

TRIBAL ENROLLMENT OF PARENTS

	Name of Father	Year	County	Name of Mother	Year	County
1	Alex Jones	Dead	Skullyville	Paralee Morgan		I.W.
2	Jim Smith		non-citz	Lou Smith		non-citz
3	No1			No2		
4						
5						
6	No3 Affidavits of birth filed May 31, 1902.					
7	Nos 1 to 3 inclusive transferred from Choctaw card #D475					
8	See decision of March 26, 1903.					
9						
10						
11						
12						
13						
14				Date of Application for Enrollment.		
15				Sept 11/99		
16					Date of Transfer to this Card.	APR 11 1903
17						

Choctaw By Blood Enrollment Cards 1898-1914

		COUNTY. **Choctaw Nation**				CARD No.
POST OFFICE: South Canadian Ind. Ter			**Choctaw Roll** (Not Including Freedmen)			FIELD No. **5661**

Dawes' Roll No.	NAME	Relationship to Person First Named	AGE	SEX	BLOOD	TRIBAL ENROLLMENT		
						Year	County	No.
14985	1 Land, Addie	First Named	20	F	1/8	1896	Tobucksy	9200
	2							
	3							
	4							
	5							
	6							
	7							
	8							
	9							
	10							
	11							
	12							
	13							
	14							
	15							
	16							
	17							

ENROLLMENT OF NOS. 1 HEREON APPROVED BY THE SECRETARY OF INTERIOR OCT 15 1903

TRIBAL ENROLLMENT OF PARENTS

Name of Father	Year	County	Name of Mother	Year	County
1 C. J. Mᶜ Duff		Tobucksy	Rachel Mᶜ Duff		Creek
2					
3					
4					
5					
6 No1 transferred from Choctaw card #D497					
7 See decision of March 26, 1903.					
8 See affidavit of Simon E Lewis as to degree of Choctaw blood [possessed by No1, filed July 3, 1903					
9					
10					
11					
12					
13					
14			Date of Application for Enrollment.		
15					
16			Sept 14/99	Date of Transfer to this Card. APR 11 1903	
17					

Choctaw By Blood Enrollment Cards 1898-1914

RESIDENCE: Tobucksy   COUNTY. **Ch**▮▮▮▮▮**cta**▮   CARD NO.

POST OFFICE: South Canadian Ind. Ter   *cludin*   FIELD NO. **5662**

Dawes' Roll No.	NAME	Relationship to Person First Named	AGE	SEX	BLOOD	TRIBAL ENROLLMENT Year		No.
14986	1 Mc Duff, Mary M	First Named	15	F	1/8	1896	Tobucksy	
14987	2 " Charles L	Bro	13	M	1/8	1896	"	920▮
14988	3 " Emma	Sis	10	F	1/8	1896	"	9203
14989	4 " Robert L	Bro	7	M	1/8	1896	"	9204
14990	5 " Andrew J	"	5	"	1/8			
	6							
	7							
	8							
	9							
	10							
	11							
	12							
	13							
	14							
	15							
	16							
	17							

ENROLLMENT
OF NOS. 1,2,3,4,& 5 HEREON
APPROVED BY THE SECRETARY
OF INTERIOR   OCT 15 1903

TRIBAL ENROLLMENT OF PARENTS

		ar	County	Name of Mother	Year	County
		R. 225	Tobucksy	Rachel Mc Duff		Creek
2	"	"	"	"	"	
3	"	"	"	"		"
4	"	"	"	"	"	
5	"	"	"	"	"	
6						

7   No1 on 1896 Choctaw census roll as Myrtle M Mc Duff

   No2 " 1896 " " " " Chas L "

8   No4 " 1896 " " " " Robt L "

9   Nos 1 to 5 inclusive transferred from Choctaw card #D498

10   See decision of March 26, 1903.

11   See copy of affidavit of S. E. Lewis as to degree of Choctaw blood possessed by Nos 1 to 5 inclusive filed July 3, 1903

12   Nos 1 to 5, inclusive are children of Charles L Mc Duff, Choctaw Card No. 4789

13   No5 Proof of birth filed Sept 14, 1899.

14				Date of Application for Enrollment.		
15						
16				Sept 14/99	Date of transfer to this card. APR 11	
17						

Choctaw By Blood Enrollment Cards 1898-1914

RESIDENCE: Jackson COUNTY.	**Choctaw Nation**	Choctaw Roll	CARD NO.
POST OFFICE: Bennington Ind Ter		(Not Including Freedmen)	FIELD NO. **5663**

Dawes' Roll No.	NAME	Relationship to Person First Named	AGE	SEX	BLOOD	TRIBAL ENROLLMENT Year	TRIBAL ENROLLMENT County	TRIBAL ENROLLMENT No.
IW163	1 Gardner, Zora	First Named	19	F	I.W.			
	2							
	3							
	4							
	5							
	6							
	7							
	8							
	9							
	10							
	11							
	12							
	13							
	14							
	15							
	16							
	17							

ENROLLMENT
OF NOS. 1 HEREON
APPROVED BY THE SECRETARY
OF INTERIOR JUN 13 1903

TRIBAL ENROLLMENT OF PARENTS

Name of Father	Year	County	Name of Mother	Year	County
1 Richard McDaniel		non-citz	Eliz. McDaniel		non-citz
2					
3					
4					
5					
6 No1 transferred from Choctaw card #D520 See					
7 decision of April 20, 1903.					
8 No.1 is wife of William Gardner on Choctaw card #3458					
9					
10					
11					
12					
13					
14				.	
15			Date of Application for Enrollment.		
16			Nov 14/99		
17				MAY 6 1903	

263

Choctaw By Blood Enrollment Cards 1898-1914

RESIDENCE: Choctaw Nation ~~COUNTY.~~ **Choctaw Nation** Choctaw Roll CARD NO.
POST OFFICE: Stigler, Ind. Ter. *(Not Including Freedmen)* FIELD NO.

Dawes' Roll No.	NAME	Relationship to Person First Named	AGE	SEX	BLOOD	TRIBAL ENROLLMENT		
						Year	County	No.
I.W. 536	1 Gilstrap, J. F.		31	M	I.W.	1896	Skullyville	14558
14991	2 " Ida	Wife	29	F	1/8	1896	"	4670
14992	3 " Clara	Dau	8	"	1/16	1896	"	4671
14993	4 " Wheeler	Son	2	M	1/16			
14994	5 " Luke	"	9mo	"	1/16			
	6							
	7							
	8	ENROLLMENT						
	9	OF NOS. 2,3,4 and 5 HEREON						
	10	APPROVED BY THE SECRETARY						
	11	OF INTERIOR OCT 15 1903						
	12	ENROLLMENT						
	13	OF NOS. 1 HEREON						
	14	APPROVED BY THE SECRETARY OF INTERIOR DEC 24 1903						
	15							
	16							
	17							

TRIBAL ENROLLMENT OF PARENTS

	Name of Father	Year	County	Name of Mother	Year	County
1	L. D. Gilstrap		non-citz	Lizzie Gilstrap	Dead	non-citz
2	Jno. H. Wilson		" "	Sarah Wilson		
3	No1			No2		
4	No1			No2		
5	No1			No2		

6 No2 admitted by Act of Choctaw council of Oct 30, 1890 under the name of Isaac Wilson
7 No1 and 3 Admitted by the Commission in 1896 in Choctaw case #263. No appeal.
8 No4 proof of birth filed Nov. 6, 1900
No5 Born July 13, 1902, enrolled Dec. 23, 1902
9 Nos 1 to 5 inclusive transferred from Choctaw card #D586
10 See decision of March 26, 1903.

11						
12						
13						
14			Date of Application for Enrollment.			
15						
16			Oct 25/1900			
17						APR

Choctaw By Blood Enrollment Cards 1898-1914

RESIDENCE: Skullyville   COUNTY. **Choctaw Nation**   **Choctaw Roll**   CARD NO.
POST OFFICE: Panther Ind. Ter.   *(Not Including Freedmen)*   FIELD NO. **5665**

Dawes' Roll No.	NAME	Relationship to Person First Named	AGE	SEX	BLOOD	TRIBAL ENROLLMENT		
						Year	County	No.
I.W. 197	1 Coleman, James M		71	M	I.W.	1896	Skullyville	14381
	2							
	3							
	4							
	5							
	6							
	7							
	8							
	9							
	10							
	11	ENROLLMENT						
	12	OF NOS. 1 HEREON APPROVED BY THE SECRETARY						
	13	OF INTERIOR JUN 13 1903						
	14							
	15							
	16							
	17							

TRIBAL ENROLLMENT OF PARENTS

Name of Father	Year	County	Name of Mother	Year	County
1 Spilsby Coleman	Dead	non-citz	Anna J Coleman	Dead	non-citz
2					
3					
4					
5					
6 No1 on 1896 Choctaw census roll as Jas. M Coleman					
7 No1 transferred from Choctaw card #D.242					
8 See decision of April 25, 1903.					
9					
10					
11					
12					
13					
14			Date of Application for Enrollment.		
15					
16			6/14/99		
17			Date of Transfer to this Card.		MAY 10 1903

265

Choctaw By Blood Enrollment Cards 1898-1914

RESIDENCE: Chickasaw Nation ~~COUNTY.~~
POST OFFICE: Purdy, Ind. Ter.

Choctaw Nation

Choctaw Roll *(Not Including Freedmen)*

CARD NO.
FIELD NO. **5666**

Dawes' Roll No.	NAME	Relationship to Person First Named	AGE	SEX	BLOOD	TRIBAL ENROLLMENT Year	TRIBAL ENROLLMENT County	TRIBAL ENROLLMENT No.
I.W. 198	1 Bell, Lizzie		37	F	I.W.			
	2							
	3							
	4							
	5							
	6							
	7							
	8							
	9							
	10							
	11	ENROLLMENT						
	12	OF NOS. 1 HEREON APPROVED BY THE SECRETARY						
	13	OF INTERIOR JUN 13 1903						
	14							
	15							
	16							
	17							

TRIBAL ENROLLMENT OF PARENTS

	Name of Father	Year	County	Name of Mother	Year	County
1	Alex Mayfield	Dead	non-citz	Roxanna Mayfield		non-citizen
2						
3						
4						
5						
6	No1 admitted by Dawes Commission in 1896 Choctaw					
7	citizenship case #638. No appeal.					
8	No1 transferred from Choctaw card #D81. See decision					
9	of May 1, 1903.					
10						
11						
12						
13						
14			Date of Application for Enrollment.			
15						
16			Oct 17/98	Date of Transfer		
17				To this Card.	MAY 16 1903	

Choctaw By Blood Enrollment Cards 1898-1914

RESIDENCE: Chickasaw Nation ~~COUNTY.~~ **Choctaw Nation** **Choctaw Roll** CARD NO.
POST OFFICE: Rush Springs Ind. Ter *(Not Including Freedmen)* FIELD NO.

Dawes' Roll No.	NAME	Relationship to Person First Named	AGE	SEX	BLOOD	TRIBAL ENROLLMENT		
						Year	County	No.
I.W. 199	1 Blakely, F. C.		46	M	I.W.			
	2							
	3							
	4							
	5							
	6							
	7							
	8							
	9							
	10							
	11	ENROLLMENT						
	12	OF NOS. 1 HEREON APPROVED BY THE SECRETARY						
	13	OF INTERIOR JUN 13 1903						
	14							
	15							
	16							
	17							

TRIBAL ENROLLMENT OF PARENTS

	Name of Father	Year	County	Name of Mother	Year	County
1	Milton C. Blakely	Dead	non-citz	Catherine C. Blakely	Dead	non-citz
2						
3						
4						
5						
6	No1 was admitted by Dawes Commission in 1896 as an intermarried					
7	citizen, as F. C. Blakeley[sic], Choctaw citizenship case #865. No appeal.					
8	No1 transferred from Choctaw card #D85. See decision of May 1, 1903. ~~For children of No1 see NB (Apr 26 '06) #1100~~					
9						
10						
11						
12						
13						
14				Date of Application for Enrollment.		
15						
16				Oct 18/99	Date of Transfer to this Card.	MAY 16 1903
17						

Choctaw By Blood Enrollment Cards 1898-1914

RESIDENCE: Tobucksy	COUNTY.	**Choctaw Nation**		**Choctaw Roll** (Not Including Freedmen)		CARD NO.		
POST OFFICE: Canadian Ind Ter						FIELD NO.		

Dawes' Roll No.	NAME	Relationship to Person First Named	AGE	SEX	BLOOD	TRIBAL ENROLLMENT		
						Year	County	No.
I.W. 200	1 Costen, Thomas J	First Named	49	M	I.W.	1896	Tobucksy	14392
	2							
	3							
	4							
	5							
	6							
	7							
	8							
	9							
	10							
	11	ENROLLMENT OF NOS. 1 HEREON APPROVED BY THE SECRETARY OF INTERIOR JUN 13 1903						
	12							
	13							
	14							
	15							
	16							
	17							

TRIBAL ENROLLMENT OF PARENTS

	Name of Father	Year	County	Name of Mother	Year	County
1	William Costen	Dead	Non-citizen	Cassie Costen	Dead	Non-citizen
2						
3						
4						
5						
6	No1 on 1896 Choctaw census roll as Thomas J Coston[sic]					
7	No1 admitted in 1896 by Dawes Commission as an intermarried					
8	citizen in Choctaw citizenship case #710. No appeal. No1 transferred from Choctaw card #D 152. See decision of May 1, 1903.					
9						
10						
11						
12						
13						
14			Date of Application for Enrollment.			
15			5/10/99			
16				Date of Transfer to this Card. MAY 16 1903		
17						

Choctaw By Blood Enrollment Cards 1898-1914

RESIDENCE: Tobucksy   COUNTY. **Choctaw** ▉ **on**   **Choctaw Roll**   CARD No.
POST OFFICE: Krebs, Ind Ter   *(Not Including Freedmen)*   FIELD No. **5669**

Dawes' Roll No.	NAME	Relationship to Person First Named	AGE	SEX	BLOOD	TRIBAL ENROLLMENT	
						Year	County
I.W. 201	1 Gleason, Michael H	First Named	60	M	I.W.	1896	Tobucksy ...5
	2						
	3						
	4						
	5						
	6						
	7						
	8						
	9						
	10						
	11	ENROLLMENT					
	12	OF NOS. 1 HEREON APPROVED BY THE SECRETARY					
	13	OF INTERIOR JUN 13 1903					
	14						
	15						
	16						
	17						

TRIBAL ENROLLMENT OF PARENTS

	Name of Father	Year	County	Name of Mother	Year	County
1	Michael Gleason		non-citz	Biddy Gleason		
2						
3						
4						
5						
6	No1 admitted by Dawes Commission in 1896 as an intermarried					
7	citizen in Choctaw citizenship case #1012: no appeal					
8	No1 transferred from Choctaw card #D446. See decision of May 1, 1903.					
9						
10						
11						
12						
13						
14			Date of Application for Enrollment.	9/6/99		
15						
16			Date of Transfer to this Card.	MAY 16 1903		
17						

269

Choctaw By Blood Enrollment Cards 1898-1914

RESIDENCE: Chickasaw Nation COUNTY. **Cho███ Nation** Choctaw Roll CARD NO.
Stonewall Ind. Ter. *(Not Including Freedmen)* FIELD NO. **5670**

	NAME	Relationship to Person First Named	AGE	SEX	BLOOD	TRIBAL ENROLLMENT		
						Year	County	No.
I.W. 202	1 Cochran, W. L.		68	M	I.W.	1896	Chickasaw Nation	14450
2								
3								
4								
5								
6								
7								
8								
9								
10								
11	ENROLLMENT							
12	OF NOS. 1 HEREON APPROVED BY THE SECRETARY							
13	OF INTERIOR JUN 13 1903							
14								
15								
16								
17								

TRIBAL ENROLLMENT OF PARENTS

	Name of Father	Year	County	Name of Mother	Year	County
1	A. O. Cochran	Dead	non-citizen	Frances B Cochran	Dead	non-citizen
2						
3						
4						
5						

6 No1 admitted by Dawes Commission in 1896 as an intermarried
7 citizen in Choctaw case #962 - no appeal.
8 No1 Transferred from Choctaw card #D 84. See decision
of May 5, 1903.

Date of Application for Enrollment. 9/3/99

MAY **20** 1903

270

RESIDENCE: Red River	COUNTY.							
POST OFFICE: Arkinda, Ark.	**Choctaw Nation**				Choctaw Roll (Not Including Freedmen)		CARD NO. FIELD NO. **5671**	

Dawes' Roll No.	NAME	Relationship to Person First Named	AGE	SEX	BLOOD	TRIBAL ENROLLMENT		
						Year	County	No.
I.W. 203	1 De Laughter, George		43	M	I.W.			
	2							
	3							
	4							
	5							
	6							
	7							
	8							
	9							
	10							
	11	ENROLLMENT						
	12	OF NOS. 1 HEREON APPROVED BY THE SECRETARY						
	13	OF INTERIOR JUN 13 1903						
	14							
	15							
	16							
	17							

	TRIBAL ENROLLMENT OF PARENTS						
Name of Father	Year	County	Name of Mother	Year	County		
1 David De Laughter	Dead	non-citz	Bettie De Laughter	Dead	non-citz		
2							
3							
4							
5							
6 No1 admitted by Dawes Commission in 1896 as an intermarried							
7 citizen in Choctaw citizenship case #852, no appeal.							
8 Admitted as Geo. De Lautry							
9 No1 transferred from Choctaw card #D 132. See decision of May 5, 1903.							
10							
11							
12							
13							
14			Date of Application for Enrollment.				
15							
16			Apr 28/99			MAY 2	
17							

271

Choctaw By Blood Enrollment Cards 1898-1914

RESIDENCE: Blue COUNTY. **Choctaw Nation** Choctaw Roll CARD No.
POST OFFICE: Utica Ind Ter *(Not Including Freedmen)* FIELD No. **5672**

Dawes' Roll No.	NAME	Relationship to Person First Named	AGE	SEX	BLOOD	TRIBAL ENROLLMENT Year	County	No.
I.W. 204	1 Benson, Eugene R		51	M	I.W.			
	2							
	3							
	4							
	5							
	6							
	7							
	8							
	9							
	10							
	11	ENROLLMENT						
	12	OF NOS. 1 HEREON APPROVED BY THE SECRETARY						
	13	OF INTERIOR JUN 13 1903						
	14							
	15							
	16							
	17							

TRIBAL ENROLLMENT OF PARENTS

	Name of Father	Year	County	Name of Mother	Year	County
1	George Benson	Dead	non-citz	Manda Benson	Dead	non-citz
2						
3						
4						
5						
6	No1 admitted by Dawes Commission in 1876 as					
7	E.R. Benson, Choctaw citizenship case #534: no appeal					
8	No1 transferred from Choctaw card #D325. See decision of May 5, 1903.					
9	For child of No1 see NB (Apr 26 '06) #1099.					
10						
11						
12						
13						
14						
15						
16			Aug 16/99	Date of transfer to this card.	MAY 20 1903	
17			Date of Application for Enrollment.			

Choctaw By Blood Enrollment Cards 1898-1914

RESIDENCE: Chickasaw Nation ~~COUNTY.~~ **Choctaw Nation**   **Choctaw Roll** CARD NO.
POST OFFICE: Bee, Ind. Ter   *(Not Including Freedmen)*   FIELD NO. **5673**

Dawes' Roll No.	NAME	Relationship to Person	AGE	SEX	BLOOD	TRIBAL ENROLLMENT Year	County	No.
I.W. 205	1 Stalcup, Thomas	First Named	32	M	I.W.			
	2							
	3							
	4							
	5							
	6							
	7							
	8							
	9							
	10							
	11	ENROLLMENT						
	12	OF NOS. 1 HEREON APPROVED BY THE SECRETARY						
	13	OF INTERIOR JUN 13 1903						
	14							
	15							
	16							
	17							

TRIBAL ENROLLMENT OF PARENTS

Name of Father	Year	County	Name of Mother	Year	County
1 Peter Stalcup		non-citz	Sarah Stalcup		non-citz
2					
3					
4					
5					
6 No1 transferred from Choctaw card #D380. See					
7 decision of May 5, 1903.					
8 For child of No1 see NB (Apr 26 '06) #1246.					
9					
10					
11					
12					
13					
14					
15					
16		Aug 28/99		Date of transfer to this card.	MAY 20 1903
17		Date of Application for Enrollment.			

273

Choctaw By Blood Enrollment Cards 1898-1914

RESIDENCE: Choctaw Nation   COUNTY, **Choctaw Nation**   **Choctaw Roll**   CARD NO.

POST OFFICE: Sterrett, I.T;   *(Not Including Freedmen)*   FIELD NO. **5674**

Dawes' Roll No.	NAME	Relationship to Person First Named	AGE	SEX	BLOOD	TRIBAL ENROLLMENT		
						Year	County	No.
I.W.937	1 Rhea, James	First Named	48	M	I.W.	1896	Chickasaw Dist	15004
15031	2 " Eugenie	Wife	34	F	1/8	1896	" "	10953
15032	3 " Willie	Dau	12	F	1/16	1896	" "	10954
15033	4 " Elizabeth	Dau	3	F	1/16			
	5							
	6							
	7	ENROLLMENT						
	8	OF NOS. 2,3 and 4 HEREON APPROVED BY THE SECRETARY						
	9	OF INTERIOR Oct 15 1903						
	10							
	11							
	12	No3 is a girl. Change made						
	13	under departmental instructions of				ENROLLMENT HEREON		
	14	July 2 1904 (D.C. #23418-1904)				OF NOS. 1 APPROVED BY THE SECRETARY OF INTERIOR Aug 3 1904		
	15							
	16							
	17							

TRIBAL ENROLLMENT OF PARENTS

	Name of Father	Year	County	Name of Mother	Year	County
1						
2			[No information given]			
3						
4						

5   Nos 1,2,3 and 4 refused enrollment by Commission Dec 8, 1902: on grounds of non-residence

No2 on 1896 census roll as Eugene Rhea

6   No3 also on 1896 Choctaw census roll Page 49 No. 2023

7   Nos 1-2 and 3 were admitted by Dawes Commission in 1896 Choctaw Case #690

8   Nos 1-4 inclusive transferred from Choctaw card D #74 under departmental decision of May 21, 1903

See Departmental notice of rehearing Oct 26, 1903: D.C. No. 30235-1903

9   Land offices notified to with hold issuance of citizenship certificates: Nov. 3, 1903

10   Feby 23rd, 1904: The Secty of Interior denied motion of attorneys for Choctaw and Chickasaw

11   nations for a re-adjudication and directed that Departmental decision of May 21, 1903 be adhered

12   to and applicants enrolled and allotted.

13			
14			
15			Date of transfer to this card.
16		Date of Application for Enrollment. Oct 13/98	Jun 2, 1903
17			

Choctaw By Blood Enrollment Cards 1898-1914

RESIDENCE: Chickasaw Nation COUNTY. **Choctaw Nation**   **Choctaw Roll**   CARD NO.
POST OFFICE: Rush Springs IT 4/26/04   *(Not Including Freedmen)*   FIELD NO. **5675**

Dawes' Roll No.	NAME	Relationship to Person First Named	AGE	SEX	BLOOD	TRIBAL ENROLLMENT Year	County	No.
14995	1 Martin, Sam	First Named	38	M	3/8	1896	Chickasaw Dist	8941
14996	2 " Willie	Dau	10	F	3/16	1896	"	8942
	3							
	4							
	5							
	6							
	7							
	8							
	9							
	10							
	11	ENROLLMENT						
	12	OF NOS. 1 and 2 HEREON APPROVED BY THE SECRETARY						
	13	OF INTERIOR OCT 15 1903						
	14							
	15							
	16							
	17							

TRIBAL ENROLLMENT OF PARENTS

	Name of Father	Year	County	Name of Mother	Year	County
1	Louis Martin	Dead	Choctaw roll	Sophie Winters	Dead	Choctaw roll
2	No1			Nora Martin		Noncitizen
3						
4						
5						
6	Nos 1 and 2 transferred from Choctaw card D13					
7	See decision of July 20, 1903.					
8	Former wife of No1 & mother of No2 on Choc. card No. 6077					
9						
10	(Name of No.2 now Martin 45993-1911)					
11						
12						
13						
14						
15						
16	No2 P.O. Comanche, Okla 12/6/11					
17						

Sept 12/98
Date of Application for Enrollment.

Date of Transfer to this Card.   AUG

275

Choctaw By Blood Enrollment Cards 1898-1914

RESIDENCE: Chickasaw Nation COUNTY. **Choctaw Nation** Choctaw Roll CARD NO.
POST OFFICE: Millcreek, I.T. (Not Including Freedmen) FIELD NO.

Dawes' Roll No.	NAME	Relationship to Person First Named	AGE	SEX	BLOOD	TRIBAL ENROLLMENT Year	County	No.
14997	1 Cotten, Robert L	First Named	22	M	1/16	1896	Chickasaw District	3079
IW 1225	2 " Maud	Wife	22	F	I.W.			
	3							
	4							
	5							
	6							
	7	ENROLLMENT						
	8	OF NOS. 1 HEREON						
	9	APPROVED BY THE SECRETARY OF INTERIOR OCT 15 1903						
	10							
	11	ENROLLMENT						
	12	OF NOS. 2 HEREON APPROVED BY THE SECRETARY						
	13	OF INTERIOR DEC 13 1904						
	14							
	15							
	16							
	17							

TRIBAL ENROLLMENT OF PARENTS

	Name of Father	Year	County	Name of Mother	Year	County
1	David B. Cotten	Dead	noncitizen	Susan L Cotten	Dead	Choctaw roll
2	William Dougherty	"	" "	Adelaide Dougherty	"	non citizen
3						
4						
5	No1 on Choctaw roll as Robert Cotten					
6	No1 is now husband of Maud Cotten on Choctaw card D761					
7	No1 transferred from Choctaw card #D47. See decision of July 10, 1903.					
8	No2 was married to Robert L Cotten April 16, 1902 under U.S. license					
9	See testimony of July 18, 1902.					
10	No2 originally listed for enrollment on Choctaw card #D-761 Jul 18, 1902: transferred to this card Nov. 26, 1904. See decision of No. 9, 1904.					
11						
12						
13						
14						
15			Sept 23/98			
16			Date of Application for Enrollment.	Date of Transfer to this Card.	AUG 5 1903	
17						

Choctaw By Blood Enrollment Cards 1898-1914

RESIDENCE: Kiamitia COUNTY. **Choctaw Nation**

POST OFFICE: Antlers, I.T.

Choctaw Roll *(Not Including Freedmen)*

CARD NO.

FIELD NO. **5677**

Dawes' Roll No.	NAME	Relationship to Person First Named	AGE	SEX	BLOOD	TRIBAL ENROLLMENT		
						Year	County	No.
IW998	1 Isaac, George	First Named	14	M	Full	1896	Kiamitia	13761
	2							
	3							
	4							
	5							
	6							
	7							
	8							
	9							
	10							
	11	ENROLLMENT						
	12	OF NOS. 1 HEREON APPROVED BY THE SECRETARY						
	13	OF INTERIOR Oct 15 1903						
	14							
	15							
	16							
	17							

TRIBAL ENROLLMENT OF PARENTS

	Name of Father	Year	County	Name of Mother	Year	County
1	William Isaac	dead	Choctaw Roll	Lucy Isaac	Dead	Choctaw Roll
2						
3						
4						
5						
6	No1 also on 1893 Pay Roll Kiamitia County Page 52 No. 418					
7						
8	No.1 transferred from Choctaw card D 169. See decision of July 20, 1903					
9						
10						
11						
12						
13						
14						
15						
16						
17						

5/18/99

Date of Application for Enrollment.

Date of Transfer to this Card. Aug 5-1903

Choctaw By Blood Enrollment Cards 1898-1914

RESIDENCE: **Blue** COUNTY. **Choctaw Nation** Choctaw Roll *(Not Including Freedmen)* CARD NO. FIELD NO. **5678**
POST OFFICE: **Caddo, I.T.**

Dawes' Roll No.	NAME	Relationship to Person First Named	AGE	SEX	BLOOD	TRIBAL ENROLLMENT		
						Year	County	No.
14999	₁ Ward, Joseph M		28	M	1/32	1896	Blue	13873
IW 537	₂ " Minnie	Wife	27	F	I.W.			
15000	₃ " Alice	Dau	4	F	1/64			
15001	₄ " Martha	Dau	1	F	1/64			
	₅							
	₆							
	₇ ENROLLMENT							
	₈ OF NOS. 1,3 and 4 HEREON							
	₉ APPROVED BY THE SECRETARY OF INTERIOR Oct 15 1903							
	₁₀							
	₁₁							
	₁₂							
	₁₃ ENROLLMENT							
	₁₄ OF NOS. 2 HEREON APPROVED BY THE SECRETARY							
	₁₅ OF INTERIOR Dec 24 1903							
	₁₆							
	₁₇							

TRIBAL ENROLLMENT OF PARENTS

	Name of Father	Year	County	Name of Mother	Year	County
₁	W. G. Ward		Blue	Eliza Ward		Cherokee
₂	Marion Head		Noncitizen	Mary Head		Noncitizen
₃	No1			No2		
₄	No1			No2		
₅						
₆	Nos 1 to 4 inclusive transferred from Choctaw card D370					
₇	See decision of July 20, 1903.					
₈	No3 Proof of birth filed Oct 31, 1899 No4 Proof of birth filed Oct 20, 1902					
₉						
₁₀	For child of nos 1 & 2 see NB (Apr 26-06) Card #484					
₁₁						
₁₂						
₁₃						
₁₄						
₁₅			Date of Application for Enrollment.		Date of Transfer to this Card.	
₁₆			Aug 22/99			Aug 5-1903
₁₇						

278

Choctaw By Blood Enrollment Cards 1898-1914

RESIDENCE: Choctaw Nation   COUNTY. **Choctaw Nation**   **Choctaw Roll**   CARD No.

POST OFFICE: Red Oak I.T.   (Not Including Freedmen)   FIELD No. **5679**

Dawes' Roll No.	NAME	Relationship to Person First Named	AGE	SEX	BLOOD	TRIBAL ENROLLMENT		
						Year	County	No.
15002	1 Green, Ida	First Named	27	F	Full	1896	Sans Bois	2164
15003	2 " Robert	Son	5	M	1/2			
	3							
	4							
	5							
	6							
	7							
	8							
	9							
	10							
	11	ENROLLMENT						
	12	OF NOS. 1 and 2 HEREON APPROVED BY THE SECRETARY						
	13	OF INTERIOR OCT 15 1903						
	14							
	15							
	16							
	17							

TRIBAL ENROLLMENT OF PARENTS

	Name of Father	Year	County	Name of Mother	Year	C
1	Ben Alberson		Chick residing in Choctaw N, 1st Dist	Tennessee Alberson	Dead	Ch
2	Morris Green	1896	Sugar Loaf	No.1		
3						
4						
5						
6	No1 on 1896 Choctaw census roll as Ida Colbert					
7						
8	Nos 1-2 transferred from Chickasaw card #1400. July 21, 1903.			See decision of		
9	No2 Proof of birth filed June 19, 1899.					
10	For child of No.1 see NB (March 3 1905) #1420					
11						
12						
13						
14						
15						
16				March 21/99	Date of Transfer to this Card.	AU
17				Date of Application for Enrollment.		

Choctaw By Blood Enrollment Cards 1898-1914

| RESIDENCE: | Kiamitia | COUNTY. | **Choctaw Nation** | | **Choctaw Roll** | CARD No. | |
| POST OFFICE: | Grant I.T. | | | | *(Not Including Freedmen)* | FIELD No. | |

Dawes' Roll No.	NAME	Relationship to Person First Named	AGE	SEX	BLOOD	TRIBAL ENROLLMENT		
						Year	County	No.
15004	1 Parshall, Lula	First Named	21	F	1/8	1896	Kiamitia	10458
	2							
	3							
	4							
	5							
	6							
	7							
	8							
	9							
	10							
	11	ENROLLMENT						
	12	OF NOS. 1 HEREON APPROVED BY THE SECRETARY						
	13	OF INTERIOR OCT 15 1903						
	14							
	15							
	16							
	17							

TRIBAL ENROLLMENT OF PARENTS

	Name of Father	Year	County	Name of Mother	Year	County
1	L. B. Parshall	Dead	noncitizen	Virginia Parshall	Dead	Chickasaw roll
2						
3						
4						
5						
6	No1 transferred from Chickasaw card #1431. See decision of					
7	July 30, 1903.					
8						
9						
10						
11						
12						
13						
14						
15						
16				5/19/99 Date of Application for Enrollment.		AUG 15 1903
17						

Choctaw By Blood Enrollment Cards 1898-1914

RESIDENCE: Atoka
POST OFFICE: Allen, I.T.
COUNTY. **Choctaw Nation**
Choctaw Roll *(Not Including Freedmen)*
CARD NO.
FIELD NO. **5681**

Dawes' Roll No.	NAME	Relationship to Person First Named	AGE	SEX	BLOOD	TRIBAL ENROLLMENT		
						Year	County	No.
15005	1 Williams, Robert	First Named	22	M	1/2	1896	Atoka	14028
	2							
	3							
	4							
	5							
	6							
	7							
	8							
	9							
	10							
	11	ENROLLMENT OF NOS. 1 HEREON APPROVED BY THE SECRETARY OF INTERIOR OCT 15 1903						
	12							
	13							
	14							
	15							
	16							
	17							

TRIBAL ENROLLMENT OF PARENTS

	Name of Father	Year	County	Name of Mother	Year	County
1	Edward Williams	Dead	Chickasaw roll	Julia Haynes	1896	Chick residing in Choctaw N. 1st Dist
2						
3						
4						
5						
6	No1 transferred from Chickasaw card #32. See decision of					
7	July 30, 1903.					
8	For child of No1 see Chickasaw NB (Apr 26-06) Card #134					
9						
10						
11						
12						
13						
14						
15						
16					transferred to this card	AUG 15 1903
17						

Choctaw By Blood Enrollment Cards 1898-1914

RESIDENCE: Atoka	COUNTY.	Choctaw Nation	Choctaw Roll	CARD No.
POST OFFICE: Citra, I.T.			(Not Including Freedmen)	FIELD No. 5682

Dawes' Roll No.	NAME	Relationship to Person First Named	AGE	SEX	BLOOD	TRIBAL ENROLLMENT		
						Year	County	No.
15006	1 Johnson, Frances	First Named	25	F	Full	1896	Atoka	13999
	2							
	3							
	4							
	5							
	6							
	7							
	8							
	9							
	10							
	11	ENROLLMENT						
	12	OF NOS. 1 HEREON APPROVED BY THE SECRETARY						
	13	OF INTERIOR OCT 15 1903						
	14							
	15							
	16							
	17							

TRIBAL ENROLLMENT OF PARENTS

Name of Father	Year	County	Name of Mother	Year	County
1 Ah-wan-tan-tubby	Dead	Chickasaw roll	Chim-ho-c▒		▒
2					
3					
4					
5					
6 No1 on 1896 Choctaw census roll as Frances Wa▒					
7					
8 No1 transferred from Chickasaw card #1042. See decision of July 30, 1903.					
9					
10					
11					
12					
13					
14					
15					
16			Date of Transfer to this Card.	AUG 15 1903	
17					

Choctaw By Blood Enrollment Cards 1898-1914

RESIDENCE: Blue COUNTY. **Choctaw Nation**   **Choctaw Roll** (Not Including Freedmen)   CARD No.

POST OFFICE: Caddo, I. T.   FIELD No. **5683**

Dawes' Roll No.	NAME	Relationship to Person First Named	AGE	SEX	BLOOD	TRIBAL ENROLLMENT		
						Year	County	No.
IW538	1 Fandree, Howard	First Named	32	M	I.W.	1896	Blue	14534
15007	2 " Annie L	Dau	6	F	1/64			
15008	3 " Lola P	Dau	4	F	1/64			
15009	4 " Ross Howard	Son	2	M	1/64			
	5							
	6							
	7	ENROLLMENT						
	8	OF NOS. 2, 3 and 4 HEREON APPROVED BY THE SECRETARY						
	9	OF INTERIOR Oct 15, 1903						
	10							
	11	ENROLLMENT						
	12	OF NOS. 1 HEREON APPROVED BY THE SECRETARY						
	13	OF INTERIOR Dec 24, 1903						
	14							
	15							
	16							
	17							

TRIBAL ENROLLMENT OF PARENTS

	Name of Father	Year	County	Name of Mother	Year	County
1	R.P. Fandree		Non-citizen	Eliza V Fandree		non-citizen
2	No.1			Martha Fandree	Dead	Blue
3	No.1			" "	"	"
4	No.1			" "	"	"
5						
6	No1 on 1896 roll as Howard Fordree[sic]					
7	Nos 1-4 inclusive transferred from Choctaw card D371. See decision of July 30, 1903.					
8	No.2 Born June 1, 1897, enrolled Sept 2, 1899					
9	No.3 Born April 10, 1899, enrolled Sept. 2, 1899					
10	No.4 Born Dec. 14, 1901 enrolled Jany 2, 1902					
11						
12						
13						
14				Date of Application for Enrollment.		
15						
16				Sept 14/99	Date of Transfer to this Card.	AUG 15 1903
17						

Choctaw By Blood Enrollment Cards 1898-1914

RESIDENCE: Atoka COUNTY. **Choctaw Nation** **Choctaw Roll** CARD NO.
POST OFFICE: Mᶜ Curtain, I.T. (Not Including Freedmen) FIELD NO. **5684**

Dawes' Roll No.		NAME	Relationship to Person First Named	AGE	SEX	BLOOD	TRIBAL ENROLLMENT		
							Year	County	No.
15010	1	Nevins, Floyd	First Named	28	M	1/4	1896	Atoka	9851
IW854	2	" Vivian Scott	Wife	22	F	I.W.			
	3								
	4								
	5								
	6								
	7	ENROLLMENT OF NOS. 1 HEREON							
	8	APPROVED BY THE SECRETARY							
	9	OF INTERIOR OCT 15 1903							
	10								
	11	ENROLLMENT							
	12	OF NOS. 2 HEREON APPROVED BY THE SECRETARY							
	13	OF INTERIOR MAY 21 1904							
	14								
	15								
	16								
	17								

TRIBAL ENROLLMENT OF PARENTS

	Name of Father	Year	County	Name of Mother	Year	County
1	Mose Nevins		Cherokee	Julia Nevins		Choctaw
2	George W Scott		noncitizen	Stella O Scott		Cherokee
3						
4						
5						
6	No1 transferred from Choctaw card D533. No2 transferred from					
7	Choctaw card D95. See decisions of July 30, 1903.					
8						
9						
10						
11						
12						
13						
14			Date of Application for Enrollment.			
15						
16			Dec 4/99	Date of Transfer to this Card.	AUG 15 1903	
17						

284

Choctaw By Blood Enrollment Cards 1898-1914

Dawes' Roll No.	NAME	Relationship to Person First Named	AGE	SEX	BLOOD	TRIBAL ENROLLMENT		
						Year	County	No.
15011	1 Huddleston, Frank	First Named	24	M	1/4	1896	Atoka	6072
15012	2 " Sophia	Sister	19	F	1/4	1896	"	6074
15013	3 " Lucy J	Sister	17	F	1/4	1896	"	6075
15014	4 " Walter J	Bro	14	M	1/4	1896	"	6-76
15015	5 " May	Sister	12	F	1/4	1896	"	6077
15016	6 Floyd, Eliza	Sister	22	F	1/4	1896	"	6073
15017	7 " Huddleston	Neph.	2	M	1/4			
IW 1047	8 " Charles W	Husband of No6	26	"	I.W.			
IW 1610	9 Huddleston, May	Wife	18	F	I.W.			
	10					ENROLLMENT OF NOS. 8 HEREON APPROVED BY THE SECRETARY OF INTERIOR Oct 21 1904		
	11	ENROLLMENT OF NOS. 1,2,3,4,5,6 and 7 HEREON APPROVED BY THE SECRETARY						
	12	OF INTERIOR Oct 15 1903						
	13	No7 born April 10, 1901, enrolled April 19-1901						
	14	No.6 is wife of Charles W. Floyd on Choctaw card D. 457						
	15	For child of No.3 see NB (Apr 26-06) Card #433.						
	16	Nos. 1-7 inclusive transferred from Choctaw card D311. See decision of July 30, 1903						
	17							

(left margin, vertical:) For child of No 6 & 8 see NB (Mar 3/05) #414, " " #420, For child " " 189, For children "*

	TRIBAL ENROLLMENT OF PARENTS					
	Name of Father	Year	County	Name of Mother	Year	County
1	Jas. Huddleston	Dead	non citizen	Sinie Huddleston	Dead	Atoka
2	" "	"	"	" "	"	"
3	" "	"	"	" "	"	"
4	" "	"	"	" "	"	"
5	" "	"	"	" "	"	"
6	" "	"	"	" "	"	"
7	Chas W Floyd		"	No.6		
8	D.S. Floyd		"	Jane Floyd		non-citz
9	Billy Smith			Emma Smith		
10	No.1 on 1896 roll as Frank Hudlson					
11	No.2 " " " " Sophia					
12	No.3 " " " " Lucy					
13	No.4 " " " " Walter J					
14	No.5 " " " " May					
15	No.6 " " " " Eliza					
16						
17						

ENROLLMENT OF NOS. 9 HEREON APPROVED BY THE SECRETARY OF INTERIOR Feb 12 1907

No.8 transferred from Choctaw card D457. See decision of August 31, 1904. Sept 15, 1904

No.9 transferred from Choc. card #D-966. Jan 15, 1907 see decision of Dec. 31, 1906

Date of Application for Enrollment. Aug 9/99

Date of transfer to this card. Aug 15 1903

Choctaw By Blood Enrollment Cards 1898-1914

RESIDENCE: Chickasaw Nation COUNTY. **Choctaw Nation**   Choctaw Roll ░░░ ARD NO.
POST OFFICE: *(Not Including Freedmen)*   FIELD NO. **5686**

Dawes' Roll No.	NAME	Relationship to Person	AGE	SEX	BLOOD	TRIBAL ENROLLMENT		
						Year	County	No.
15018	1 Bailey, Ida L	First Named	40	F	1/16	1896	Chickasaw Dist	2019
15019	2 " Tobias J	Son	19	M	1/32	1896	" "	2020
15020	3 " Viola	Dau	14	F	1/32	1896	" "	2021
	4							
	5							
	6							
	7	ENROLLMENT						
	8	OF NOS. 1, 2 and 3 HEREON APPROVED BY THE SECRETARY						
	9	OF INTERIOR OCT 15 1903						
	10							
	11							
	12							
	13							
	14							
	15							
	16							
	17							

TRIBAL ENROLLMENT OF PARENTS

	Name of Father	Year				Year	County
1	John Stewart		Noncitizen	Nancy J Stewart		Dead	Atoka
2	I. J. Bailey		"	No.1			
3	" "		"	No.1			
4							
5							
6	No2 on 1896 roll as Tobias Bailey						
7							
8	Nos 1-3 transferred from Choctaw card D5. See decision of July 30, 1903.						
9	Nos 1-2 admitted by U.S. Indian Agent Oct. 12, 1889.						
10							
11							
12							
13							
14							
15							Date of transfer
16				Date of Application for Enrollment. 9/3/98			to this card. AUG 15 1903
17							

286

Choctaw By Blood Enrollment Cards 1898-1914

RESIDENCE: Chickasaw Nation COUNTY.
POST OFFICE: Ardmore, I.T.

Choctaw Nation

Choctaw Roll (Not Including Freedmen)

CARD NO.
FIELD NO. **5687**

Dawes' Roll No.	NAME	Relationship to Person First Named	AGE	SEX	BLOOD	TRIBAL ENROLLMENT Year	County	No.
IW1359	₁ Douglas, Seigel McClellan	First Named	41	M	I.W.			
15021	₂ Stewart, Bailey	step son	24	M	1/16			
15022	₃ " James	" "	17	M	1/16			
15023	₄ " Newton	" "	16	M	1/16			
15024	₅ " Bonny	" Dau	13	F	1/16			
NB688	₆ " Purcell							
NB764	₇ Mᶜ Gee, Annice							
	₈ Douglas, Jessie							
	₉ " Marvin Paul	ENROLLMENT						
	₁₀ " Beulah Lillian	OF NOS. 2,3,4 and 5 HEREON APPROVED BY THE SECRETARY						
	₁₁	OF INTERIOR Oct 15 1903						
	₁₂							
	₁₃	ENROLLMENT						
	₁₄	OF NOS. 1 HEREON APPROVED BY THE SECRETARY						
	₁₅	OF INTERIOR Mar 14 1905						
	₁₆							
	₁₇							

TRIBAL ENROLLMENT OF PARENTS

	Name of Father	Year	County	Name of Mother	Year	County
₁	Alex Douglas	Dead	non citizen	Sarah A. Douglas		
₂	John Stewart		" "	Mollie Douglas	Dead	Choctaw
₃	" "		" "	" "	"	"
₄	" "		" "	" "	"	"
₅	" "		" "	" "	"	"
₆	No.3			Rinnie B Stewart	Born	Sep 6-05
₇	John F Mᶜ Gee			No.5	"	Jul 17-05
₈	No.1					
₉	"					
₁₀	Nos2-3-4 and 5 admitted by Dawes Commission in 1896 case #815. No appeal taken					
₁₁	No1 transferred from Choctaw card D-75. See decision of Jan 10-1905					
₁₂	Nos2-5 inclusive transferred from Choctaw card D75. See decision of July 30, 1903.					
₁₃	No.1 formerly husband of Mollie Douglas. (formerly Stewart) who was admitted as a citizen by blood of the Choctaw Nation by the Commission in 1896, case #815 and who died about 1899.					
₁₄	For child of No3 see NB (Apr 26-06) card #688					
₁₅	" " No5 " " " " #764					
₁₆	" children "No1 " " " " #1110					
₁₇						

Oct 13/98
Date of Application for Enrollment.

Date of transfer
to this card. Aug 15 1903

Choctaw By Blood Enrollment Cards 1898-1914

RESIDENCE: Blue
POST OFFICE: Durant, I.T.

COUNTY. **Choctaw Nation**

Choctaw Roll
(Not Including Freedmen)

CARD NO.
FIELD NO. **5688**

Dawes' Roll No.	NAME	Relationship to Person First Named	AGE	SEX	BLOOD	TRIBAL ENROLLMENT		
						Year	County	No.
IW 1467	1 Walker, Naomi	First Named	50	F	I.W.	1896	Blue	15061
15862	2 " Cynthia	Dau	19	F	A.W.			
15863	3 " Rose	Son	16	M	A.W.			
DP 8/30/06	4 Guion, Harry	son	25	M	White			
	5					No.4 Refused Oct. 2, 1906		
	6					Copy of Decision Forwarded Applicant Oct. 2, 1906		
	7 Record and decision of Commission of July 30, 1903							
	8 enrolling Nos 1,2 and 3 forwarded Dept Feby 13, 1904					Copy of Decision forwarded Attorney for Applicant. Oct 2, 1906		
	9							
	10							
	11 ENROLLMEN					Copy of Decision forwarded		
	12 OF NOS. 2 and 3 HEREON					Attorneys for Choctaw and		
	13 APPROVED BY THE SECRETARY					Chickasaw Nations. Oct. 2, 1906		
	14 OF INTERIOR Jun 12 1905					Record Forwarded Department.		
	15 ENROLLMENT OF NOS. 1 HEREON					Oct. 2, 1906		
	16 APPROVED BY THE SECRETARY							
	17 OF INTERIOR Jun 12, 1905							

TRIBAL ENROLLMENT OF PARENTS

Name of Father	Year	County	Name of Mother	Year	County
1 J J Gardner	dead	Non Citz	Emiline Gardner	dead	Non-citz
2 Rose Walker	"	"	No.1		
3 "	"	"	No.1		
4 Frank H. Guion		non-citizen	No.1		
5					
6					

7 Nos 1-2&3 Transferred from Choctaw card D320. See decision of July 30th 1903.

8 Decision of Commission enrolling Nos 1,2 and 3 affirmed by Secty of Interior April 5, 1905

Name of No4 placed hereon under direction of Secty of Interior of April 5, 1905

9 May 5, 1905: Report to Department as to No.4 No.4 Feb. 18, 1907 Report to Dept.

10 No.1 admitted by Com in 1896 as intermarried citizen Choc. case No. 516

11 No2 and 3 " " " " " " citizens " " " 502.

12

13 J.G. Ralls, Atoka, I.T.

14 J.B. Dickinson To McAlester I.T.

15

16 Date of Application for Enrollment. Nos 1,2 and 3 Listed for Enrollment Aug 15/99

17 P.O. Address of No4 Sterrett, I.T. Listed on this card Aug 15 1903

288

Choctaw By Blood Enrollment Cards 1898-1914

RESIDENCE: Towson   COUNTY, **Choctaw Nation**   **Choctaw Roll**   CARD NO.

POST OFFICE: Doaksville I.T.   (Not Including Freedmen) FIELD NO. **5689**

Dawes' Roll No.	NAME	Relationship to Person First Named	AGE	SEX	BLOOD	TRIBAL ENROLLMENT Year	County	No.
IW1483	1 Holly, James		39	M	I.W.			
15063	2 " Frances E	Wife	27	F	1/8	1896	Towson	1106
	3							
	4							
	5							
	6							
	7	ENROLLMENT						
	8	OF NOS. 2 HEREON						
	9	APPROVED BY THE SECRETARY OF INTERIOR Feb 16 1904						
	10							
	11							
	12							
	13	ENROLLMENT						
	14	OF NOS. One HEREON						
	15	APPROVED BY THE SECRETARY OF INTERIOR Aug 22, 1905						
	16							
	17							

TRIBAL ENROLLMENT OF PARENTS

	Name of Father	Year	County	Name of Mother	Year	County
1	Bryant Holly	dead	Non Citz	Nancy Holly	dead	Non Citz
2						
3						
4						
5	Decision of Commission enrolling Nos 1 and 2 of July 30, 1903					
6	forwarded Department, Feby 13, 1904					
7						
8						
9	June 28, 1905 Decision of Commission of July 30, 1903					
10	enrolling No.1 affirmed by Department (I.T.D. 5448-1904) D.C. #32464-1905					
11						
12	Nos. 1&2 Transferred from Choctaw card D162.					
13	See decision of July 30, 1903.					
14						
15						
16			5/16/99			
17	P.O. Swink, I.T. 4/13/05		Date of Application for Enrollment	Date of Transfer to this Card Aug 15 1903		

289

Choctaw By Blood Enrollment Cards 1898-1914

Choctaw Nation

Choctaw Roll (Not Including Freedmen)

CARD NO. FIELD NO. **5690**

Dawes' Roll No.		NAME	Relationship to Person First Named	AGE	SEX	BLOOD	TRIBAL ENROLLMENT		
							Year	County	No.
15864	1	Davis, Zachary T		50	M	1/4	1893	Red River	P.R. 161
IW 1457	2	" Mary Elizabeth	Wife	39	F	I.W.			
15865	3	" Buford	Dau	11	F	1/8	1896	Red River	3440
15866	4	" Anis	Dau	9	F	1/8	1896	" "	3441
15867	5	" Seemenigh	Son	3mo	M	1/8			
	6								
	7	ENROLLMENT							
	8	OF NOS. 1,3,4 and 5 HEREON APPROVED BY THE SECRETARY							
	9	OF INTERIOR Jun 12, 1905							
	10								
	11	ENROLLMENT							
	12	OF NOS. 2 HEREON							
	13	APPROVED BY THE SECRETARY OF INTERIOR Jun 12, 1905							
	14								
	15	For child of Nos 1&2 see NB (Apr 26-06) Card #448							
	16								
	17								

TRIBAL ENROLLMENT OF PARENTS

	Name of Father	Year	County	Name of Mother	Year	County
1	Art Davis	Dead	Non Citz	Amy Davis	Dead	Non Citz
2	Willian Hudson	"	" "	Paralee Hudson	"	" "
3	No.1			Fanny Davis	"	" "
4	No.1			" "	"	" "
5	No.1			No.2		
6	Decision of Commission of July 30, 1903 enrolling Nos. 1 to 5 approved by secretary of					
7	Interior February 10, 1905, (I.T.D. #4009 5039-1904) D.C. #7748-1905					
8	Nos 1-3-4&5 Transferred from Choctaw card No. D.124					
9	No 2 Transferred from Choctaw Card No D.611 Sex of No.3 Buford Davis changed					
10	See decision of July 30, 1903. from male to female under					
11	No.4 on 1896 Roll as Zack Davis Departmental authority of					
12	Protest of Choctaw Nation, Nov. 9, 1903. Aug 21, 1905 (I.T.D.10364-1905)					
13	Record forwarded Department Nov 11, 1903					
14						
15						
16				April 24/99		
17	P.O. Goodwater, I.T. 12/30/04			Date of Application for Enrollment. transferred Aug 15 1903		

Choctaw By Blood Enrollment Cards 1898-1914

RESIDENCE: Red River   COUNTY, ~~Goodwater~~ I.T.
POST OFFICE: ~~Cerrogordo~~ Ark

Choctaw Nation

Choctaw Roll
(Not Including Freedmen)

CARD NO.
FIELD NO. **5691**

Dawes' Roll No.	NAME	Relationship to Person First Named	AGE	SEX	BLOOD	TRIBAL ENROLLMENT		
						Year	County	No.
15868	1 Davis, Sherwood	First Named	21	M	1/8	1896	Red River	3442
IW 1458	2 " Laura	Wife	19	F	I.W.			
15869	3 " Theodore Winston	Son	1mo	M	1/16			
	4							
	5	ENROLLMENT						
	6	OF NOS. 1 and 3 HEREON						
	7	APPROVED BY THE SECRETARY OF INTERIOR Jun 12 1905						
	8							
	9							
	10	ENROLLMENT						
	11	OF NOS. 2 HEREON						
	12	APPROVED BY THE SECRETARY OF INTERIOR Jun 12 1905						
	13							
	14							
	15							
	16							
	17							

TRIBAL ENROLLMENT OF PARENTS

	Name of Father	Year	County	Name of Mother	Year	County
1	Zachary T. Davis			Fanny Davis	Dead	Non Citz
2	France Willis		non citz	Sarah Willis		" "
3	No.1			No.2		
4						
5						
6						
7						
8	Decision of Commission of July 30, 1903 enrolling Nos. 1 to 3 inclusive, approved by					
9	Secretary of Interior February 10, 1905, (I.T.D. #4009 5037-1904) D.C. #7748-1905					
10	For child of Nos 1&2 see NB S(Apr 26-06) Card #748					
	Nos 1 and 3 Transferred from Choctaw card No. D.124					
11	No. 2 " " " " No. D.608					
12	See Decision of July 30, 1903, filed with Choctaw No. 5690					
13						
14	Protest of Choctaw Nation Nov. 9, 1903.					
	Record forwarded Department Nov. 11, 1903					
15	Protest of attorneys for Choctaw and Chickasaw Nations of Jany 23,					
16	forwarded Secty of Interior, Feby 6, 1904.					
17	Date of Application for Enrollment. April 24/99			Trans		

291

Choctaw By Blood Enrollment Cards 1898-1914

RESIDENCE: Choctaw COUNTY. **Choctaw Nation** Choctaw Roll CARD No.
POST OFFICE: Goodwater, I.T. *(Not Including Freedmen)* FIELD No. **5692**

Dawes' Roll No.		NAME	Relationship to Person First Named	AGE	SEX	BLOOD	TRIBAL ENROLLMENT		
							Year	County	No.
IW 1459	1	Bishop, Hugh A		24	M	I.W.			
15870	2	" Eunice	Wife	17	F	1/8	1896	Red River	3438
15871	3	" Fannie Lundie	Dau	3wks	F	1/16			
	4								
	5								
	6								
	7	ENROLLMENT							
	8	OF NOS. 2 and 3 HEREON							
	9	APPROVED BY THE SECRETARY							
		OF INTERIOR Jun 12 1905							
	10								
	11								
	12								
	13	ENROLLMENT							
	14	OF NOS. 1 HEREON							
		APPROVED BY THE SECRETARY							
	15	OF INTERIOR Jun 12 1905							
	16								
	17								

TRIBAL ENROLLMENT OF PARENTS

	Name of Father	Year	County	Name of Mother	Year	County
1	Solon B. Bishop		Non Citz	Nannie H. Bishop		Non Citz
2	Zachary T Davis	1893		Fanny Davis	Dead	" "
3	No.1			No.2		
4						
5	Decision of Commission of July 30, 1903 enrolling Nos. 1 to 3 inclusive, approved by					
6	Department February 10, 1905, (I.T.D. #4009 5037-1904) D.C. #7748-1905					
7	No.1 transferred from Choctaw card No. D.688					
8	No.2 and 3 " " " " No.D.124					
9	See Decision of July 30, 1903, filed with Choctaw No. 5690					
10	Protest of Choctaw Nation Nov. 9, 1903					
11	Record forwarded Department Nov 11, 1903					
12	Protest of attorneys for Choctaw and Chickasaw Nation of Jan 23, 1904 forwarded Secty of Interior Feby 6, 1904.					
13	For children (twins) of Nos 1&2 see NB (Apr 26/06) Card #708					
14						Nov 19/1901
15						Date of Application for Enrollment.
16						Aug 15 1903
17	P.O. Tupelo I.T. 4/7/05				Transferred	

292

Choctaw By Blood Enrollment Cards 1898-1914

RESIDENCE: Choctaw   COUNTY. **Choctaw Nation**   **Choctaw Roll** *(Not Including Freedmen)*   CARD NO.

POST OFFICE: Goodwater I.T.   FIELD NO. **5693**

Dawes' Roll No.	NAME	Relationship to Person First Named	AGE	SEX	BLOOD	TRIBAL ENROLLMENT Year	County	No.
IW 1460	1 Roberts, Joseph J	First Named	27	M	I.W.			
15872	2 " Carrie	Wife	15	F	1/8	1896	Red River	3439
	3							
	4							
	5							
	6 ENROLLMENT							
	7 OF NOS. 2 HEREON APPROVED BY THE SECRETARY							
	8 OF INTERIOR JUN 12 1905							
	9							
	10							
	11 ENROLLMENT							
	12 OF NOS. 1 HEREON APPROVED BY THE SECRETARY							
	13 OF INTERIOR JUN 12 1905							
	14							
	15							
	16							
	17							

TRIBAL ENROLLMENT OF PARENTS

	Name of Father	Year	County	Name of Mother	Year	County
1	Henry F Roberts		Non Citz	Matilda Roberts	Dead	Non Citz
2	Zachary T. Davis	1893	Red River	Fanny Davis	"	" " "
3						
4						
5						
6						
7	Decision of Commission of July 30, 1903 enrolling [illegible] approved by Secretary of Interior February 14, 1905. (I.T.D. #4009 5017 1904) D.C. #7718 1905					
8	For child of No.1 see NB (Apr 26, 1906) Card No. 13					
9	No1 transferred from Choctaw Card No. D. 583					
10	No2 " " " " No. D.124 See Decision of July 30, 1903, filed with Choctaw No. 5690.					
11						
12	Protest of Choctaw Nation Nov. 9, 1903					
13	Record forwarded Department Nov 11, 1903 Protest of attorneys for Choctaw and Chickasaw Nation of Jany 23, 1904					
14	forwarded Secty of Interior Feby 6, 1904.				9/28/00	
15					Date of Application for Enrollment.	
16						
17					Transferred - AUG 15 1903	

Choctaw By Blood Enrollment Cards 1898-1914

RESIDENCE: Sugar Loaf POST OFFICE: Page I.T.	COUNTY.	**Choctaw Nation**				**Choctaw Roll** *(Not Including Freedmen)*	CARD NO. FIELD NO. **5694**	

Dawes' Roll No.	NAME	Relationship to Person First Named	AGE	SEX	BLOOD	TRIBAL ENROLLMENT		
						Year	County	No.
15597	1 Davis, Joe		24	M	1/8	1896	Sugar Loaf	3255
	2							
	3							
	4							
	5							
	6 Decision of Commission of July 30, 1903							
	7 enrolling No.1 approved by Secretary of Interior , July 14, 1904 (I.T.D. 8291-1905)							
	8							
	9							
	10							
	11							
	12							
	13							
	14							
	15 ENROLLMENT OF NOS. 1 HEREON							
	16 APPROVED BY THE SECRETARY OF INTERIOR SEP 22 1905							
	17							

TRIBAL ENROLLMENT OF PARENTS

Name of Father	Year	County	Name of Mother	Year	County
1 Zach Davis	Dead	Non Citz	Emily Davis	Dead	Eagle
2					
3					
4					
5 Transferred from Choctaw Card No. D. 193 Aug. 15, 1903					
6 See decision of July 30, 1903.					
7 Protest of Choctaw Nation Nov. 9, 1903					
8 Record forwarded Department Nov 11, 1903					
9 Protest of attorneys for Choctaw and Chickasaw Nation of Jan 23, 1904					
10 forwarded Secty of Interior Feby 6, 1904					
11					
12					
13					Date of Application for Enrollment.
14					
15					6/5/99
16					
17				Transferred	AUG 15 1903

Choctaw By Blood Enrollment Cards 1898-1914

RESIDENCE: Red River   COUNTY. **Choctaw Nation**   Choctaw Roll   CARD NO.
POST OFFICE: ~~Cerrogordo~~ Ark   Goodwater I.T. 2/04   *(Not Including Freedmen)*   FIELD NO. **5695**

Dawes' Roll No.		NAME	Relationship to Person First Named	AGE	SEX	BLOOD	TRIBAL ENROLLMENT		
							Year	County	No.
IW1461	1	Robinson, J. W.	Named	27	M	I.W.			
15873	2	" Rose Ella	Wife	29	F	1/8	1893	Eagle	P.R. 703
15874	3	Willis, Doda C	S.Son	7	M	1/16	1893	"	705
15875	4	" Ethel V	S.Dau	1	F	1/16			
15876	5	Robinson, Matie Lillian	Dau	6mo	F	1/16			
15877	6	" Maudie E	Dau	2mo	F	1/16			
	7								
	8								
	9	ENROLLMENT							
	10	OF NOS. 2,3,4,5 and 6 HEREON APPROVED BY THE SECRETARY							
	11	OF INTERIOR JUN 12 1905							
	12								
	13	ENROLLMENT							
	14	OF NOS. 1 HEREON APPROVED BY THE SECRETARY							
	15	OF INTERIOR JUN 12 1905							
	16	For child of Nos 1&2 see NB (Apr 26-06) Card #398							
	17								

TRIBAL ENROLLMENT OF PARENTS

	Name of Father	Year	County	Name of Mother	Year	County
1	Levi Robinson	Dead	Non Citz	Mahale Robinson	Dead	Non Citz
2	Z. T. Davis	1896	Red River	Fanny Davis	1896	Intermarriage
3	Francis M Willis	1896	Adopted	No.2		
4	" "	1896	"	No.2		
5	No.1			No.2		
6	No.1			No.2		
7	Decision of Commission of July 30, 1903 enrolling Nos 1 to 6 approved by Secretary					
8	of Interior February 10, 1905 (I.T.D. #4009 5037-1904) D.C. #7749-1905					
9	Transferred from Choctaw Card No. D. 125					
	See decision of July 30, 1903, filed with Choctaw No. 5690.					
10	Francis M Willis former husband of No2 and the father of Nos 3&4 on Choctaw Card #1284					
11	Protest of Choctaw Nation Nov. 9, 1903					
12	Record forwarded Department Nov 11, 1903					
13	Protest of attorneys for Choctaw and Chickasaw Nation of Jany 23, 1904					
14	forwarded Secty of Interior Feby 6, 1904.	Date of Application for Enrollment. April 24/99				
15						
16				Date of Transfer to this Card.		
17	PO Boswell IT 3/18/05			Transferred AUG 15 1903		

PO [Illegible] I.T. 5/21/05

5696 IS MISSING
[Even missing in the Dawes Packets]

Choctaw By Blood Enrollment Cards 1898-1914

RESIDENCE:		COUNTY.				Choctaw Roll		CARD NO.	
POST OFFICE: Washington, D.C. U.S. Treasury Dept		**Choctaw Nation**				*(Not Including Freedmen)*		FIELD NO. **5697**	

Dawes' Roll No.	NAME	Relationship to Person First Named	AGE	SEX	BLOOD	TRIBAL ENROLLMENT		
						Year	County	No.
15064	1 Pitchlynn, Lee	First Named	42	M	1/4	1896	Nashoba	10399
	2							
	3							
	4							
	5							
	6							
	7							
	8							
	9							
	10							
	11	ENROLLMENT						
	12	OF NOS. 1 HEREON APPROVED BY THE SECRETARY						
	13	OF INTERIOR FEB 16 1904						
	14							
	15							
	16							
	17							

TRIBAL ENROLLMENT OF PARENTS

	Name of Father	Year	County	Name of Mother	Year	County
1	Peter P Pitchlynn	Dead	Eagle	Carrie Pitchlynn	Dead	Eagle
2						
3						
4						
5						
6	No.1 transferred from Choctaw R #234. See decision of October 10, 1903.					
7						
8						
9						
10						
11						
12						
13						
14						
15					10/10/03	on this card
16					Date of Application	
17					for Enrollment.	OCT 26 1903

297

Choctaw By Blood Enrollment Cards 1898-1914

RESIDENCE:
POST OFFICE: Washington D.C. 1104 6th St. N.W.

COUNTY. **Choctaw Nation**

Choctaw Roll (Not Including Freedmen)

CARD NO.
FIELD NO. **5698**

Dawes' Roll No.	NAME	Relationship to Person First Named	AGE	SEX	BLOOD	TRIBAL ENROLLMENT		
						Year	County	No.
15065	1 Pitchlynn, Sophia		41	F	1/4	1896	Nashoba	10406
	2							
	3							
	4							
	5							
	6							
	7							
	8							
	9							
	10							
	11	ENROLLMENT OF NOS. HEREON						
	12	APPROVED BY THE SECRETARY						
	13	OF INTERIOR FEB 10 1904						
	14							
	15							
	16							
	17							

TRIBAL ENROLLMENT OF PARENTS

	Name of Father	Year	County	Name of Mother	Year	County
1	Peter P Pitchlynn	Dead	Eagle	Carrie Pitchlynn	Dead	Eagle
2						
3						
4						
5						
6						
7	No.1 transferred from Choctaw R 235. See decision of Oct. 10, 1903.					
8						
9						
10						
11						
12						
13						
14						
15						
16					Date of Application for Enrollment.	
17						OCT 26 1903

298

Choctaw By Blood Enrollment Cards 1898-1914

RESIDENCE: Chickasaw Nation COUNTY, **Choctaw Nation**   **Choctaw Roll**   CARD NO.
POST OFFICE: Hart, I.T. 12/25/05   *(Not Including Freedmen)*   FIELD NO. **5699**

Dawes' Roll No.	NAME	Relationship to Person First Named	AGE	SEX	BLOOD	TRIBAL ENROLLMENT Year	County	No.
16059	1 Burris, Samuel Sydney	First Named	23	M	1/4			
16060	2 " Hyman H	son	2	M	1/8			
IW 1611	3 " Florence	Wife	18	F	I.W.			
	4							
	5							
	6							
	7							
	8							
	9							
	10							
	11	ENROLLMENT OF NOS. 1 and 2 HEREON						
	12	APPROVED BY THE SECRETARY						
	13	OF INTERIOR Aug 22 1906						
	14	ENROLLMENT						
	15	OF NOS. 3 HEREON APPROVED BY THE SECRETARY						
	16	OF INTERIOR Feb 12 1907						
	17							

TRIBAL ENROLLMENT OF PARENTS

	Name of Father	Year	County	Name of Mother	Year	County
1	Gabriel Burris	Dead		Polly A Land		non-citz
2	No.1			Florence Burris		"
3	Bill Hays		non citizen	Boney Hayes		non-citizen
4						
5	Gabriel Burris, 69 years old, on 1885 Census Roll, Tobucksy County, No. 189					
6	No1 Original application made at Atoka I.T. in Sept. 1899					
7	No1 transferred from Choctaw Card #R478 to Choctaw card D572 June 6, 1900					
8	No2 Born May 8, 1901; evidence f birth filed Dec 28, 1901. Evidence of marriage of No.1 to Florence Hays, non-citizen, filed Dec. 28, 1901.					
9	Nos 1 and 2 transferred from Choctaw Card #D572 to M.C.R. card #7382 March 24, 1903					
10	Nos 1 and 2 transferred to this card Nov. 16, 1903				June 6, 1900	
	For children of Nos 1&3 see NB (Apr 26, 1906) Card No. 37					
11	No3 placed heron March 23, 1906 under order of Commissioner to the Five				Date of Application for Enrollment	
12	Civilized Tribes of that date, holding application was made for her enrollment					
13	within the time provided by act of Congress of July 1, 1902 (32 stat 641)				No 3 December 4, 1905	
	No.1 enrolled by special provision of Act of Congress June 21=1906					
14	(34 stats 325) ages given hereon as of September 25, 1902.					
15						
16						
17	P.O. Roff, I.T. 4/8/05				Nov. 16 1903	

299

Choctaw By Blood Enrollment Cards 1898-1914

RESIDENCE: Blue COUNTY. **Choctaw Nation** Choctaw Roll CARD NO.
POST OFFICE: Bokchito, I.T. (Not Including Freedmen) FIELD NO. **5700**

Dawes' Roll No.	NAME	Relationship to Person First Named	AGE	SEX	BLOOD	TRIBAL ENROLLMENT		
						Year	County	No.
15066	1 Ashford, James D	Named	21	M	1/4	1896	Towson	233
IW 1360	2 " Lizzie	Wife	21	F	I.W.			
15067	3 " Bertie M	Dau	8mo	"	1/8			
15068	4 " Florence Lela	"	4mo	"	1/8			
	5							
	6							
	7							
	8							
	9							
	10							
	11							
	12							
	13							
	14							
	15							
	16							
	17							

ENROLLMENT
OF NOS. 1-3-4 HEREON
APPROVED BY THE SECRETARY
OF INTERIOR FEB 18 1904

ENROLLMENT
OF NOS. 2 HEREON
APPROVED BY THE SECRETARY
OF INTERIOR MAR 14 1905

TRIBAL ENROLLMENT OF PARENTS

	Name of Father	Year	County	Name of Mother	Year	County
1	Thos. Ashford	1896	Non Citz	Virginia Ashford	Dead	Nashoba
2	Taylor Jacobs	1896	" "	Mollie Jacobs	"	Non Citz
3	No.1			No.2		
4	No.1			No.2		
5						
6	No1 on 1893 Leased district payroll Towson Co page 2 #9					
7	No1 on 1896 Choctaw census roll as James Ashford					
8	Evidence of marriage between Nos 1 and 2 received and filed May 8, 1899 No3 enrolled April 7, 1900					
9	No4 enrolled April 6, 1901					
10	Nos 1 to 4 transferred from Choctaw Card# D. 120					
11	For child of Nos 1&2 see NB (Apr 26" 06) Card #426					
12	" " " " " " " (Mar 3" 05) " #421					
13						
14						
15						
16						
17	PO Coalgate IT 12/17/04					

Date of Application for Enrollment.
April 24/99

on this card NOV 16 1903

Choctaw By Blood Enrollment Cards 1898-1914

RESIDENCE: Choctaw Nation   <del>COUNTY.</del>   **Choctaw Nation**   Choctaw Roll   CARD NO.

POST OFFICE: Savanna I.T.   *(Not Including Freedmen)*   FIELD NO. **5701**

Dawes' Roll No.	NAME	Relationship to Person First Named	AGE	SEX	BLOOD	TRIBAL ENROLLMENT		
						Year	County	No.
15509	1 Wilson, Cillin	First Named	14	F	Full	1893	Tobucksy	97/812
15810	2 " Stephen	Bro	16	M	"	1896	Atoka	14018
15811	3 " Robert	"	8	M	"	1896	"	14017
	4							
	5	No.3 died in Jan 1902 - Cancellation recommended 2/27/07						
	6							
	7	ENROLLMENT						
	8	OF NOS. 1 HEREON APPROVED BY THE SECRETARY						
	9	OF INTERIOR May 9 1904						
	10	No.3 died prior to September 25, 1902						
	11	Not entitled to land or money						
	12	See Indian Office letter of Mch 6, 1909.						
	13	(Land 22789-1907, 12739-1909)						
	14	ENROLLMENT						
	15	OF NOS. 2 and 3 HEREON						
	16	APPROVED BY THE SECRETARY OF INTERIOR Mar 15 1905						
	17							

TRIBAL ENROLLMENT OF PARENTS

	Name of Father	Year	County	Name of Mother	Year	County
1	Wallace Wilson	Dead	Tobucksy	Wikey Wilson	Dead	Tobucksy
2	" "	"	"	" "	"	"
3	" "	"	"	" "	"	"
4						
5						
6						
7						
8	Lives with Norris Carney.					
9	See sworn statements of B.F. Grubbs and W.S. James Dec. 24, 1902					
10	George Cann on Choctaw card #5629, is half brother of Nos. 1,2 and 3 hereon Transferred from Choctaw Card #D936					
11	Wikey Wilson, mother of Nos. 1,2 and 3, also known by name of Sophy Wilson					
12	See testimony taken January 12, 1905.					
13	Nos 2 and 3 originally listed for enrollment on Choctaw Card #D860 on Dec. 24, 1902. transferred to this card January 26 1905					
14	For child of No1 see NB (Mar 3'05) #476					
15						
16						
17				Date of Application for Enrollment.		Dec. 24, 1900

301

Choctaw By Blood Enrollment Cards 1898-1914

RESIDENCE: Choctaw Nation   <del>COUNTY.</del> **Choctaw Nation**   **Choctaw Roll**   CARD NO.
POST OFFICE: Garvin I.T.   *(Not Including Freedmen)*   FIELD NO. **5702**

Dawes' Roll No.		NAME	Relationship to Person First Named	AGE	SEX	BLOOD	TRIBAL ENROLLMENT		
							Year	County	No.
15069	1	Forbis[sic], William Eddie	First Named	32	M	1/2	1896	Red River	4197
	2								
	3								
	4								
	5								
	6								
	7								
	8								
	9								
	10								
	11								
	12								
	13								
	14								
	15								
	16								
	17								

ENROLLMENT
OF NOS. 1 HEREON
APPROVED BY THE SECRETARY
OF INTERIOR Feb 16 1904

TRIBAL ENROLLMENT OF PARENTS

	Name of Father	Year	County	Name of Mother	Year	County
1	Albert Forbes	1896	Red River	Jane Forbes		White woman
2						
3						
4						
5						
6	Father and mother both on Final Roll card #750					
7	No.1 also on 1893 Leased district pay roll Red River Co,					
8	page 23 #189 as Addie Forbbis.					
	No.1 is father of Nancy Forbbis Choctaw Card #887					
9	No.1 Transferred from Choctaw Card# D 937					
10						
11						
12						
13						
14						
15						Date of Application for Enrollment.
16						Nov. 28, 1902
17						

Choctaw By Blood Enrollment Cards 1898-1914

RESIDENCE: Towson COUNTY. **Choctaw Nation**   **Choctaw Roll**   CARD No.
POST OFFICE: Fowlerville, I.T.   *(Not Including Freedmen)*   FIELD No. **5703**

Dawes' Roll No.	NAME	Relationship to Person First Named	AGE	SEX	BLOOD	TRIBAL ENROLLMENT		
						Year	County	No.
15070	1 Gardner, Dodie		12	F	1/4	1896	Towson	4747
IW1146	2 Wright, Ida	Mother	37	F	I.W.	1896	"	4746
	3							
	4							
	5							
	6							
	7	ENROLLMENT OF NOS. 1 HEREON APPROVED BY THE SECRETARY OF INTERIOR FEB 16 1904						
	8							
	9							
	10							
	11	ENROLLMENT OF NOS. 2 HEREON APPROVED BY THE SECRETARY OF INTERIOR NOV 16 1904						
	12							
	13							
	14							
	15							
	16							
	17							

TRIBAL ENROLLMENT OF PARENTS

	Name of Father	Year	County	Name of Mother	Year	County
1	James Gardner	Dead	Towson	Ida Wright		noncitizen
2	Nicholas Lick	dead	non-Citz	Harriet E Hicks	dead	" "
3						
4						
5						
6						
7						
8						
9						
10						
11						
12						
13						
14						
15						
16						
17	P.O. Valliant I.T. 11/28/02					

Choctaw By Blood Enrollment Cards 1898-1914

RESIDE[...] lue
POST O[...] addo, I.T.

COUNTY. **Choctaw Nation**

Choctaw Roll
(Not Including Freedmen)

CARD No.
FIELD NO. **5704**

Dawes Roll N[...]	NAME	Relationship to Person First Named	AGE	SEX	BLOOD	TRIBAL ENROLLMENT Year	TRIBAL ENROLLMENT County	TRIBAL ENROLLMENT No.
	hlynn, Grace M	First Named	40	F	I.W.	1896	Eagle	10405
	" Paul P	Son	21	M	1/8	1896	"	10404
	" Earnest L	Son	19	M	1/8	1896	"	10403
15073 4	" Garland A	Son	17	M	1/8	1896	"	10400
15074 5	" Carlisle M	Son	9	M	1/8	1896	"	10401
6								
7								
8								
9								
10								
11								
12								
13								
14								
15								
16								
17								

ENROLLMENT
OF NOS. 2,3,4 and 5 HEREON
APPROVED BY THE SECRETARY
OF INTERIOR FEB 16 1904

ENROLLMENT
OF NOS. 1 HEREON
APPROVED BY THE SECRETARY
OF INTERIOR MAR 26 1904

TRIBAL ENROLLMENT OF PARENTS

	Name of Father	Year	County	Name of Mother	Year	County
1	Augustus Dorsey		Noncitizen	Frances Dorsey		Noncitizen
2	Thomas Pitchlynn	Dead	Eagle	No.1		
3	" "	"	"	No.1		
4	" "	"	"	No.1		
5	" "	"	"	No.1		
6						
7	6/18/15 - Ages given hereon as of September 25, 1902 - CHD					
8						
9	No.2 on 1896 Choctaw roll as Paul Peter Pitchlynn					
10	No.3 on 1896 Choctaw roll as Ernest Pitchlynn					
	No.5 on 1896 Choctaw roll as Carlisle L Pitchlynn					
11						
12	Nos. 1-5 transferred from Choctaw Card # D.349. See decision of December 5, 1903.					
13						
14						Date of Application for Enrollment. 7/30/98
15						Date of Transfer to this Card.
16						
17						DEC 21 1903

304

Choctaw By Blood Enrollment Cards 1898-1914

RESIDENCE: Tobucksy   COUNTY. **Choctaw Nation**   **Choctaw Roll** *(Not Including Freedmen)*   CARD NO.
POST OFFICE: Canadian   FIELD NO. **5705**

Dawes' Roll No.	NAME	Relationship to Person First Named	AGE	SEX	BLOOD	TRIBAL ENROLLMENT		
						Year	County	No.
IW984	1 Heskett, Emery E	First Named	53	M	I.W.	1896	Tobucksy	14614
	2							
	3							
	4							
	5 Take no further action relative to enrollment of No1							
	6 Protest of Attys for Choctaw and Chickasaw Nations							
	7	Jan 23 '04						
	8							
	9							
	10							
	11							
	12							
	13	ENROLLMENT						
	14	OF NOS. 1 HEREON APPROVED BY THE SECRETARY						
	15	OF INTERIOR Sep 22 1904						
	16							
	17							

TRIBAL ENROLLMENT OF PARENTS

	Name of Father	Year	County	Name of Mother	Year	County
1	Elijah Heskett	Dead	Non citizen	Elizabeth Heskett	Dead	Non citizen
2						
3						
4						
5	No1 on 1896 Choctaw roll as Elisha E. Heskett					
6						
7	No.1 transferred from Choctaw Card # D.504. See decision of January 4, 1904.					
8						
9	Record and decision forwarded Department Feb 13 1904 with					
10	protest of attorneys for Choctaw and Chickasaw Nations of Jan 23, 1904 Decision of Commission of Jany. 4, 1904 enrolling Emery E. Heskett					
11	as an intermarried Choctaw, affirmed by Secty of Interior July 7, 1904					
12	(I.T.D. 5368-1904) D.C. No. 23870-1904					
13						
14						
15						
16						Date of transfer on this card.
17			Sept 12/99	Date of Application for Enrollment.		Jan 21 1904

Choctaw By Blood Enrollment Cards 1898-1914

RESIDENCE:	COUNTY.					Choctaw Roll	CARD NO.
POST OFFICE: Crowder, I.T.	**Choctaw Nation**					*(Not Including Freedmen)*	FIELD NO. **5706**

Dawes' Roll No.	NAME	Relationship to Person First Named	AGE	SEX	BLOOD	TRIBAL ENROLLMENT		
						Year	County	No.
IW692	1 Dowland, Frank	First Named	26	M	I.W.			
	2							
	3							
	4							
	5							
	6							
	7							
	8							
	9							
	10	ENROLLMENT OF NOS. 1 HEREON						
	11	APPROVED BY THE SECRETARY OF INTERIOR Mar 26 1904						
	12							
	13							
	14							
	15							
	16							
	17							

TRIBAL ENROLLMENT OF PARENTS

Name of Father	Year	County	Name of Mother	Year	County
1 Jack Dowland	Dead	Non citizen	Rachel Dowland	Dead	Non citizen
2					
3					
4					
5					
6					
7 No1 is the husband of Mattie Dowland on Choctaw card #1458					
8					
9 No1 transferred from Choctaw Card # D.730. See decision of January 4, 1904.					
10 For children of No1 see NB (March 3, 1905) #5706 [illegible]					
11					
12					
13					
14					
15					
16			May 29/02 Date of Application for Enrollment.		on this card Jan 21 1904
17					

Choctaw By Blood Enrollment Cards 1898-1914

RESIDENCE: Atoka   COUNTY. **Choctaw Nation**   **Choctaw Roll** CARD No. ▮▮▮
POST OFFICE: Lane, I.T.   *(Not Including Freedmen)* FIELD No.

Dawes' Roll No.	NAME	Relationship to Person First Named	AGE	SEX	BLOOD	TRIBAL ENROLLMENT		
						Year	County	No.
15510	1 Billy, Nancy Mintubbe	Named	30	F	Full	1893	Atoka	PR 762
	2							
	3							
	4							
	5							
	6							
	7							
	8							
	9							
	10							
	11							
	12							
	13							
	14							
	17							

ENROLLMENT
OF NOS. 1 HEREON
APPROVED BY THE SECRETARY
OF INTERIOR MAY 9 1904

TRIBAL ENROLLMENT OF PARENTS

	Name of Father	Year	County	Name of Mother	Year	County
1	David Mintubbe	Dead		Phobe[sic] Mintubbe	Dead	
2						
3						
4						
5						
6	On 1893 Leased district payroll, Atoka County No 762 as Nancy Meantubbe					
7	Also on 1896 Choctaw census roll page 367 No 14024 as Nancy Wats					
8	Transferred from Choctaw Card # D.827					
9						
10						
11						
12						
13						
14						
15						
16					Date of Application for Enrollment.	11-19-02 on this card.
17						JAN 20 1904

307

Choctaw By Blood Enrollment Cards 1898-1914

RESIDENCE:
POST OFFICE: Leflore I.T.
COUNTY. **Choctaw Nation**
Choctaw Roll (Not Including Freedmen)
CARD NO.
FIELD NO. **5708**

Dawes' Roll No.	NAME	Relationship to Person First Named	AGE	SEX	BLOOD	TRIBAL ENROLLMENT		
						Year	County	No.
IW693	1 Harris, James F		24	M	IW			
	2							
	3							
	4							
	5							
	6							
	7							
	8							
	9							
	10							
	11							
	12							
	13							
	14							
	15							
	16							
	17							

ENROLLMENT OF NOS. 1 HEREON APPROVED BY THE SECRETARY OF INTERIOR MAR 26 1904

TRIBAL ENROLLMENT OF PARENTS

	Name of Father	Year	County	Name of Mother	Year	County
1	Mathew H Harris		Noncitizen	Elizabeth Harris		Noncitizen
2						
3						
4						
5						
6	No1 is husband of Nellie H Harris on Choctaw card #3016					
7	No1 transferred from Choctaw Card # D.605. See decision of					
8	January 4, 1904					
9	For child of No1 see NB (March 3, 1905) #1477					
10						
11						
12						
13						
14						
15						
16						
17			Jan 11/01	Date of Application for Enrollment.	JAN 21 1904	

Choctaw By Blood Enrollment Cards 1898-1914

RESIDENCE:
POST OFFICE: Cowlington I.T.

COUNTY. **Choctaw Nation**

Choctaw Roll
(Not Including Freedmen)

CARD NO.
FIELD NO. **5709**

Dawes' Roll No.	NAME	Relationship to Person First Named	AGE	SEX	BLOOD	TRIBAL ENROLLMENT		
						Year	County	No.
IW694	1 Overstreet, Lillian P	First Named	19	F	IW			
	2							
	3							
	4							
	5							
	6							
	7							
	8							
	9							
	10	ENROLLMENT OF NOS. 1 HEREON APPROVED BY THE SECRETARY OF INTERIOR MAR 26 1904						
	11							
	12							
	13							
	14							
	15							
	16							
	17							

TRIBAL ENROLLMENT OF PARENTS

	Name of Father	Year	County	Name of Mother	Year	County
1	R.A. Rabon		Noncitizen	L.C. Rabon		noncitizen
2						
3						
4						
5						
6	No1 is wife of Charles A Overstreet on Choctaw card #2683					
7						
8	No1 transferred from Choctaw Card D.736. See decision of					
9	January 6, 1904.					
10						
11						
12						
13						
14						
15						
16						
17			June 27/02	Date of Application for Enrollment	JAN 23 1904	

Choctaw By Blood Enrollment Cards 1898-1914

| | | | | | | RESIDENCE: | POST OFFICE: Thurman, I.T. | COUNTY. Choctaw Nation (Not Including Freedmen) | Choctaw Roll | CARD NO. FIELD NO. 5710 |

Dawes' Roll No.	NAME	Relationship to Person First Named	AGE	SEX	BLOOD	TRIBAL ENROLLMENT		
						Year	County	No.
15511	1 Beams, John J	First Named	27	M	1/4	1896	Tobucksy	901
15512	2 " William T	Bro	23	M	1/4	1896	"	902
15513	3 Brown, Ida F	Sis	21	F	1/4	1896	"	903
15514	4 " Hettie A	Sis	20	F	1/4	1896	"	904
15515	5 Beams, Viola Victoria	Niece	2	F	1/8			
15516	6 Brown, Pearlie Catherine	Niece	1	F	1/8			
IW1147	7 Staton, Phoebe C	Mother	49	F	I.W.	1896	Tobucksy	15036
	8							
	9 No.5 born November 9, 1900: Evidence of							
	10 birth filed March 22, 1902							
	No.6 born December 28, 1901: Evidence of							
	11 birth filed March 22, 1902							
	12							
	13		For child of No4 see NB (Apr 26-06) Card 624					
	14		" " " " " (Mar 3-05) " 422					
	15 ENROLLMENT							
	16 OF NOS. 1-2-3-4-5-6- HEREON APPROVED BY THE SECRETARY							
	17 OF INTERIOR May 9 1904							

TRIBAL ENROLLMENT OF PARENTS

Name of Father	Year	County	Name of Mother	Year	County	
1 Wm Beams	Dead	Choctaw	Phoebe C. Staton			
2 Wm Beams	Dead	"	" "			
3 " "	"	"	" "			
4 " "	"	"	" "			For child of No3 see NB (Mar 3-05) #749 #1305
5 No.2			Lavinia V. Beams		non citizen	
6 Elm Brown		non citizen	No.3			
7 Henry Stewart		" "	Susan Stewart		non-citizen	
8 No2 is now the husband of Lavinia Victoria Beams Choc card #5943 March 22, 1902						
9 No3 is now wife of Elm Brown a noncitizen March 22, 1902						
10 No4 is now wife of Foster Brown a non citizen December 24, 1902						
For child of No3 see NB (April 26, 1906) No. 533						
11 No1 on Choctaw 1896 roll as James Beams			ENROLLMENT			
12 No2 on Choctaw 1896 roll as Wm F. Beams			OF NOS 7 HEREON			
13 No3 on Choctaw 1896 roll as Ida T. Beams			APPROVED BY THE SECRETARY OF INTERIOR Nov 16 1904			
14 No4 on Choctaw 1896 roll as Hattie A Beams						
15 Nos 1 to 6 inclusive transferred from Choctaw Card # D.444						
16 No7 transferred from Choctaw Card # D-444 Oct 31, 1904. See decision of Oct. 15, 1904						
No4 P.O. So. McAlester I.T						
No3 P.O. Choate I.T.			Date of Application	9/6/99		
17 No2&4 P.O. Indianola I.T. 12/9/04			for Enrollment. Jan 24 1904 on this card			

Choctaw By Blood Enrollment Cards 1898-1914

| RESIDENCE: | COUNTY. | Choctaw Nation | Choctaw Roll | CARD No. |
| POST OFFICE: Silo I.T. | | | (Not Including Freedmen) | FIELD No. 5711 |

Dawes' Roll No.	NAME	Relationship to Person First Named	AGE	SEX	BLOOD	TRIBAL ENROLLMENT		
						Year	County	No.
IW695	1 O'Neil, Cassandra Frances	First Named	72	F	IW	1896	Chickasaw	75
	2							
	3							
	4							
	5							
	6							
	7							
	8							
	9							
	10							
	11	ENROLLMENT OF NOS. 1 HEREON APPROVED BY THE SECRETARY OF INTERIOR MAR 26 1904						
	12							
	13							
	14							
	15							
	16							
	17							

TRIBAL ENROLLMENT OF PARENTS

	Name of Father	Year	County	Name of Mother	Year	County
1	A.T. Davis	Dead	noncitizen	Rachel Davis	Dead	noncitizen
2						
3						
4						
5						
6	No1 transferred from Chickasaw Card # D.152 See decision of					
7	January 7, 1904					
8						
9						
10						
11						
12						
13						
14						
15						
16				5/10/99 Date of Application for Enrollment.	Date of transfer on this card.	
17					JAN 25 1904	

311

Choctaw By Blood Enrollment Cards 1898-1914

RESIDENCE:
POST OFFICE: Sulphur, I.T. COUNTY. **Choctaw Nation** **Choctaw Roll** *(Not Including Freedmen)* FIELD NO. **5712**

Dawes' Roll No.	NAME	Relationship to Person First Named	AGE	SEX	BLOOD	TRIBAL ENROLLMENT		
						Year	County	No.
15598	₁ Standley, James Franklin	First Named	22	M	1/8			
ᴵᵂ1612	₂ " Ella	Wife	26	F	I.W.			
	₃							
	₄					No1 admitted in 96 Case #822		
	₅ Decision of Commission of Jan 9, 1904 enrolling							
	₆ No.1 forwarded Department							
	₇ Decision of Commission of Jan. 9, 1904 approved by Department July 22, 1904							
	₈							
	₉							
	₁₀							
	₁₁ ENROLLMENT OF NOS. 2 HEREON							
	₁₂ APPROVED BY THE SECRETARY							
	₁₃ OF INTERIOR FEB 12 1907							
	₁₄ ENROLLMENT							
	₁₅ OF NOS. 1 HEREON APPROVED BY THE SECRETARY							
	₁₆ OF INTERIOR SEP 22 1904							
	₁₇							

TRIBAL ENROLLMENT OF PARENTS

Name of Father	Year	County	Name of Mother	Year	County
₁ Frank Standley	Dead	Choctaw	Silvia Standley	Dead	noncitizen
₂ Isaac Ralph	Dead	Non Citz	Jane Ralph		
₃					
₄					
₅ Transferred from Choctaw card D825. See decision of January 9, 1904					
₆					
₇ Protest of attorneys for Choctaw and Chickasaw Nation of Jany 23, 1904 with record in case forwarded Sec'ty of Interior Feby 12, 1904.					
₈					
₉					
₁₀ No2 places hereon under order of the Commissioner to the Five Civilized Tribes of Dec 17.06 holding that application was made for her enrollment within the time provided by the Act of					
₁₁ Congress approved April 26' 1906					
₁₂					
₁₃					
₁₄					
₁₅					
₁₆				on this card.	
₁₇ P.O. Coalgate IT 2/17/04			Nov 14/02	Date of Application for Enrollment.	JAN 26 1904

Choctaw By Blood Enrollment Cards 1898-1914

RESIDENCE: Chickasaw Nation COUNTY. **Choctaw Nation**   Choctaw Roll
POST OFFICE: Minco, Ind. Ter.   *(Not Including Freedmen)*

Dawes' Roll No.	NAME	Relationship to Person First Named	AGE	SEX	BLOOD	TRIBAL ENROLLMENT		
						Year	County	No.
15075	1 Foster, Ephraim	First Named	71	M	1/4		Sugar Loaf	C.C.R.#2 167
IW 1566	2 " Eliza Jane	Wife	41	F	IW			
	3							
	4							
	5							
	6	ENROLLMENT						
	7	OF NOS. 1 HEREON APPROVED BY THE SECRETARY						
	8	OF INTERIOR MAR 26 1904						
	9							
	10							
	11							
	12							
	13							
	14							
	15							
	16							
	17							

TRIBAL ENROLLMENT OF PARENTS

	Name of Father	Year	County	Name of Mother	Year	County
1	James Foster	dead	Choctaw	Millie Foster	dead	non-citizen
2	Hosea Stuart	"	noncitizen	Sophia S Foster	"	" "
3						
4						

5 No.1 admitted by act of Choctaw council, approved Nov. 5, 1888.
6 No.1 on 1896 Choctaw roll, Sugar Loaf Co #3952.
7 Originally enrolled on Chickasaw Card D.93 Oct. 21, 1898: transferred
8 to this card Feby. 24, 1904

ENROLLMENT
OF NOS. 2 HEREON
APPROVED BY THE SECRETARY
OF INTERIOR AUG 2 1906

11 No.2 placed hereon under an order of the Commissioner to the Five Civilized Tribes
12 January 11, 1906, holding that application was made for her enrollment within the time
13 provided by the Act of Congress approved July 1, 1902 (32 Stat 64)

GRANTED

July 1/02   APR 25 1906
Date of Application for Enrollment.   Feby 24, 1904

17 P.O. Newcastle, I.T. 8/23/05

313

Choctaw By Blood Enrollment Cards 1898-1914

Choctaw Nation

Choctaw Roll ▮▮▮
(Not Including Freedmen) FIELD NO.

Dawes' Roll No.		NAME	Relationship to Person First Named	AGE	SEX	BLOOD	TRIBAL ENROLLMENT		
							Year	County	No.
15076	1	Hallmark, Lulu		18	F	1/16		Choctaw residing in Chickasaw Dist	C.C.R.#2 195
15077	2	" Ervin A	Son	1	M	1/32			
	3								
	4								
	5								
	6								
	7								
	8								
	9								
	10								
	11	ENROLLMENT OF NOS. 1 and 2 HEREON APPROVED BY THE SECRETARY OF INTERIOR MAR 26 1904							
	12								
	13								
	14								
	15								
	16								
	17								

TRIBAL ENROLLMENT OF PARENTS

	Name of Father	Year	County	Name of Mother	Year	County
1	James Foster	dead	Choctaw	Edna Foster	dead	non-citizen
2	Jas. W. Hallmark		non-citizen	No.1		
3						
4						
5	No.1 admitted by act of Choctaw council, approved Nov. 5, 1888					
6	No.1 on 1896, Choctaw roll, Chickasaw district #4589 as Lula Foster					
7	No.1 named in Act of Council as Lula Foster					
8	No.1 married to James W Hallmark a non-citizen, July 3d, 1900 No.2 born April 29, 1901; evidence of birth filed Aug. 9, 1901.					
9	Nos. 1 and 2 originally enrolled on Choctaw Card #D.93: transferred to this card Oct. 21, 1902. card, Feby 24, 1904.					
10	For child of No1 see NB (Mar 3' 05) #423					
11						
12						
13						
14						
15						
16			Oct 21/98 Date of Application for Enrollment.	Date of Transfer to this Card.		Feby. 24, 19
17						

Choctaw By Blood Enrollment Cards 1898-1914

RESIDENCE: Tobucksy County COUNTY.
POST OFFICE: Calvin Ind. Ter Sept 14/98 **Choctaw Nation** Choctaw Roll *(Not Including Freedmen)* CARD NO. FIELD No. **5715**

Norman Oklahoma Mar 9 01

Dawes' Roll No.	NAME	Relationship to Person First Named	AGE	SEX	BLOOD	TRIBAL ENROLLMENT		
						Year	County	No.
15078	1 Foster, W. F.		46	M	1/4		Tobucksy	C.C.R#2 171
IW985	2 " Mary A	Wife	40	F	I.W.		"	C.F.Roll 30
15079	3 " John A	Son	22	M	1/8		"	C.C.R#2 171
15080	4 " Robt E	"	20	M	1/8		"	
15081	5 " Maude E	Dau	14	F	1/8		"	
15082	6 " Claude F	Son	10	M	1/8		"	
15083	7 " James O	"	7	M	1/8		"	
15084	8 " Ida O	Dau	6	F	1/8		"	
15085	9 " Martin T	Son	4	M	1/8			
15086	10 " Earl Clyde	Son	2	M	1/8			
	11 No2 See Decision of July 19'04							
	12 No1 1896 Tobucksy 4018							
	13 No2 1896 " 14524							
	14 No3 1896 " 4019							
	No4 1896 " 4020							
	15 No5 1896 " 4021							
	16 No6 1896 " 4022							
	No7 1896 " 4023							
	17 No8 Affidavit as to birth - Received 6/13/99							

ENROLLMENT OF NOS. 1,3,4,5,6,7,8,9and10 HEREON APPROVED BY THE SECRETARY OF INTERIOR MAR 26 1904

PO Minco IT 2/13/05
PO [Illegible] IT 7/13/05

TRIBAL ENROLLMENT OF PARENTS

Name of Father	Year	County	Name of Mother	Year	County	
1 Ephraim Foster		Sugar Loaf	Mandy Foster	Dead	Non Citizen	For children of Nos 1&2 see NB (Mar 3-05) #822
2 Robt Britton	Dead	Non-Citizen	"	"	"	
3 No.1			No.2			
4 No.1			No.2			
5 No.1			No.2			
6 No.1			No.2			
7 No.1			No.2			
8 No.1		ENROLLMENT OF NOS 2 HEREON	No.2			
9 No.1		APPROVED BY THE SECRETARY OF INTERIOR SEP 22 1904	No.2			
10 No.1			No.2			
11 No2 restored to roll by Departmental authority of January 19, 1909 (File 55)						
12 Nos1,2,3,4 and 5 Adopted by Act of Choctaw Council approved Nov, 5, 1888 Choctaw Commission notifies Dawes Commission that the action of the Legislature admitting						
13 these parties is to be contested						
14 No2 was rejected by Dawes Commission in 1896 No Appeal Choctaw Case #437						
No9 Born Jan 28" 1899 Enrolled June 13" 1899						
15 No10 Born Jan 22 1901 Evidence of Birth filed March 9" 1901						
16 Nos 1to10 inclusive originally enrolled on Choctaw D20. Transferred to this card Feby 24 '04						
17 Enrollment of No2 cancelled by order of Department March 4 1904		Feb. 24 '04				

315

RESIDENCE: Chickasaw Nation COUNTY. **Choctaw Nation** Choctaw Roll CARD No.
POST OFFICE: Newcastle I.T. 12/18/02 *(Not Including ___)* FIELD No. **5716**

Dawes' Roll No.	NAME	Relationship to Person First Named	AGE	SEX	BLOOD	TRIBAL ENROLLMENT		
						Year	County	No.
15087	1 Foster, John Abe		44	M	1/8	1896	Chickasaw Dist	4598
IW938	2 " Minnie B	Wife	40	F	I.W.	1896	" "	14553
15088	3 " John Wesley	Son	13	M	1/16	1896	" "	4600
	4							
	5							
	6							
	7	ENROLLMENT OF NOS. 1 and 3 HEREON APPROVED BY THE SECRETARY OF INTERIOR MAR 26 1904						
	8							
	9							
	10							
	11							
	12	ENROLLMENT OF NOS. 2 HEREON APPROVED BY THE SECRETARY OF INTERIOR AUG 3 1904						
	13							
	14							
	15							
	16							
	17							

TRIBAL ENROLLMENT OF PARENTS

	Name of Father	Year	County	Name of Mother	Year	County
1	Ephraim Foster		S___ Loaf	Amanda Foster	Dead	Non-Citizen
2	Wm Paul	Dead	No___zen	Marella Paul	"	" "
3	No1			No2		
4						
5						
6	No1 on 96 Roll as Jno A Foster					
7	No2 " 96 " " Minnie "					
8	No3 " 96 " " Jno W "					
	No 1 and 2 admitted by Act of Choctaw Council approved Nov 5 1888					
9	No1 married in Texas before his admission by Council					
10	Nos 1,2 and 3 originally enrolled on Choctaw Card D #96 transferred to this card Feb 24 '04					
	See memorandum of testimony of Mattie Bell Foster taken Nov 3 1902					
11						
12						
13						
14						
15						
16				Oct 21/98		on this card.
17				Date of Application for Enrollment.		Feb 24 '04

Choctaw By Blood Enrollment Cards 1898-1914

RESIDENCE: Chickasaw Nation ~~County.~~
POST OFFICE: Newcastle I.T. 12/18/02 · **Choctaw Nation** · **Choctaw Roll** *(Not Including Freedmen)*

Dawes' Roll No.	NAME	Relationship to Person First Named	AGE	SEX	BLOOD	TRIBAL ENROLLMENT Year	County	No.
15089	1 Foster, William Thomas	First Named	20	M	1/16	1896	Chick. Dist	4599
15090	2 " Eva May	Dau	1	F	1/32			
IW 1226	3 " Mattie Bell	Wife	24	F	I.W.			
	4							
	5	For child of Nos 1&3 see NB (Mar 3 '05) #424						
	6							
	7							
	8	ENROLLMENT						
	9	OF NOS. 1 and 2 HEREON APPROVED BY THE SECRETARY						
	10	OF INTERIOR MAR 26 1904						
	11							
	12	ENROLLMENT						
	13	OF NOS. 3 HEREON APPROVED BY THE SECRETARY						
	14	OF INTERIOR DEC 13 1904						
	15							
	16							
	17							

TRIBAL ENROLLMENT OF PARENTS

	Name of Father	Year	County	Name of Mother	Year	C...
1	John Abe Foster		Chick Dist	Minnie B Foster		Chick
2	No.1			Mattie B. Foster		Non Citz
3	Robert Crotzer		Non Citizen	Joanna Crotzer		" "
4						
5	No1 on 96 Roll as Wm Foster					
6	No1 is married to Mattie B Foster non-citizen: Evidence of marriage filed Jan 6-1902					
	~~No2 Born Nov 12 1901.~~					
7	~~Evidence of Birth filed Jan 6-1902~~					
8	See memorandum of testimony of Mattie Bell Foster taken Nov 3, 1902					
9	No1 admitted by act of Choctaw Council Nov 5 1888					
10	~~Nos 1 & 2 originally enrolled on Choctaw card D#96 transferred to this card Feb 24 '04~~					
	~~Wife of No1 is Mattie Bell Foster on Choctaw card #D1002~~					
11	Nos 1and 3 were married at El Reno Oklahoma Territory Dec 19, 1900 License issued					
12	under laws of Oklahoma Territory					
	~~Further evidence taken in this case Oct. 13, 1904~~					
13	~~No3 originally listed for enrollment on Choctaw card #D-1002 Nov. 3, 1902;~~					
14	transferred to this card Nov. 26, 1904. See decision of Nov. 9, 1904.					
15						
16						
17	PO Ardmore IT 3/14/05			Oct 21/98	Date of Application for Enrollment.	Feb 24 '04 on this card

Choctaw By Blood Enrollment Cards 1898-1914

RESIDENCE: Chickasaw Nation ~~COUNTY.~~ **Choctaw Nation**   Choctaw Roll   CARD NO.
POST OFFICE: Duncan I.T.   (Not Including Freedmen)   FIELD NO. **5718**

Dawes' Roll No.	NAME	Relationship to Person First Named	AGE	SEX	BLOOD	TRIBAL ENROLLMENT Year	County	No.
IW1148	1 Paul, William Albert	First Named	44	M	I.W.	1896	Chick. Dist	14950
15091	2 " Delia	Dau	18	F	1/16	1896	" "	10633
15092	3 " Claude	Son	16	M	1/16	1896	" "	10634
	4							
	5							
	6							
	7							
	8	ENROLLMENT OF NOS. 2 and 3 HEREON APPROVED BY THE SECRETARY OF INTERIOR MAR 26 1904						
	9							
	10							
	11							
	12	ENROLLMENT OF NOS. 1 HEREON APPROVED BY THE SECRETARY OF INTERIOR NOV 16 1904						
	13							
	14							
	15							
	16							
	17							

TRIBAL ENROLLMENT OF PARENTS

	Name of Father	Year	County	Name of Mother	Year	County
1	G.W. Paul	Dead	Non Citizen	M.B. Paul		Non Citizen
2	No.1			Matilda Ann Paul	Dead	Choctaw Roll
3	No.1			" " "	"	" " "
4						
5						
6	No1 on 1896 Roll as W. A. Paul					
7	No2 " 1896 " " Delilah					
8	No3 " 1896 " " Claudie					
	No1 married in Texas under U.S. Law before himself and wife, Matilda Ann were admitted by Council					
9	Nos 1,2 and 3 were admitted by Act of Choctaw Council Nov 5 1888.					
10	All living in Texas at [Illegible] of admin					
11	Nos 1,2 and 3 originally enrolled on Choctaw Card D # 94 transferred to this card Feb 24 '04					
12	For children of No1 see NB (Apr 26 '06) Card #1129.					
13						
14						
15						
16				Oct 21/98 Date of Application for Enrollment.	Date of Transfer to this Card.	Feb 24 '04
17						

318

Choctaw By Blood Enrollment Cards 1898-1914

RESIDENCE: Chickasaw Nation ~~COUNTY.~~ **Choctaw Nation** **Choctaw Roll**
POST OFFICE: Duncan IT   *(Not Including Freedmen)*

Dawes' Roll No.	NAME	Relationship to Person First Named	AGE	SEX	BLOOD	TRIBAL ENROLLMENT		
						Year	County	No.
15093	₁ Isbell, Belle Paul	First Named	22	F	1/16	1896	Chick. Dist	10631
15094	₂ " Charles George	Son	1	M	1/32			
	₃							
	₄							
	₅							
	₆							
	₇							
	₈							
	₉							
	10							
	11	ENROLLMENT						
	12	OF NOS. 1 and 2 HEREON						
	13	APPROVED BY THE SECRETARY OF INTERIOR MAR 20 1904						
	14							
	15							
	16							
	17							

TRIBAL ENROLLMENT OF PARENTS

Name of Father	Year	County	Name of Mother	Year	County
₁ W.A. Paul (IW)		Choctaw residing in Chickasaw Dist	Matilda A Paul	Dead	Choctaw residing in Chickasaw Dist
₂ Bert Isbell		Non Citizen	No.1		
₃					
₄					
₅					
₆ No1 Daughter of W.A. Paul Card #5718					
₇ No1 Admitted by Act of Choctaw Council Nov 5 1888					
₈ ~~No1 Evidence of marriage to Bert Isbell filed Aug 20 1901~~ ~~No2 Born Aug 1" 1901 Proof of Birth filed Aug 3 1901~~					
₉ Nos 1 and 2 originally enrolled on Choctaw Card D # 109 transferred to this card Feb 24 '04					
10					
11					
12					
13					
14					
15					
16			Oct 22/98		
17			Date of Application for Enrollment.	Feb 24 '04	

319

Choctaw By Blood Enrollment Cards 1898-1914

RESIDENCE: Chickasaw Nation ~~COUNTY.~~ **Choctaw Nation**
POST OFFICE: Duncan IT

Choctaw Roll (Not Including Fr...)   CARD NO. 5720

Dawes' Roll No.	NAME	Relationship to Person First Named	AGE	SEX	BLOOD	TRIBAL ENROLLMENT		
						Year	County	No.
15095	1 Marshall, Ludie Paul	First Named	20	F	1/16	1896	Chick. Dist	10632
15096	2 " Osburn Gilbert	Son	1	M	1/32			
	3							
	4							
	5							
	6							
	7							
	8							
	9							
	10							
	11							
	12							
	13							
	14							
	15							
	16							
	17							

ENROLLMENT
OF NOS. 1 and 2 HEREON
APPROVED BY THE SECRETARY
OF INTERIOR MAR 26 1904

TRIBAL ENROLLMENT OF PARENTS

	Name of Father	Year	County	Name of Mother	Year	County
1	W. A. Paul		Choctaw residing ~~in Chickasaw Dist~~	Matilda A Paul	Dead	Choctaw residing in Chickasaw Dist
2	Henry L Marshall		Non-Citizen	No.1		
3						
4						
5						
6	No1 Father of, William A Paul, on Card #5718					
7	No1 on 96 Roll as Lutia Paul					
8	~~No1 Admitted by Act of Choctaw Council Nov 5 1888~~ ~~No2 Born April 26 1901 Enrolled Oct 22 1902~~					
9	Nos 1 and 2 originally enrolled on Choctaw Card D # 108 Transferred to this card Feb 24 '04					
10						
11						
12						
13						
14						
15				10/22/98 Date of Application for Enrollment.		on this card Feb 24 '04
16						
17						

Choctaw By Blood Enrollment Cards 1898-1914

RESIDENCE: Chickasaw Nation ~~COUNTY~~. **Choctaw Nation**   Choctaw Roll
POST OFFICE: Minco I.T.   *(Not Including Freedmen)*

Dawes' Roll No.	NAME	Relationship to Person First Named	AGE	SEX	BLOOD	TRIBAL ENROLLMENT		
						Year	County	No.
IW939	1 Williams, William Franklin	First Named	44	M	IW	1896	Chick. Dist	15201
15097	2 " Mollie E	Wife	36	F	1/8	1896	" "	14148
15098	3 " Lulu	Dau	18	"	1/16	1896	" "	14149
15099	4 " Ollie	"	16	"	1/16	1896	" "	14150
15100	5 " Athel	Son	14	M	1/16	1896	" "	14151
15101	6 " Lottie	Dau	8	F	1/16	1896	" "	14152
	7							
	8 ENROLLMENT							
	9 OF NOS. 2,3,4,5 and 6 HEREON APPROVED BY THE SECRETARY							
	10 OF INTERIOR MAR 26 1904							
	11							
	12 ENROLLMENT							
	13 OF NOS. 1 HEREON APPROVED BY THE SECRETARY							
	14 OF INTERIOR AUG 3 1904							
	15							
	16							
	17							

TRIBAL ENROLLMENT OF PARENTS

	Name of Father	Year	County	Name of Mother	Year	County
1	W. T. Williams	Dead	Non Citizen	Dorcas Williams		Non Citizen
2	Ephraim Foster		Sugar Loaf	Amanda Foster	Dead	" "
3	No.1			No.2		
4	No.1			No.2		
5	No.1			No.2		
6	No.1			No.2		
7						

8 Nos1,2,3 and 4 admitted by Act of Choctaw Council Nov 5 1888
9 No1 married in Texas before said admission
No2 daughter of Ephraim Foster Choctaw Card #5713
10 Nos 1 to 6 inclusive originally enrolled on Choctaw Card D # 97 Transferred to this

				10/21/98 Date of Application for Enrollment.	transfer date Feb 24 '04

Choctaw By Blood Enrollment Cards 1898-1914

RESIDENCE: Chickasaw Nation <s>COUNTY.</s> **Choctaw Nation**
POST OFFICE: Minco I.T.

Choctaw Roll NO.
(Not Including Freedmen) 5722

Dawes Roll No	NAME	Relationship to Person First Named	AGE	SEX	BLOOD	TRIBAL ENROLLMENT		
						Year	County	No.
1510	ley, Edna A	First Named	31	F	1/8	1896	Chick Dist	11068
151	" Frank	Son	1	M	1/16			
6								
7								
8								
9								
10								
11		ENROLLMENT						
12		OF NOS. 1 and 2 HEREON						
13		APPROVED BY THE SECRETARY OF INTERIOR MAR 26 1904						
14								
15								
16								
17								

TRIBAL ENROLLMENT OF PARENTS

	Name of Father	Year	County	Name of Mother	
1	Ephraim Foster		Sugar Loaf	Amanda Fost	
2	B. F. Henley		Non-Citizen	No1	
3					
4					

5 No1 Daughter of Ephraim Foster Choctaw Card 5713
6 No1 On 96 Roll as Edna F. Reynolds
7 No1 Admitted by Act of Choctaw Council Nov 5 1888
No1 is the wife of B.F. Henley Non-Citz. Evidence of marriage filed Aug 8 1901
8 No2 Born April 30 1901 Proof of Birth filed Aug 8 1901
9 Nos 1 and 2 originally enrolled on Choctaw Card D 97 Transferred to this card Feb 24 '04
10
11 For child of No.1 see NB (Mar 3, 1905) #477
12
13
14
15
16   10/21/98
17 PO Amber IT 3/27/05   Date of Application for Enrollment.   Feb 24 '04

Choctaw By Blood Enrollment Cards 1898-1914

RESIDENCE: Chickasaw Nation COUNTY. **Choctaw Nation**
POST OFFICE: Minco I.T.

5723
Choctaw Roll
(Not Including Freedmen)

Dawes' Roll No.	NAME	Relationship to Person First Named	AGE	SEX	BLOOD	TRIBAL ENROLLMENT		
						Year	County	No.
15104	1 Enloe, Wade	First Named	27	F	1/16	1896	Chick Dist	10630
15105	2 " Maye	dau	2	F	1/32			
	3							
	4							
	5							
	6							
	7							
	8							
	9							
	10							
	11	ENROLLMENT						
	12	OF NOS. 1 and 2 HEREON APPROVED BY THE SECRETARY						
	13	OF INTERIOR MAR 26 1904						
	14							
	15							
	16							
	17							

TRIBAL ENROLLMENT OF PARENTS

	Name of Father	Year	County	Name of Mother	Year	County
1	Wade, Mardes	Dead	Non Citizen	Caldinia Wade	Dead	Choctaw
2	Wᵐ G Enloe		Non-Citz	No1		
3						
4						
5	No1 on 1896 Roll as Wade W Paul					
6	No1 Admitted by Act of Choctaw Council Nov 5 1888 as Wade Mardis Paul					
7	No1 Grand daughter of Ephraim Foster Choctaw Card #5713					
8	No1 wife of Wᵐ G Enloe, non-citizen					
	No2 Born Aug 24 1900 Proof of Birth filed Sept 4 1900					
9	Nos 1 and 2 originally enrolled on Choctaw Card D # 97 Transferred to this card Feb 24 '04					
10	For child of No1 see NB (March 3, 1905) #868					
11						
12						
13						
14						
15					Oct 21/98	Transfer date
16					Date of Application for Enrollment	Feb 24 '04
17						

323

Choctaw By Blood Enrollment Cards 1898-1914

RESIDENCE: Chickasaw Nation COUNTY. **Choctaw Nation** Choctaw ~~~~ ARD No.
POST OFFICE: Minco Ind. Ter. *(Not Including Freedmen)* FIELD No. **5724**

Dawes' Roll No.	NAME	Relationship to Person First Named	AGE	SEX	BLOOD	TRIBAL ENROLLMENT Year	County	No.
IW940	1 Thomas, John F	First Named	41	M	I.W.	1896	Chick Dist	15119
15106	2 " Alice	Wife	33	F	1/8	1896	" "	12569
15107	3 " Jesse W	Son	16		1/16	1896	" "	12570
15108	4 " Ethel	Dau	14	F	1/16	1896	" "	12571
	5							
	6							
	7							
	8	ENROLLMENT OF NOS. 2,3 and 4 HEREON						
	9	APPROVED BY THE SECRETARY						
	10	OF INTERIOR MAR 26 1904						
	11							
	12	ENROLLMENT OF NOS. 1 HEREON						
	13	APPROVED BY THE SECRETARY						
	14	OF INTERIOR AUG 3 1904						
	15							
	16							
	17							

TRIBAL ENROLLMENT OF PARENTS

	Name of Father	Year	County	Name of Mother	Year	County
1	Jesse Thomas	Dead	Non-Citizen	Polly Ann Thomas	Dead	Non Citizen
2	Ephraim Foster		Sugar Loaf	Amanda Foster	"	" " "
3	No1			No2		
4	No1			No2		
5						
6	Nos 1,2 and 3 admitted by Act of Choctaw Council Nov 4 1888					
7	No1 married in Texas under U.S. Law before admission of himself and wife Alice					
8	No2 Daughter of Ephraim Foster on Choctaw Card #5713 ~~No1 See testimony of, taken Oct 15 1902~~					
9	Nos 1 to 4 originally enrolled on Choctaw Card ID # 92 Transferred to this card Feb 24 '04					
10						
11						
12						
13						
14						
15						
16					Oct 21/98 Date of Application for Enrollment.	Transfer date Feb 24 '04
17						

Choctaw By Blood Enrollment Cards 1898-1914

RESIDENCE: Chickasaw Nation COUNTY. **Choctaw Nation**   **Choctaw Roll** CARD NO.

POST OFFICE: Purcell, I.T.   (Not Including Freedmen)   FIELD NO. **5725**

Dawes' Roll No.	NAME	Relationship to Person First Named	AGE	SEX	BLOOD	TRIBAL ENROLLMENT		
						Year	County	No.
15109	1 Foster, Samuel	First Named	27	M	1/16	1896	Chick. Dist	4597
	2							
	3							
	4							
	5							
	6							
	7							
	8							
	9							
	10							
	11	ENROLLMENT						
	12	OF NOS. 1 HEREON APPROVED BY THE SECRETARY						
	13	OF INTERIOR MAR 26 1904						
	14							
	15							
	16							
	17							

TRIBAL ENROLLMENT OF PARENTS

Name of Father	Year	County	Name of Mother	Year	County
1 S. D. Foster	Dead	Choctaw Indian	Mattie Pierson		Non Citizen
2					
3					
4					
5					
6 No1 Admitted by Act of Choctaw Council Nov 5 1888					
7 No1 Grand-son of Ephraim Foster Choctaw Card #5713					
8 No1 originally enrolled on Choctaw Card D # 99, Transferred to this card Feb 24 '04					
9					
10					
11					
12					
13					
14					
15					
16			Oct 21/98		Transfer date
17			Date of Application for Enrollment.		Feb 24 '04

325

Choctaw By Blood Enrollment Cards 1898-1914

Choctaw Nation   **Choctaw Roll** *(Not Including Freedmen)*   CARD NO. FIELD NO. **5726**

POST OFFICE: Minco Ind. Ter.

Dawes' Roll No.	NAME	Relationship to Person First Named	AGE	SEX	BLOOD	TRIBAL ENROLLMENT Year	County	No.
15110	1 Foster, William F	First Named	25	M	1/16	1896	Chick Dist	4596
	2							
	3							
	4							
	5							
	6							
	7							
	8							
	9							
	10							
	11	ENROLLMENT OF NOS. 1 HEREON						
	12	APPROVED BY THE SECRETARY						
	13	OF INTERIOR MAR 26 1904						
	14							
	15							
	16							
	17							

TRIBAL ENROLLMENT OF PARENTS

	Name of Father	Year	County	Name of Mother	Year	County
1	S. D. Foster	Dead	Choctaw Indian	Mattie Foster		Non Citizen
2						
3						
4						
5						
6	No1 Admitted by Act of Choctaw Council Nov 5 1888					
7	No1 Grand-son of Ephraim Foster on Choctaw Card #5713					
8	No1 originally enrolled on Choctaw Card D #98 Transferred to this card Feb 24 '04					
9						
10						
11						
12						
13						
14						
15						
16			10/21/98			
17			Date of Application for Enrollment.	Date of Transfer to this Card.	Feb 24 '04	

Choctaw By Blood Enrollment Cards 1898-1914

RESIDENCE: Chickasaw Nation ~~COUNTY.~~ Tuttle I.T. 10/16/02 **Choctaw Nat**

CARD NO.

POST OFFICE: Minco Ind Ter Oct21/98

FIELD NO. **5727**

Dawes' Roll No.	NAME	Relationship to Person	AGE	SEX	BLOOD	TRIBAL ENROLLMENT		
						Year	County	No.
IW941	1 Park, Robert Lee	First Named	36	M	I.W.			
15111	2 " Ida M	Wife	29	F	1/8	1896	Chick Dist	10627
15112	3 " Edgar Lee	Son	8	M	1/16	1896	" "	10628
15113	4 " Mary Blanche	Dau	6	F	1/16	1896	" "	10629
	5							
	6							
	7							
	8	ENROLLMENT						
	9	OF NOS. 2,3 and 4 HEREON						
	10	~~APPROVED BY THE SECRETARY~~ OF INTERIOR MAR 26 1904						
	11							
	12	ENROLLMENT						
	13	OF NOS. 1 HEREON						
	14	APPROVED BY THE SECRETARY OF INTERIOR AUG 3 1904						
	15							
	16							
	17							

TRIBAL ENROLLMENT OF PARENTS

Name of Father	Year	County	Name of Mother	Year	County
1 W.O. Park	Dead	Non Citizen	Mary E Park		Non Citizen
2 Ephraim Foster		Sugar Loaf	Amanda Foster	Dead	" "
3 No 1			No 2		
4 No 1			No 2		
5					
6 No2 Admitted by Act of Choctaw Council Nov 5 1888					
7 No2 is daughter of Ephraim Foster Choctaw Card #5713					
8 Nos 1,2,3 and 4 originally enrolled on Choctaw Card D # 95 Transferred to this card Feb 24 '04					
9					
10					
11					
12					
13					
14					
15					
16				Oct 21/98		Transfer date
17				Date of Application for Enrollment.		Feb 24 '04

327

Choctaw By Blood Enrollment Cards 1898-1914

RESIDENCE: Chickasaw Nation ~~COUNTY.~~
POST OFFICE: Minco IT 8/16/98

Choctaw Nation

Choctaw Roll
(Not Including Freedmen)

CARD NO.
FIELD NO. **5728**

Dawes' Roll No.	NAME Norman O.T. 7/29/03	Relationship to Person First Named	AGE	SEX	BLOOD	TRIBAL ENROLLMENT		
						Year	County	No.
15134	1 Foster, E. A		28	M	1/8	1896	Chick. Dist.	4594
IW942	2 " Ida Adella	Wife	28	F	I.W.	1896	" "	
15135	3 " Roy	Son	7	M	1/16	1896	Chick. Dist.	4595
15136	4 " Dewey F	"	5	"	1/16			
15137	5 " Ruth Adella	Dau	2	F	1/16			
	6							
	7							
	8	ENROLLMENT OF NOS. 1,2,3 and 5 HEREON						
	9	APPROVED BY THE SECRETARY						
	10	OF INTERIOR MAR 26 1904						
	11							
	12	ENROLLMENT						
	13	OF NOS. 2 HEREON APPROVED BY THE SECRETARY						
	14	OF INTERIOR AUG 3 1904						
	15							
	16							
	17							

TRIBAL ENROLLMENT OF PARENTS

	Name of Father	Year	County	Name of Mother	Year	County
1	E. Foster		Sugar Loaf	Amanda Foster	Dead	Non-Citizen
2	W. F. Armstrong		Non-citizen	Tonney Armstrong		" "
3	No.1			No.2		
4	No.1			No.2		
5	No.1			No.2		
6						
7	No1 Admitted by Act of Choctaw Council Nov 5 1888					
8	No1 Son of Ephraim Foster Card #5713					
	No4 Affidavit of attending physician to be supplied Received March 6 '99					
9	No5 Born Feb 26 '01 Evidence of birth filed August 2 1901					
10	Nos 1 to 5 incl. originally enrolled on Choctaw Card D # 29 transferred to this card Feb 24 '04					
11	No2 admitted by Com., 1896, case #436: no appeal					
12						
13						
14						
15						
16						
17	Norman O.T. 5/29/06					Feb 24 '04

328

Choctaw By Blood Enrollment Cards 1898-1914

RESIDENCE: Chickasaw Nation ~~COUNTY.~~ **Choctaw Nation**   Choctaw Roll   CARD NO.
POST OFFICE: Minco, Ind. Ter.   *(Not Including Freedmen)*   FIELD NO. **5729**

Dawes' Roll No.		NAME	Relationship to Person First Named	AGE	SEX	BLOOD	TRIBAL ENROLLMENT		
							Year	County	No.
15114	1	Campbell, James M	First Named	55	M	1/8	1896	Chick. Dist.	3126
IW943	2	" Susan Frances	Wife	55	F	I.W.	1896	" "	14446
15115	3	" Samuel S	Son	19	M	1/16	1896	" "	3128
15116	4	" Minnie	Dau	16	F	1/16	1896	" "	3129
15117	5	" William	Son	14	M	1/16	1896	" "	3130
15118	6	" Dillard	"	10	"	1/16	1896	" "	3131
IW1613	7	" Clara S	Wife of No3	18	F	I.W.			
	8								
	9	ENROLLMENT OF NOS. 1,3,4,5 and 6 HEREON							
	10	APPROVED BY THE SECRETARY OF INTERIOR Mar 26 1904							
	11								
	12	ENROLLMENT OF NOS. 2 HEREON							
	13	APPROVED BY THE SECRETARY OF INTERIOR Aug 3 1904							
	14			ENROLLMENT OF NOS. 7 HEREON						
	15			APPROVED BY THE SECRETARY OF INTERIOR Feb 12 1907						
	16								
	17								

TRIBAL ENROLLMENT OF PARENTS

	Name of Father	Year	County	Name of Mother	Year	County
1	Lee Campbell	Dead	Non Citizen	Ellen Foster Campbell	Dead	Choctaw Ind
2	Jim Ferguson	"	" " "	Telitha Womack		Non-Citz
3	No1			No2		
4	No1			No2		
5	No1			No2		
6	No1			No2		
7	Nos. 1,2,3 and 4 Admitted by Act of Choctaw Council Nov 5 1888					
8	No1 on 96 Roll as Jno M Campbell					
9	No2 married in Texas before admission by Council Transferred from Choctaw Card # D.100					
10	No7 placed on this card July 14, 1906 under order of Commissioner to the Five Civilized					
11	Tribes of July 10, 1906 holding that application was made for her enrollment within the time					
12	limited by the provisions of the Act of Congress approved April 26, 1906					
13	9/4/19 For children of Nos 3&7 see NB (March 3, 1905) #862					
14	Date in lower right corner is in error so far as it relates to ages of Nos 1 to 6, for correct date					
15	see Choc. D. Card 100 W.H.A.					

	#1 to 6
	Date of Application for Enrollment. Oct 21/99
No3 P.O. Tuttle I.T. 3/29/05	Listed on this card Feb 24 '04

329

Choctaw By Blood Enrollment Cards 1898-1914

RESIDENCE: Chickasaw Nation COUNTY. **Choctaw Nation**   **Choctaw Roll**   CARD NO.

POST OFFICE: Minco, Ind. Ter.   (Not Including Freedmen)   FIELD NO. **5730**

Dawes' Roll No.	NAME	Relationship to Person	AGE	SEX	BLOOD	TRIBAL ENROLLMENT Year	County	No.
15132	1 Jones, Maggie	First Named	22	F	1/16	1896	Chick Dist	3127
15133	2 " Ernest E	Son	3	M	1/32			
	3							
	4							
	5							
	6							
	7							
	8							
	9							
	10							
	11	ENROLLMENT OF NOS. 1 and 2 HEREON						
	12	APPROVED BY THE SECRETARY						
	13	OF INTERIOR MAR 26 1904						
	14							
	15							
	16							
	17							

TRIBAL ENROLLMENT OF PARENTS

Name of Father	Year	County	Name of Mother	Year	County
1 James M Campbell		Chick. Dist.	Susan F. Campbell		(I.W.)
2 Frank H. Jones		Non citizen	No.1		
3					
4					
5					
6 No.1 Admitted by Act of Council Nov 5 1888					
7 No.1 wife of Frank H. Jones, non citizen. Evidence of marriage filed April 23, 02					
8 No.2 born in New Mexico Feb. 24, 1900: evidence of birth filed April 23, '02					
Nos 1 and 2 originally enrolled on Choctaw Card D # 100:					
9 Transferred to this card Feb 24 '04					
10					
11					
12					
13					
14					
15					
16					
17					Feb 24 '04

Choctaw By Blood Enrollment Cards 1898-1914

RESIDENCE: Chickasaw Nation COUNTY. **Choctaw Nation**   **Choctaw Roll**   CARD NO.
POST OFFICE: Minco Ind. Ter.   *(Not Including Freedmen)*   FIELD NO. **5731**

Dawes' Roll No.	NAME	Relationship to Person First Named	AGE	SEX	BLOOD	TRIBAL ENROLLMENT		
						Year	County	No.
15119	1 Campbell, James Lee	First Named	31	M	1/16	1896	Chick. Dist.	3132
IW944	2 " Katie	Wife	33	F	I.W.	1896	" "	14447
15120	3 " Henry L. D	Son	7	M	1/32	1896	" "	3134
15121	4 " Irene	Dau	5	F	1/32			
15122	5 " Eva Francis	"	2	"	1/32			
	6							
	7 ENROLLMENT							
	8 OF NOS. 1,3,4 and 5 HEREON							
	APPROVED BY THE SECRETARY							
	9 OF INTERIOR MAR 26 1904							
	10							
	11 ENROLLMENT							
	12 OF NOS. 2 HEREON							
	APPROVED BY THE SECRETARY							
	13 OF INTERIOR AUG 3 1904							
	14							
	15							
	16							
	17							

TRIBAL ENROLLMENT OF PARENTS

Name of Father	Year	County		Year	County
1 J. M. Campbell		Chic▇	▇(IW)		Chick Dist
2 George Denny		Non Citizen	Kate De▇▇		Non Citizen
3	No.1		No.2		
4	No.1		No.2		
5	No.1		No.2		
6					

7 No1 Admitted by Act of Choctaw Council Nov 5 1888
8 No1 Son of James M Campbell Card #5729
No4 Affidavit of attending physician to be supplied - Received Nov 30/98
9 No5 Born June 20 1900: Evidence of birth filed August 6" 1900
10 Nos 1&2 Affidavits as to marriage filed Dec 29 02
11 Nos 1 to 5 inclusive originally enrolled on Choctaw Card D # 104
12 transferred to this card Feb 24 '04
13 For child of Nos 1 and 2 see NB (Mar 3 '05) #425
14
15
16   Oct 21/98   transfer date
17 PO Tuttle I.T. [?]/12   Date of Application for Enrollment.   Feb 24 '04

Choctaw By Blood Enrollment Cards 1898-1914

RESIDENCE: Chickasaw Nation ~~COUNTY.~~
POST OFFICE: Minco I.T.

Choctaw Nation

Choctaw Roll
(Not Including Freedmen)

CARD NO.
FIELD NO. **5732**

Dawes' Roll No.	NAME	Relationship to Person First Named	AGE	SEX	BLOOD	TRIBAL ENROLLMENT Year	County	No.
15123	1 Campbell, Charles R	First Named	28	M	1/16	1896	Chick. Dist.	3135
15124	2 " Annie D	Dau	7	F	1/32	1896	" "	3136
15125	3 " John M	Son	6	M	1/32	1896	" "	3137
15126	4 " Agnes	Dau	4	F	1/32			
15127	5 " Chas Carroll	Son	3	M	1/32			
IW 1561	6 " Susan Josephine	Wife	25	F	I.W.			
	7							
	8 ENROLLMENT							
	9 OF NOS. 1,2,3,4 and 5 HEREON APPROVED BY THE SECRETARY							
	10 OF INTERIOR MAR 26 1904							
	11							
	12 ENROLLMENT OF NOS. 6 HEREON							
	13 APPROVED BY THE SECRETARY							
	14 OF INTERIOR AUG 2 1906							
	15 No6							
	16 GRANTED							
	17 JUN 13 1906							

TRIBAL ENROLLMENT OF PARENTS

	Name of Father	Year	County	Name of Mother	Year	County
1	J. M. Campbell		Chick. Dist.	Susan F. Campbell (I.W.)		Chick. Dist.
2	No.1			Susan J. Campbell		Non Citizen
3	No.1			" " "		" "
4	No.1			" " "		" "
5	No.1			" " "		" "
6	John N Jones		noncitizen	Ann Jones	Dead	noncitizen
7						
8						

9 No1 Son of J.M. Campbell Choctaw Card #5729
No1 Admitted by Act of Choctaw Council Nov 5 1888
10 No4 Affidavit of attending physician to be supplied. Received Nov. 3 '98
11 No5 Born Jan 3' 1900. Evidence of Birth filed May 24 1900
12 Nos 1 to 5 incl. originally enrolled on Choctaw Card D # 103. Transferred to this card Feb 24 '04
For children of Nos 1&6 see NB (Mar 3 '05) #426
13 ~~No.6 is placed hereon under order of Commissioner to the Five Civilized Tribes of January~~
14 ~~11, 1906 holding that application was made for her enrollment within the time provided by the~~
15 ~~Act of Congress approved July 1, 1902 (32 Stats 641)~~

16
17 PO Tuttle I.T. 8/14/05

Date of Application for Enrollment.

Choctaw By Blood Enrollment Cards 1898-1914

RESIDENCE: Chickasaw Nation ~~COUNTY~~ ▪▪▪ **Nation** ▪▪▪ Roll   CARD NO.

POST OFFICE: Minco Ind. Ter.   *(Not Including Freedmen)*   FIELD NO. **5733**

Dawes' Roll No.	NAME	Relationship to Person First Named	AGE	SEX	BLOOD	TRIBAL ENROLLMENT Year	County	No.
15128	1 Campbell, Thomas A	First Named	26	M	1/16	1896	Chick. Dist.	3138
15129	2 " James A	Son	6	"	1/32	1896	" "	3139
15130	3 " Samuel Augustus	"	5	"	1/32			
15131	4 " May Dean	Dau	1	F	1/32			
IW 1562	5 " Sarah A	Wife	23	F	I.W.			
	6							
	7							
	8	ENROLLMENT						
	9	OF NOS. 1,2,3 and 4 HEREON APPROVED BY THE SECRETARY						
	10	OF INTERIOR MAR 26 1904						
	11	ENROLLMENT						
	12	OF NOS. 5 HEREON						
	13	APPROVED BY THE SECRETARY OF INTERIOR AUG 2- 1906						
	14							
	15							
	16							
	17							

TRIBAL ENROLLMENT OF PARENTS

Name of Father	Year	County	Name of Mother	Year	County
1 James M. Campbell		Chick. Dist.	Susan F. Campbell (I.W.)		Chick. Dist.
2 No.1			Sarah A. Campbell		Non Citizen
3 No.1			" " "		" "
4 No.1			" " "		" "
5 John N Jones		noncitizen	Ann Jones	Dead	" "
6					
7					

8 No1 Admitted by Act of Choctaw Council Nov 5 1888

No1 Son of James M Campbell on Choctaw Card #5729

9 ~~Evidence of marriage between No1 and mother of children on this Card filed April 4 '02~~

10 No2 Born April 28" 1896

11 No3 Born Jany 17 1898 Affidavit of attending physician to be supplied. Received Nov 18/98

12 No4 Born August 11 '01. Evidence of birth filed April 4, 1902

13 ~~Nos 1 to 4 inclusive originally enrolled on Choctaw Card D # 110. Transferred to this card Feb 24 04~~

14 No 5 placed hereon under order of Commissioner to the Five Civilized Tribes of January 11,

15 1906 holding that application was made for her enrollment within the time provided by the Act of Congress approved July 1, 1902 (32 Stats 641)

16   Oct 24/98   No5   on this card

17 PO Tuttle, I.T.   Date of Application for Enrollment.   **GRANTED**   Feb 24 '04

~~APR 25 1906~~

Choctaw By Blood Enrollment Cards 1898-1914

Choctaw Nation

CARD No.
FIELD No. **5734**

Dawes' Roll No.	NAME	Relationship to Person First Named	AGE	SEX	BLOOD	TRIBAL ENROLLMENT Year	County	No.
15138	1 Bedingfield, Mollie	First Named	25	F	1/16	1896	Chick. Dist	35
15139	2 " Mary F	Dau	8	"	1/32	1896	" "	36
15140	3 " Clyde	Son	7	M	1/32	1896	" "	37
15141	4 " Laura M	Dau	6	F	1/32			
15142	5 " Claude A	Son	4	M	1/32			
15143	6 " Nona Thelma	Dau	2	F	1/32			
	7							
	8							
	9							
	10							
	11	ENROLLMENT OF NOS. 1,2,3,4,5 and 6 HEREON						
	12	APPROVED BY THE SECRETARY						
	13	OF INTERIOR MAR 26 1904						
	14							
	15							
	16							
	17							

TRIBAL ENROLLMENT OF PARENTS

	Name of Father		County	Name of Mother	Year	County
1	J. M. Campbell		Chick. Dist.	Susan F. Campbell (I.W.)		Chick. Dist.
2	Milas Bedingfield		Non Citizen	No.1		
3	" "		" "	No.1		
4	" "		" "	No.1		
5	" "		" "	No.1		
6	" "		" "	No.1		
7						
8	No1 Admitted by Act of Choctaw Council Nov 5 1888					
9	No1 Parents on Choctaw Card 5729					
10	No4 Born Feb 26 '99 Proof of birth filed Oct 6/99 No5 Born Oct 13 1900 " " " " April 29 '01					
11	No6 Born Aug 22, '02 " " " " Sept 6, 1902					
12	Nos 1 to 6 inclusive originally enrolled on Choctaw Card D #111. Transferred to this card Feb 24 '04					
13						
14						
15						
16				Date of Application for Enrollment.		transfer date on this card
17				Oct 22/98		Feb 24 '04

Choctaw By Blood Enrollment Cards 1898-1914

Choctaw Nation

Dawes' Roll No.	NAME	Relationship to Person First Named	AGE	SEX	BLOOD	TRIBAL ENROLLMENT		
						Year		
[15200 White, James] Edward		First Named	50	M	I.W.	189		
[15144 " Ella]		Wife	30	F	1/16	189		
15145 ₃ " James Edward Jr		Son	15	M	1/			14146
15146 ₄ " Katie		Dau	11	F	1/			14147
15147 ₅ " Esther		"	5	"	1/			
6								
7								
8	ENROLLMENT							
9	OF NOS. 2,3,4 and 5 HEREON							
10	APPROVED BY THE SECRETARY OF INTERIOR MAR 26 1904							
11								
12	ENROLLMENT							
13	OF NOS. 1 HEREON							
14	APPROVED BY THE SECRETARY OF INTERIOR AUG 3 1904							
15								
16								
17								

TRIBAL ENROLLMENT OF PARENTS

	Name of Father	Year	County	Name of Mother	Year	County
		ad	Non citizen	Martha White (IW)	Dead	Non Citizen
	[James M Campbell]		Chick Dist	Susan F. Campbell		Chick Dist
3	No1			No2		
4	No1			No2		
5	No1			No2		
6						
7	No1 married in Texas before admission					
8	Nos 1 and 2 Admitted by Act of Choctaw Council Nov 5 1888					
9	~~No2 Daughter of 1 and 2 on Choctaw Card #5729~~					
	No3 not named in Act of Council					
10	No5 Born Aug 5, 1897 Affidavit of Attending physician filed					
11	Nos 1 to 5 incl. originally enrolled on Choctaw Card D #105 Transferred to this card Feb 24 '04					
12						
13						
14						
15						
16				lication ment.	Date of Transfer to this Card.	Feb 24 '04
17				/98		

Choctaw By Blood Enrollment Cards 1898-1914

RESIDENCE: Chickasaw Nation COUNTY.
POST OFFICE: Minco, Ind. Ter.

Choctaw Nation
(Not Including Freedmen)

Choctaw Roll

CARD NO.
FIELD NO. **5736**

Dawes' Roll No.	NAME	Relationship to Person First Named	AGE	SEX	BLOOD	TRIBAL ENROLLMENT		
						Year	County	No.
IW946	1 Kirkendall, Joseph	First Named	51	M	I.W.	1896	Chick. Dist	14734
15148	2 " Jane	Wife	47	F	1/8	1896	" "	7664
15812	3 " Willie Inez	Dau	17	"	1/16	1896	" "	7668
15813	4 " Ada Lee	"	15	"	1/16	1896	" "	7667
15149	5 " Sarah Amanda	"	13	"	1/16	1896	" "	7669
15150	6 " William Edward	Son	10	M	1/16	1896	" "	7672
	7							
	8							
	9							
	10	ENROLLMENT OF NOS. 2, 5 and 6 HEREON APPROVED BY THE SECRETARY OF INTERIOR MAR 26 1904						
	11							
	12							
	13							
	14	ENROLLMENT OF NOS. 1 HEREON APPROVED BY THE SECRETARY OF INTERIOR AUG 3 1904		ENROLLMENT OF NOS. 3 and 4 HEREON APPROVED BY THE SECRETARY OF INTERIOR MAR 15 1905				
	15							
	16							
	17							

TRIBAL ENROLLMENT OF PARENTS

	Name of Father	Year	County	Name of Mother	Year	County
1	Ben Kirkendall	Dead	Non-Citizen	Polly Kirkendall	Dead	Non Citizen
2	L. J. Campbell	"	" "	Ellen Foster Campbell	"	Choctaw Ind.
3	No.1			No.2		
4	No.1			No.2		
5	No.1			No.2		
6	No.1			No.2		
7						
8	Nos 1 and 2 Admitted by Act of Choctaw Council Nov 5 1888					
9	Nos 3 and 4 Not " " " " " " " "					
10	Nos 1 to 6 incl originally enrolled on Choctaw Card D #101 Transferred to this card Feb 24 '04					
11						
12						
13						
14						
15					Date of Application for Enrollment.	
16						
17	PO Box 367 Chickasha IT 4/30/04		Oct 21/98		Date of Transfer to this Card.	Feb 24 '04

9/7/20 This notation in error should read Feb 24, 1903

Choctaw By Blood Enrollment Cards 1898-1914

RESIDENCE: Chickasaw Nation COUNTY. **Choctaw Nation** Choctaw Roll CARD NO.
POST OFFICE: Purcell I.T. (Not Including Freedmen) FIELD NO. **5737**

Dawes' Roll No.	NAME	Relationship to Person First Named	AGE	SEX	BLOOD	TRIBAL ENROLLMENT		
						Year	County	No.
15246	1 Buckholts, Rebecca	First Named	26	F	1/32	1896	Blue	1537
	2							
	3							
	4							
	5							
	6							
	7							
	8							
	9							
	10							
	11	ENROLLMENT						
	12	OF NOS. 1 HEREON APPROVED BY THE SECRETARY						
	13	OF INTERIOR MAY 9 1904						
	14							
	15							
	16							
	17							

TRIBAL ENROLLMENT OF PARENTS

	Name of Father	Year	County	Name of Mother	Year	County
1	James M. Buckholts	1896	Blue	Jennetta Buckholts		non-citizen
2						
3						
4						
5						
6	No1 transferred from Choctaw Card # D.357					
7	See decision of July 20, 1903, approved by Department Feby 24, 1904					
8						
9	For child of No1 see NB (Apr 26-06) Card #358					
10	" " " " " (Mar 3-05) " #828					
11						
12						
13						
14						
15						
16			Date of Application for Enrollment. 8/24/99			transfer date on this card
17						MAR 3 1904

337

Choctaw By Blood Enrollment Cards 1898-1914

RESIDENCE: Chickasaw Nation COUNTY. **Choctaw Nation** Choctaw Roll CARD NO.
POST OFFICE: Purcell Ind. Ter. (Not Including Freedmen) FIELD NO. **5738**

Dawes' Roll No.	NAME	Relationship to Person First Named	AGE	SEX	BLOOD	TRIBAL ENROLLMENT		
						Year	County	No.
15247	1 Buckholts, James M	First Named	56	M	1/16	1896	Blue	1536
IW 1537	2 " Jennetta H		55	F	I.W.	1896	"	14338
	3							
	4							
	5							
	6							
	7	ENROLLMENT						
	8	OF NOS. 1 HEREON						
	9	APPROVED BY THE SECRETARY OF INTERIOR MAY 9 1904						
	10							
	11	ENROLLMENT						
	12	OF NOS. 2 HEREON						
	13	APPROVED BY THE SECRETARY OF INTERIOR MAR 14 1906						
	14							
	15							
	16							
	17							

TRIBAL ENROLLMENT OF PARENTS

	Name of Father	Year	County	Name of Mother	Year	County
1	Wᵐ Buckholts		Blue	Matilda Buckholts	Dead	non-citizen
2	Wᵐ Perryman	Dead	noncitizen	Elizabeth Perryman	Dead	noncitizen
3						
4						
5	Wᵐ Buckholts father of No1 admitted by Supreme Court Choctaw Nation Oct, 1872					
6	No1 transferred from Choctaw Card # D. 357					
7	See decision of July 20 1903, approved by Department Feby 24 1904					
8	No2 Transferred from D724 to this card January 12 1906: see decision of December 27 1905					
9	No2 was denied by the Dawes Commission in 1896 Choc case #943. No appeal.					
10	Enrollment of No.2 cancelled by order of Department March 22, 1907					
11	No2 restored to roll by Departmental authority of January 19, 1909 (File 551)					
12						
13						
14						
15				Date of Application for Enrollment.		transfer date on this date[sic]
16						
17				Aug 24/99		MAR 3 1904

338

Choctaw By Blood Enrollment Cards 1898-1914

RESIDENCE: Choctaw Nation COUNTY.
POST OFFICE: Ego, I.T.

Choctaw Nation
(Not Including Freedmen)

Choctaw Roll Card No.
Roll No. 339

Dawes' Roll No.	NAME	Relationship to Person First Named	AGE	SEX	BLOOD	TRIBAL ENROLLMENT		
						Year	County	No.
15248	1 Jones, Francis M	First Named	41	M	1/32	1896	Blue	7162
IW947	2 " Ida M	Wife	34	F	I.W.	1896	"	14704
15249	3 " Lenora M	Dau	15	"	1/64	1896	"	7163
15250	4 " Robert M	Son	13	M	1/64	1896	"	7164
15251	5 " Jesse F	"	10	"	1/64	1896	"	7165
15252	6 " Walter A	"	9	"	1/64	1896	"	7166
15253	7 " Albert L	"	7	"	1/64	1896	"	7167
15254	8 " Claude O	"	4	"	1/64			
15255	9 " Roy D	"	2	"	1/64			
	See opinion of Atty Genl of Feb 18 '04 and letter of							
	11 Secy of Interior of Feb 24 '04 in the case of							
	12 James M Buckholts							
	13							
	14							
	15							
	16							
	17							

ENROLLMENT
OF NOS. 1-3-4-5-6-7-8-9 HEREON
APPROVED BY THE SECRETARY
OF INTERIOR May 9 1904

ENROLLMENT
OF NOS. 2 HEREON
APPROVED BY THE SECRETARY
OF INTERIOR Aug 3 1904

TRIBAL ENROLLMENT OF PARENTS

Name of Father	Year	County	Name of Mother	Year	County
1 R T Jones		intermarried	Lurena E Jones		Blue
2 Frank Melton		non-citz	Candis Melton		non-citz
3	No1		No2		
4	No1		No2		
5	No1		No2		
6	No1		No2		
7	No1		No2		
8	No1		No2		
9	No1		No2		
10	No3 on 1896 Choctaw census roll as Leonora Jones				
11	No7 " 1896 " " " " Albert Lee "				
12	No2 admitted in 1896 by Dawes Commission in Choctaw case #1041 No appeal No9 Enrolled Dec. 7 1900				
13	Transferred from Choctaw Card # D.354				
14					Date of Application for Enrollment.
15	For child of No 3 see NB #1057 (Act Apr 26 '06)		Date of application for enrollment Aug 24/99		
16	" " " " " " #542 (Act Mar 3,1905)				Date of transfer on this card.
17			Date of transfer to this card. Mar 4 1903		

339

Choctaw By Blood Enrollment Cards 1898-1914

Dawes' Roll No.	NAME	Relationship to Person First Named	AGE	SEX	BLOOD	TRIBAL ENROLLMENT		
						Year	County	No.
IW948	1 Simmons, Nathaniel H	First Named	38	M	I.W.			
15256	2 " Matilda E	Wife	33	F	1/32	1896	Blue	7172
15257	3 " Viola May	Dau	2	"	1/64			
15258	4 " Nathaniel Roddom	Son	1mo	M	1/64			
	5							
	6 See opinion of Atty Genl of Feb 18 '04 and letter of Secy of Interior of							
	7 Feb 24 '04 in the case of James M Buckholts et al 7-5738							
	8							
	9							
	10							
	11 ENROLLMENT							
	12 OF NOS. 2 - 3 - 4 HEREON APPROVED BY THE SECRETARY							
	13 OF INTERIOR MAY 9 1904							
	14 ENROLLMENT							
	15 OF NOS. 1 HEREON APPROVED BY THE SECRETARY							
	16 OF INTERIOR AUG 3 1904							
	17							

	TRIBAL ENROLLMENT OF PARENTS					
	Name of Father		County	Name of Mother	Year	County
1	Nath Simmons	Dead		Margaret Simmons		non-citz
2	R. T. Jones			Lurenda E Jones		Blue
3	No1			No2		
4	No1			No2		
5						
6						
7	No2 on 1896 Choctaw census roll as Lizzie Jones					
8	No3 Born June 6 1900. Evidence of birth filed June 26 1900					
9	No4 Born May 28, 1902. Evidence of birth filed July 8, 1902.					
10	Transferred from Choctaw Card # D. 355.					
11						
12	For child of Nos 1 and 2 see NB (Mar 3 '05) #427					
13						
14						
15				Date of Application for Enrollment.		transfer date on this card
16						
17	PO Aylesworth IT 3/17/05			Aug 24/99		MAR 4 1903

340

Choctaw By Blood Enrollment Cards 1898-1914

RESIDENCE: Choctaw Nation COUNTY. **Choctaw Nation** Choctaw Roll CARD NO.
POST OFFICE: Caddo I.T. (Not Including Freedmen) FIELD NO. **5741**

Dawes' Roll No.	NAME	Relationship to Person	AGE	SEX	BLOOD	TRIBAL ENROLLMENT		
						Year	County	No.
15259	1 Hamilton, Rebecca	First Named	45	F	1/16	1896	Blue	5835
15260	2 " Mary M	Dau	24	"	1/32	1896	"	5836
15261	3 " Vercy	"	20	"	1/32	1896	"	5837
15262	4 " Rufus	Son	18	M	1/32	1896	"	5838
	5							
	6 See opinion of Atty Genl of Feb 18 '04 and letter of Secy of Interior of							
	7 Feb 24 '04 in the case of James M Buckholts et al 7-5738							
	8							
	9							
	10							
	11 ENROLLMENT							
	12 OF NOS. 1 - 2 - 3 - 4 HEREON APPROVED BY THE SECRETARY							
	13 OF INTERIOR MAY 9 1904							
	14							
	15							
	16							
	17							

TRIBAL ENROLLMENT OF PARENTS

Name of Father	Year	County	Name of Mother	Year	County
1 John Null	Dead	White man	Sarah Null	Dead	Choctaw
2 Oscar Hamilton	"	non-citz	No 1		
3 " "	"	" "	No 1		
4 " "	"	" "	No 1		
5					
6 Transferred from Choctaw Card # D.309					
7 For child of No.3 see NB (Mar 3, 1905) #676					
8					
9					
10					
11					
12					
13					
14					
15					
16			Aug 25/99 Date of Application for Enrollment.		transfer date on this card MAR 4 1903
17					

Choctaw By Blood Enrollment Cards 1898-1914

RESIDENCE: Choctaw Nation   <del>COUNTY.</del>   **Choctaw Nation**   **Choctaw Roll**   CARD No.
POST OFFICE: Ego,   I.T.   *(Not Including Freedmen)*   FIELD No. **5742**

Dawes' Roll No.	NAME	Relationship to Person First Named	AGE	SEX	BLOOD	TRIBAL ENROLLMENT		
						Year	County	No.
15263	1 Jones, William T	First Named	44	M	1/32	1896	Blue	7181
	2							
	3							
	4							
	5 See opinion of Atty Genl of Feb 18 '04 and letter of Secy of Interior of							
	6 Feb 24 '04 in the case of James M Buckholts et al 7-5738							
	7							
	8							
	9							
	10							
	11	ENROLLMENT						
	12	OF NOS. 1 HEREON APPROVED BY THE SECRETARY						
	13	OF INTERIOR MAY 9 1904						
	14							
	15							
	16							
	17							

TRIBAL ENROLLMENT OF PARENTS

	Name of Father	Year	County	Name of Mother	Year	County
1	R. T. Jones		intermarried	Lizabeth Jones		Blue
2						
3						
4						
5						
6	On 1896 Choctaw census roll as W.T. Jones also as Wᵐ T Jones					
7	Wife and family on Choctaw card #3952					
8	No1 transferred from Choctaw Card # D376					
9						
10						
11						
12						
13						
14						
15				~~Date of Application for Enrollment.~~		transfer date on this card
16						MAR 4 1903
17				Aug 25/99		

Choctaw By Blood Enrollment Cards 1898-1914

RESIDENCE: Choctaw Nation   COUNTY.

POST OFFICE: Doaksville I.T.

Dawes' Roll No.	NAME	Relationship to Person First Named	AGE	SEX	BLOOD	TRIBAL ENROLLMENT		
						Year	County	No.
15517	1 Lowe Minnie	First Named	21	F	Full	1896	Nashoba	7975
15518	2 " George	Bro	17	M	"	1896	"	7976
	3							
	4							
	5							
	6							
	7							
	8							
	9							
	10							
	11	ENROLLMENT						
	12	OF NOS. 1 & 2 HEREON APPROVED BY THE SECRETARY						
	13	OF INTERIOR MAY 9 1904						
	14							
	15							
	16							
	17							

TRIBAL ENROLLMENT OF PARENTS

	Name of Father	Year	County	Name of Mother	Year	County
1	Impson Lowe	Dead	Choctaw	Josie Lowe	Dead	Choctaw
2	" "		"	" "		"
3						
4						
5						
6	No1 on 1896 Choctaw census roll as Mellie Low					
7	No2 " 1896 " " " " George "					
8	See testimony of Nov. 28, 1902 Nos 1 and 2 transferred from Choctaw freedman card # 451 March 10, 1904					
9						
10						
11						
12						
13						
14						
15					Date of Application for Enrollment.	
16				9/7/99	MAR 10 1904	
17	PO Tishomingo IT 6/6/04			Date of Application for Enrollment.	transfer date	

343

Choctaw By Blood Enrollment Cards 1898-1914

RESIDENCE: Choctaw Nation		COUNTY. **Choctaw Nation**					**Choctaw Roll** (Not Including Freedmen)	CARD NO.	
POST OFFICE: Cowlington I.T.								FIELD NO. **5744**	

Dawes' Roll No.	NAME	Relationship to Person First Named	AGE	SEX	BLOOD	TRIBAL ENROLLMENT		
						Year	County	No.
IW776	1 Overstreet, Alice E	First Named	26	F	I.W.			
	2							
	3							
	4							
	5							
	6							
	7							
	8							
	9							
	10							
	11	ENROLLMENT OF NOS. 1 HEREON APPROVED BY THE SECRETARY OF INTERIOR MAY -7 1904						
	12							
	13							
	14							
	15							
	16							
	17							

TRIBAL ENROLLMENT OF PARENTS

	Name of Father	Year	County	Name of Mother	Year	County
1	Jim Cremeens	dead	non-citizen	Rebecca O'Brian		non-citizen
2						
3						
4						
5						
6	No 1 is wife of Clayton N Overstreet Choctaw card #2683 Roll #7816					
7	No 1 transferred from Choctaw Card # D. 689 March 17, 1904					
8	See decision of Feby 27, 1904					
9						
10						
11						
12						
13						
14						
15				Date of Application for Enrollment.		transfer date on this card
16						MAR 17 1904
17				Nov 29/01		

344

Choctaw By Blood Enrollment Cards 1898-1914

RESIDENCE: Tobucksy COUNTY.
POST OFFICE: Canadian I.T.

Choctaw Nation

Choctaw Roll
(Not Including Freedmen)

CARD NO.
FIELD NO. 574

Dawes' Roll No.	NAME	Relationship to Person First Named	AGE	SEX	BLOOD	TRIBAL ENROLLMENT		
						Year	County	No.
IW777	1 Smith, Anna E	First Named	34	F	I.W.	1896	Tobucksy	15142
15519	2 " Orlean	Son	10	M	1/32	1896	"	11286
15520	3 " Frances	Dau	8	F	1/32	1896	"	11287
15521	4 " Fulton	Son	2	M	1/32			
	5							
	6							
	7							
	8							
	9	ENROLLMENT						
	10	OF NOS. 1 HEREON						
	11	APPROVED BY THE SECRETARY OF INTERIOR MAY - 7 1904						
	12							
	13							
	14	ENROLLMENT						
	15	OF NOS. 2 - 3 -4 HEREON APPROVED BY THE SECRETARY						
	16	OF INTERIOR MAY 9 1904						
	17							

TRIBAL ENROLLMENT OF PARENTS

	Name of Father	Year	County	Name of Mother	Year	
1	Stephen F Wade		non citz	B. M. Wade		non-cit
2	Freeman R Smith		Choctaw	No1		
3	" "		"	No1		
4	" "		"	No1		
5						
6	No1 admitted in '96 Can #838					
7	No4 Born July 29 1900 Enrolled Sept 10 1900					
8	Transferred from Choctaw Card # D. 494 See decision of Feby 29, 1904					
9	No1 is wife of Freeman R Smith Roll #13207 Card #4781					
10						
11						
12	For child of No1 see NB (Mar 3 '05) #383					
13						
14						
15						
16			Date of Application for Enrollment.			
17			Sept 14/99	Date of Transfer to this Card MAR 17 1904		

Choctaw By Blood Enrollment Cards 1898-1914

RESIDENCE:	Choctaw Nation										

RESIDENCE: Choctaw Nation COUNTY. **Choctaw Nation** **Choctaw Roll** (Not Including Freedmen) CARD No. FIELD No. **5746**
POST OFFICE: Antlers I.T.

Dawes' Roll No.		NAME	Relationship to Person First Named	AGE	SEX	BLOOD	TRIBAL ENROLLMENT		
							Year	County	No.
IW778	1	Locke, Victor M	First Named	56	M	I.W.	1896	Jacks Fork	14791
	2								
	3								
	4								
	5								
	6								
	7								
	8								
	9								
	10								
	11	ENROLLMENT OF NOS. 1 HEREON APPROVED BY THE SECRETARY OF INTERIOR MAY -7 1904							
	12								
	13								
	14								
	15								
	16								
	17								

TRIBAL ENROLLMENT OF PARENTS

	Name of Father	Year	County	Name of Mother	Year	County
1			non-citizen			non-citizen
2						
3						
4						
5						
6	No 1 transferred from Choctaw Card # D. 524 See decision of Feby 29, 1904					
7						
8						
9						
10						
11						
12						
13						
14						
15				Date of Application for Enrollment.		transfer date on this card
16						MAR 17 1904
17				Nov 15/99		

346

Choctaw By Blood Enrollment Cards 1898-1914

RESIDENCE: Choctaw Nation COUNTY. **Choctaw Nation** **Choctaw Roll** CARD NO.
POST OFFICE: Durant I.T. (Not Including Freedmen) FIELD NO. **5747**

Dawes' Roll No.	NAME	Relationship to Person First Named	AGE	SEX	BLOOD	TRIBAL ENROLLMENT		
						Year	County	No.
IW779	1 Seeley, George W	First Named	39	M	I.W.			
	2							
	3							
	4							
	5							
	6							
	7							
	8							
	9							
	10							
	11	ENROLLMENT						
	12	OF NOS. 1 HEREON APPROVED BY THE SECRETARY						
	13	OF INTERIOR MAY -7 1904						
	14							
	15							
	16							
	17							

TRIBAL ENROLLMENT OF PARENTS

	Name of Father	Year	County	Name of Mother	Year	County
1	Ralph Seeley		non-citz	Mary Seeley		non citz
2						
3						
4						
5						
6	No1 is husband of Birdie Seeley on Choctaw card #3527. #10020 on final Roll					
7	No1 transferred from Choctaw Card # D.616 See decision of Feby 29, 1904					
8	For child of No.1 see NB (Mar 3-1905) Card #247					
9						
10						
11						
12						
13						
14						
15				Date of Application for Enrollment.		transfer date to this card
16						MAR 17 1904
17				Feb. 13/01		

Choctaw By Blood Enrollment Cards 1898-1914

RESIDENCE: Choctaw Nation COUNTY.
POST OFFICE: Kennady I.T.

Choctaw Nation
(Not Including Freedmen)

Choctaw Roll

FIELD NO. 5748

Dawes' Roll No.	NAME	Relationship to Person First Named	AGE	SEX	BLOOD	TRIBAL ENROLLMENT		
						Year	County	No.
IW780	1 McAlvain, Mollie Belle	First Named	23	F	I.W.			
	2							
	3							
	4							
	5							
	6							
	7							
	8							
	9							
	10							
	11	ENROLLMENT						
	12	OF NOS. 1 HEREON APPROVED BY THE SECRETARY						
	13	OF INTERIOR MAY 7 1904						
	14							
	15							
	16							
	17							

TRIBAL ENROLLMENT OF PARENTS

	Name of Father	Year	County	Name of Mother	Year	County
1	Wm Brazeal	dead	non-citizen	Adeline Brazeal		non-cit
2						
3						
4						
5						
6	No1 is wife of Robert McAlvain Choctaw card #2225 #6447 on final Roll					
7	Transferred from Choctaw Card # D. 632 See decision of Feby 29, 1904					
8	For child of No.1 see NB (Apr 26, 1906) Card No. 28					
9						
10						
11						
12						
13						
14						
15				Date of Application for Enrollment.	transfer date on this card	
16						
17				May 13/01	MAR 17 1904	

348

Choctaw By Blood Enrollment Cards 1898-1914

RESIDENCE: Choctaw Nation   COUNTY. **Choctaw Nation**   Choctaw
POST OFFICE: *(Not Including Fr*   **5749**

Dawes' Roll No.	NAME	Relationship to Person First Named	AGE	SEX	BLOOD	TRIBAL ENROLLMENT		
						Year	County	No.
IW781	1 Simpson, Edward	First Named	58	M	I.W.			
	2							
	3							
	4							
	5							
	6							
	7							
	8							
	9							
	10							
	11	ENROLLMENT						
	12	OF NOS. 1 HEREON APPROVED BY THE SECRETARY						
	13	OF INTERIOR MAY 17 1904						
	14							
	15							
	16							
	17							

TRIBAL ENROLLMENT OF PARENTS

	Name of Father	Year	County	Name of Mother	Year	County
1	Reuben Simpson	Dead	non-citz	Sarah Simpson	Dead	non-citz
2						
3						
4						
5						
6	Transferred from Choctaw Card # D. 362 See decision of Feby 27, 1904					
7	Husband of Elizabeth H Simpson #10973 on final Roll Choctaw Card #3900					
8						
9						
10						
11						
12						
13						
14						
15				Date of Application for Enrollment.		transfer date on this card
16						MAR 17 1904
17	PO Caddo Ind. Ter. March 30, 1904			8/24/99		

Choctaw By Blood Enrollment Cards 1898-1914

Choctaw Nation

POST OFFICE, Bee Ind Ter

Choctaw Roll
(Not Including Freedmen)

CARD NO.
FIELD NO. **5750**

	NAME	Relationship to Person First Named	AGE	SEX	BLOOD	TRIBAL ENROLLMENT		
						Year	County	No.
IW782	1 Hamilton, William H	First Named	42	M	I.W.			
	2							
	3							
	4							
	5							
	6							
	7							
	8							
	9							
	10							
	11							
	12							
	13							
	14							
	15							
	16							
	17							

ENROLLMENT
OF NOS. 1 HEREON
APPROVED BY THE SECRETARY
OF INTERIOR MAY -7 1904

TRIBAL ENROLLMENT OF PARENTS

	Name of Father	Year	County	Name of Mother	Year	County
1	John Hamilton	Dead	Non-Citz	Mary A Hamilton		Non-citz
2						
3						
4						
5						
6	No 1 transferred from Choctaw Card # D. 383. See decision of Feby 27, 1904					
7	Husband of Mamie Hamilton #11139 on final Roll Choctaw card #3977					
8						
9						
10						
11						
12						
13						
14						
15						
16				Aug 28/99 Date of Application for Enrollment.		Date of transfer on this card. MAR 17 1904
17						

350

Index

www.ingramcontent.com/pod-product-compliance
Lightning Source LLC
Chambersburg PA
CBHW030234030426
42336CB00009B/96

Other Books and Series by Jeff Bowen

1901-1907 Native American Census Seneca, Eastern Shawnee, Miami, Modoc, Ottawa, Peoria, Quapaw, and Wyandotte Indians (Under Seneca School, Indian Territory)

1932 Census of The Standing Rock Sioux Reservation with Births And Deaths 1924-1932

Census of The Blackfeet, Montana, 1897- 1901 Expanded Edition

Eastern Cherokee by Blood, 1906-1910, Volumes I thru XIII

Choctaw of Mississippi Indian Census 1929-1932 with Births and Deaths 1924-1931   Volume I
Choctaw of Mississippi Indian Census 1933, 1934 & 1937, Supplemental Rolls to 1934 & 1935 with Births and Deaths 1932-1938, and Marriages 1936-1938 Volume II

Eastern Cherokee Census Cherokee, North Carolina 1930-1939
Census 1930-1931 with Births And Deaths 1924-1931 Taken By Agent L. W. Page Volume I
Eastern Cherokee Census Cherokee, North Carolina 1930-1939
Census 1932-1933 with Births And Deaths 1930-1932 Taken By Agent R. L. Spalsbury   Volume II
Eastern Cherokee Census Cherokee, North Carolina 1930-1939
Census 1934-1937 with Births and Deaths 1925-1938 and Marriages 1936 & 1938 Taken by Agents R. L. Spalsbury And Harold W. Foght Volume III

Seminole of Florida Indian Census, 1930-1940 with Birth and Death Records, 1930-1938

Texas Cherokees 1820-1839 A Document For Litigation 1921

Starr Roll 1894 (Cherokee Payment Rolls) Districts: Canadian, Cooweescoowee, and Delaware Volume One
Starr Roll 1894 (Cherokee Payment Rolls) Districts: Flint, Going Snake, and Illinois   Volume Two
Starr Roll 1894 (Cherokee Payment Rolls) Districts: Saline, Sequoyah, and Tahlequah; Including Orphan Roll   Volume Three

Cherokee Intruder Cases Dockets of Hearings 1901-1909 Volumes I & II

Indian Wills, 1911-1921 Records of the Bureau of Indian Affairs
Books One thru Seven
Native American Wills & Probate Records 1911-1921

Turtle Mountain Reservation Chippewa Indians 1932 Census with Births & Deaths, 1924-1932

Other Books and Series by Jeff Bowen

Chickasaw By Blood Enrollment Cards 1898-1914 Volume I thru V

Cherokee Descendants East An Index to the Guion Miller Applications Volume I
Cherokee Descendants West An Index to the Guion Miller Applications Volume II (A-M)
Cherokee Descendants West An Index to the Guion Miller Applications Volume III (N-Z)

Applications for Enrollment of Seminole Newborn Freedmen, Act of 1905

Eastern Cherokee Census, Cherokee, North Carolina, 1915-1922, Taken by Agent James E. Henderson   *Volume I (1915-1916)*
                                Volume II (1917-1918)
                                Volume III (1919-1920)
                                Volume IV (1921-1922)

Complete Delaware Roll of 1898

Eastern Cherokee Census, Cherokee, North Carolina, 1923-1929, Taken by Agent James E. Henderson   *Volume I (1923-1924)*
                                Volume II (1925-1926)
                                Volume III (1927-1929)

Applications for Enrollment of Seminole Newborn Act of 1905 Volumes I & II

North Carolina Eastern Cherokee Indian Census 1898-1899, 1904, 1906, 1909-1912, 1914 Revised and Expanded Edition

1932 Hopi and Navajo Native American Census with Birth & Death Rolls (1925-1931) Volume 1 - Hopi
1932 Hopi and Navajo Native American Census with Birth & Death Rolls (1930-1932) Volume 2 - Navajo

Western Navajo Reservation Navajo, Hopi and Paiute 1933 Census with Birth & Death Rolls 1925-1933

Cherokee Citizenship Commission Dockets 1880-1884 and 1887-1889 Volumes I thru V

Applications for Enrollment of Chickasaw Newborn Act of 1905 Volumes I thru VII

Cherokee Intermarried White 1906 Volume I thru X

Applications for Enrollment of Creek Newborn Act of 1905 Volumes I thru XIV